DIGITAL

nude photography

A step-by-step guide to creating perfect photos

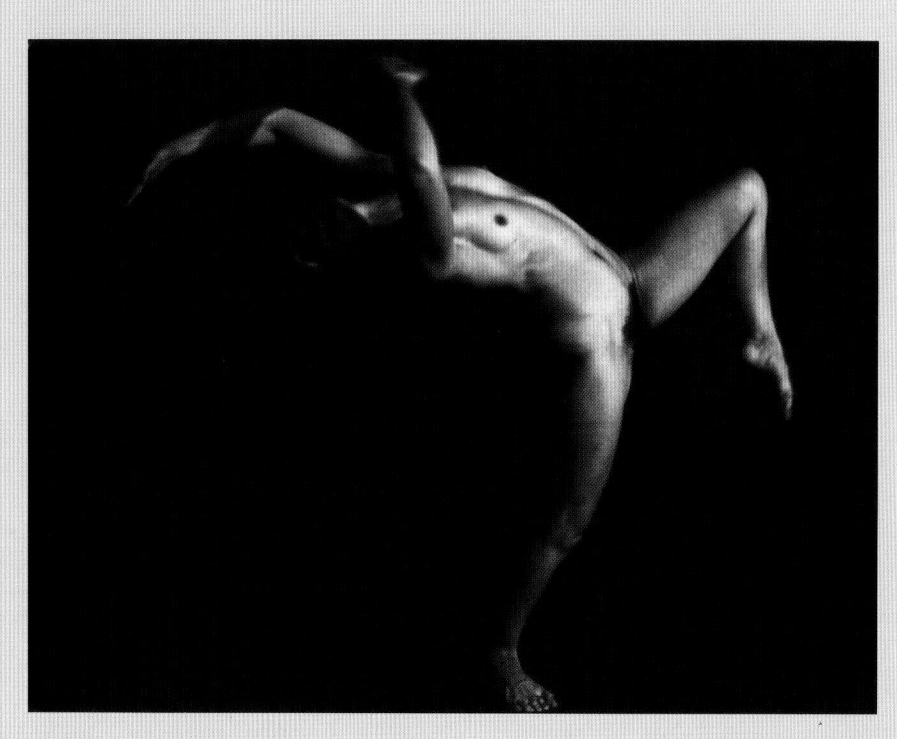

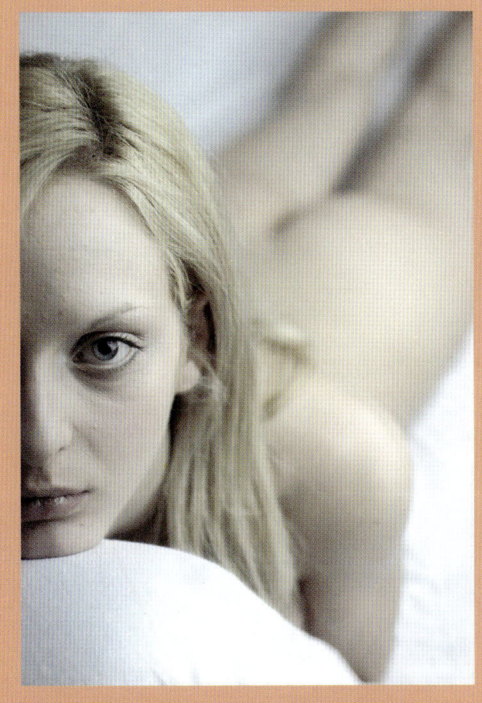

DIGITAL

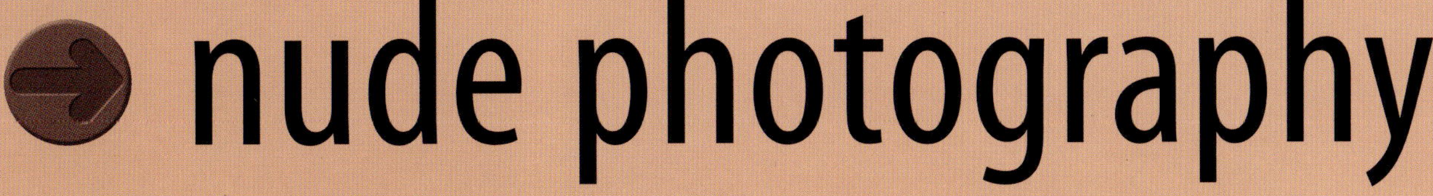

nude photography

A step-by-step guide to creating perfect photos

RODERICK MACDONALD

First published in the United States by Muska & Lipman Publishing, a division of Course Technology, in 2003.

For Muska & Lipman Publishing:
Publisher: Stacy L. Hiquet
Senior Marketing Manager: Sarah O'Donnell
Marketing Manager: Heather Hurley
Associate Marketing Manager: Kristin Eisenzopf
Senior Aquisitions Editor: Kevin Harreld
Manager of Editorial Services: Heather Talbot
Senior Editor: Mark Garvey
Retail Market Coordinator: Sarah Dubois

ISBN 1-59200-105-X

5 4 3 2 1

Cataloging-in-Publication Data is available

Educational facilities, companies, and organizations interested in multiple copies or licensing of this book should contact the publisher for quantity discount information. Training manuals, CD-ROMs, and portions of this book are also available individually or can be tailored for specific needs.

MUSKA & LIPMAN PUBLISHING,
a Division of Course Technology (www.course.com)
25 Thomson Place
Boston, MA 02210

www.muskalipman.com
publisher@muskalipman.com

This book was conceived, designed, and produced by
ILEX
The Barn, College Farm
1 West End, Whittlesford
Cambridge CB2 4LX
England

Sales Office:
The Old Candlemakers
West Street
Lewes
East Sussex BN7 2NZ
England

Publisher: Alastair Campbell
Executive Publisher: Sophie Collins
Creative Director: Peter Bridgewater
Editorial Director: Steve Luck
Series Editor: Stuart Andrews
Editor: Nicola Hodgson
Design Manager: Tony Seddon
Designer: Kevin Knight
Development Art Director: Graham Davis
Technical Art Editor: Nicholas Rowland

Printed in China

For more information on this title please visit:
www.ssnuus.web-linked.com

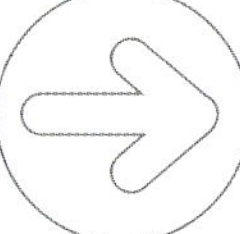

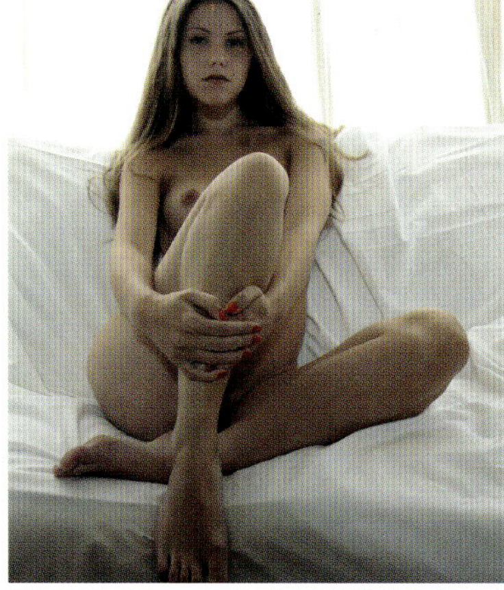

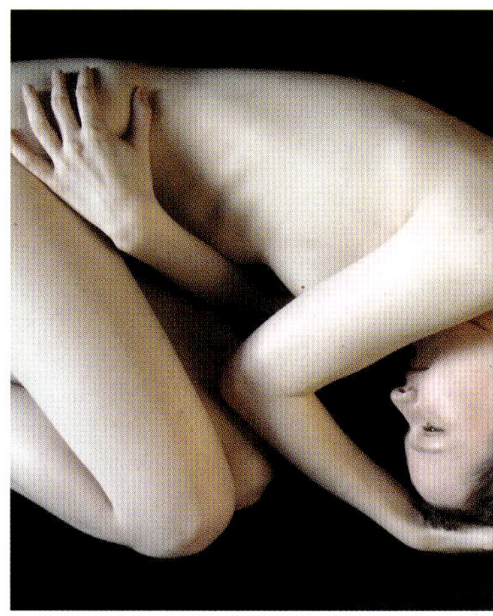

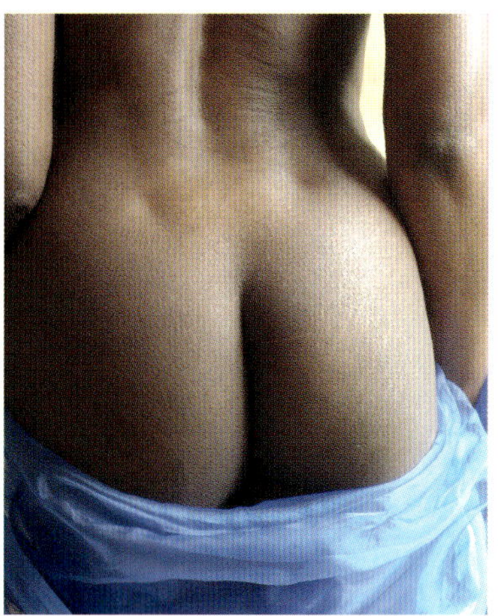

Contents

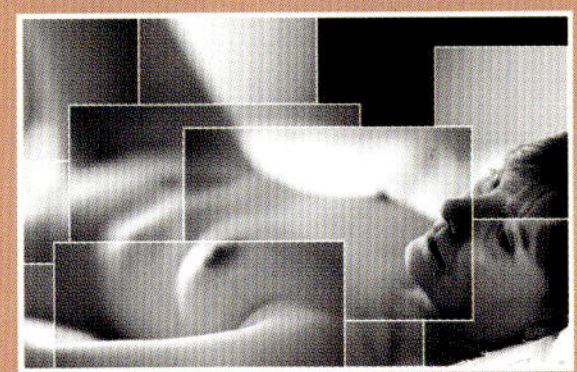

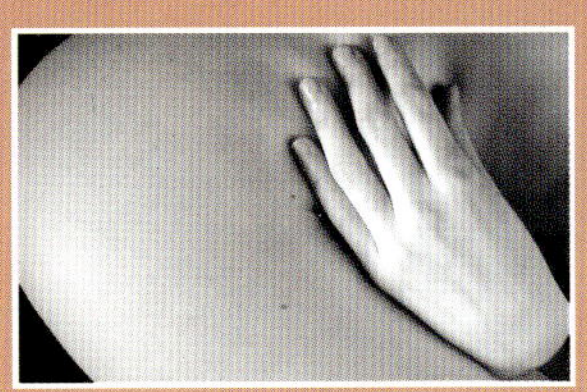

Introduction

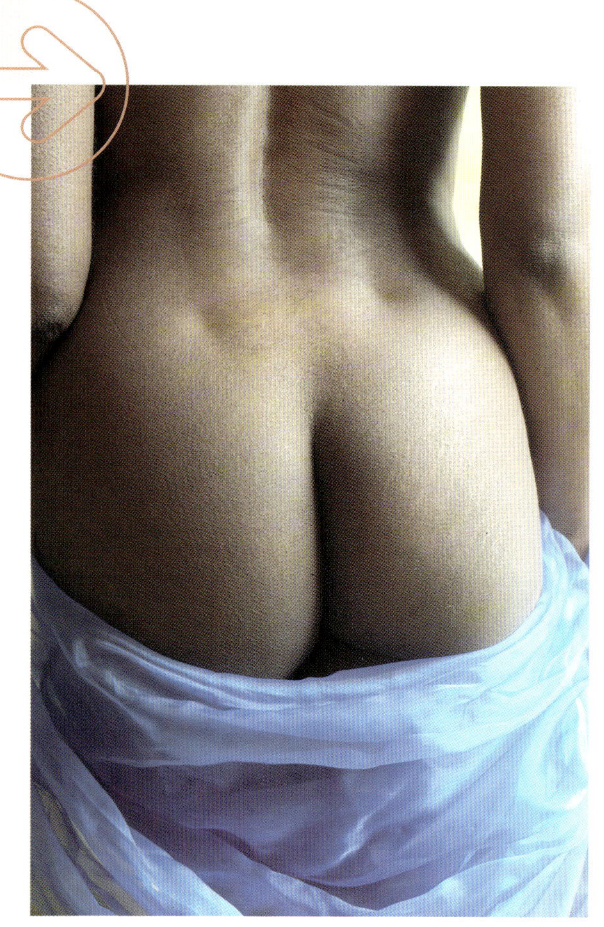

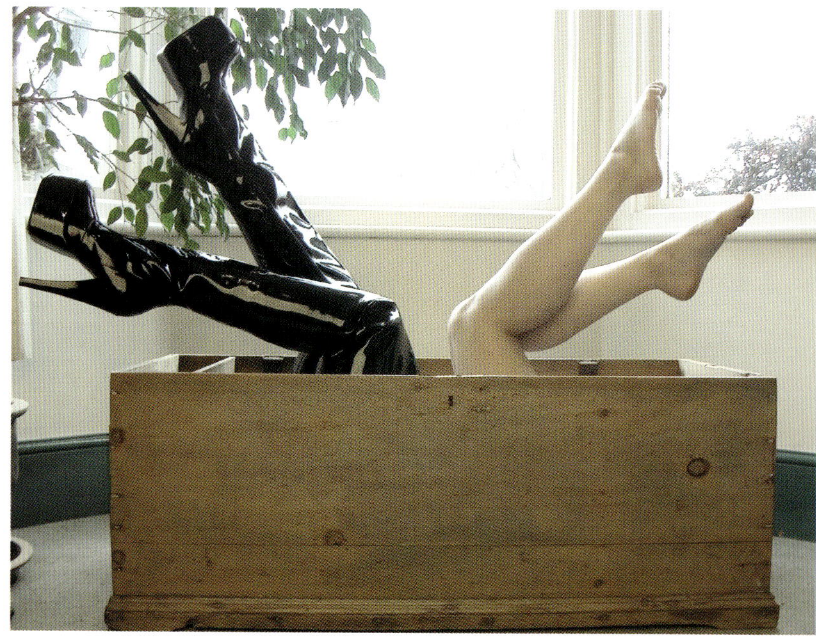

Oblique lighting and intense hues give vitality to this image, in which no attempt is made to glamorize the model by softening or removing her slight imperfections.

Part of a spread of thumbnail images generated by a computer, which can be used just like a photographic contact sheet.

An amusing "double take," easily and seamlessly assembled using image-editing software.

The nude is a long-established photographic subject. Images of the naked human form, while sometimes the subject of controversy and debate, remain popular with photographers and viewers for their power to move us. Digital photography has in many ways given new life to this theme, particularly for amateur photographers. This book discusses the whole process of making images of the nude using digital technology: from finding a model and a location; shooting and editing the pictures; to exhibiting your work.

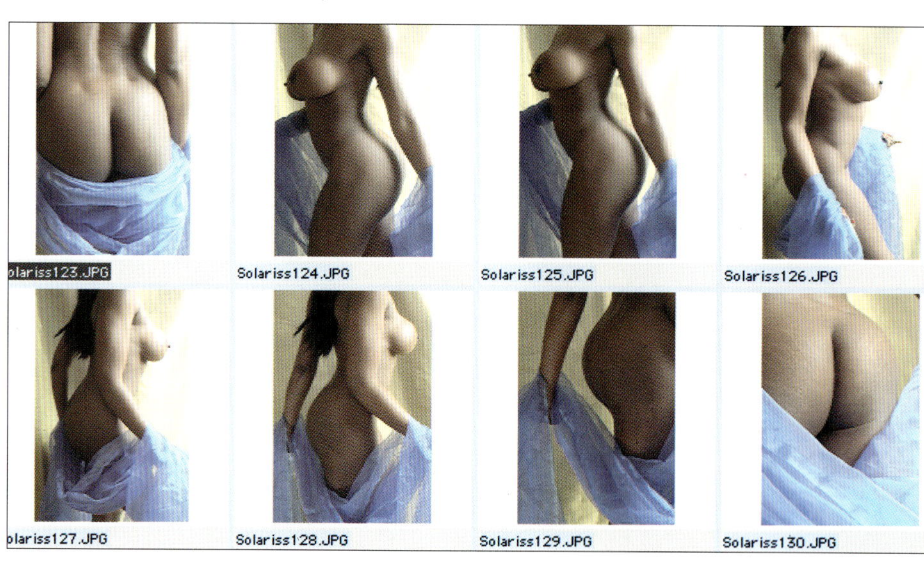

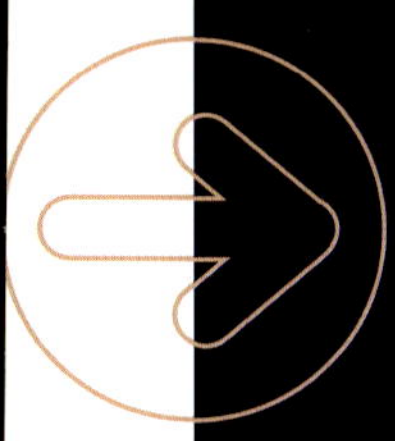

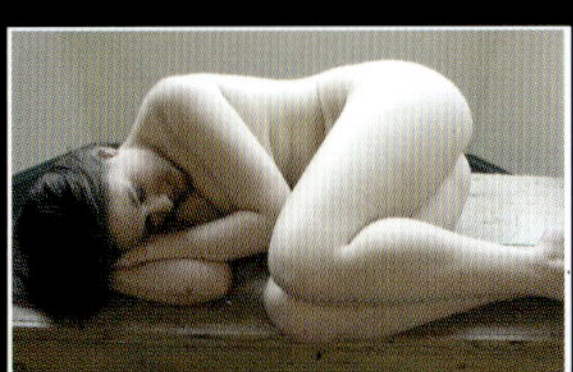

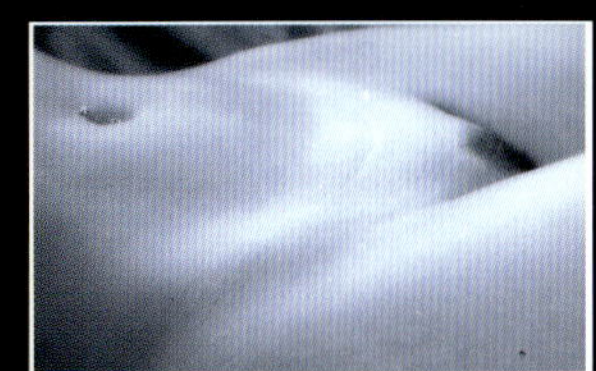

Digital photography has a number of advantages over traditional film photography, but the most important is the sense of immediacy that the medium brings. This is particularly appropriate when shooting the nude.

THE ADVANTAGES OF DIGITAL PHOTOGRAPHY

▶ Digital photography is immediate. With a digital camera, you can see what you have shot as soon as you've taken it, make any adjustments, and reshoot it until you've obtained the image you want.

▶ Digital photography is powerful. Once you've taken your digital pictures, you move them from the camera onto the computer, where you can edit and manipulate them. This means not only tidying the image up (cropping, removing distracting details, fixing blemishes, etc), but altering it creatively. Your computer enables you to create effects that would be difficult or impossible to achieve even in the most expensive darkroom.

▶ Digital photography is flexible. You can show your pictures in many different ways: you can print them on a good-quality printer, then frame and exhibit them, as you would conventional photographs; you can e-mail them to friends; or you can display them over the internet in a number of ways *(see page 137)*.

▶ Digital photography is cheap to run. It's not cheap to set up *(see page 8)*, but once you've bought the equipment, you don't pay for film stock or processing. This means that you can take more pictures than you might with a film camera, which in turn frees up your imagination to take more chances and be more experimental. When you print your work, your paper costs will be low. You will print a picture only when you are certain, from what you see on the computer screen, that the picture is exactly how you want it—there is no need for test prints. If you decide to show your work on the internet, you have no materials costs (apart from phone charges).

▶ You can use the computer to work on images taken with a film camera. Using either a film or a paper scanner, you can create a digital version of images on film (negative or transparency, color or black-and-white) or prints, and then edit them on the computer.

▶ Digital is all under your control. You don't have to rely on processing labs to handle your film properly and make your prints the way you want them. And—with nude photography—you don't have to worry about the processing lab handling your work discreetly. You have complete creative control over every phase of the process.

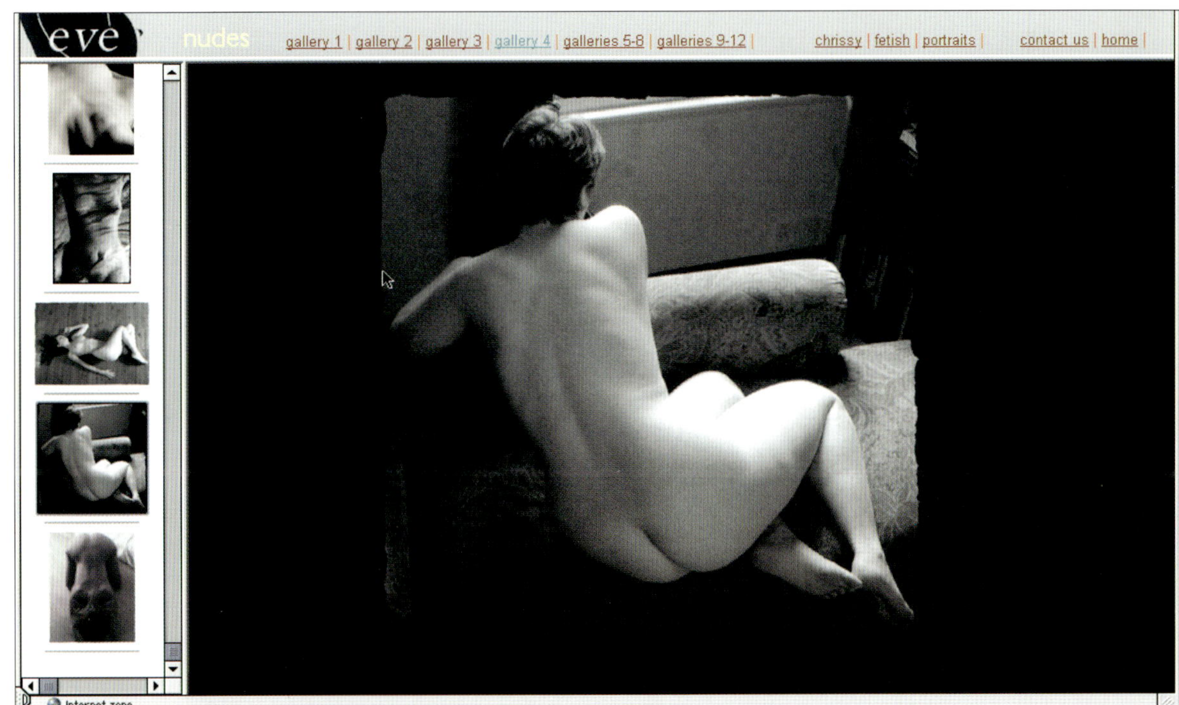

An example from my website. Note the black background on which the main image is displayed.

THE DRAWBACKS OF DIGITAL

▶ Digital is not cheap to set up. The arrival of digital cameras in the marketplace has driven down the price of many high-quality film cameras, but digital cameras of reasonable quality are still quite expensive. Also, if you don't already have access to a computer, you'll need to buy one to edit your pictures. But, as explained already, digital photography is cheap to run compared to film photography, and prices for digital cameras and their peripherals, while still high, are falling all the time.

▶ Buying a digital camera can be confusing. As well as traditional camera-makers like Olympus and Nikon, companies with a background in other technologies (Sony, Minolta) now produce high-quality cameras. New cameras appear all the time. Choosing a digital camera requires familiarity with a new technical vocabulary. However, there are good magazines and websites available that can help you decide which camera to buy.

▶ *Some viewers might find this image confrontational, as it draws attention to the lifestyle and values suggested by the model's choice to have her nipple pierced—and the photographer's decision to work with her.*

▼ *This image uses strongly contrasted elements of black and white in a composition that matches shapes (the gloved hand and the high-heeled shoe) and patterns (the parallel lines of the model's thigh and shin and the shadow of the hand).*

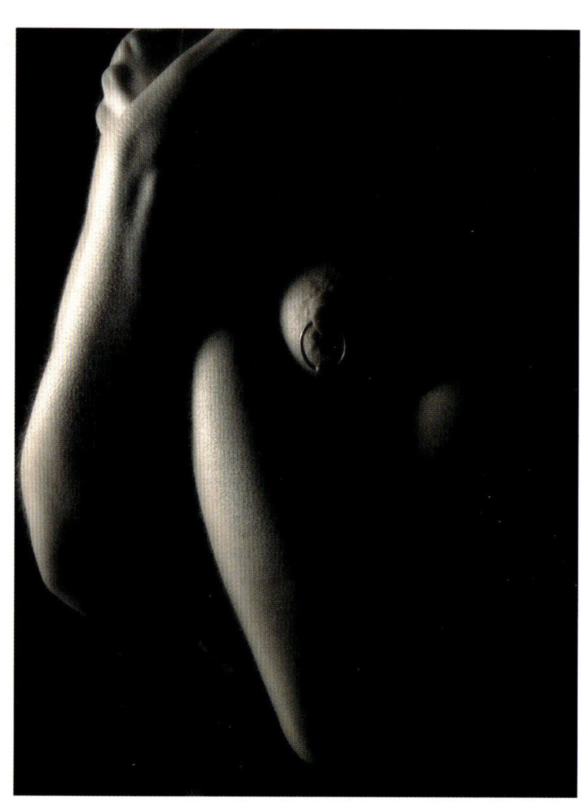

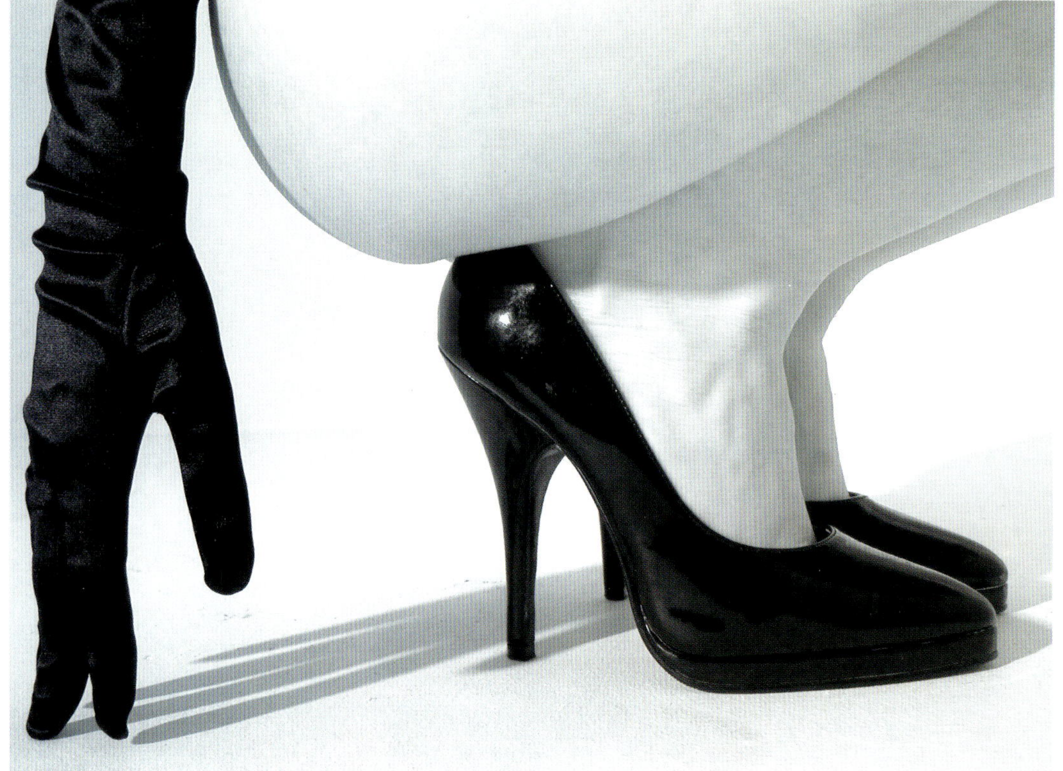

THE SCOPE OF THIS BOOK

This book is not about "glamor" or "adult" photography, but about the many different forms of nude photography that exist outside of them. These forms employ the same resources—light, camerawork, location, composition, the model, the pose, the moment, manipulation of the image—to create a visual form based on the human body that moves the viewer through its form, skill, and beauty, rather than simply being sexually arousing.

The kind of photography that has these ambitions is often monochrome, as a way of simplifying form and pattern and separating the image from the "real" world in which it was made. Yet color can add its own interest, as later examples will show.

This book also draws on the range of alternative lifestyles that exist in Western cultures today. Some of the images in the book use models who are tattooed or have body-piercings. These alterations to the body are rarely the central feature in the image, but their presence can add an extra, often quite provocative element to a nude image.

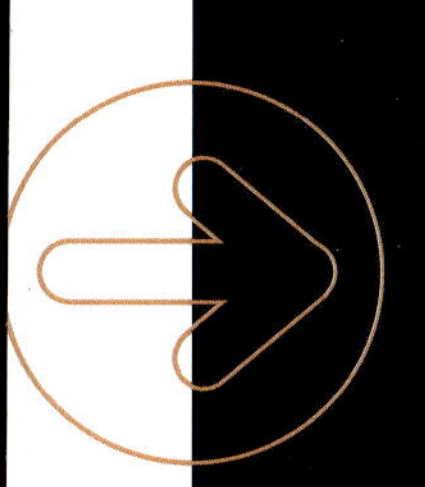

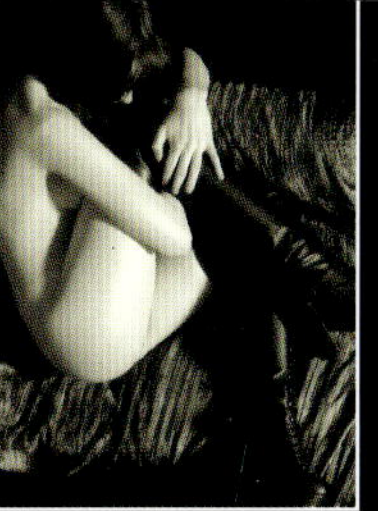

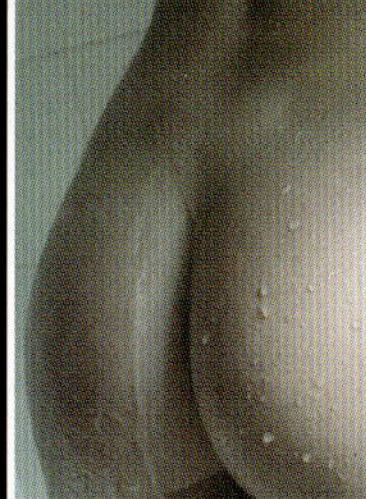

Moving to digital photography does not need to be expensive, and the long-term benefits are enormous. In addition to cheaper production costs, digital photography offers scope for infinite experimentation.

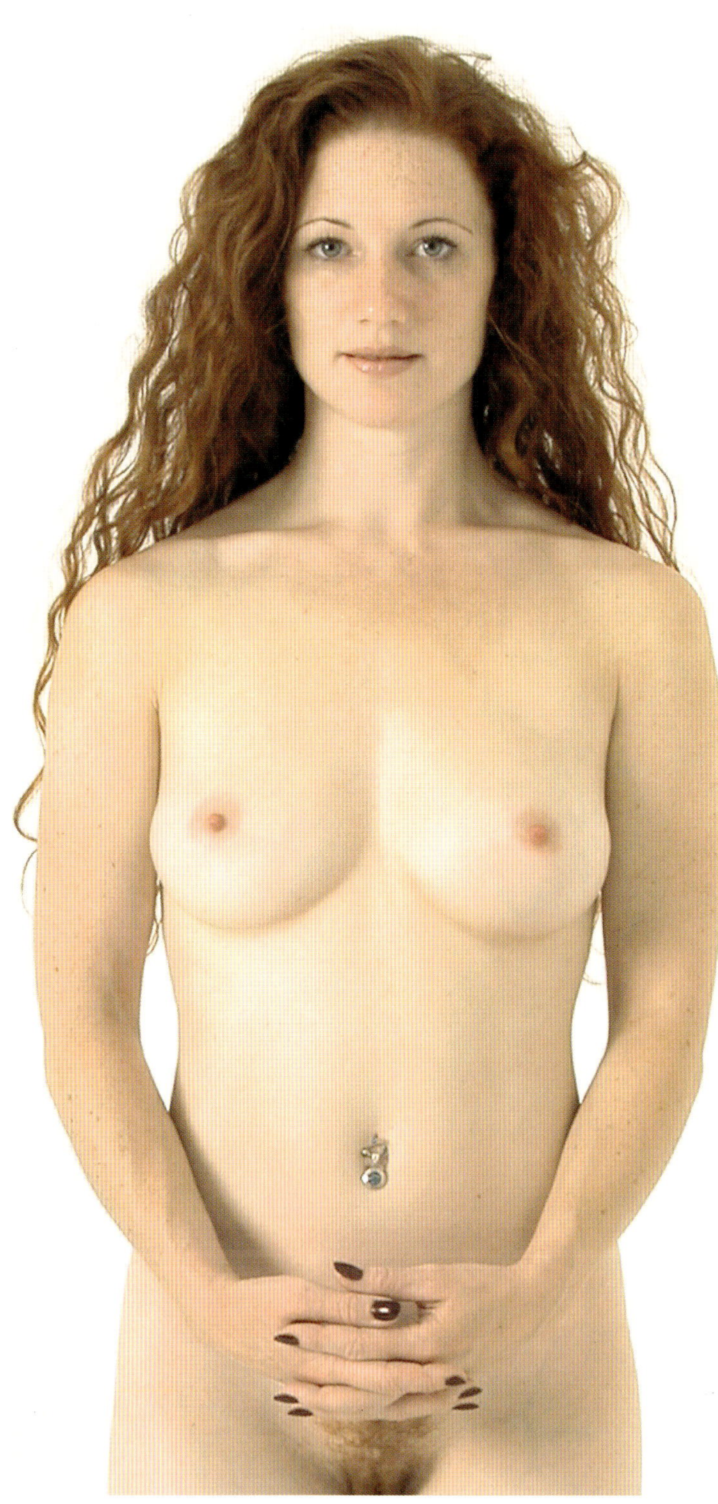

This image relies for its impact on the symmetry of the model's pose and the strength and confidence of her gaze, combined with very even lighting in a featureless white studio space.

This photograph transforms the body into a pattern of monochrome light and shade, formed by the model's limbs under the lighting conditions that the photographer has created. No attempt has been made to make the model look more "perfect" by removing the birthmark below her throat, although this could easily have been done on the computer.

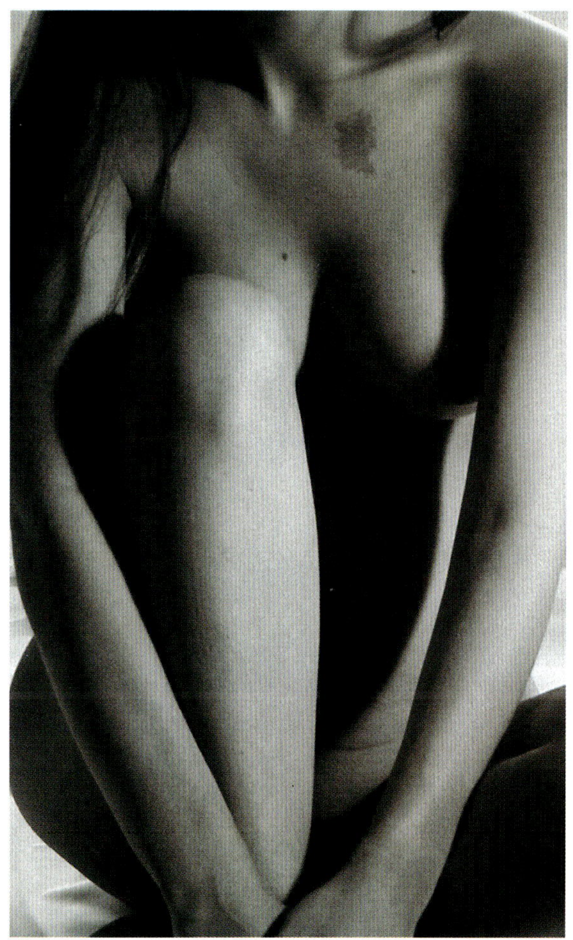

Introduction

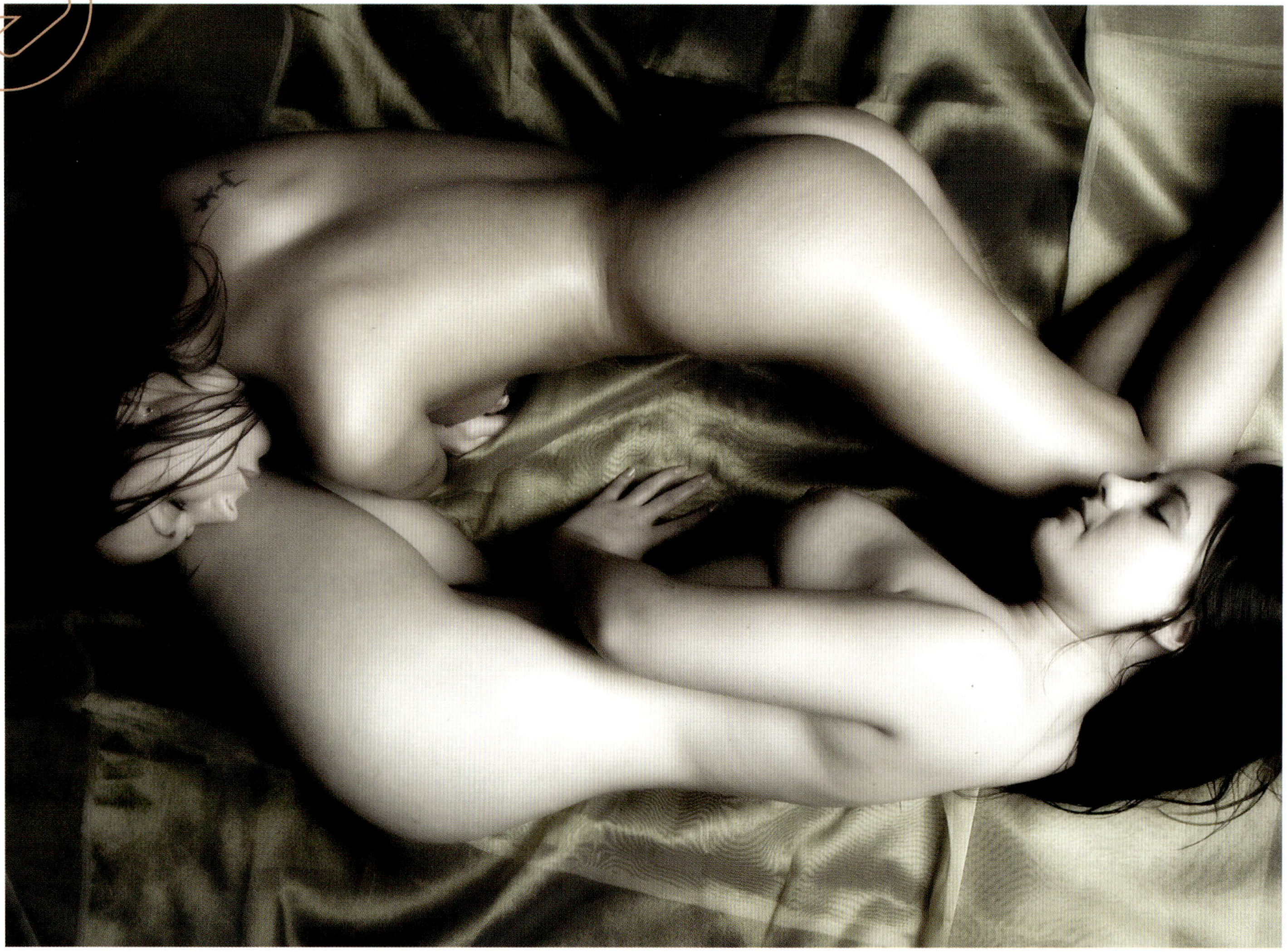

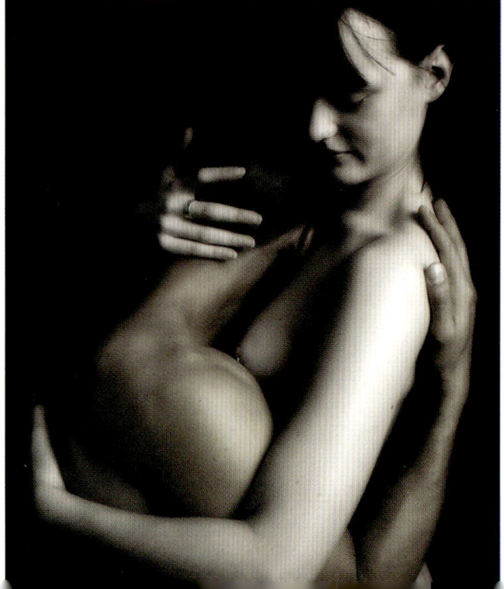

THE PHOTOGRAPHER AND THE MODEL

In this book you'll see pictures of individual female and male models, and shots that use two models together. Working with different models and combinations of models provides a continuous challenge to the photographer. Pages 34–39 look in detail at selecting and working with models.

Working with two models enables you to explore new worlds of symmetry, similarity, and contrast.

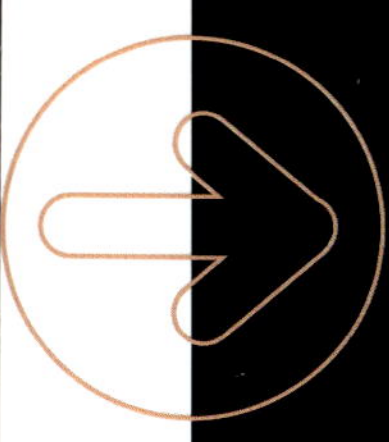

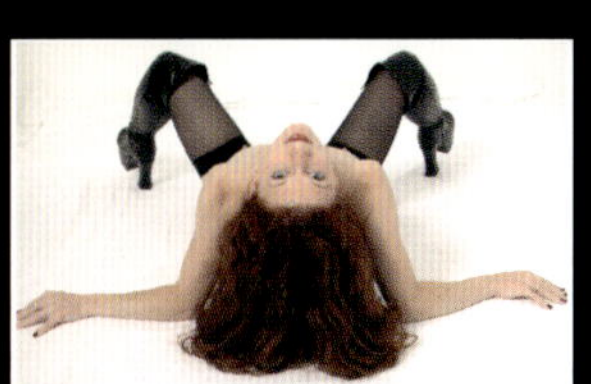

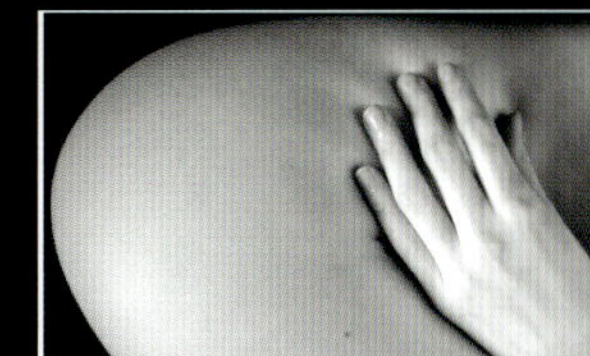

The relationship between photographer and model is not altered by digital photography. In fact, the opportunity to produce thought-provoking, evocative images has been increased by the flexibility of digital techniques.

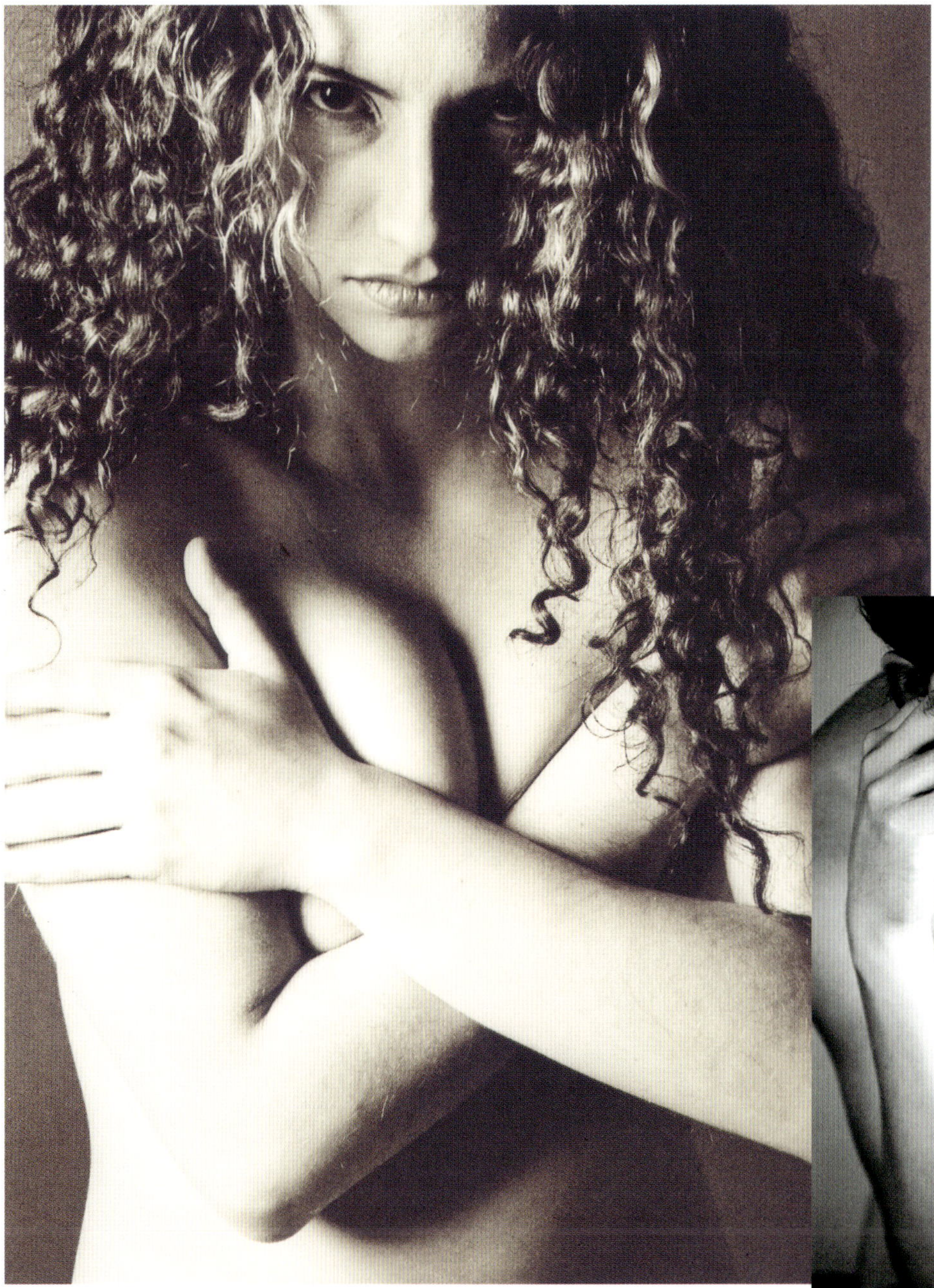

Traditionally, most nudes have been taken by male photographers using female models, but there's a growing number of female photographers whose subjects include the nude. These two examples are by American photographer Doreen Alvarez.

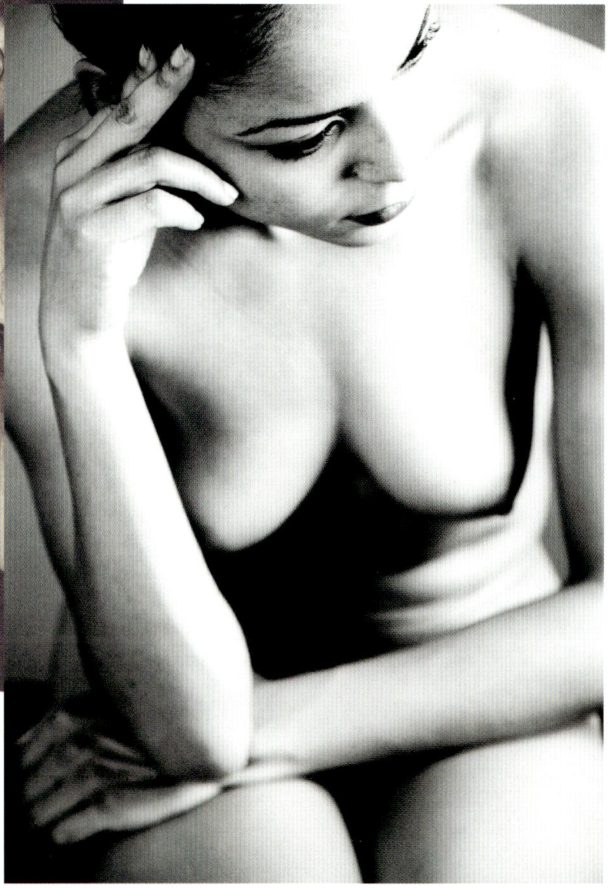

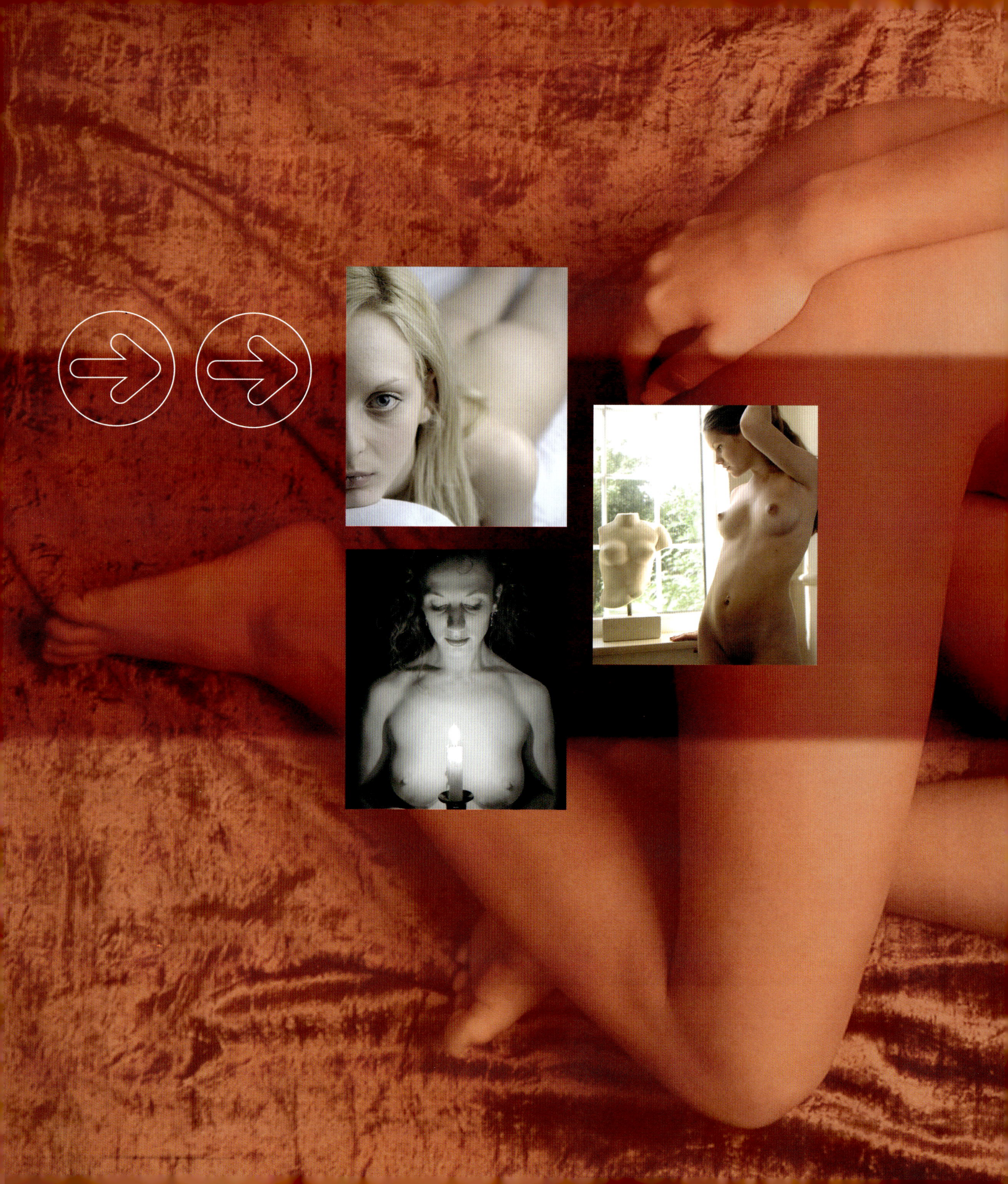

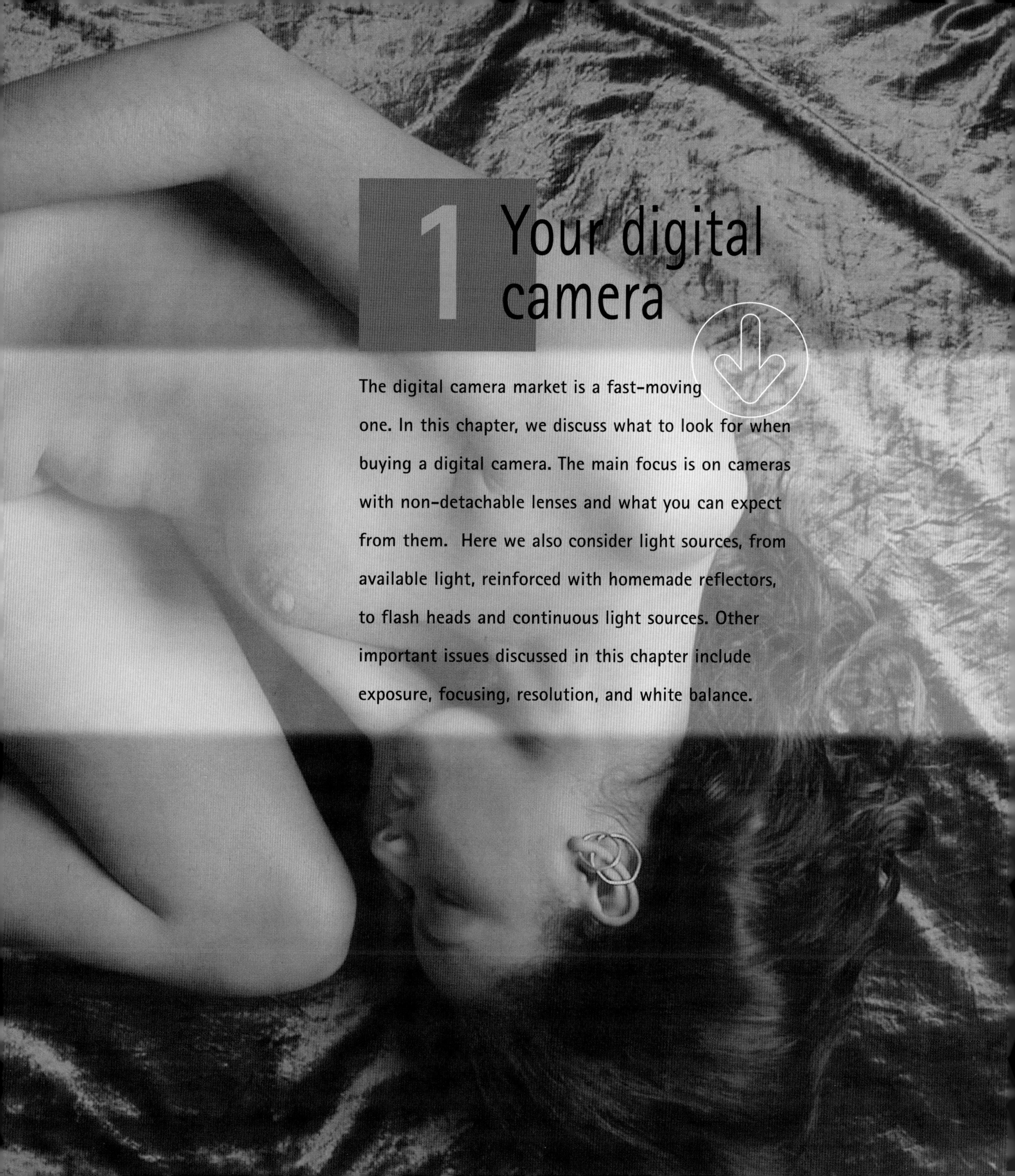

1 Your digital camera

The digital camera market is a fast-moving one. In this chapter, we discuss what to look for when buying a digital camera. The main focus is on cameras with non-detachable lenses and what you can expect from them. Here we also consider light sources, from available light, reinforced with homemade reflectors, to flash heads and continuous light sources. Other important issues discussed in this chapter include exposure, focusing, resolution, and white balance.

Choosing a camera

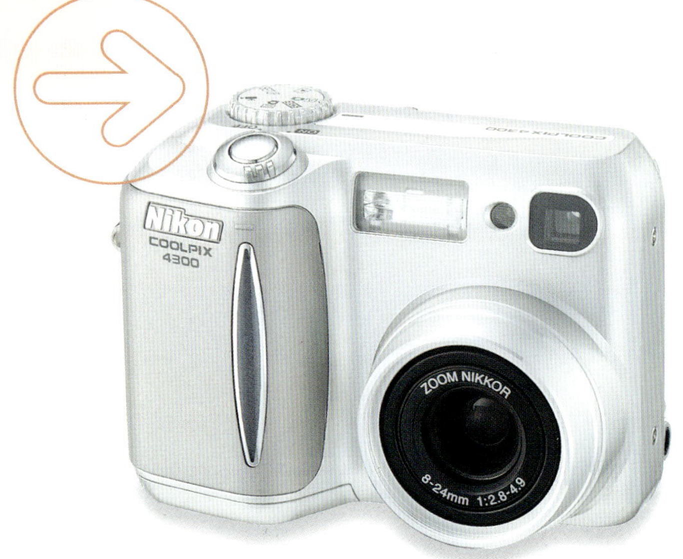

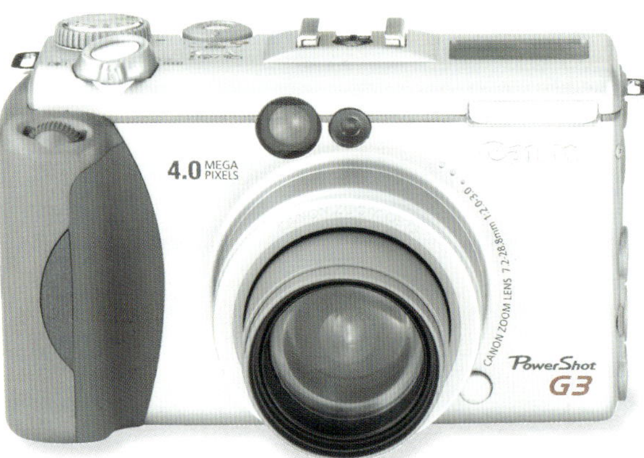

Less expensive digital cameras are still capable enough for serious nude photography. 4 megapixels should be your minimum resolution, and aim for some level of manual control.

There is a bewildering array of digital cameras on the market, with new models appearing daily. It's a good idea, therefore, to have a clear idea of what you're looking for, and to spend time researching what's available, before parting with your cash. Here we look at a typical midprice camera with an image size of 5 megapixels (see pages 16–17 for an explanation of pixels and their significance).

THE BACK OF THE CAMERA

The camera has an electronic viewfinder (in effect, a small, very sharp TV screen) and also a monitor, which is a larger version of the viewfinder. You will probably use the monitor rather than the viewfinder to set up and frame each shot, and to check each picture as you take it. The monitor also lets you play back pictures to review them as you work. On some cameras, you can flip or rotate the monitor to use it when you are shooting from ground level or holding the camera above your head.

The viewfinder is necessary only when you are working under very bright ambient light conditions that can "wash out" the image in the monitor. The viewfinder should have a diopter adjustment control so that you can set it to match your eyesight.

The zoom buttons enable you to zoom the lens in and out, as well as zooming in and out on pictures when you're playing back. The multiselector is used to navigate through the camera's menus, and also to pan across pictures when you're playing back.

On the back of the camera you are also likely to find buttons to activate the camera's control menus and to delete images that you have decided you don't want to keep. The slot that holds the memory card is also on the back.

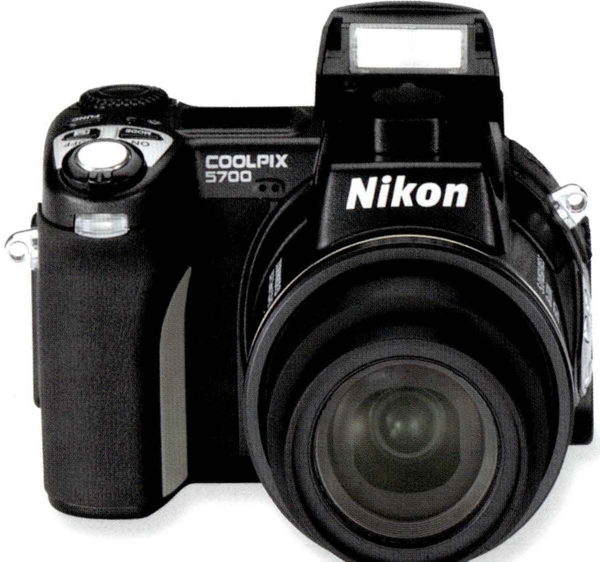

The front of the Nikon Coolpix 5700, showing the zoom lens, flash, and shutter release.

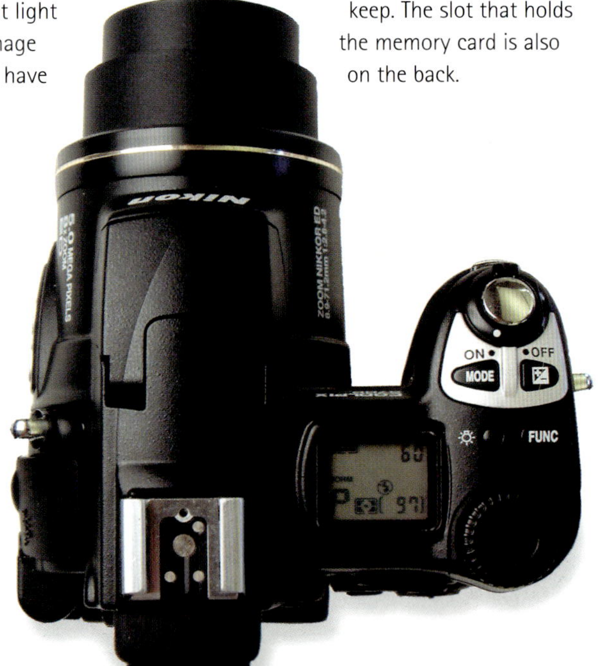

The top of the same camera, showing the accessory shoe, LCD information panel, and mode dial.

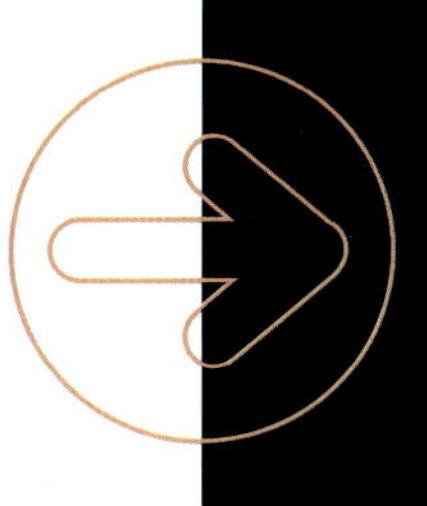

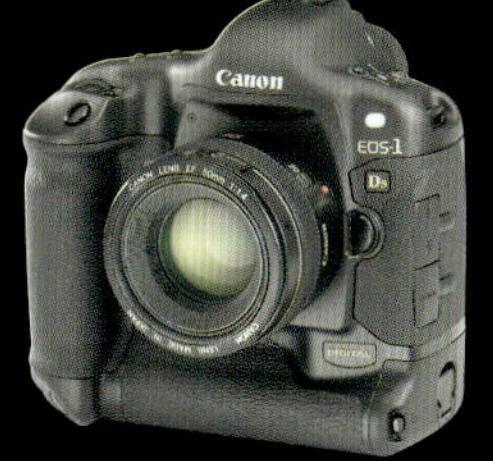

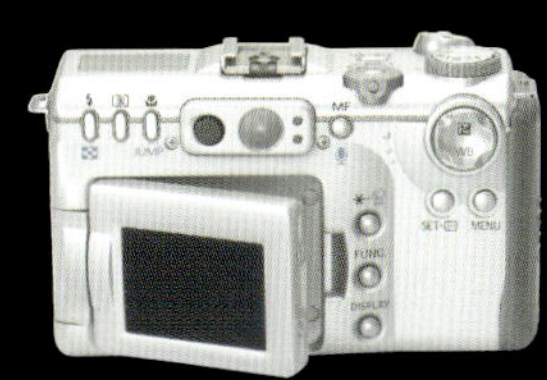

There is a bewildering array of dig
cameras available on the market.
selecting a camera, read equipme
reviews in magazines and on web
Even if you are on a tight budget,
can still find a capable model.

THE TOP OF THE CAMERA

On the top of the camera there may be an accessory shoe to which you can connect a flash unit or an adaptor to let you use studio flash heads. The shutter release button and power switch are also on top, as is the control panel in which information about the camera's setup is displayed. When the lens is in autofocus mode, applying half pressure to the shutter release will bring the lens into focus. Close to the shutter release you will find the command dial. This is used to adjust the camera's setup and also to control shutter speed and aperture when the camera is not in a fully automatic mode.

The control panel displays a wealth of information about the camera. Typically, this would include some indication of battery status, recording mode, image size, flash mode, an estimate of frames remaining on the current memory card, and information on the exposure mode.

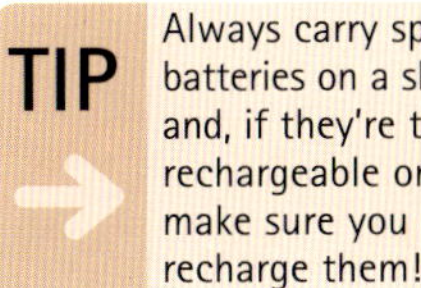

TIP Always carry spare batteries on a shoot, and, if they're the rechargeable ones, make sure you do recharge them!

THE FRONT OF THE CAMERA

On the front of the camera you find the zoom lens, the built-in flash, and a redeye reduction lamp. Some digital cameras in this price range have lenses that can be focussed manually by rotating a ring on the lens itself, but most use "focus by wire" systems, where you focus manually by rotating the command dial.

On the underside of the camera, as well as the tripod socket, you'll find the battery compartment.

INFORMATION ABOUT CAMERAS

There are several magazines and websites devoted to digital photography. Magazines include *PC Photo* and *Digital Camera*, while *Popular Photography* has plenty of relevant digital content. All of these have their own websites, containing helpful tips and equipment reviews. A useful online resource for information about digital photography is *www.dpreview.com*. This contains thorough reviews of cameras and a buying guide that identifies for you all the available cameras that have the features you are looking for. The site also includes a valuable glossary to explain digital jargon.

The Nikon D100, a 6-megapixel camera, is one of the first affordable digital SLRs—and it helps if you have a number of Nikkor lenses from an old conventional SLR. The results are outstanding.

FACT FILE

Extra storage

Digital cameras store their images on electronic cards. When you buy a camera, it will usually be supplied with a low-capacity card—32 or sometimes only 16MB (megabytes)—that will hold about 20 or 10 images respectively. It makes good sense to buy a bigger card—at least 128MB, or 256MB if a card that big is available for your camera—at the same time as you buy the camera. You will find the extra storage invaluable, and storage cards are usually cheaper when you buy them with the camera.

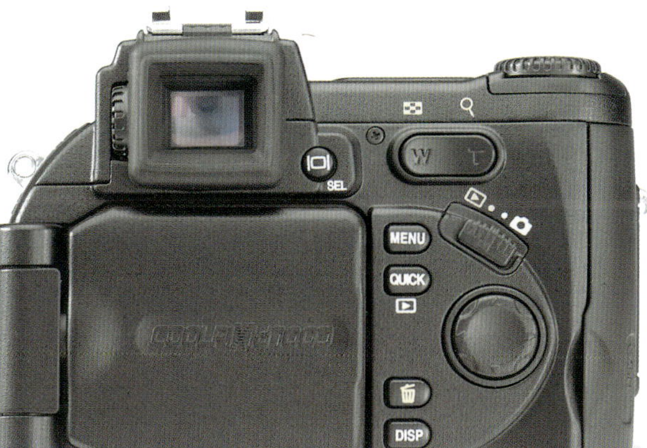

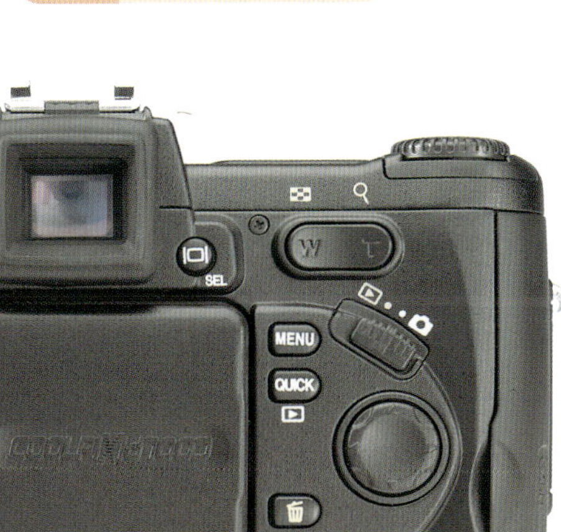

The back of the Coolpix 5700. The LCD screen flips out underneath the viewfinder, and the Zoom controls are also visible.

Resolution

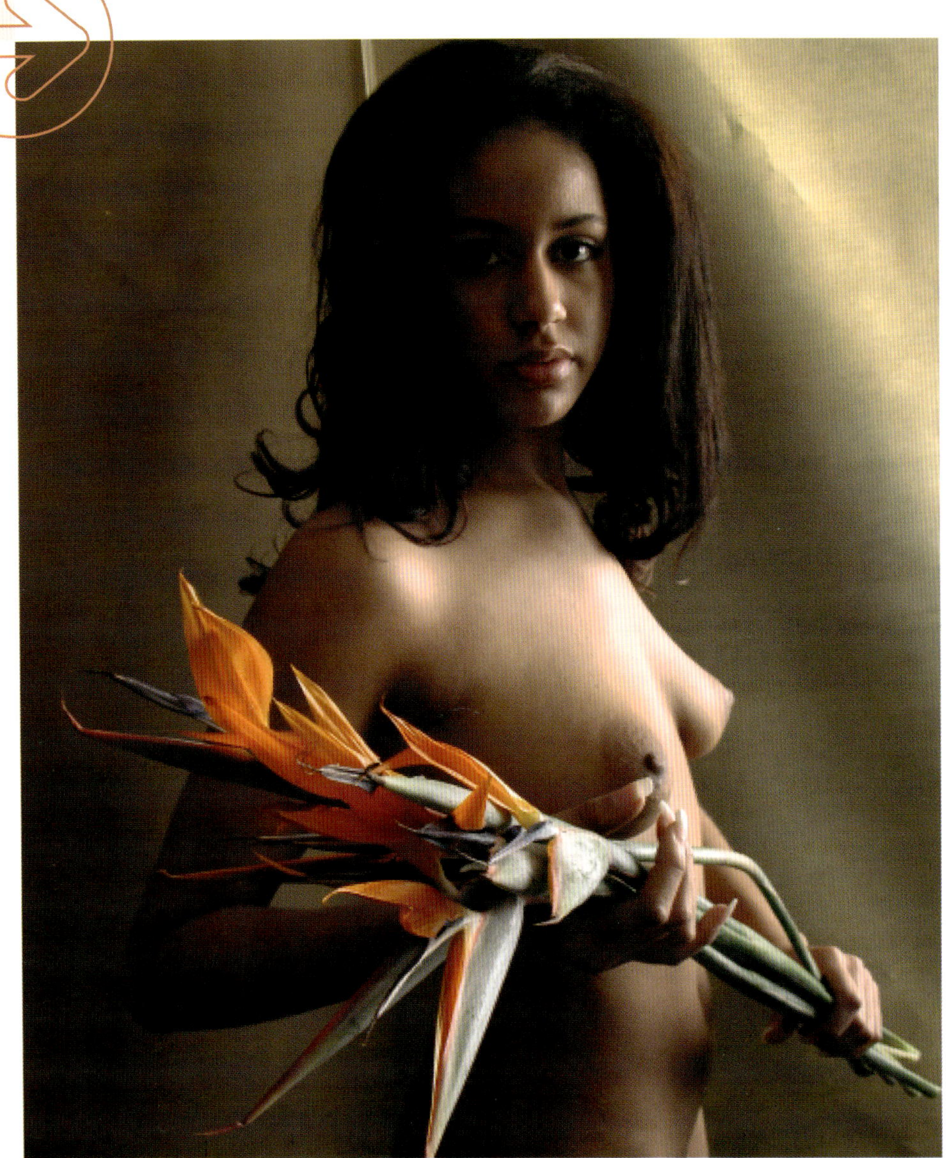

The red, green and blue components that make up this image.

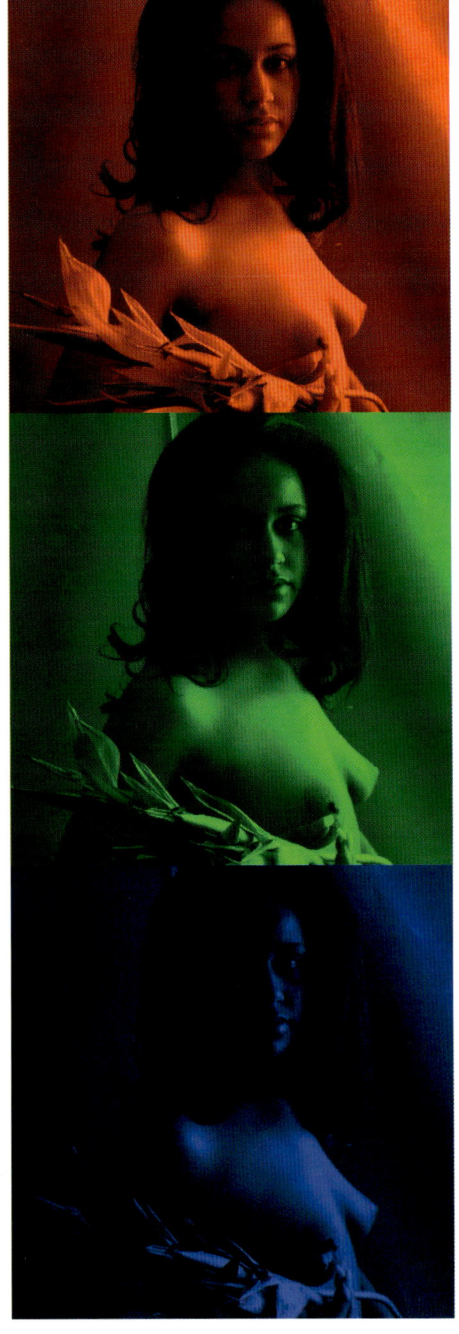

In digital photography, the size of an image is measured in pixels. Think of a pixel as one of the colored dots that makes up a digital image. Each pixel is made up of a combination of red, green, and blue (RGB). Each color can have an intensity from 0 (that is, the color is not present at all in the pixel) to 255 (the color is present in the pixel at full intensity). A pixel with the RGB values 255, 0, 0 will be pure red; a pixel with the values 255, 255, 255 will be white; and a pixel with the values 0, 0, 0 will be black. Altogether, the RGB model gives a range of about 16.7 million different colors for every pixel.

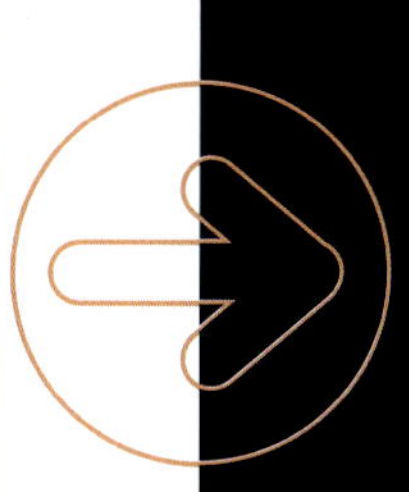

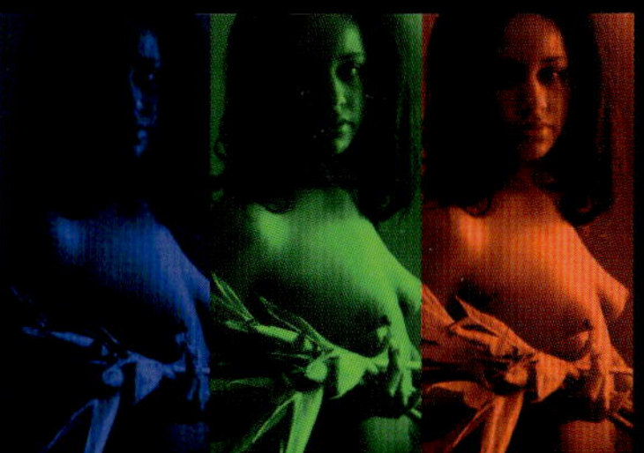

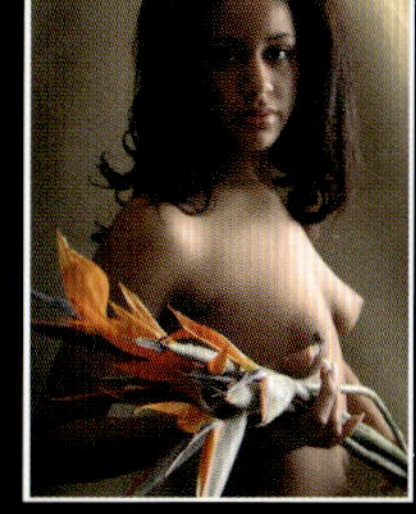

Digital photos are made up of pixels, tiny blocks made up from a combination of red, green, and blue colors. The more pixels that your camera can capture, the greater the resolution will be when you come to print out your images.

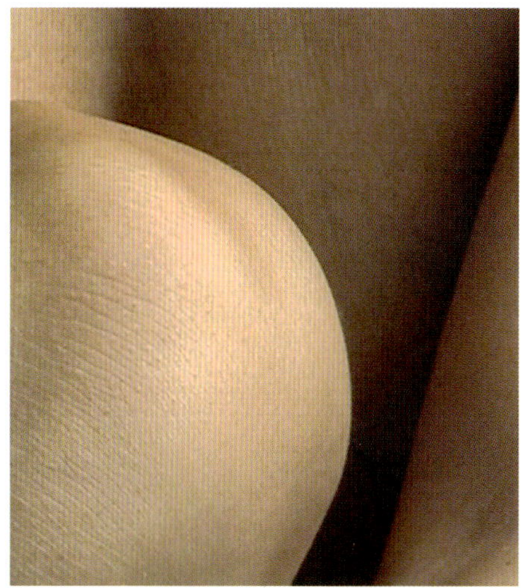

2560 x 1920 pixels at high quality

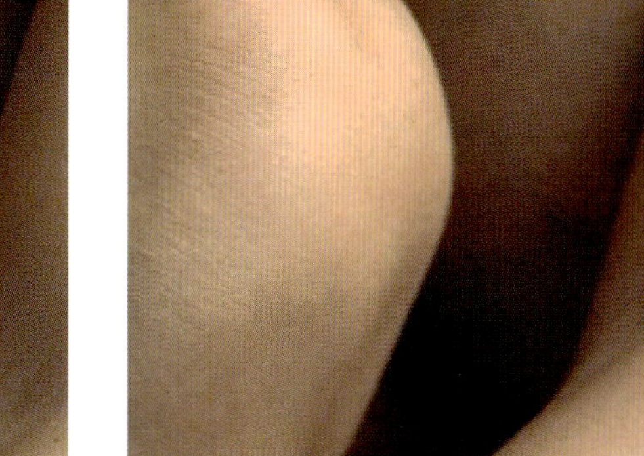

1024 x 768 pixels at medium quality

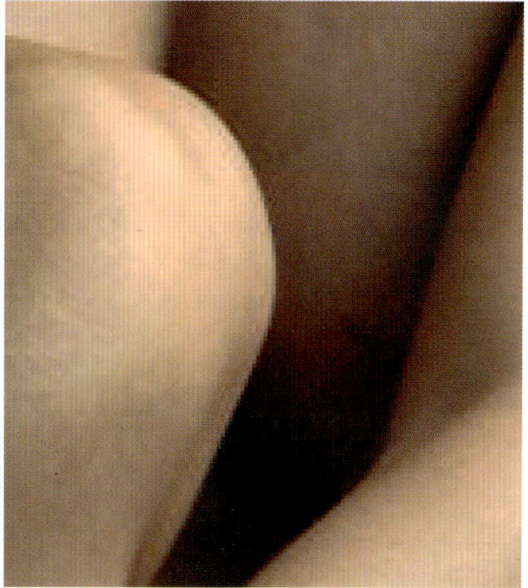

640 x 480 pixels at lowest quality

Sections cropped from three pictures, taken at different image sizes and qualities.

Left: full image size 2560 x 1920 pixels at high quality. This section of the image measures 600 x 800 pixels. Note the smoothness of the model's skin and of the curves of her knee.

Center: full image size 1024 x 768 pixels at medium quality. This section measures 424 by 576 pixels. Some jaggedness is visible around the curve of the model's knee.

Right: full image size 640 x 480 pixels at lowest quality. This section measures 150 x 200 pixels. Note the very jagged edges, and the very obvious loss of detail in skin texture.

NUMBER OF PIXELS

On a midprice camera, the maximum image size might be 2560 pixels wide and 1920 pixels high; that is, 4,915,200 pixels altogether. This image size is referred to as about 5 megapixels (in computer jargon, a million is represented by the prefix "mega"). The more pixels, the higher the resolution of the camera—in other words, the more pixels, the better.

COMPRESSION

Images are normally compressed before the camera stores them on its card. Compression means discarding information from the picture to make the file smaller, but without making the picture look unattractive or "unreal." The usual method for doing this is JPEG compression. JPEG compression can be applied in different strengths. High-quality images can be achieved even with a compression ratio of around 1: 8; for example, a 5-megapixel image is compressed from about 14.1MB to about 1.7MB.

Your camera may offer a range of different image sizes or different quality settings (that is, compression ratios), or both. The smaller the image size and the lower the quality you select, the more images you can store on the card. (Whatever size/quality combination you choose, the camera always forms the image using the whole of its imaging chip at maximum resolution. The compression takes place as the image is being stored on the card.

Why does image size matter? The smaller the image size you choose when you set up your camera, the smaller you can print the image or display it on the internet. The three examples above demonstrate what happens if you print three pictures at the same size that were shot at three different resolutions.

There are limitations to how much you can enlarge an image to print it: the smaller it was when stored on the camera's card, the less you can enlarge it. On the other hand, it's always possible to reduce the size of an image to print it. Storage cards for digital cameras aren't expensive, and they are getting cheaper all the time. Taking all these factors into account, it makes best sense to shoot JPEGs at the highest resolution and quality that your camera provides.

Most cameras also offer other ways of storing images on the card: as RAW data or as a TIFF file. RAW data is all the data produced by the camera's imaging chip, stored without any compression. RAW data requires the camera manufacturer's own software to convert it to a format that picture-editing programs can use. TIFF is another file format that stores uncompressed data.

Unless you want to produce very large prints of your images, you will obtain good results working at the largest image size and the best quality JPEG compression that your camera offers, without using either RAW or TIFF formats. TIFF comes into its own as a format when you start to edit and manipulate your pictures.

Lenses

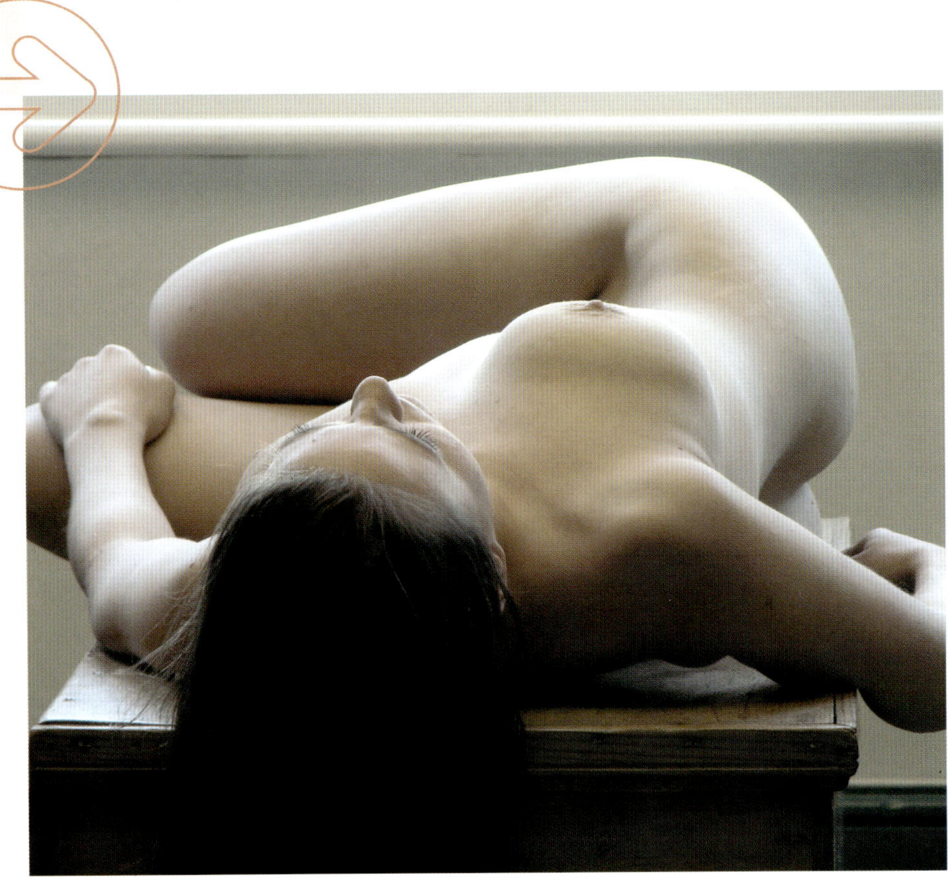

Zooming in compresses the distance between background and foreground.

Zooming right out can produce a distorting effect on the foreground.

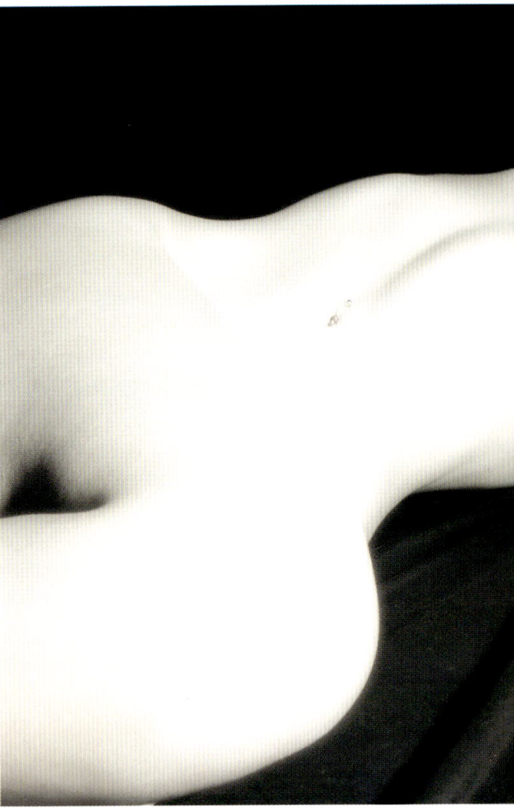

When you are choosing a digital camera, it's helpful to understand the way that camera manufacturers specify the power of zoom lenses. It's also helpful to understand the effect of depth of field in photography and some of the constraints that you may encounter in using depth of field.

FIXED ZOOM LENSES

Midrange digital cameras have fixed (i.e. non-detachable) zoom lenses. (Interchangeable lenses are available only on high-end models.) The focal lengths of digital camera zoom lenses are usually marked on the lens barrel. However, these figures can be confusing, as they are related to the size of the imaging chip inside the camera, which is smaller than a frame of 35mm film (often much smaller) and varies from one camera to another.

For this reason, manufacturers also specify focal length by stating the equivalent length on a 35mm camera, on the basis that most photographers will be familiar with these figures. For example, the lens on a Fujifilm FinePix 6900 Zoom is marked "7.8–46.8mm," which is stated by the manufacturer to be the equivalent to a zoom lens of 35–210mm on a 35mm camera. So the 35mm equivalent focal length for this lens is about 4.5 times what is marked on the lens barrel.

Zoom lenses on digital cameras may be either "wire-controlled" (operated by a rocker switch on the camera body) or manually operated by rotating a ring on the lens barrel. Wire-controlled lenses tend to lack the precision of adjustment of manually operated lenses.

In making sense of these figures, it's helpful to note that, again in terms of 35mm lenses:

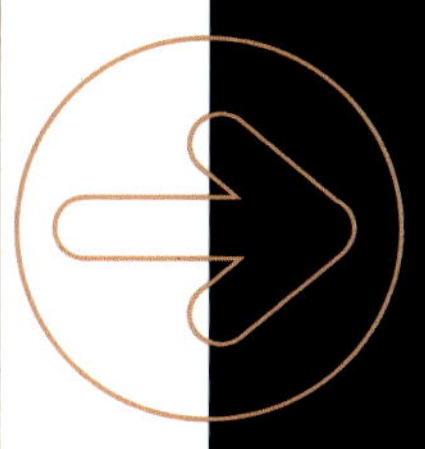

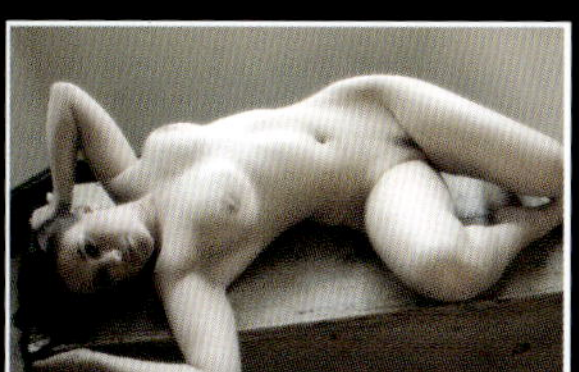

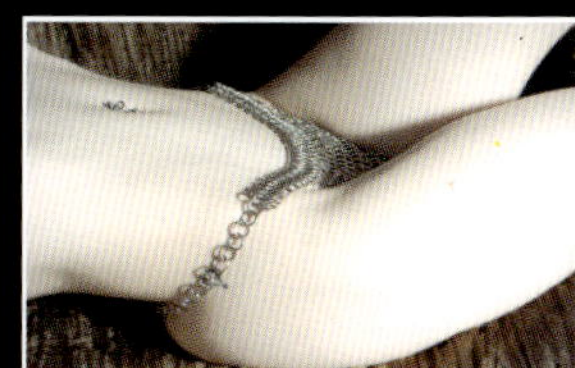

Understanding the capabilities of the camera's lens is an essential part of the photographer's art. A firm understanding of effects such as depth of field will give you greater control over the images you can produce.

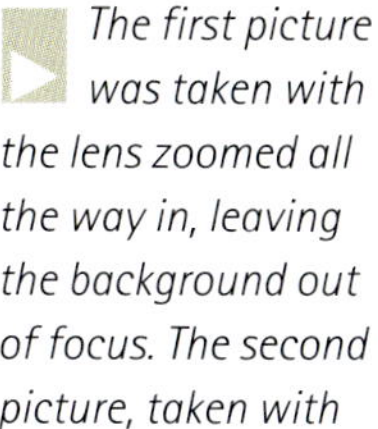

The first picture was taken with the lens zoomed all the way in, leaving the background out of focus. The second picture, taken with the lens zoomed all the way out, shows the background in focus. In addition, note how this creates a visible change of perspective.

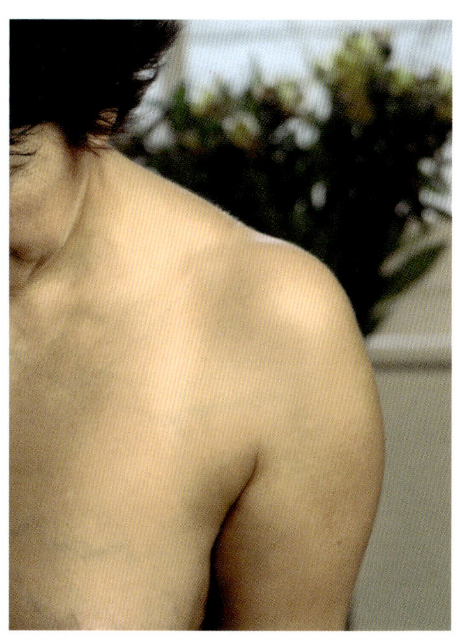

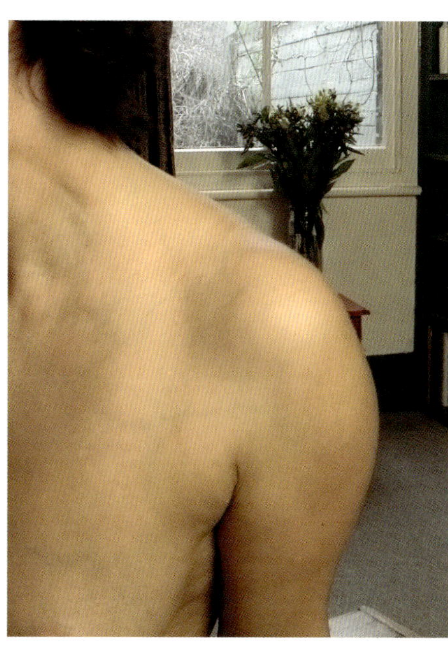

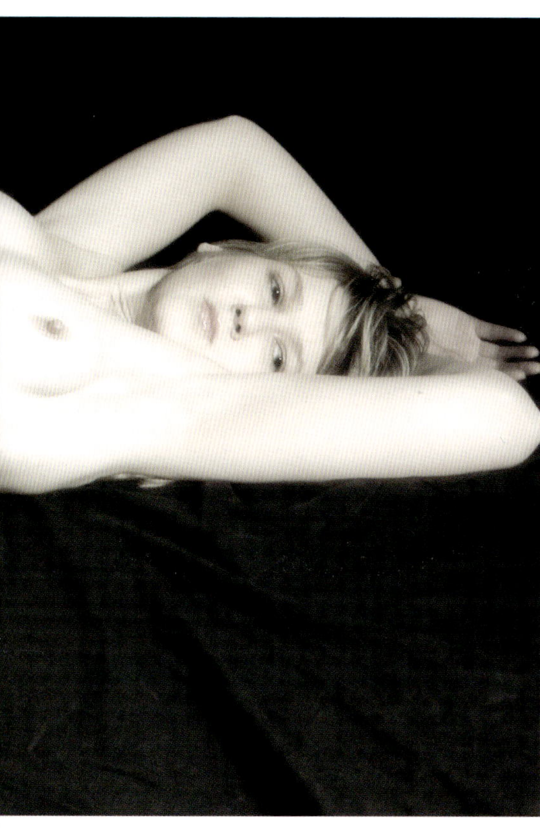

- A focal length of 50–55mm corresponds to the normal human field of vision from side to side.
- 80–90mm is reckoned to be a good focal length for portrait photography.
- 35mm or less will produce a distinct "wide-angle" feel, with the foreground distorted.
- Anything over about 105mm will produce a noticeable compression effect.

DEPTH OF FIELD

When a lens is zoomed out (and has the widest angle of view), it also has the greatest depth of field. Depth of field refers to the area of the image that is in focus in front of and behind the distance at which the lens is actually focussed. The use of shallow depth of field can be a potent tool, as it enables you to guide the eye to a certain part of the shot.

Depth of field is affected by:

- The distance to the subject—the closer the subject, the shallower the depth of field.
- The lens aperture—the larger the aperture (i.e., the smaller the f number), the shallower the depth of field.
- The focal length—the shorter the focal length (i.e. the wider the angle of view), the greater the depth of field.

It might seem that to achieve shallow depth of field all you need do is to zoom in and move as close as you can to the subject while staying in focus. Unfortunately, most non-detachable zoom lenses are designed so that as you zoom in, the aperture reduces (the f number increases), which can make it hard to control depth of field with precision *(see pages 20–23).*

FACT FILE

35mm equivalents

You may read that you should multiply the focal length of a digital lens by 1.5 to calculate its 35mm equivalent. This applies only when using a 35mm lens on a digital camera that takes interchangeable lenses.

TIP

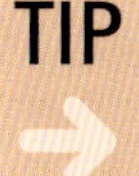

After you've taken a shot, most cameras let you zoom in on the monitor to view details of the image—a useful device for checking depth of field.

Focussing

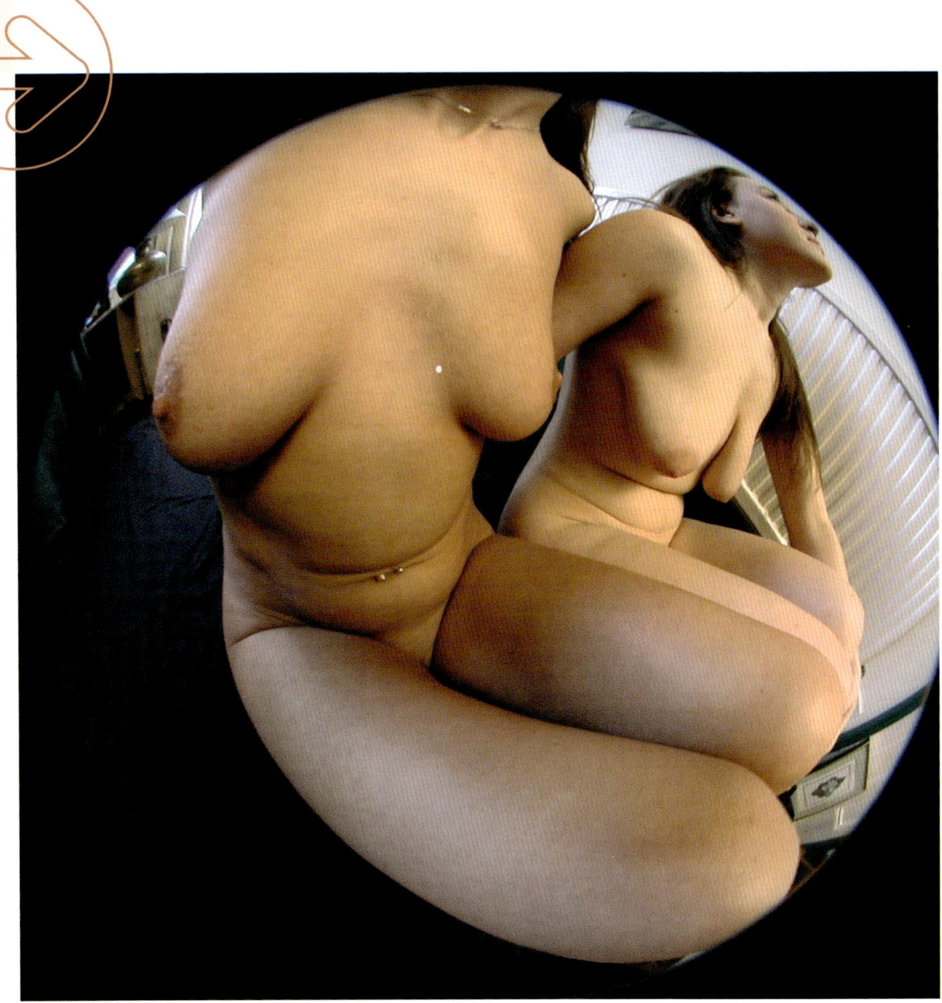

An image made with a fish-eye lens. In addition to creating extreme distortion, this sort of lens boasts an enormous depth of field.

The five focus areas on a Nikon 5700. Notice how close together they are.

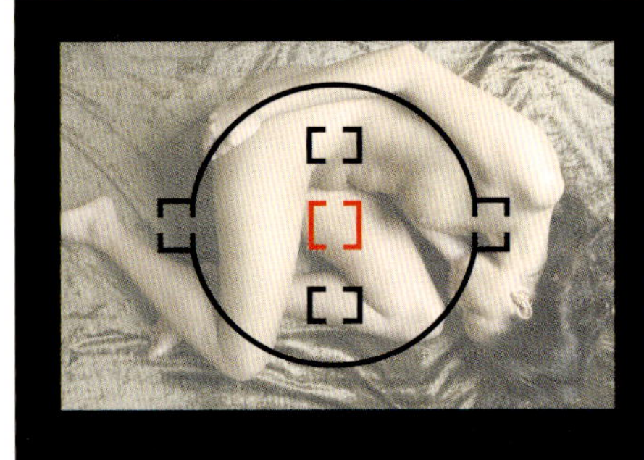

Carefully used, modern autofocus (AF) systems take care of most of the practicalities of getting focus "right." This lets you concentrate on choosing just what to focus on, and how much to have in focus.

AUTOFOCUS SYSTEMS

Pretty well all midrange digital cameras have AF systems as well as some form of manual focus control. Usually applying "half-pressure" to the shutter release button will activate the AF, with some kind of visual confirmation—a green dot in the viewfinder or an LED on the camera body lighting up—when the camera is in focus.

AF systems that are set to "continuous" will attempt to focus all the time, even when you're moving about. Because this action can quickly run down the camera's battery, it makes sense to switch this setting off, so that the camera focusses only when you half-press the shutter.

SETTING UP THE AF ON YOUR CAMERA

Your camera may have a number of modes for selecting the area on which the AF focusses. One mode may be "fully automatic': when you half-press the shutter, the camera focusses on whichever area in its field of view is closest. This is useful when you are shooting in a hurry, but not helpful otherwise. Another mode may be "manual," where you select between a number of focus areas displayed in the viewfinder. This can be useful when the model is posed at an oblique angle to the camera. The simplest setup—and the one which I find the most useful—has just one focus in the center of the viewfinder.

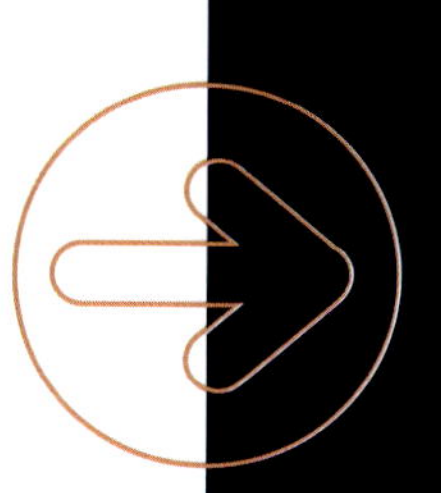

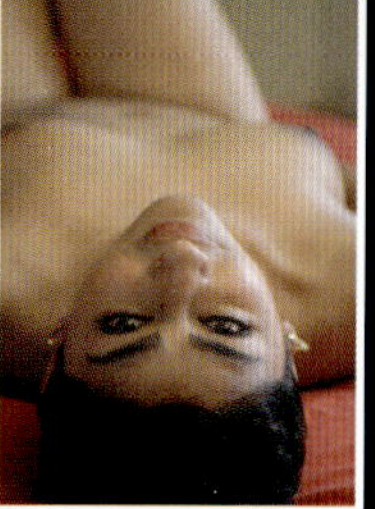

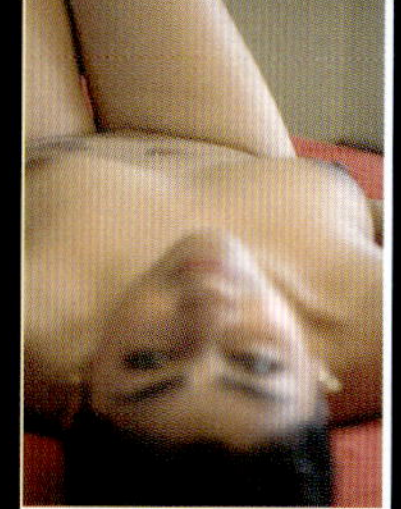

The autofocus features employed by modern digital cameras are very sophisticated, but they can make mistakes. You can learn how to avoid these, and also how to exploit focus as a part of your creative technique.

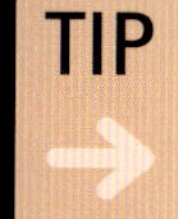

TIP Experiment with the different AF modes on your camera to decide which works best for different shots.

If you want to have the model in focus but off-center in the frame, simply:

1 Center the model in the frame. Apply and hold half-pressure on the shutter to focus.

2 Still holding half-pressure on the shutter, and without changing the distance between the lens and the model, move the camera left or right, up or down, until you have the model framed as you wish.

3 Take the picture.

DIFFERENTIAL FOCUS

Differential focus means having one plane of the image sharply focussed and another blurred. Achieving this depends on working with a shallow depth of field. On some lenses the lens stops down (the aperture reduces and the f number increases) as you zoom in. This makes it hard to produce differential focal effects, because stopping a lens down increases depth of field. The shots to the right were taken with a Nikon D100 with a Nikon 35-70mm zoom lens, which has a constant maximum aperture of f2.8 at any zoom position. (Note also the compression effect caused by zooming in.) At the other (wide) end of the zoom, depth of field is almost infinite.

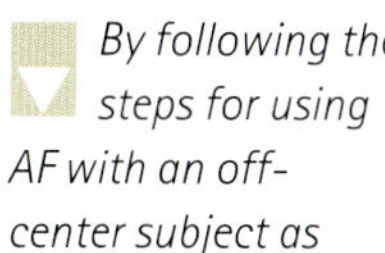

By following the steps for using AF with an off-center subject as described in the main text, the model is in focus.

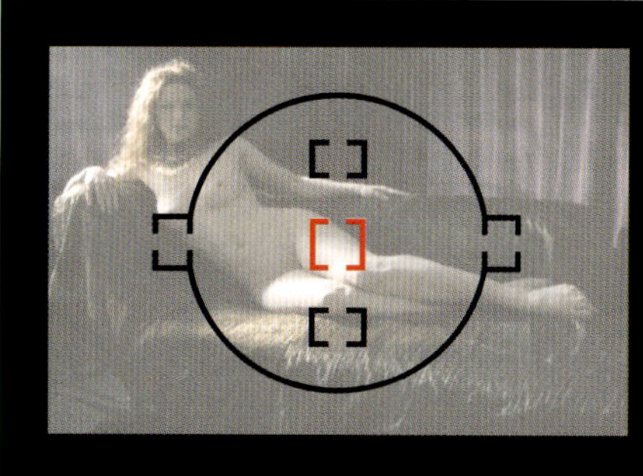

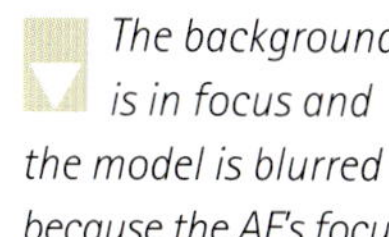

The background is in focus and the model is blurred because the AF's focus area wasn't aimed at the model when applying half-pressure on the shutter.

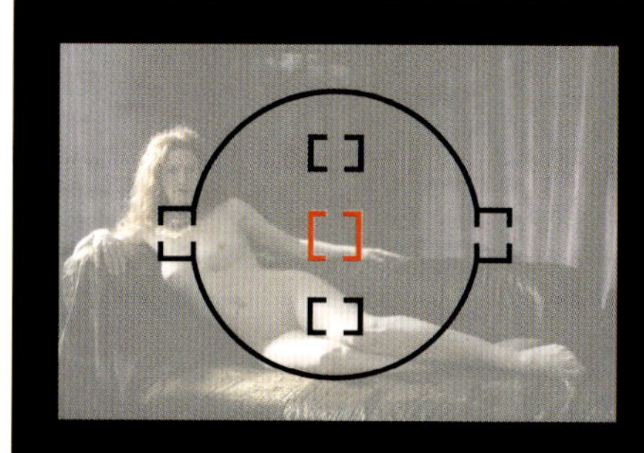

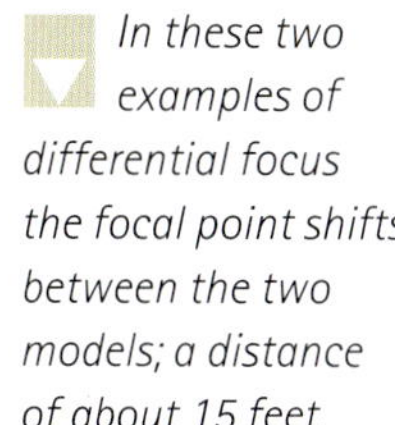

In these two examples of differential focus the focal point shifts between the two models; a distance of about 15 feet.

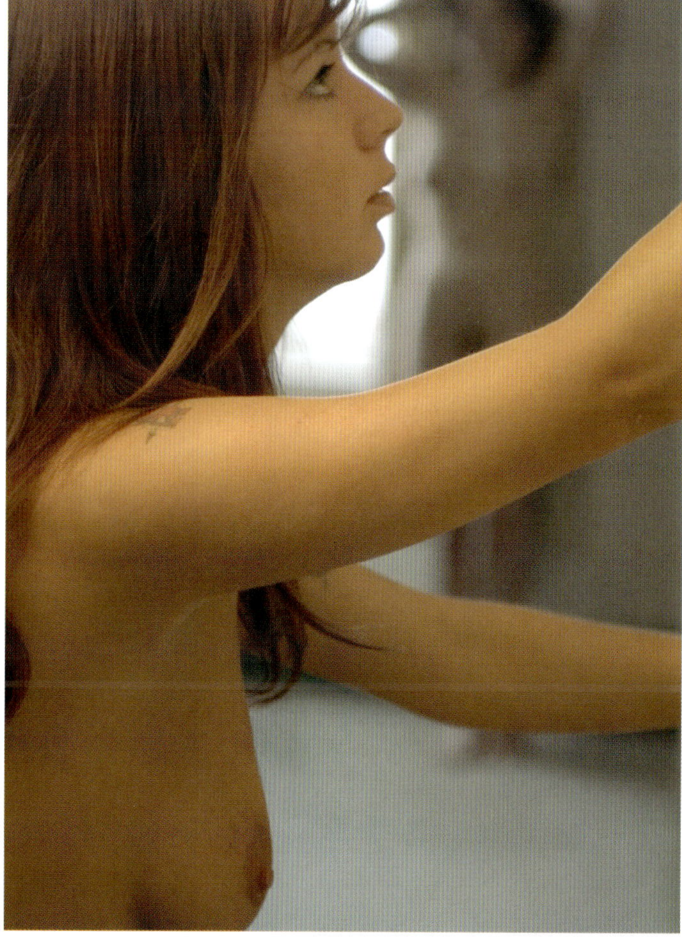

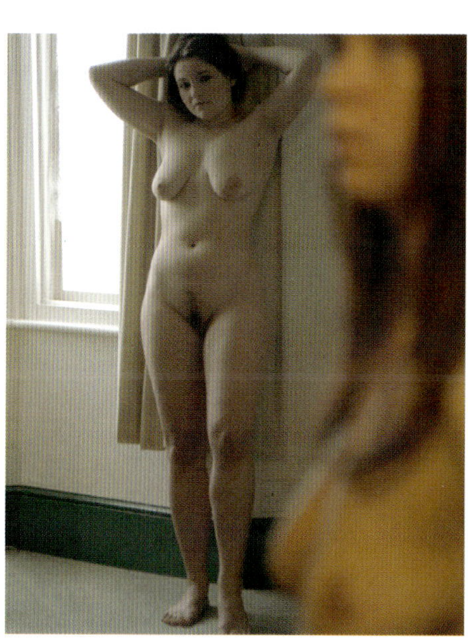

Focussing

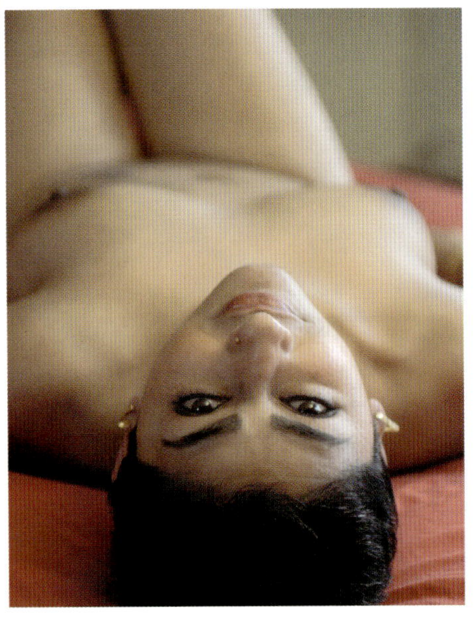

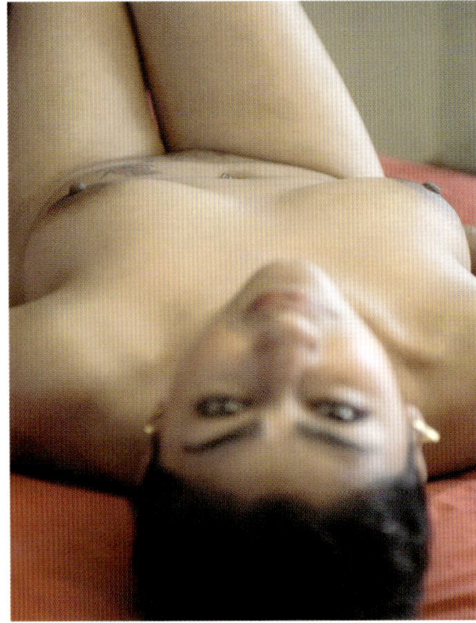

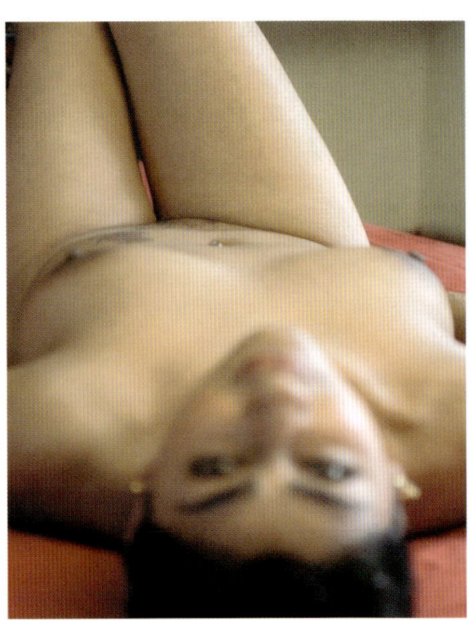

WHAT FOOLS THE AUTOFOCUS?

AF systems focus on whatever is closest in the focus area. So if the model is holding a veil in front of her, for example, or is behind a screen, the AF will focus on the veil or the screen. In these circumstances, the camera's manual focus provides a solution.

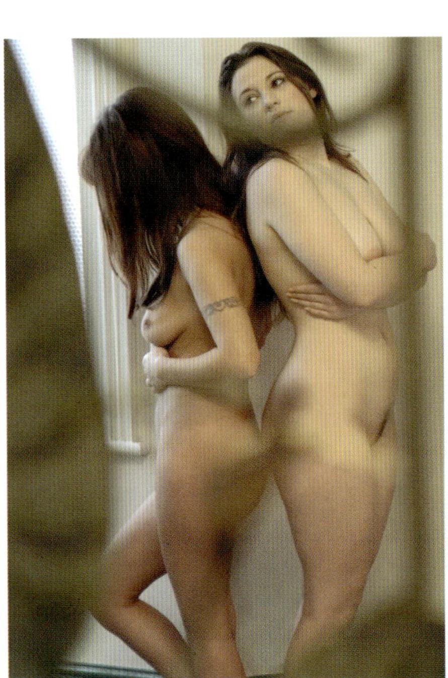

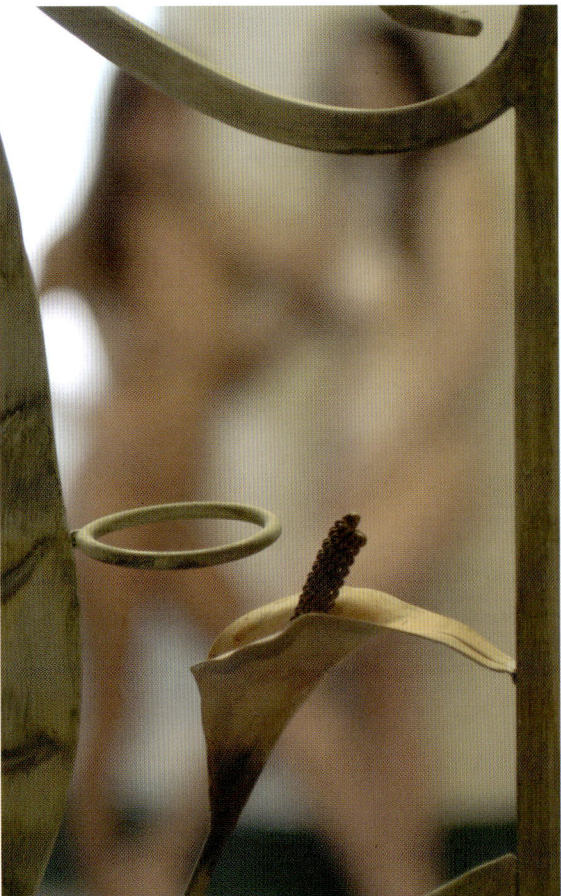

In this sequence, the focal point is moved away from the viewer a few inches at a time, along the model's body.

Manual focus lets you focus through a foreground object.

TIP

It's easy to create a "soft-focus" look over all or part of an image using the computer. It's far less easy to create convincing sharpness in an image that is soft to begin with.

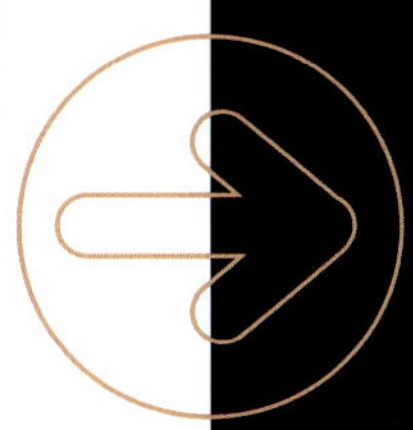

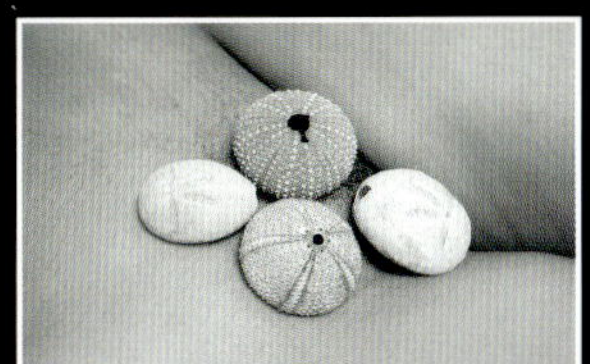

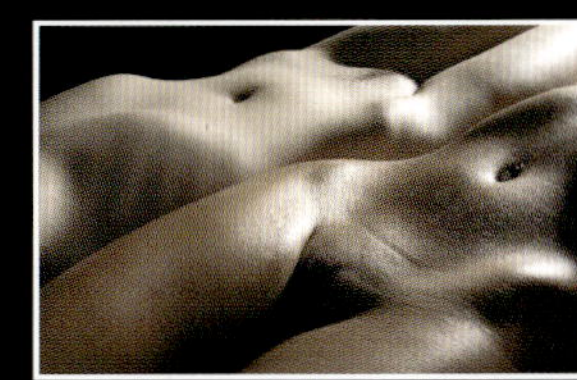

Manual focus and macro facilities can be used where you need tight control over the focal point, or in situations where the autofocus could be fooled. Macro settings, in particular, let you take advantage of natural curves and textures.

GETTING UP CLOSE

Most lenses offer a macro facility that enables you to fill the frame with a small area of your subject. You can make striking images from different skin textures, folds in the body, and other details. At the other extreme, a fisheye lens squeezes a field of view of up to 180° into the frame, with spherical distortion and almost infinite depth of field.

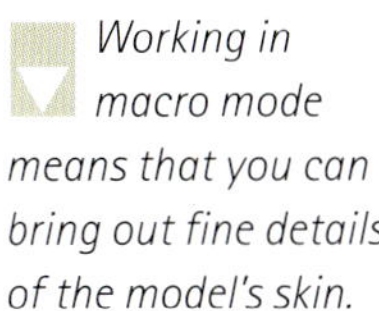

Working in macro mode means that you can bring out fine details of the model's skin.

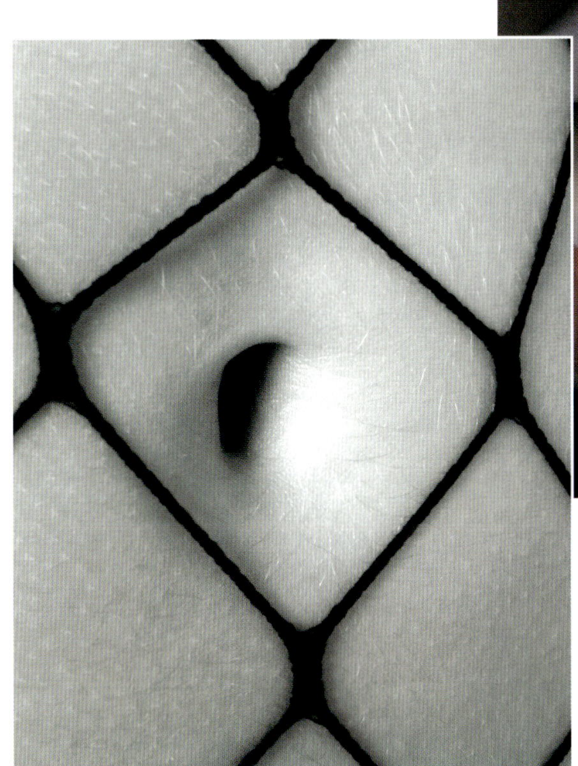

Here the fish-eye lens has been zoomed in to reduce the circular vignette seen around the image on page 20.

Exposure

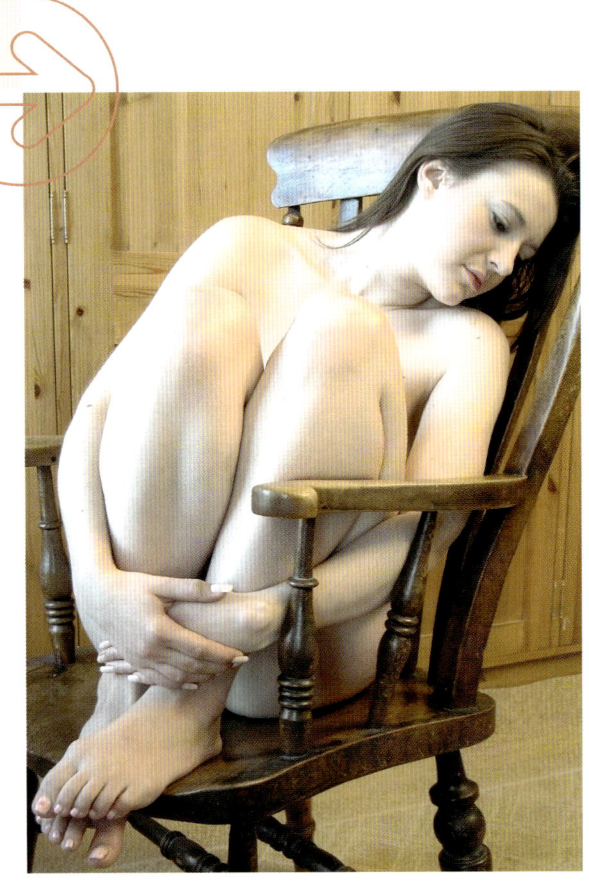

A well-exposed image captures every tone: from the whitest highlights to the darkest shadows.

The matrix method (shown by the grid) holds the highlights just below overexposure.

Center-weighted metering achieves a good balance between the drapes and the model, while retaining the subtle patterns of sunlight across the model.

Getting exposure right with a digital camera is easy, because you can check results instantly and make any adjustments. Under straightforward lighting conditions, using available light or built-in flash, you may be able to get good results just by putting your camera into its automatic mode and leaving it to the camera to work out the correct combination of shutter speed and aperture. You can gain more control over the camera by putting it into Aperture Priority, Programed Auto, Shutter Priority, or Manual mode.

DIFFERENT MODES

Programed Auto offers you by default the same combination of shutter speed and aperture you would get if you had the camera in fully automatic mode, but enables you to adjust both shutter speed and aperture together, as a way of varying the depth of field of the shot or controlling motion blur. In Aperture Priority mode, you select the aperture, and the camera adjusts the shutter speed accordingly (usually with some visible warning if this results in a combination of settings that would produce an over- or underexposed image). In Shutter Priority mode, you select the shutter speed and the camera sets the aperture (again with a visible warning for incorrect exposure). This gives some control over motion, enabling you to freeze it or create motion blur. In Manual mode, you can control both aperture and shutter speed separately, using the scale displayed in the viewfinder to get the right combination.

METERING METHODS

Once you switch the camera out of fully automatic mode, you need to decide how you want the camera to measure the light that's entering the lens. These options apply to all the modes described already, except for Manual.

The Matrix method measures the light at several hundred points in the frame and uses this data to calculate the optimal exposure. (This is also the method that the camera uses in fully automatic mode.)

The Center-weighted method measures the light across the whole frame, but assigns more importance to the central quarter of the image. This should preserve details in other parts of the picture, while exposing correctly for the central area.

If you have set the focus area to manual selection *(see pages 20–23)*, you can use the Spot AF Area method of light metering to expose correctly the area where you have focussed the camera.

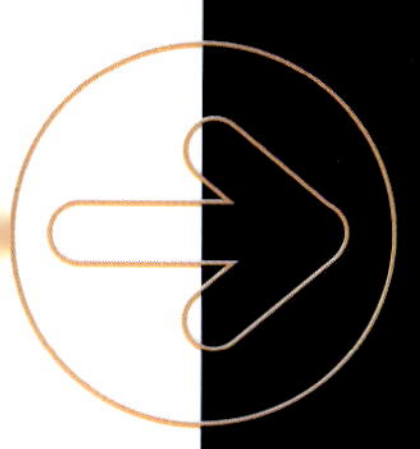

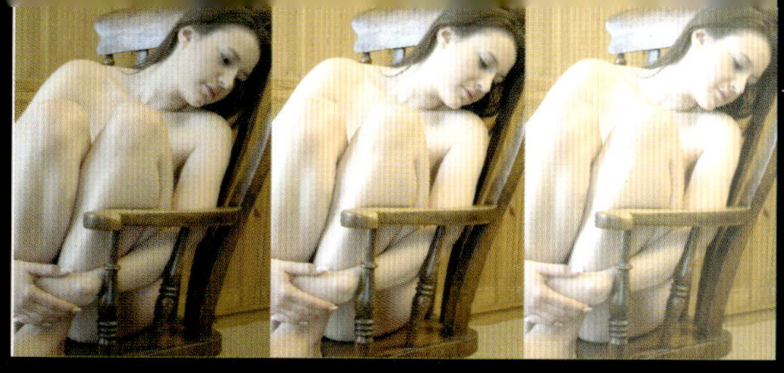

Achieving the correct exposure for your image is made simple in digital cameras. Some cameras even offer auto-bracketing, which takes a series of the same photograph at different exposures so that you can select the best image.

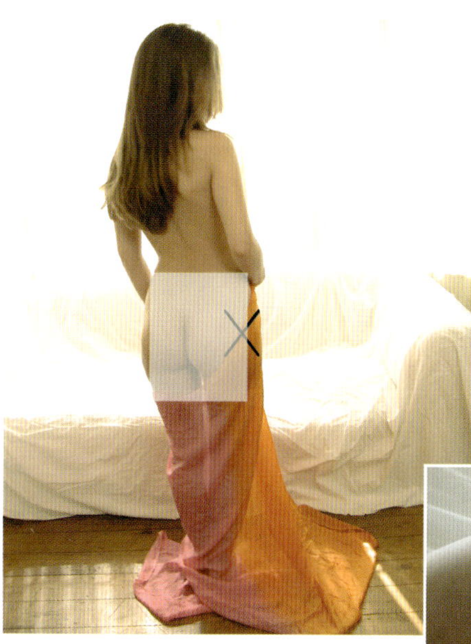

This shot was framed with the model in the center, then, with half-pressure on the shutter to lock the focus and exposure, reframed to give the desired composition.

The model's knees are in focus, as the red focus-area brackets indicate; the exposure is taken from the same area.

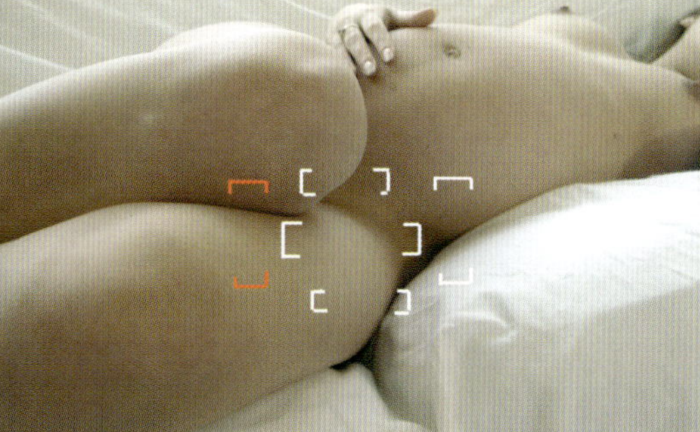

FACT FILE

Bracketing

Bracketing means taking the shot at what the camera tells you is the correct exposure, then reshooting it deliberately over- or underexposed by a stop or half a stop, just in case the camera hasn't got it completely right. There is less need to do this in digital photography, because you can always review each picture after taking it and—on many cameras—check a "Levels" histogram *(see pages 90-91).* However, it can be difficult to assess subtleties of exposure in the camera's small display screen, and sometimes it makes sense to bracket your shots.

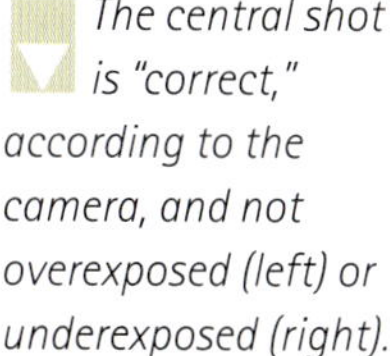

The central shot is "correct," according to the camera, and not overexposed (left) or underexposed (right).

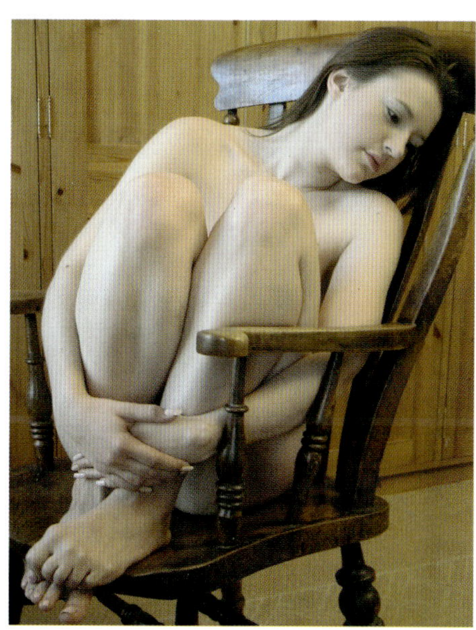

Underexposed

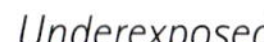

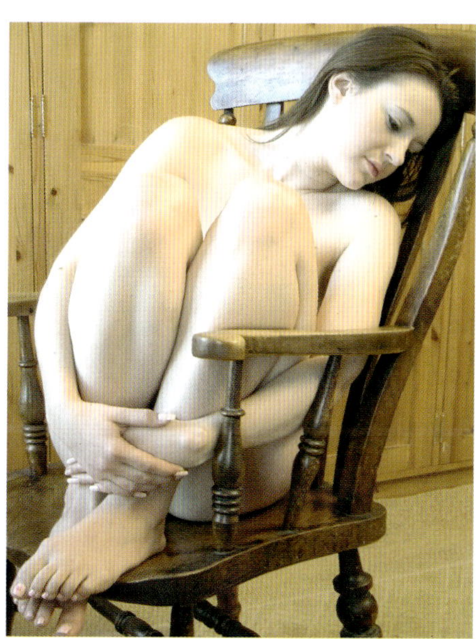

Correctly exposed

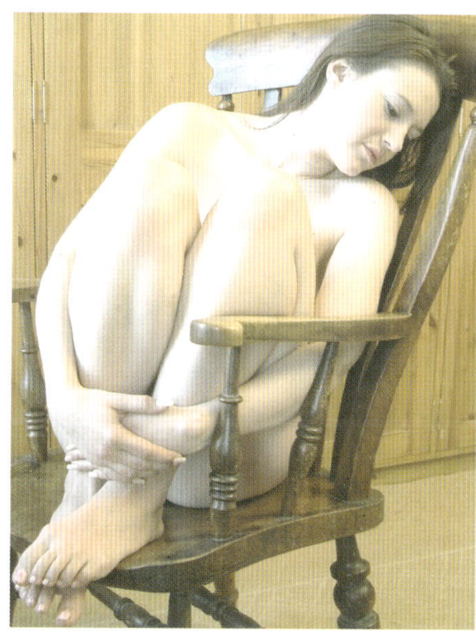

Overexposed

Low light and camera sensitivity

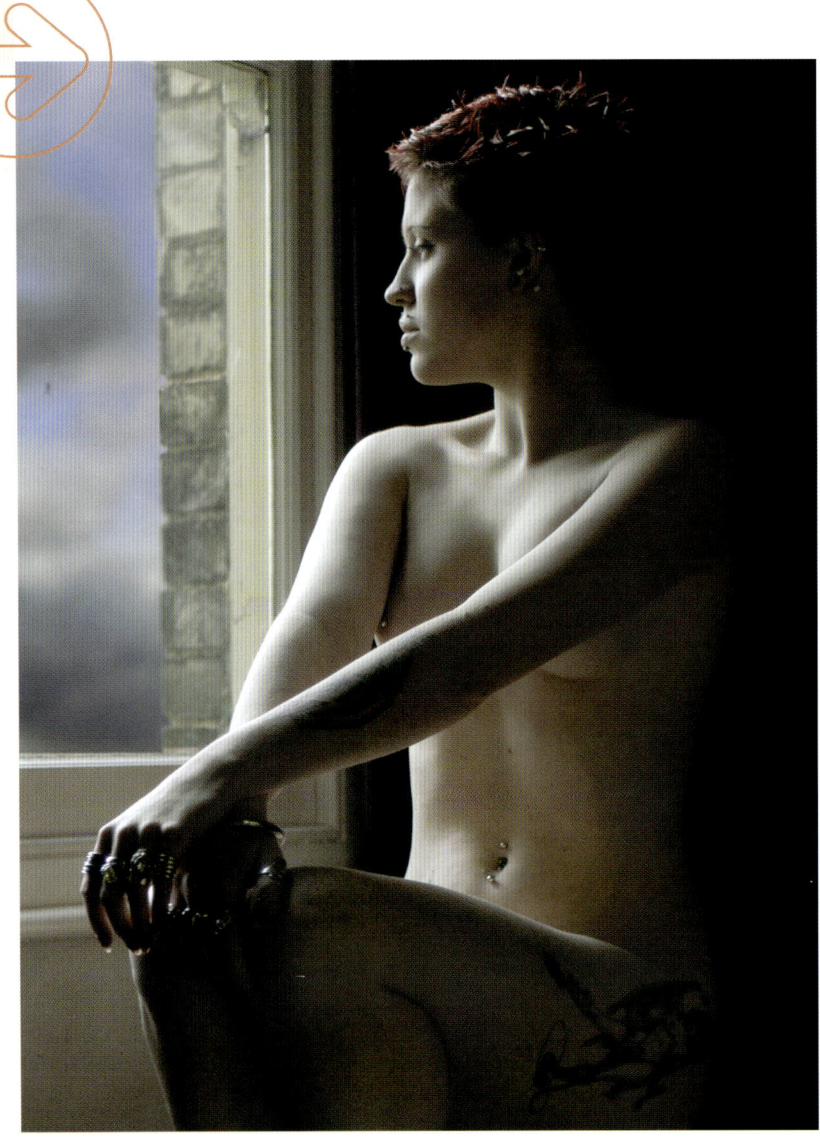

The image may look fine at the size you see it on the camera's monitor...

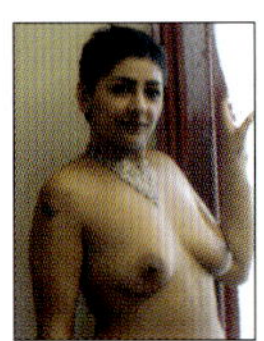

...but camera shake is evident at 100% size.

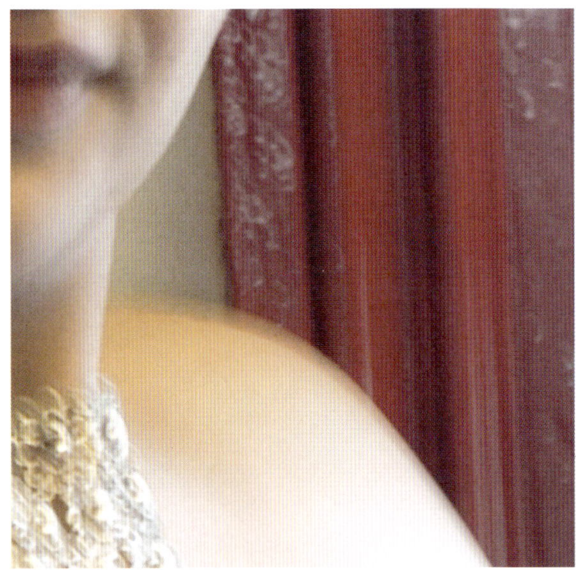

The use of a tripod keeps the camera steady and eliminates blurring.

Working indoors using available light, you will often find that, even with the aperture wide open, you need to use slow shutter speeds ("slow" here means 1/30 second or slower). It can be difficult to handhold a camera steadily under these circumstances. Increasing the sensitivity of the camera may enable you to use a faster shutter speed.

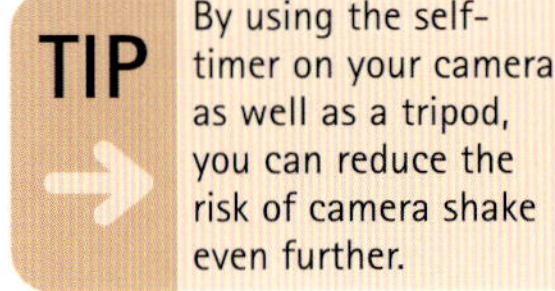

TIP By using the self-timer on your camera as well as a tripod, you can reduce the risk of camera shake even further.

DEALING WITH LOW LIGHT

The effect of camera shake may not always be visible when you glance at the playback of your picture in the camera's monitor screen, but will be all too evident when you zoom into the image on the camera monitor, or look at the image full size on your computer.

The gentle, diffused light from the window falling on the model would be lost if you added more light from the interior of the room. One solution is to use a tripod and possibly a remote-control shutter release. These steady the camera and retain the mood.

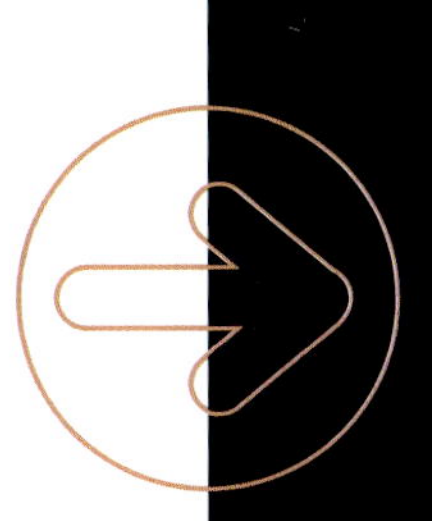

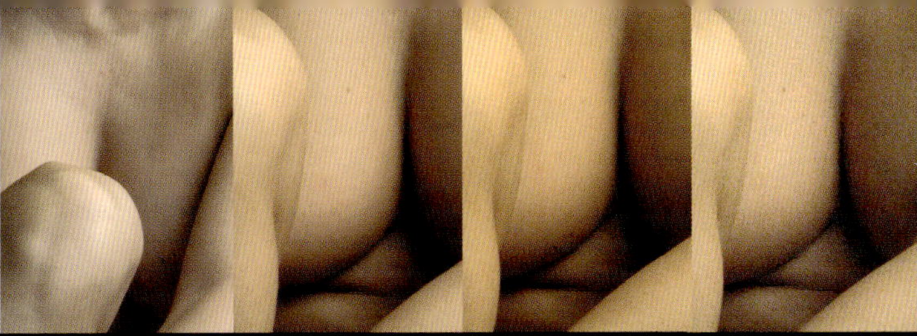

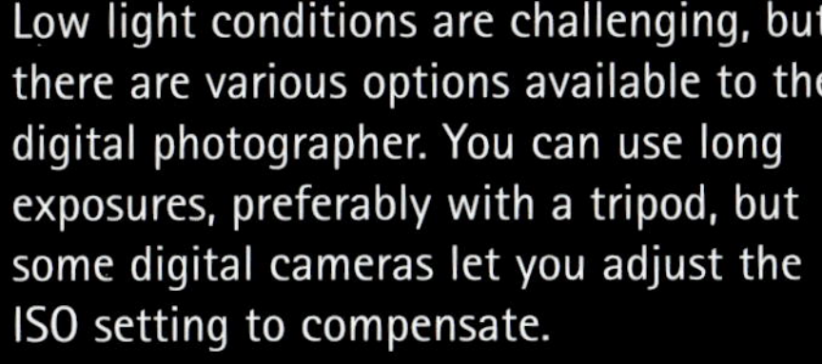

Low light conditions are challenging, but there are various options available to the digital photographer. You can use long exposures, preferably with a tripod, but some digital cameras let you adjust the ISO setting to compensate.

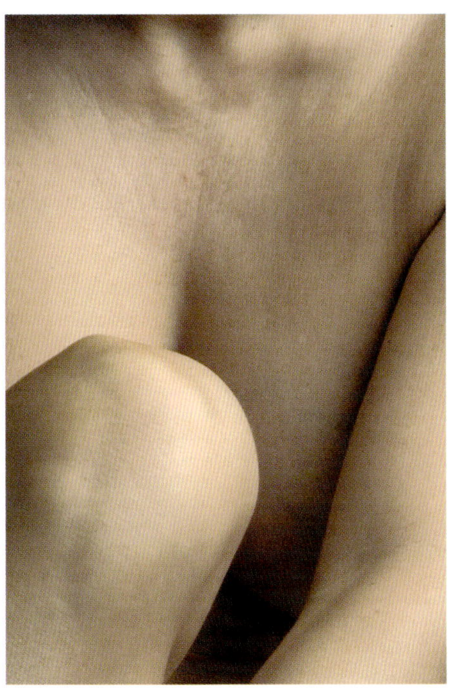

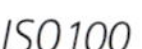

ISO100

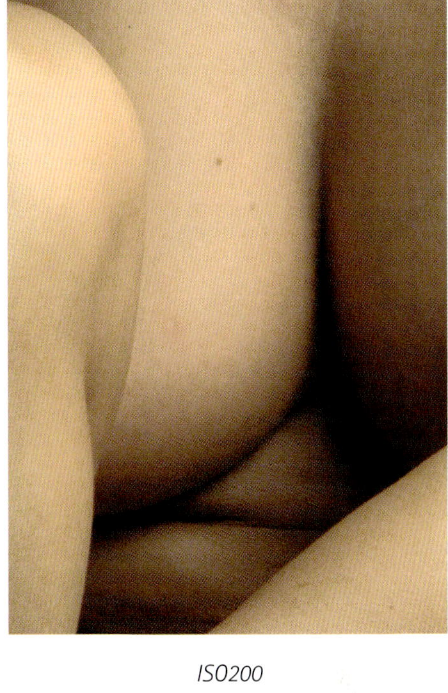

ISO200

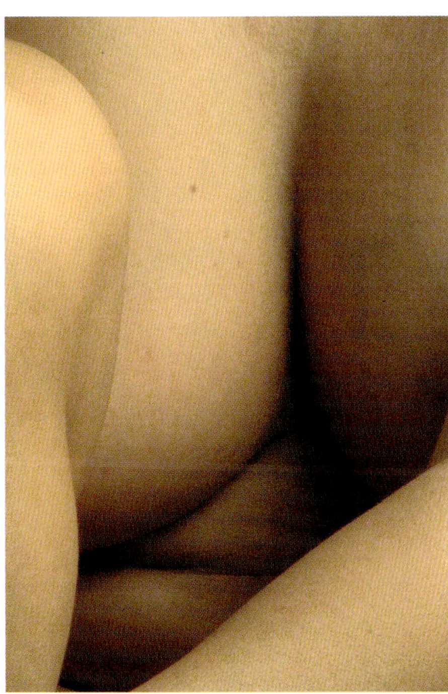

ISO400

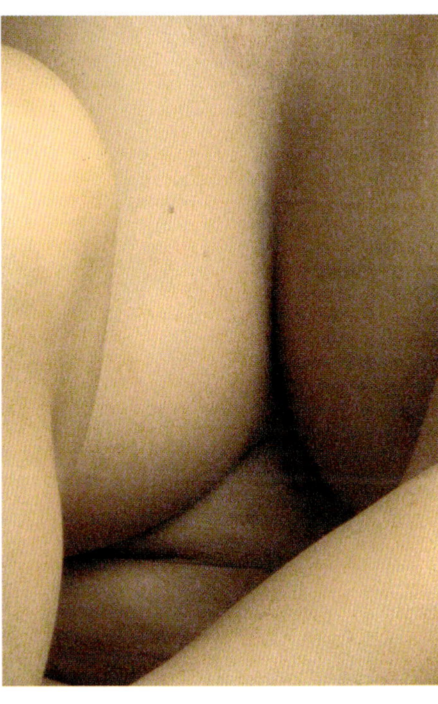

ISO800

Another way of avoiding camera shake is to increase the shutter speed by changing the sensitivity of the camera. "Sensitivity" in a digital camera corresponds to the ISO rating of film. Most midrange digital cameras offer a range of ISO equivalent sensitivities from ISO100 to ISO800. Every time you double the ISO rating from, say, ISO100 to ISO200, your shutter speed becomes twice as fast—from, say, 1/30 second to 1/60 second at the same aperture. However, you'll also see a noticeable increase in the amount of noise in the picture, particularly at ISO800.

These examples emphasize the need for caution in using any of the faster ISO ratings on your camera. There are methods of reducing the visible presence of small amounts of noise in an image (*see pages 80–81*), but they are unlikely to cure the high noise levels that go with faster ISO ratings.

Note the increase in noise from ISO100 through ISO200 and ISO400 to ISO800.

FACT FILE

The quick tripod test

If your shutter speed (expressed as a fraction of a second) exceeds the focal length at which your lens is set (expressed in millimeters) you'll avoid camera shake. So if you're using a wide-angle lens set at 24mm, you're probably OK with a shutter speed of 1/30 second. But if you're zoomed in to 200mm, you'll need a shutter speed of 1/250 sec.

Lighting

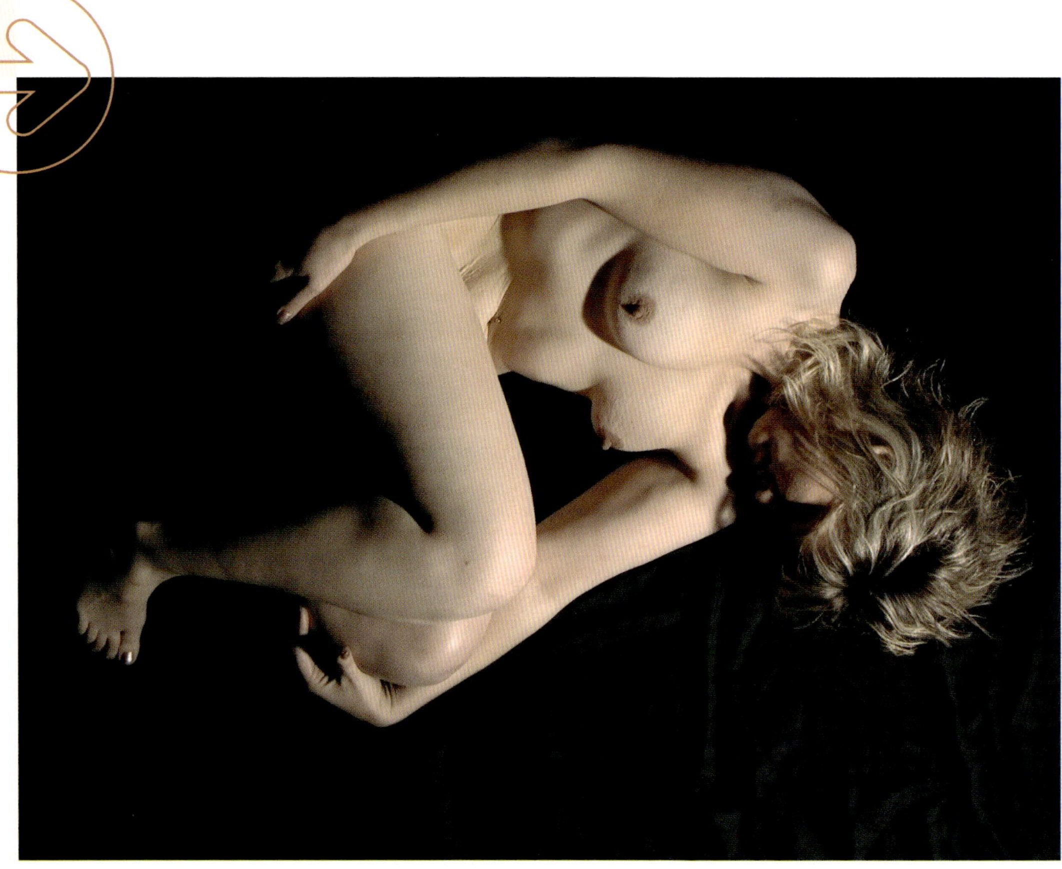

Maria is posed against a black floorcloth and lit with one large studio softlight.

Becky is lit by available light through a bay window.

Some fill light from the opposite (camera) side was provided by a 600W Arilight bounced off the ceiling.

It's a cliché to say that photography is all about lighting, but this is particularly true of photography of the nude. The same pose can be given a completely different feeling by being lit in different ways.

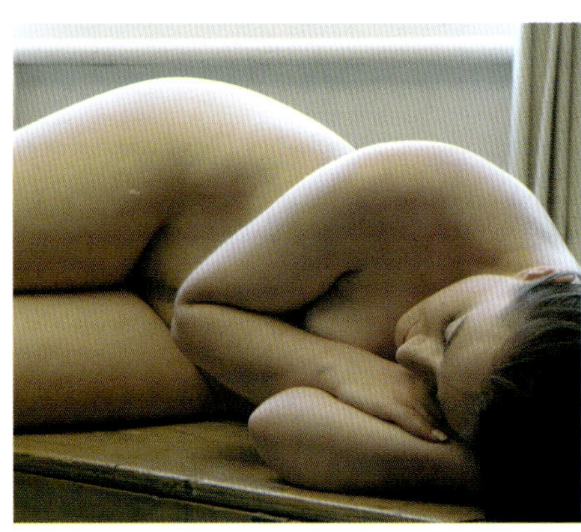

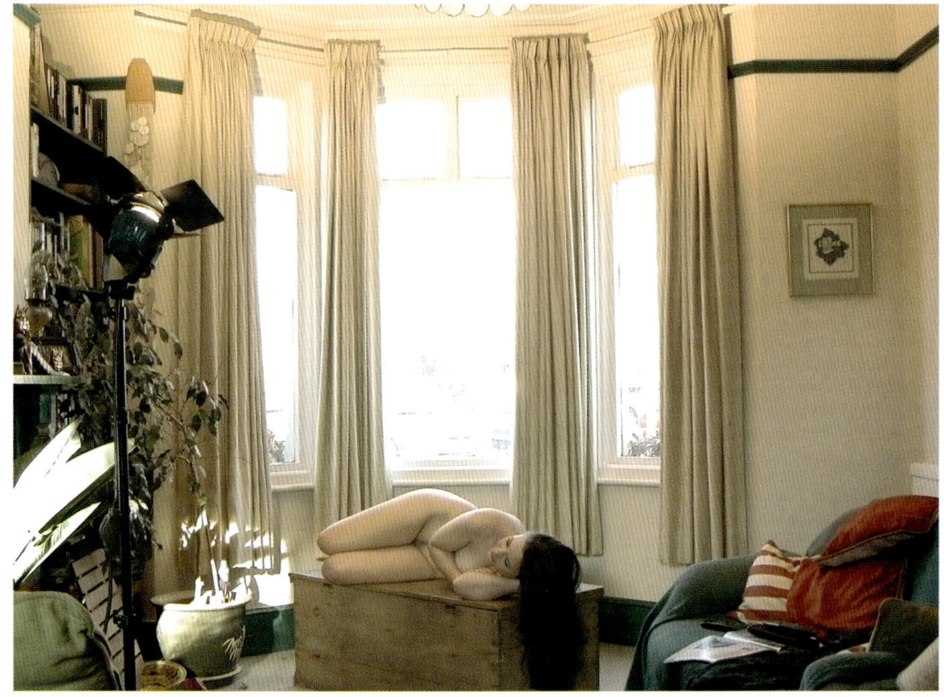

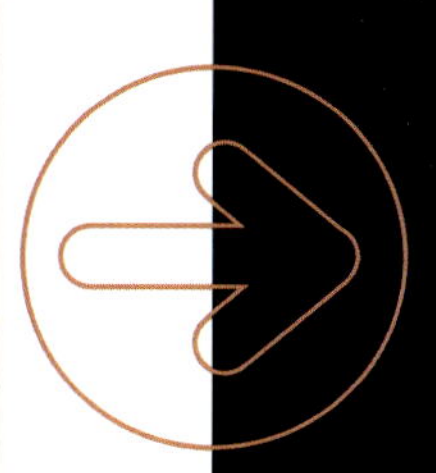

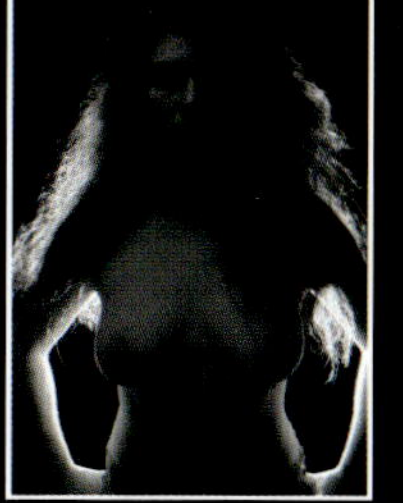

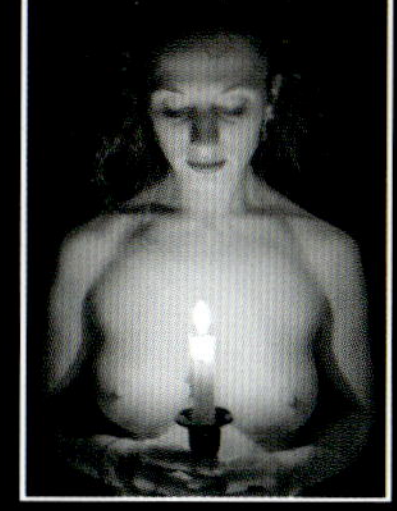

An understanding of how lighting works is essential for the photographer. Most digital cameras have a built-in flash, but available light and studio lighting will give more effective and attractive results.

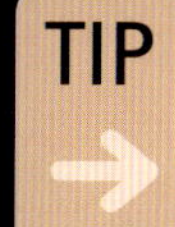

TIP The high sensitivity levels of modern digital cameras mean that you can get away with using candlelight as a source.

The model lit by daylight alone. Note how this leaves much of the face and body in shadow.

Using a basic reflector fills in the shadow areas without spoiling the feel of the shot.

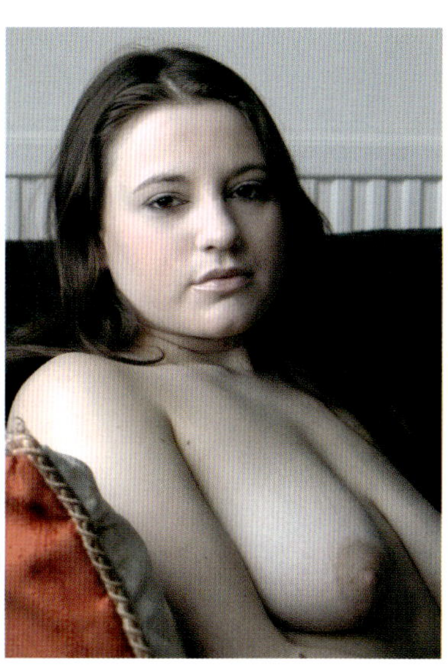

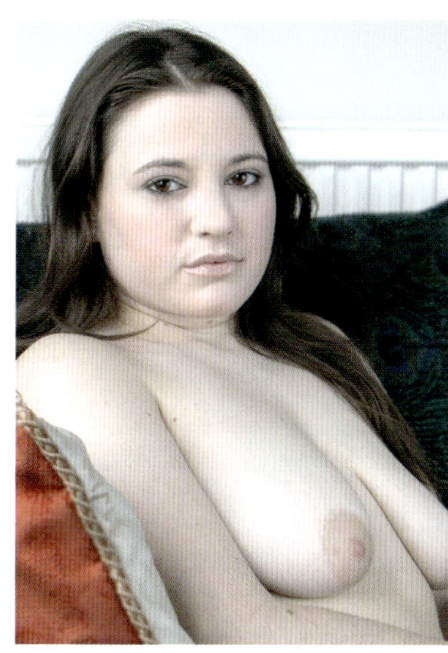

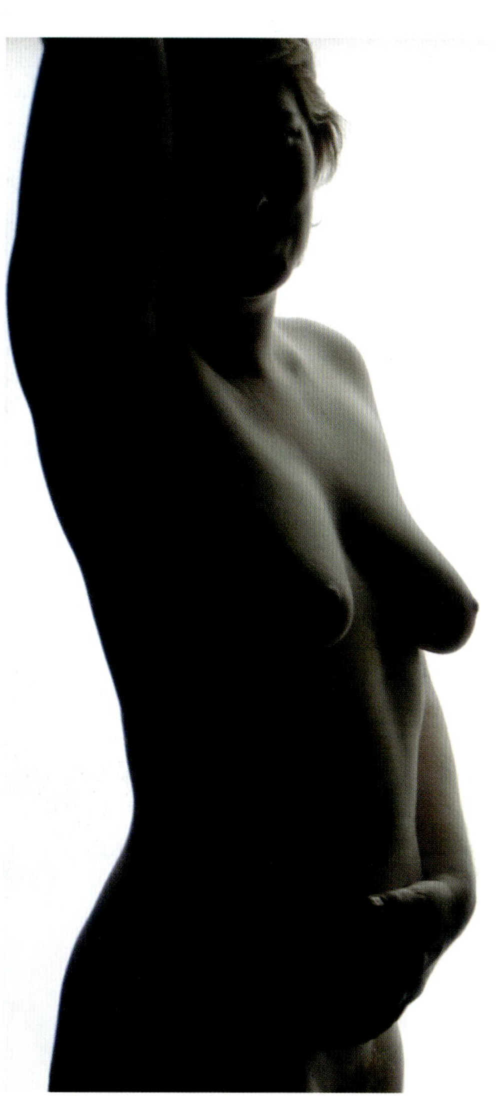

This model is lit by available north light, with the soft shapes filled in by light reflected from the white walls of the room.

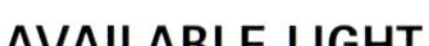

AVAILABLE LIGHT

The simplest way to light your model is with available light—the light that comes through the window, or the light outdoors. This requires no lighting equipment, although you may need a tripod to steady the camera *(see pages 26–27)*. The effects that you can achieve with window light range from the soft, even lighting of north light (daylight reflected from the sky without any direct sunlight) to more strongly contrasted images of sunlight and shadow. Available light also provides scope for silhouettes.

You can enhance your use of available light by employing a reflector to provide some "fill" light without spoiling the natural feel of the shot. You can use professional photographic reflectors, but anything white or bright will work—even a large sheet of paper, or a sheet of card wrapped in aluminum foil.

FLASH AND STUDIO LIGHTING

The built-in flash on your camera often gives disappointing results. Directly frontal lighting is harsh and unsympathetic, and does little to capture the body's shape and contours. Using an external flash unit will improve results slightly, but is still very limiting.

If you want to move beyond working with available light, the next stage might be to arrange a shoot in a local photographic studio, so that you can experiment with the the studio's lighting facilities. Studio lighting comes in two types: flash and continuous. To use flash lighting, your camera needs to have a "hot shoe" to which you can attach the cord that controls the flash heads.

Continuous lighting usually consists of tungsten or fluorescent lamps. Both systems include attachments to let you control the spread of the light and its quality, which can range from hard (producing dark shadows with crisp edges) to soft (shadowless or faint shadows with indistinct edges).

White balance

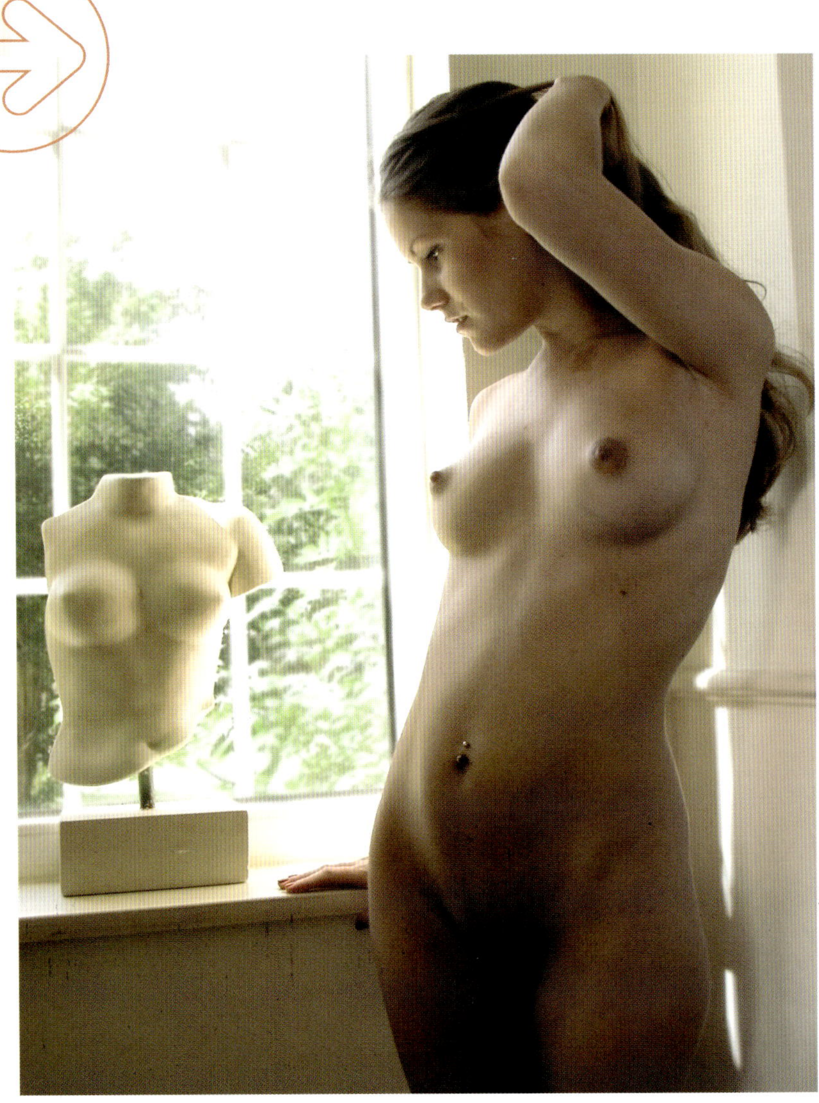

Chrissy shot using available light, including the room lights. Set to auto, the camera's white balance hasn't "correctly" rendered the white plaster bust.

This shot used a manual white balance setting. The plaster bust is white, but I prefer the golden skin tones of the image on the left.

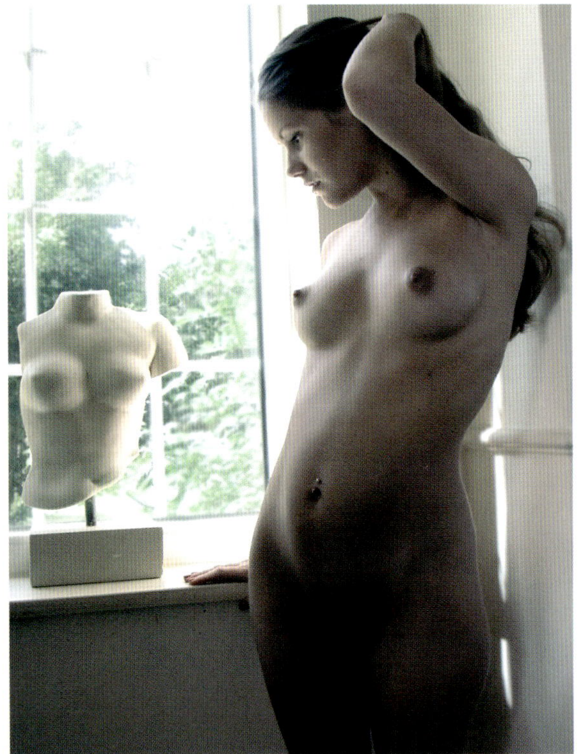

Different sources of light—sunlight, domestic light bulbs, fluorescent lights, camera flash units—produce different-colored light. We think of all these light sources as producing white light, but in fact sunlight when the sun is overhead is blue compared to ordinary light bulbs, which in turn are red compared to sunlight. When we move from one type of light to another (going indoors on a sunny day, for example), we're not aware of the change of color because our minds adjust what we see, so that we perceive everything as the "right" color.

SETTING THE WHITE BALANCE

Sometimes you need to alter camera settings in order to achieve this correct color. This is known as setting the white balance. Since white contains all the colors of the visible spectrum, if the camera is set to "see" white correctly, it will also reproduce all other colors accurately.

Your camera will have an Auto setting for white balance, as well as a range of other settings for different light sources, and possibly a "fine tuning" option for more precise control. The Auto setting will work for many situations, but sometimes you will need to intervene to get the best white balance.

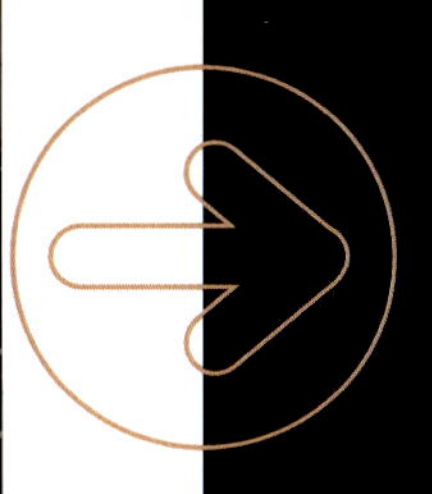
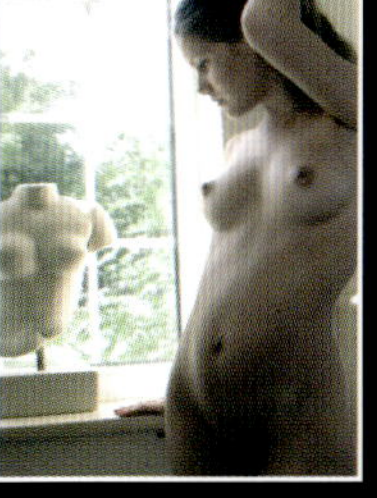
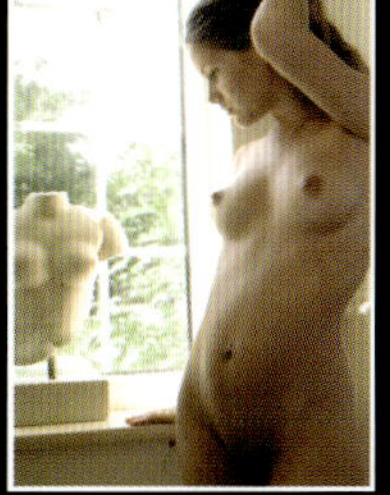

When shooting photographs indoors, control over white balance is essential. To avoid color casts, many cameras offer a range of predefined white balance settings. Alternatively, you can create your own.

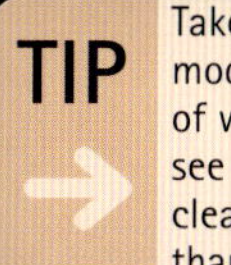

TIP Take a shot of the model holding a piece of white paper. You'll see color casts more clearly on the paper than on the skin.

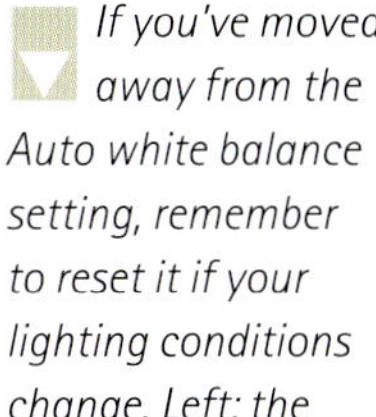

If you've moved away from the Auto white balance setting, remember to reset it if your lighting conditions change. Left: the excess of blue in the image indicates that it was shot using daylight, but with the camera set to tungsten. Center: shot under one type of fluorescent lighting with the camera set to tungsten. Right: shot under tungsten with the camera set to daylight.

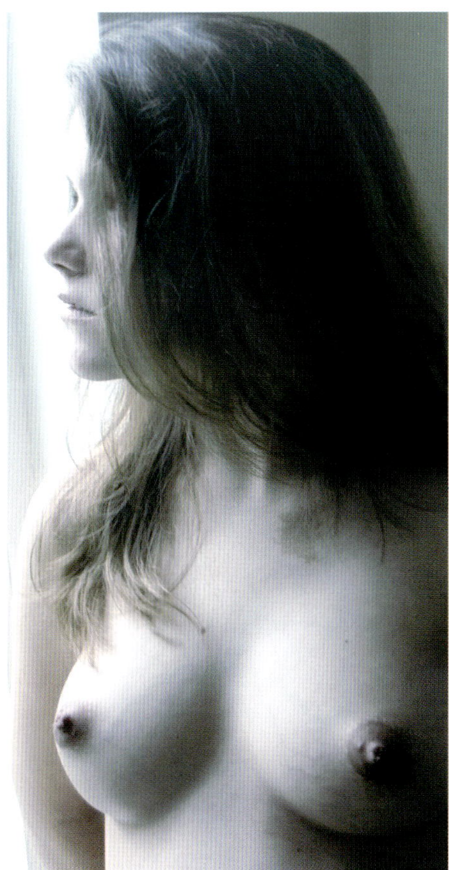

Daylight with camera set to tungsten

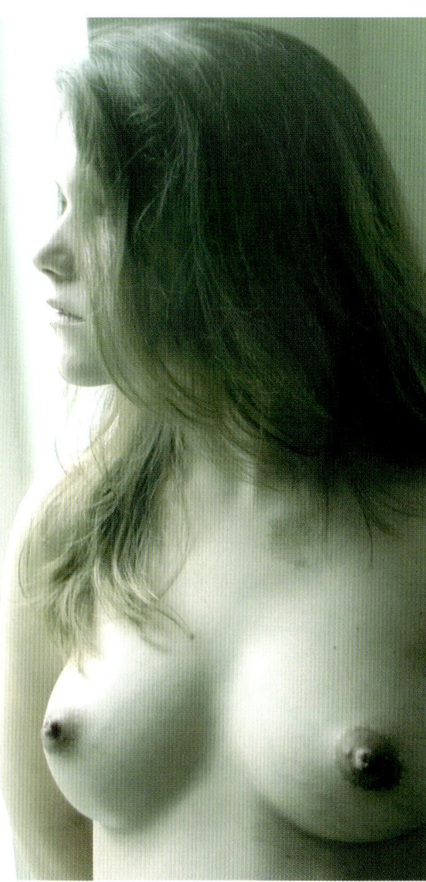

Fluorescent lighting with camera set to tungsten

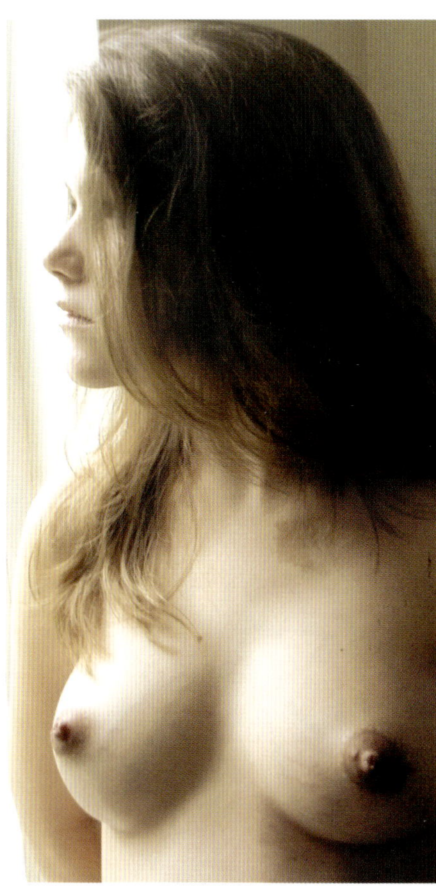

Shot under tungsten with camera set to daylight

As well as the Auto setting, most cameras offer a range of preset white balances for different lighting conditions, such as incandescent (i.e. ordinary light bulbs), fluorescent, cloudy, and flash (this usually refers to the camera maker's own flash units: it may not give good results with studio flash heads). You just set the white balance to whichever condition you're working in. Here, the camera's LCD screen comes into its own as a way of assessing whether you prefer the Auto setting or the appropriate preset.

However, you will often find yourself working under mixed conditions, where the light is a blend of, say, daylight and tungsten. The best way to get an accurate white balance under these conditions is to use a manually adjustable preset. In this mode you focus the camera on a sheet of white paper, and when you press the appropriate button the camera "learns" that this is what white looks like under the given lighting conditions. (This works only with continuous light sources, not with flash.)

Having said all that... in nude photography, it's less important to get a technically correct white balance in every shot than to use the light to achieve the effect you want.

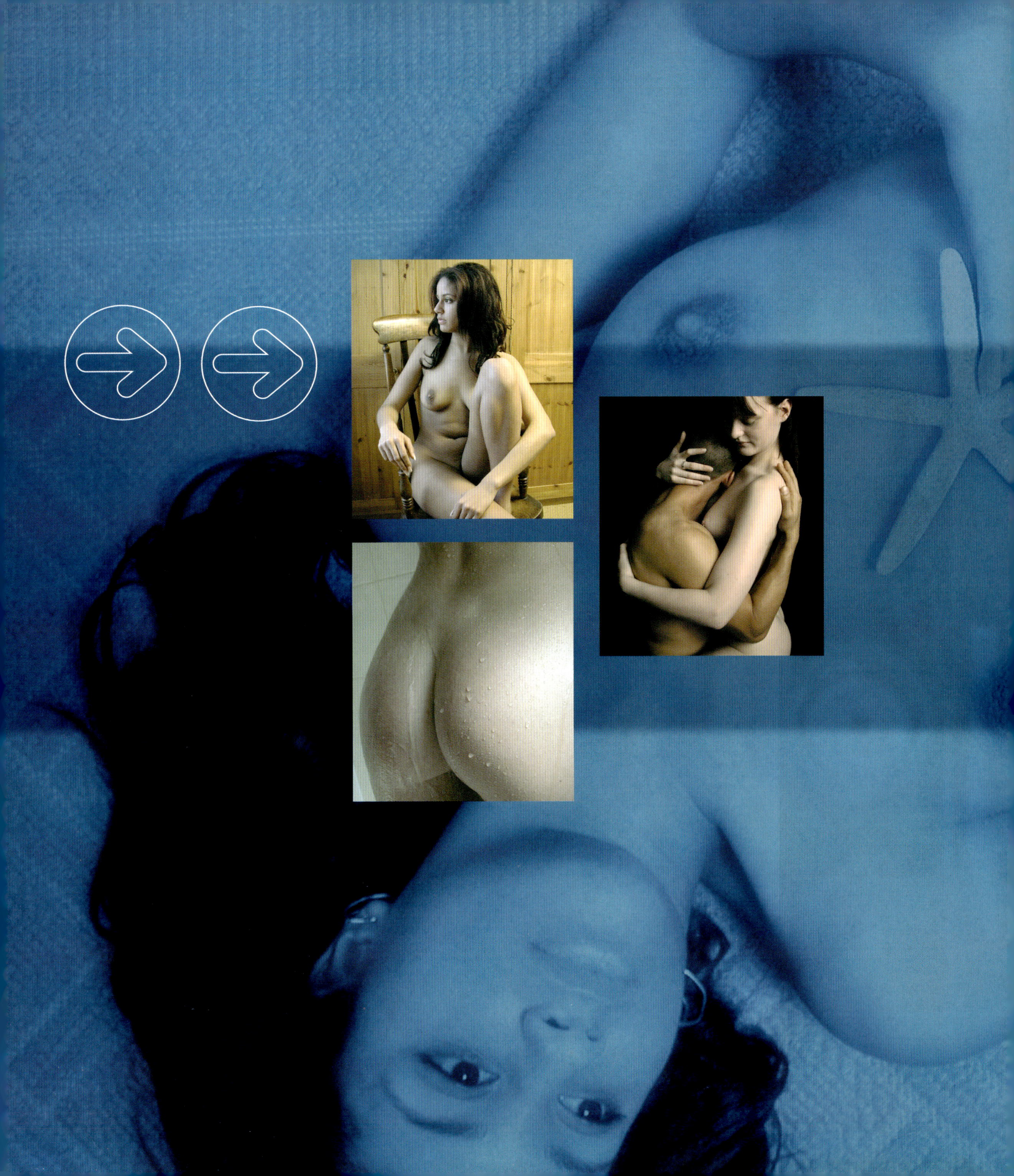

2 Taking great nude shots

We begin this chapter with a thorough look at the process of selecting, engaging, and working with a model. We then go on to explore different spaces and locations for photography, including setting up a home studio. The role of lighting in creating distinctive images is explored in detail, as are theories of composition and the arts of posing the model, and using paint, props, and materials to hide or emphasize parts of the body.

Models

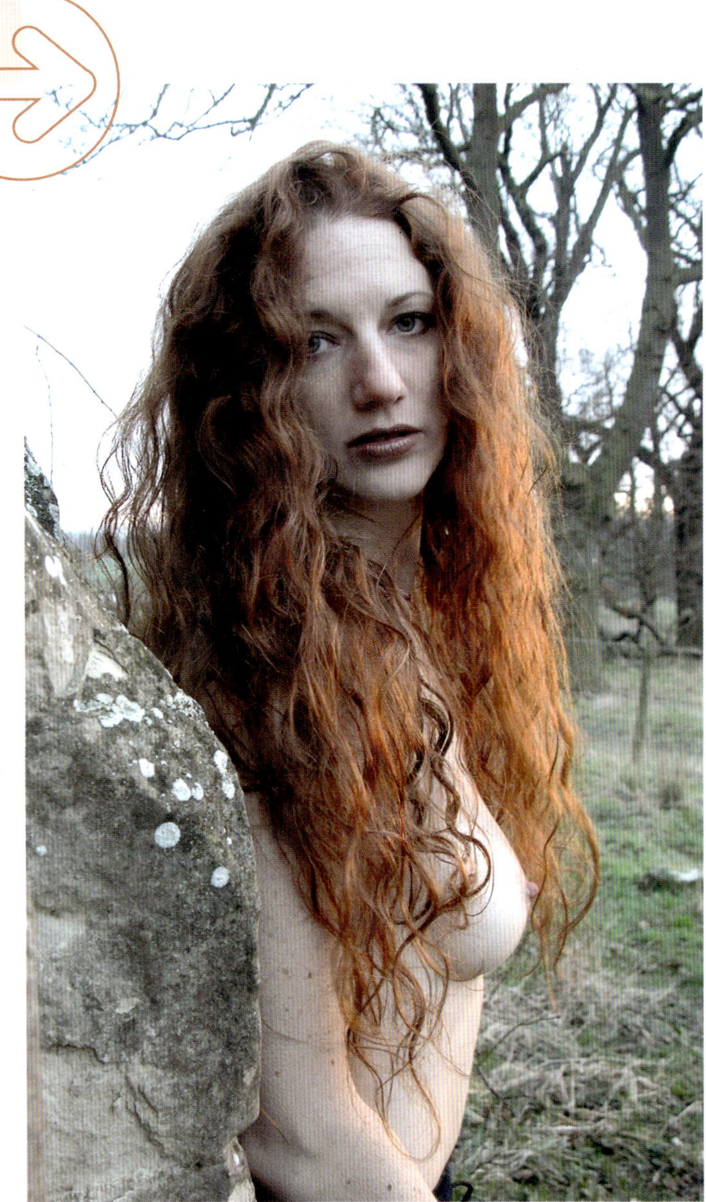

Every model has his or her own special qualities and features. Maximizing their interest and individuality will help to make your work stand out.

The form shown below is a screen grab of RedLilly's model listing on the OneModelPlace.com *website. The form clearly states her physical statistics and the type of work for which she is available. It also provides general information about her photographic preferences.*

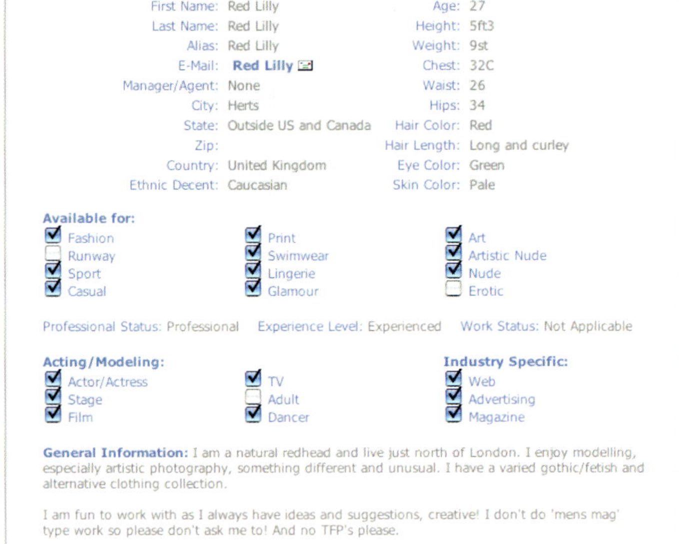

First Name:	Red Lilly	Age:	27
Last Name:	Red Lilly	Height:	5ft3
Alias:	Red Lilly	Weight:	9st
E-Mail:	**Red Lilly**	Chest:	32C
Manager/Agent:	None	Waist:	26
City:	Herts	Hips:	34
State:	Outside US and Canada	Hair Color:	Red
Zip:		Hair Length:	Long and curley
Country:	United Kingdom	Eye Color:	Green
Ethnic Decent:	Caucasian	Skin Color:	Pale

Available for:

- [x] Fashion
- [ ] Runway
- [x] Sport
- [x] Casual
- [x] Print
- [x] Swimwear
- [x] Lingerie
- [x] Glamour
- [x] Art
- [x] Artistic Nude
- [x] Nude
- [ ] Erotic

Professional Status: Professional Experience Level: Experienced Work Status: Not Applicable

Acting/Modeling:

- [x] Actor/Actress
- [x] Stage
- [x] Film
- [x] TV
- [ ] Adult
- [x] Dancer

Industry Specific:

- [x] Web
- [x] Advertising
- [x] Magazine

General Information: I am a natural redhead and live just north of London. I enjoy modelling, especially artistic photography, something different and unusual. I have a varied gothic/fetish and alternative clothing collection.

I am fun to work with as I always have ideas and suggestions, creative! I don't do 'mens mag' type work so please don't ask me to! And no TFP's please.

There are a number of ways of finding a model to work with. To start with, your partner may be willing to model for you. This can work well if your partner is comfortable in his or her new role as a model. But if it proves stressful for either of you, there are alternatives.

LOCAL STUDIOS

One possibility is to join a photographic studio in your area that offers group sessions for members. Some photography clubs run group sessions specifically for nude photography. The studio books one or more models, for anything from two hours to a whole day, and you sign up to share the shoot with other members. You make use of the studio's lighting facilities and sets, and the costs are shared among the participants. This also gives you the chance to meet other photographers and see how they work. Some studios offer photography holidays (some of them in exotic locations), which work in the same way. Studios may also offer "meet the models" evenings—food and drink and mingling and a studio session with a model.

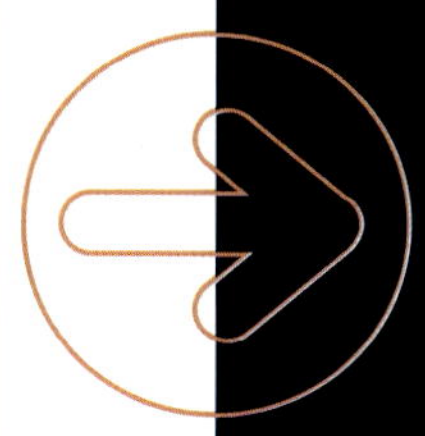

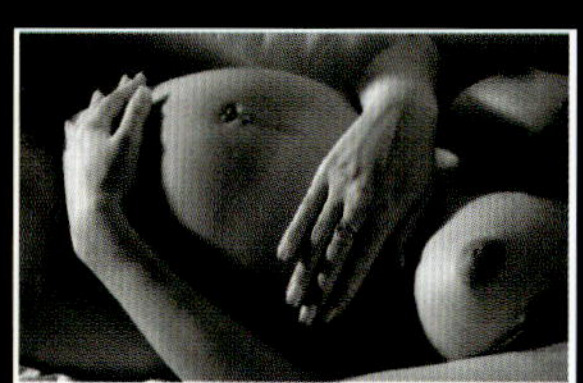

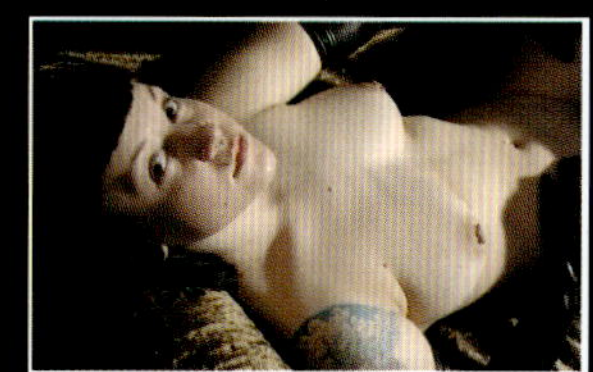

Where do you look to find a model? The internet is a good place to start searching if your partner is unwilling to model for you. Alternatively, there are a number of reputable professional agencies that provide models.

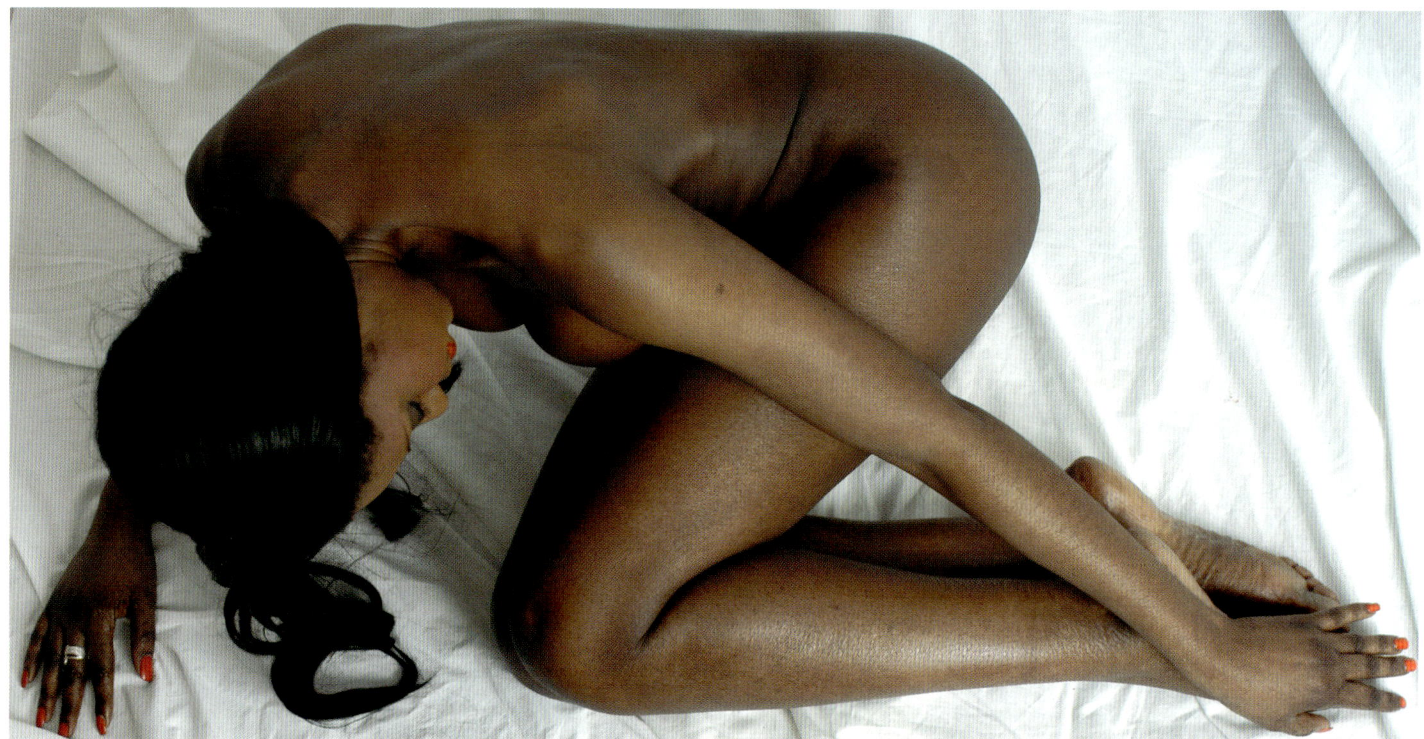

FINDING A MODEL

If you would prefer to work on your own, the internet is definitely the best resource for finding models. Typing in phrases such as "photographic models" to a search engine will provide you with hundreds of model sites. These should include some photographs of the model; details such as age, height, vital statistics, length and color of hair; and a way of contacting them. The listing may also include the model's rates.

The listing should also specify the range of work that the model is willing to undertake. This will include an indication of the model's upper limit—that is, how much exposure the model will agree to—from modeling swimwear and lingerie through to making adult videos. If the listing includes the model's fees, you will notice that usually the more exposed the model, the higher the fee.

There is no reason not to ask an "adult" model to pose for an artistic nude shoot, but those models who are specifically listed as posing only for lingerie shoots or topless shoots are most unlikely to be willing to do a nude shoot.

The largest model site currently is *www.OneModelPlace.com*. Most of the models used in this book have listings on OMP. Although based in the USA, this site covers most of the world. Some of its facilities are available only to subscribers, but it's good value for money, and as a photographer subscriber you can use OMP to display your own work on the web.

The European site *www.modelexpose.com* is also worth looking at.

A pose such as this one depends for its effectiveness on the model's very long legs.

Lighting works with the pose here to bring out the model's voluptuous curves.

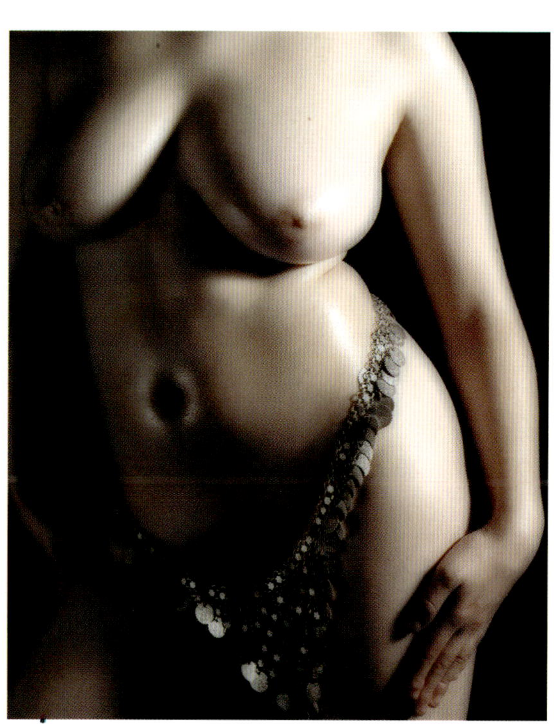

Models

Models for whom tattooing and body piercing are part of their lifestyle can inspire striking images.

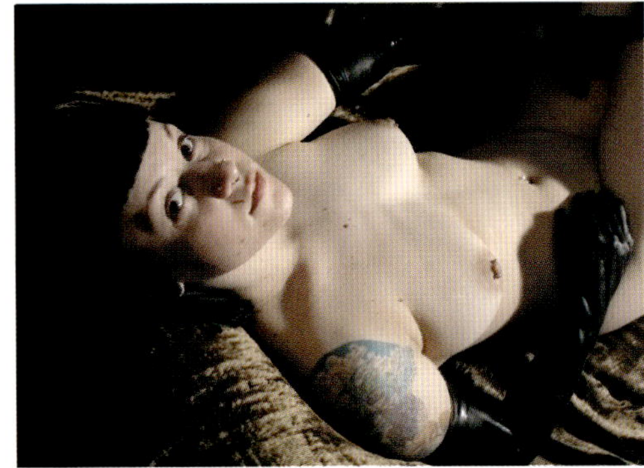

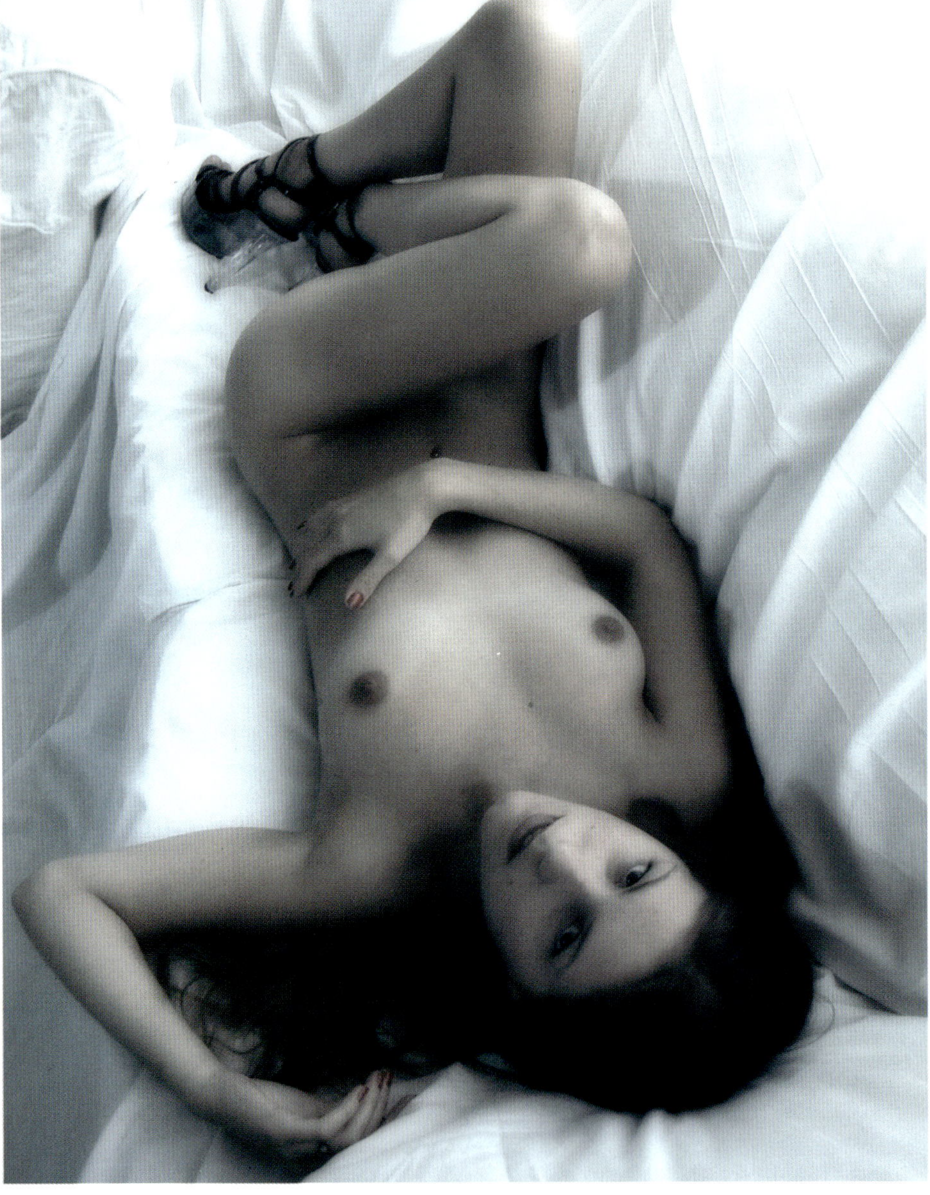

When I first met Chrissy and began to photograph her, she was just a few weeks pregnant.

WHAT TO LOOK FOR IN A MODEL

A good model is not just a passive body that you arrange. Good models bring their own personality, creativity, and experience to a shoot. You may have some idea of the physical characteristics that you're looking for, in terms of build, height, coloring, hair, ethnicity, and age. All of these will to some extent be evident from the model's pictures and details. But other factors, such as personality, individuality, experience, and invention, are just as important and harder to assess, as is the critical question of whether you will be able to work with them.

Exchanging e-mails with the model or talking to him or her on the phone can help to clarify these points. You need to develop some rapport between yourself and the model (who will also be wondering whether they can work with you) so that if you agree to do a shoot, each of you has some sense of what the other is like before you actually meet.

It's also important to keep an open mind. Youth, a good figure, and flawless skin in a model don't guarantee good photographs. The marks that life and age make on all our bodies can be an important expressive element in the images you create, and models with a different look can help to make your work stand out. However carefully you choose your model, there will be times when, although the shoot has produced some satisfactory pictures, you don't feel that you and the model "clicked." But you will also find models who inspire you to achieve images that you never knew you were capable of. They are the models you will want to go on working with.

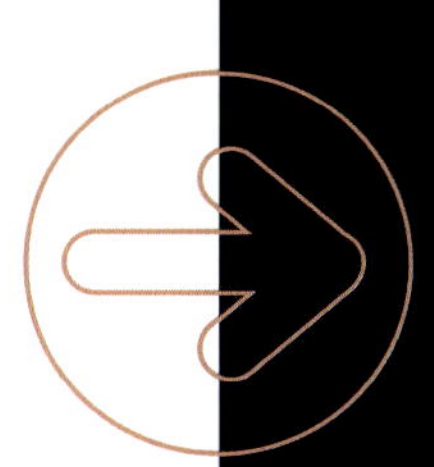

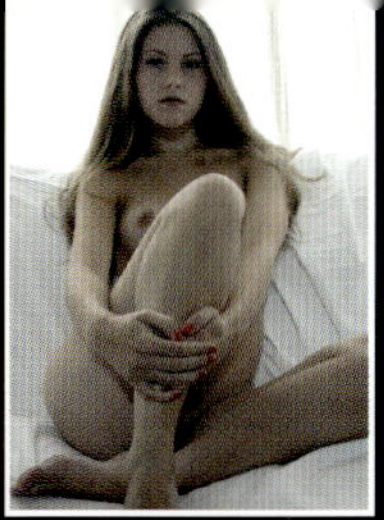

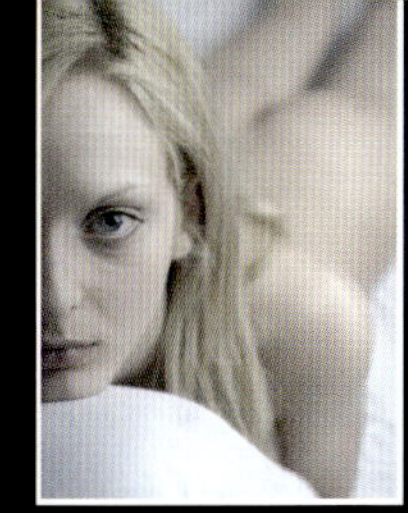

Elegance and beauty are not the sole characteristics of a good photographic model. Of equal or greater importance is personality—this can be the key to a successful photograph.

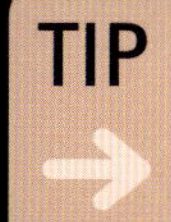

TIP Models are usually happy to recommend others to you if you're looking to extend your repertoire.

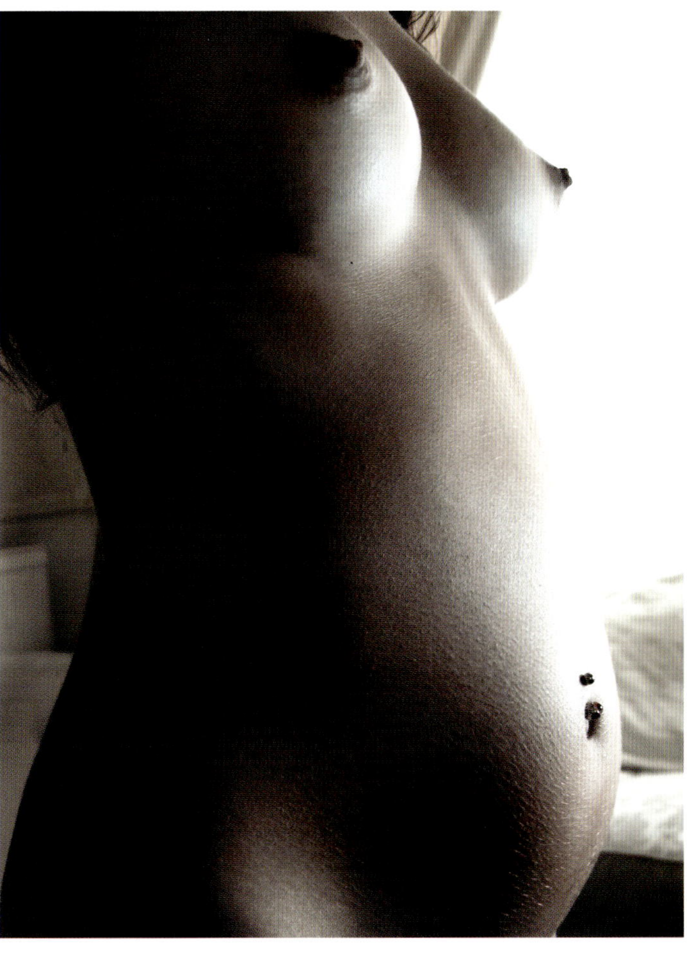

Pregnancy is a powerful, sensual, and moving theme to undertake, with its own dynamic and challenges.

Chrissy with Dillon at about 3 weeks: the start of a whole new range of photographic possibilities.

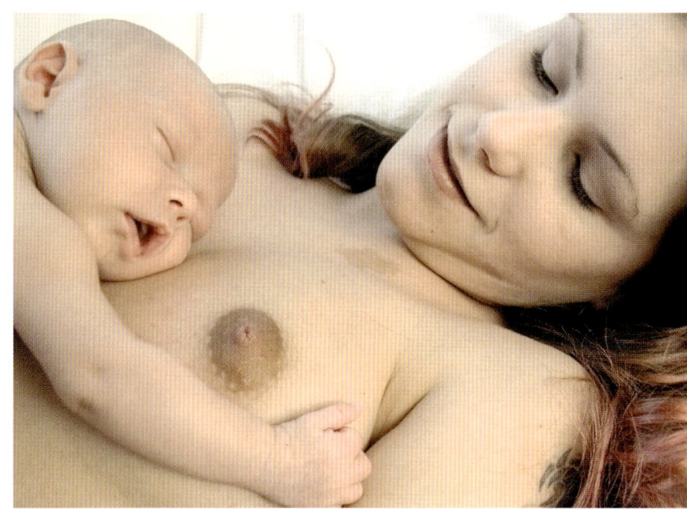

Working with Chrissy at home gave the images an appropriately domestic feeling.

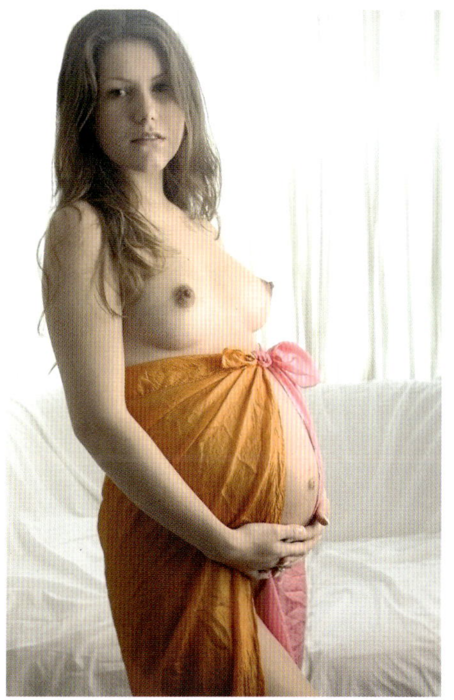

MAKING A DEAL

You are in effect negotiating a contract, so clarity, detail, and thoroughness are vital. To begin with you might specify:

- ▶ Where you saw the model's listing.
- ▶ Your status—amateur/semiprofessional.
- ▶ Where you live.
- ▶ Where you are proposing to work.
- ▶ The kind of work you want the model to do. Be clear about this, and be certain that you will not be expecting the model to work beyond his or her stated limits.
- ▶ How long a shoot you want to do and when (some models work only at weekends).
- ▶ What the model's rates are for the shoot and for a model release *(see pages 38-39)*.

You will also need to discuss with the model issues such as payment and use of the pictures, as well as sorting out the practical details of time, place, and transport. Details that need to be agreed beforehand include any garments you would like the model to bring.

MODEL'S RATES

You will notice that some models are more expensive than others. Some models are full-time professionals making their living entirely in this way. They work in a free market and charge what they believe the market will bear. Others model part-time or for the enjoyment of it and are less dependent on the work for their income.

Models

Adjusting the pose. Do ask the model's permission before you touch her for the first time.

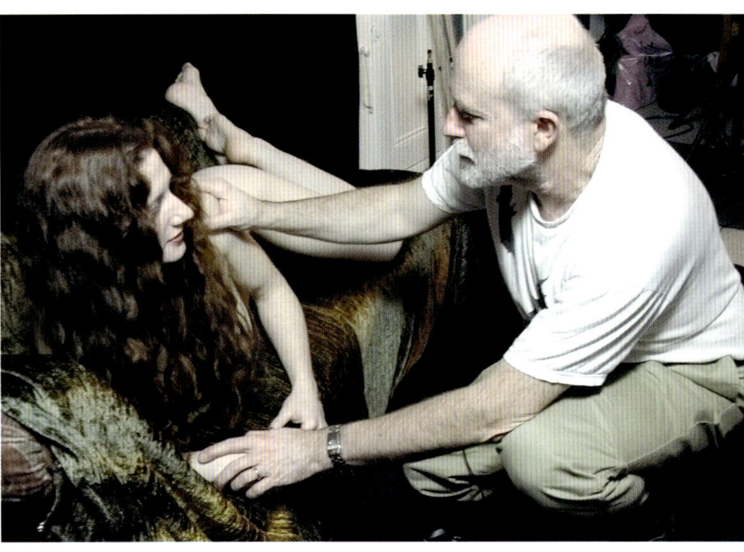

RedLilly and Bart relaxing between shots. I have to remember to check that new models aren't allergic to cats!

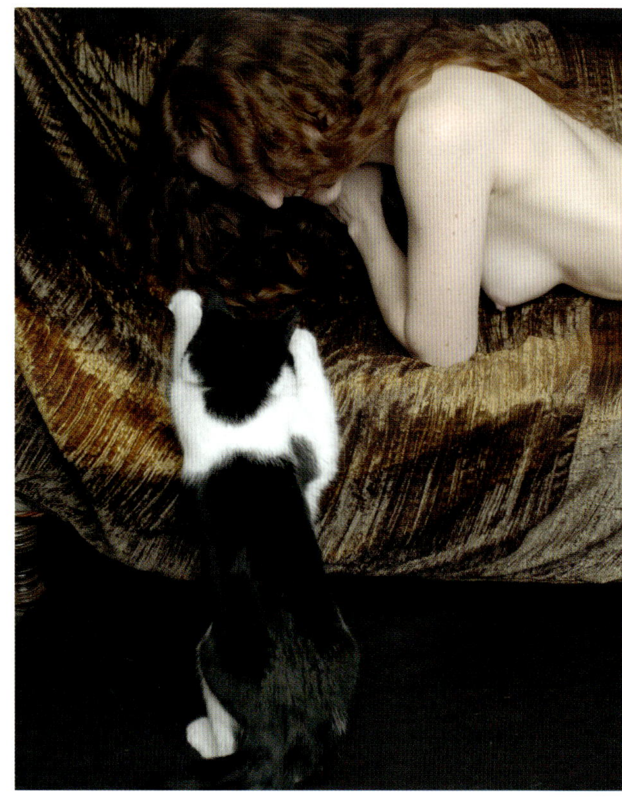

PAYING THE MODEL

There are different forms of payment. Some models will do what is known as TFP or PFT (time for prints/prints for time). You reach an agreement with the model to give her prints in exchange for the time she models for you. Specify how many prints per hours of the shoot you will provide (eight per hour is a reasonable number), what size the prints are to be, and how they are to be produced—for example, you could specify 10 x 8-inch high-quality inkjet prints. To enable the model to select the images she wants, it also makes sense to give her a CD of all the good pictures from the shoot.

More experienced models may not be interested in TFP, and may expect to be paid. Or you may be able to negotiate a split deal—a reduced payment in exchange for a smaller number of prints, perhaps. Either way, agree with them before the shoot how they are to be paid: cash, cheque, etc.

THE SHOOT

Make sure that the studio is warm. The model may be happy to prepare in the studio, or she may prefer to use a separate room to change in. She may also need a mirror in a well-lit area to check her makeup.

As you work, talk to the model: the more you explain to her what you want her to do, the easier it will be for her to give you what you are looking for, and she will often contribute useful ideas of her own. You will need to touch the model occasionally to move her hair or adjust her pose: check with her before you do this for the first time.

It's a good idea to show the model the shots on the camera's LCD screen as you work. You don't have to do this for every shot, but for those you are particularly pleased with and those where you feel the shot is not quite right: the model may have some good suggestions about what needs adjusting, or how the shot could be improved.

It's important that you respect the model's limits and don't try to get her to pose in ways that go beyond what you agreed when you booked her. All the models I spoke to while writing this section were unanimous that photographers who try to persuade them to push their boundaries in this way never succeed, but simply spoil the shoot. You may also find that the model is unhappy with some angles, which therefore need to be approached with sensitivity. For example, if she doesn't like her nose, it might be wise not to shoot large numbers of profile shots.

MODEL RELEASE

If you have agreed to pay the model, do this at the end of the shoot. You may also want to ask the model to sign a model release form. This is an agreement by which the model assigns to you the full copyright in the prints, agrees that you may publish them, and relinquishes all

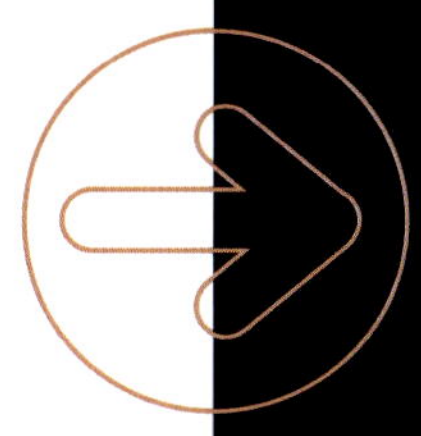
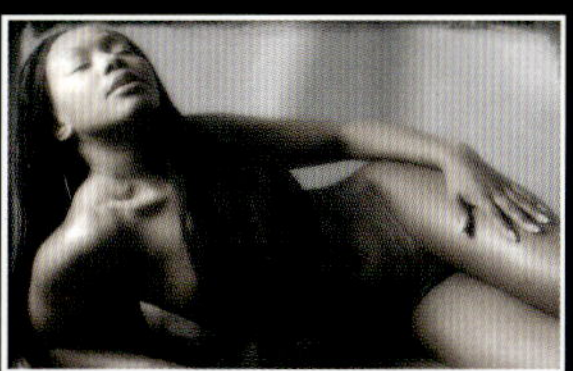
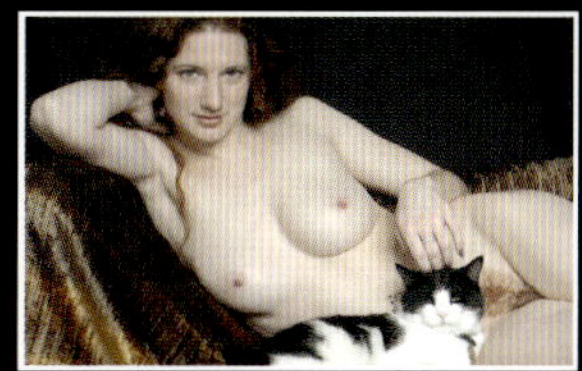

Some models may offer their time in exchange for copies of the photographs you take; others may work for a fee. In either case there are some sensible rules to be observed when working in the studio with a model.

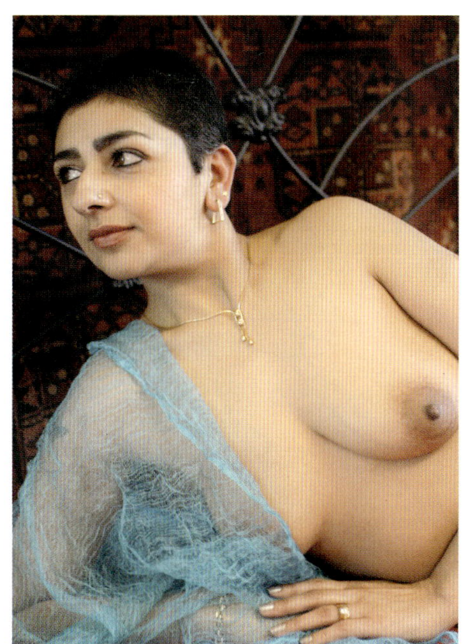

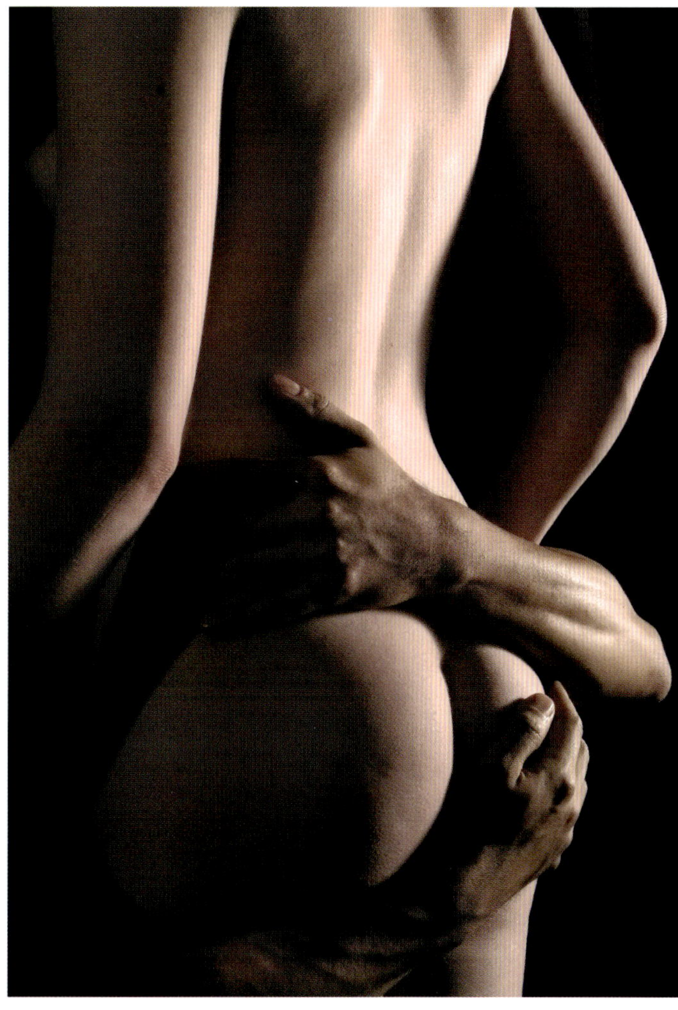

Working with models from different ethnic backgrounds will bring distinctively different "looks" to your work.

Shooting with two models is easier if the models have worked together before. If they haven't, give them time to get to know each other before the shoot gets under way.

claims to further payment for the shoot. If you search for "model release" on the internet, you will find a range of possible wordings that you can adapt to your needs.

It's important to get a release only if you are intending to sell your work. Without a model release, most models will still be happy for you to exhibit your work in a gallery or portfolio, or on the internet, although you should still ask for permission for this, verbally or in writing. Some models will expect an additional payment, usually an extra hour's fee, for signing a release.

AND AT ALL TIMES...

It's obvious but worth repeating: treat the model with respect, not only before and during the shoot but afterward as well. Apart from anything else, if the shoot has gone well, you may want to work with her again. For example, if she has told you her real name, phone number, or address, keep them confidential. Don't pass them on to anyone else without her agreement. If another photographer asks you how to get in touch with the model, you should pass the photographer's contact details on to the model, or refer the photographer to any way of contacting her that is in the public domain—her website or OMP portfolio, for example.

TIP

Give the model and yourself a break at least every 90 minutes during a photo shoot.

RECOMMENDATIONS

If you are pleased with the results of a shoot and want to help the model get further work, you could:

▶ Add a recommendation on the websites that she appears on.

▶ If you both have websites, add a link from your site to hers.

These are reciprocal arrangements: if the shoot went well, you can expect the model to do the same for you. Publicity of this kind often leads to approaches from other models who have seen and liked your work and have read the recommendations that you have received.

Locations

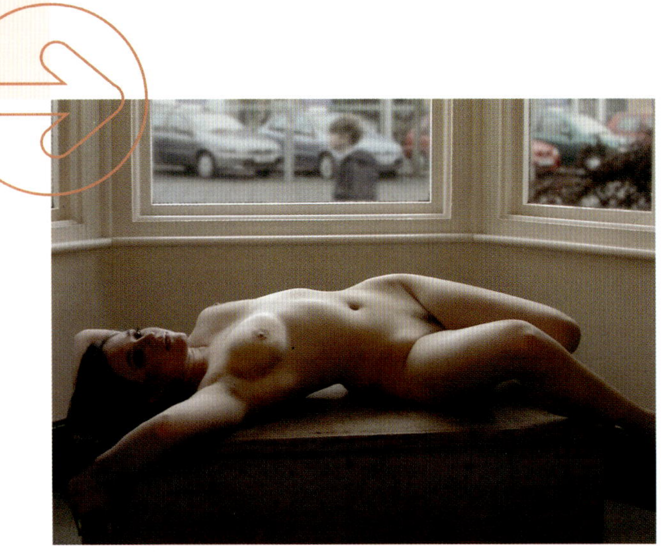

Careful positioning of the camera creates an image that combines the seclusion of an interior with the presence of the external world.

Here, the hard white walls and floor of a "white box" studio location provide scope for some interesting shadow-play.

Locations are a key element in photography: they give a context to the model. You don't have to use exotic locations; different spaces in your house can offer a good range of choices. For pure black or white environments, try out a studio. For differences of scale, try exterior locations.

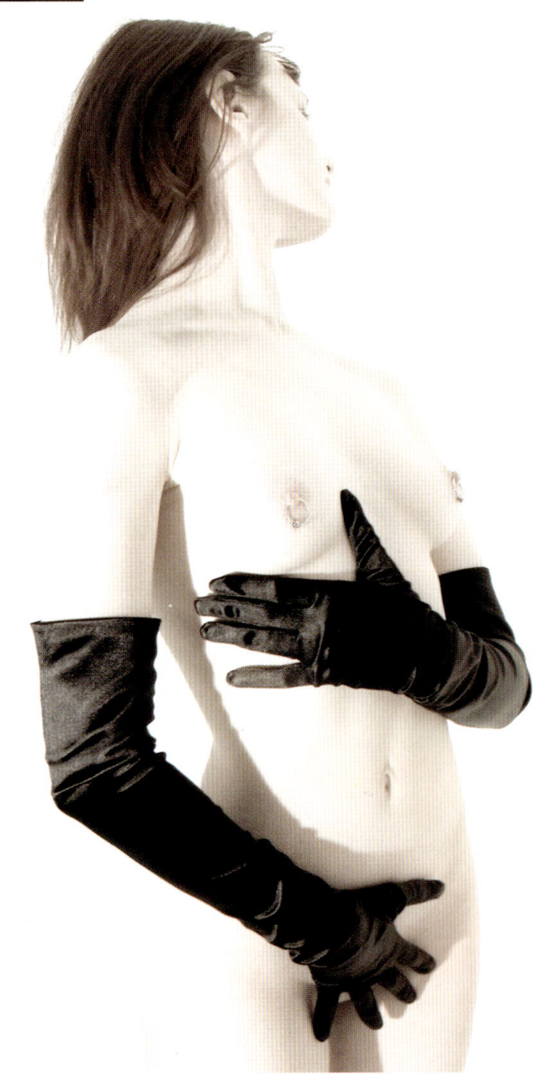

STUDIO NUDES

A good photographic studio offers one environment that is difficult to reproduce at home. This is the "white box": a space with hard walls, ceiling, and floor all painted white. Images made in this space show the model without any other elements in the composition that could distract the viewer.

DOMESTIC NUDES

Almost any part of your home can provide a "natural" location, often using just available light. Domestic interiors can make rather cluttered and distracting backgrounds, but you can use image-editing software to edit unwanted details out afterward.

OUTDOOR NUDES

External locations provide intriguing possibilities for experimenting with scale.

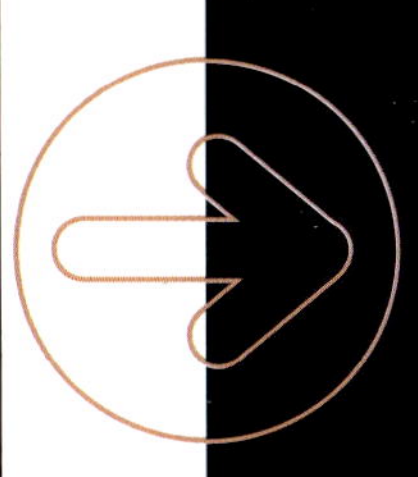

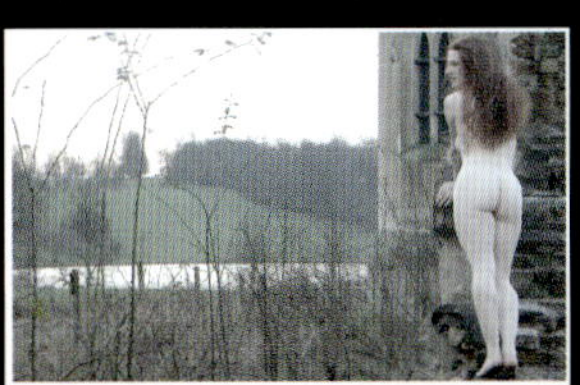

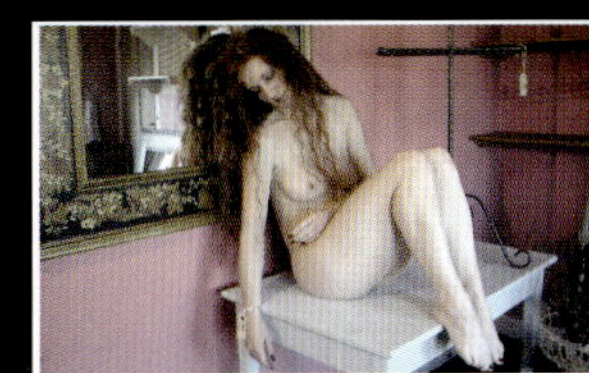

There are three main types of photographic location: studio, domestic, and outdoors. Within these three basic genres, however, you have the opportunity to create a limitless range of exciting settings for your images.

In this domestic nude image, mirrors are a way of elaborating a simple idea, as is the use of monochrome together with color in this image. The photographer makes an appearance too!

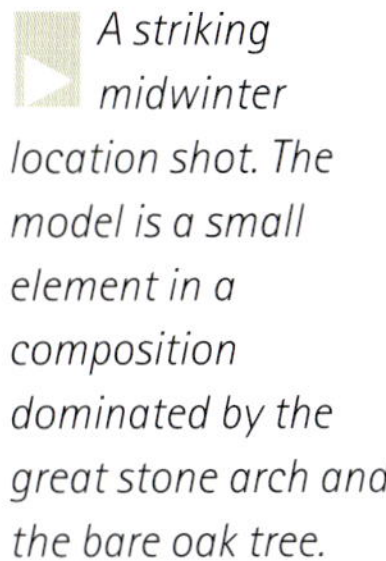

A striking midwinter location shot. The model is a small element in a composition dominated by the great stone arch and the bare oak tree.

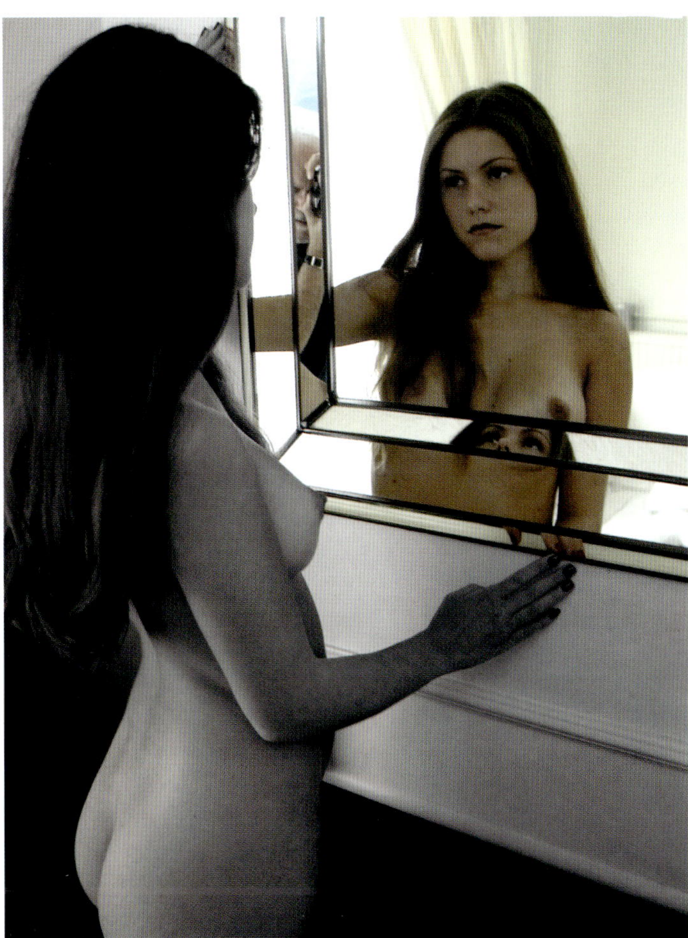

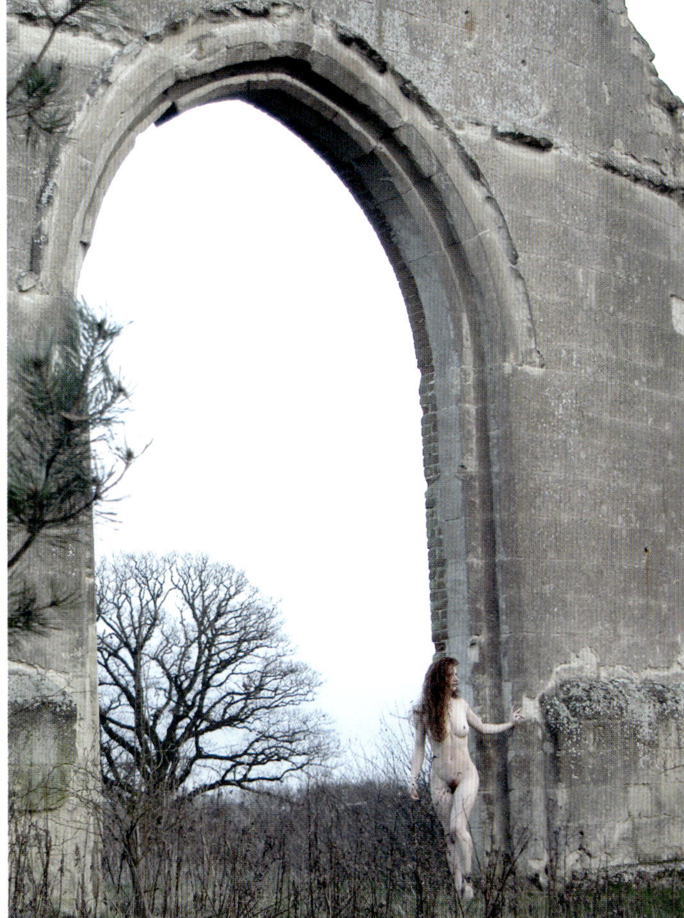

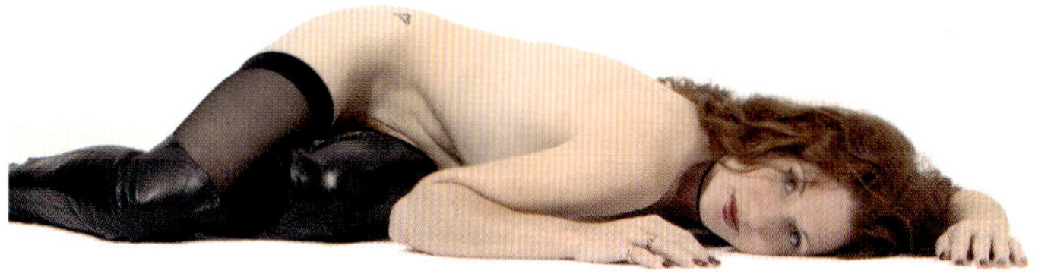

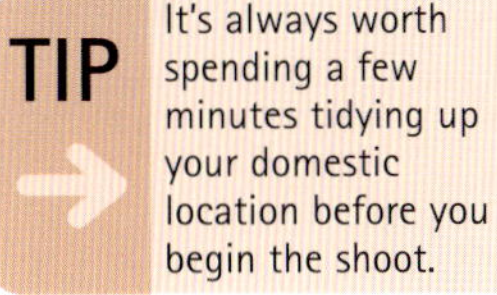

TIP It's always worth spending a few minutes tidying up your domestic location before you begin the shoot.

Here elements of costume are added, but the focal point in the white box remains the model.

The home studio

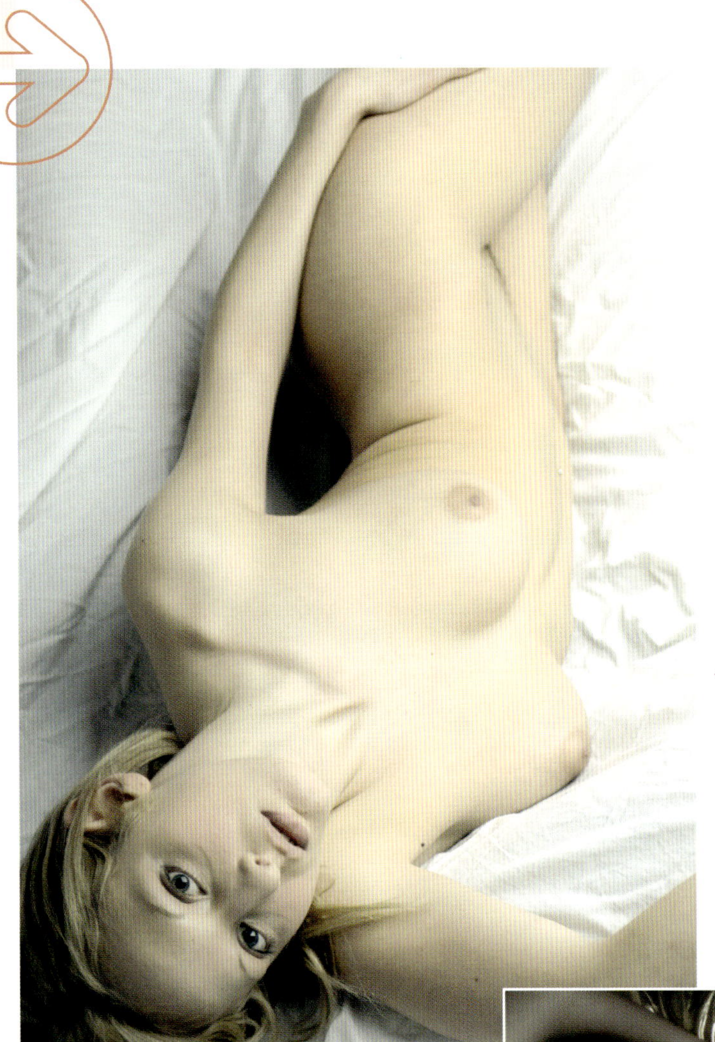

Three different "looks" with the same model, shot in the home studio. Different backgrounds—including (below) a gold reflector—and different lighting conditions can be applied to your photography in a surprisingly small studio space, which can be taken down and put away when not in use.

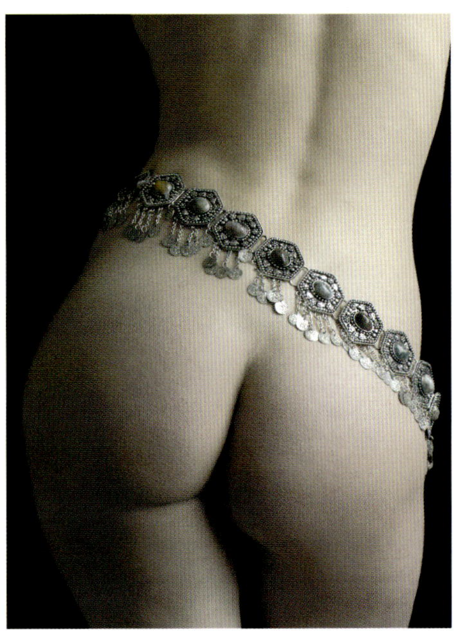

In this section we look at how you can easily make a useful studio space in even a small home. In a domestic setting, it's not easy to create the hard "white box" discussed in the previous section, but many other environments can be reproduced.

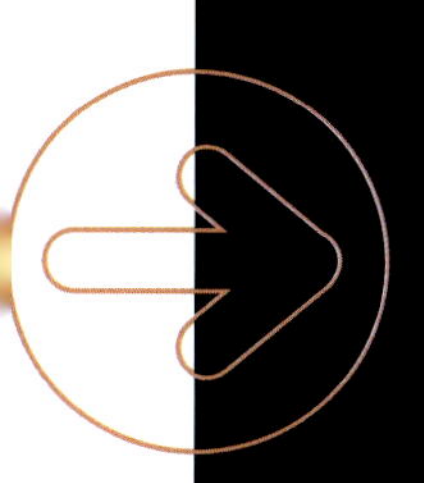
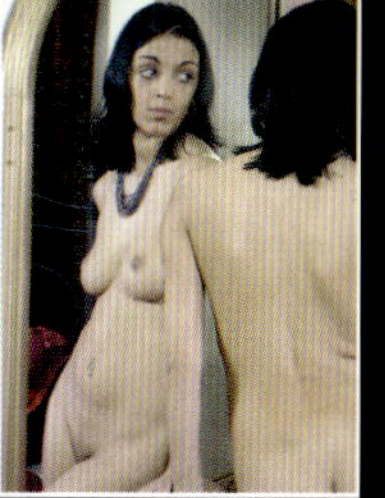
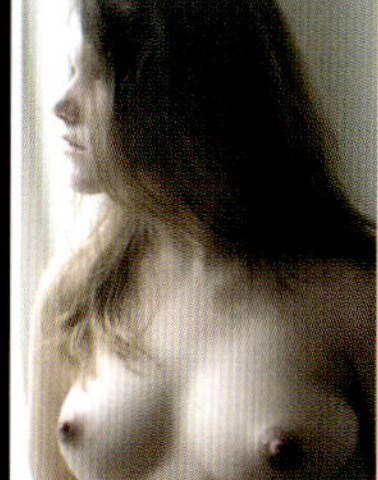

For nude photography, it's vital to create a comfortable environment where you can control the atmosphere and look. A flexible home studio does not have to be ambitious or expensive.

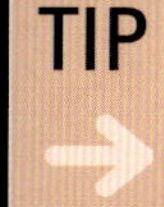

TIP

If you create a home studio, make sure you have enough power points for lights and battery chargers.

THE HOME STUDIO

The function of a home studio is to give you a controllable space in which to work, whenever you need it. Its "walls" are made of fabric, hung from floor to ceiling, and concealing the normal clutter of domestic living. It's a space into which you bring lights, props, and furniture as you need them. This enables you to work with the model in her own space, and to control the lighting effectively. The cost of setting it all up is not great, particularly when compared to the cost of hiring even a small professional studio.

STUDIO SIZE

My studio space is a little less than 11 feet square. It's part of a larger room (about 24 feet long and 13 feet wide at the widest) so that I can work from outside the studio part to achieve, for example, telephoto compression shots. It's big enough (just) to enable me to work with two models.

STUDIO CONSTRUCTION

I hang dark purple velour drapes along two adjacent walls on rods attached to the walls just below the ceiling. Each piece of fabric has a "tunnel" at the top that slides along the rod. It's important that the nap of the velour runs in the same direction in each piece of fabric, so that it lights evenly. Dark purple tends to work better than black. If you keep the light off it, it goes almost black and gives the feeling that the model is in an infinitely deep space. If you light it, it makes a sensuous background.

By pinning up different colored fabrics onto the drapes, it's possible to change the background quickly; the same can be done with the floor.

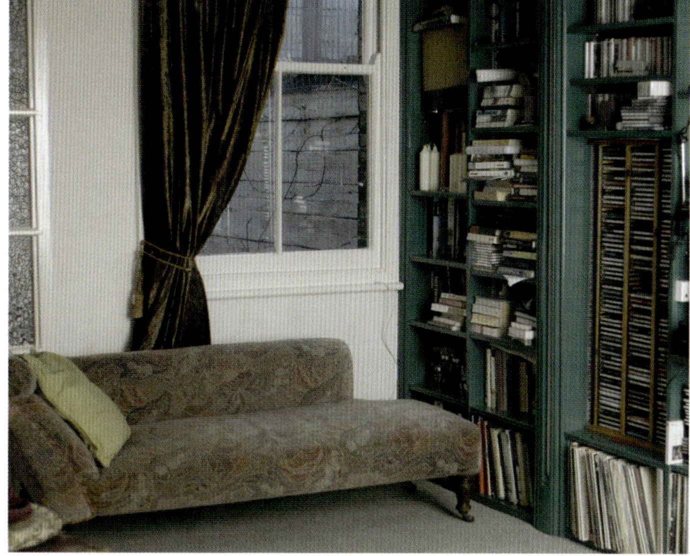

It takes just a few minutes to convert this end of the living room into an effective home studio.

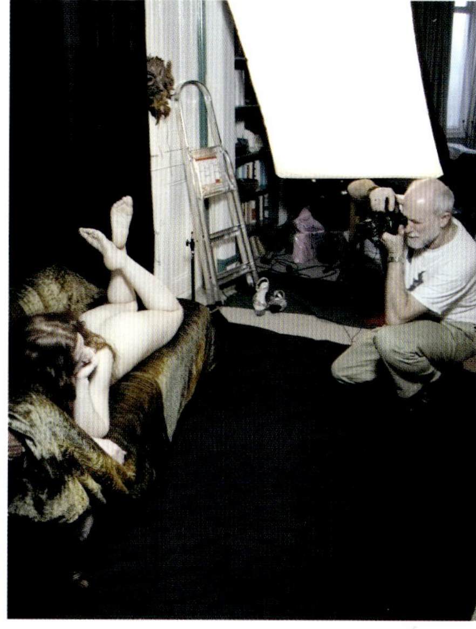

Working with Red Lilly in my home studio. Note the stepladder for overhead shots, and the masks hanging on the wall.

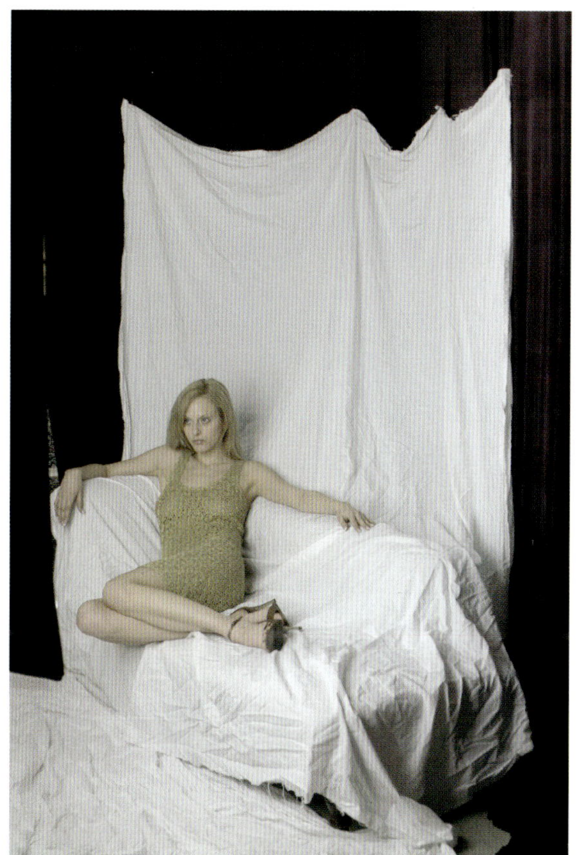

From a distance a white sheet rigged up looks messy, but working close to the model and with attention to depth of field it works.

Props

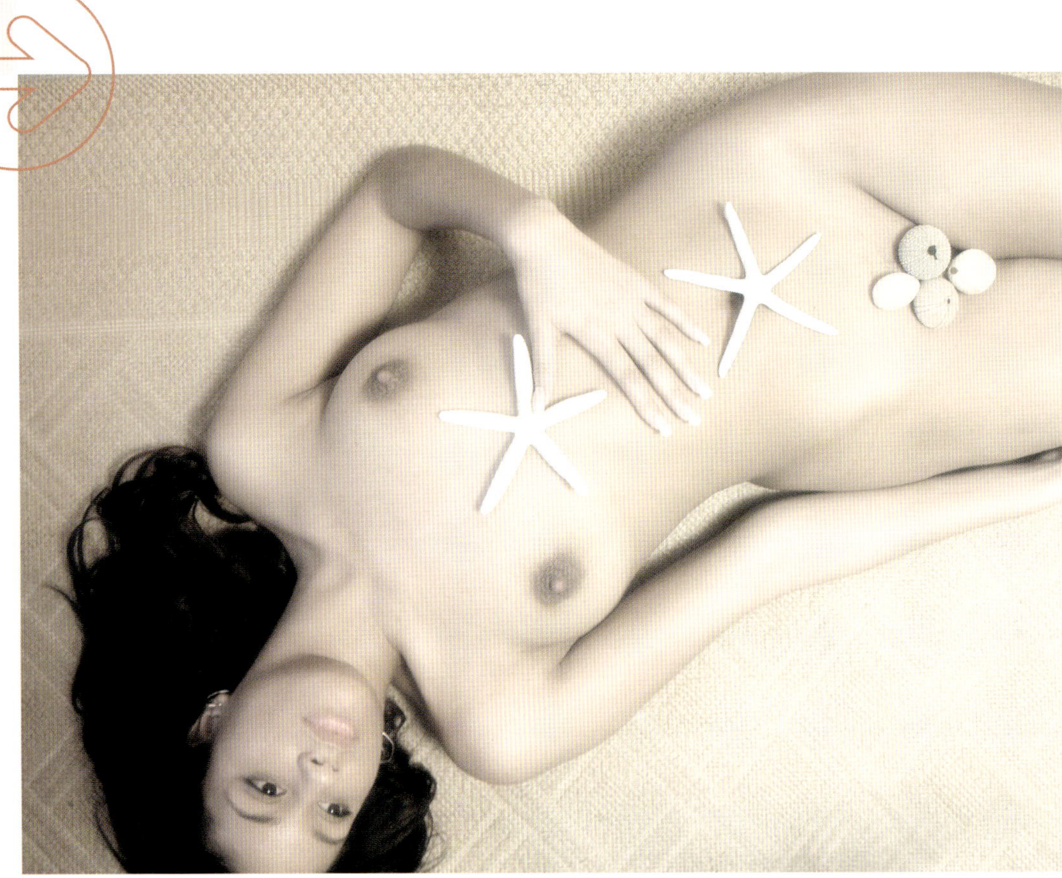

In this almost monochrome image, the arms of the starfish reflect the diamond patterns of the background.

This image features curves within curves and reflections of shape and light.

Along with the location you choose, props and furnishings help to create the context within which the model is seen, adding a touch of the exotic or the romantic to a shot. Some of the props seen here were specially acquired for use in photography, but others are everyday domestic items.

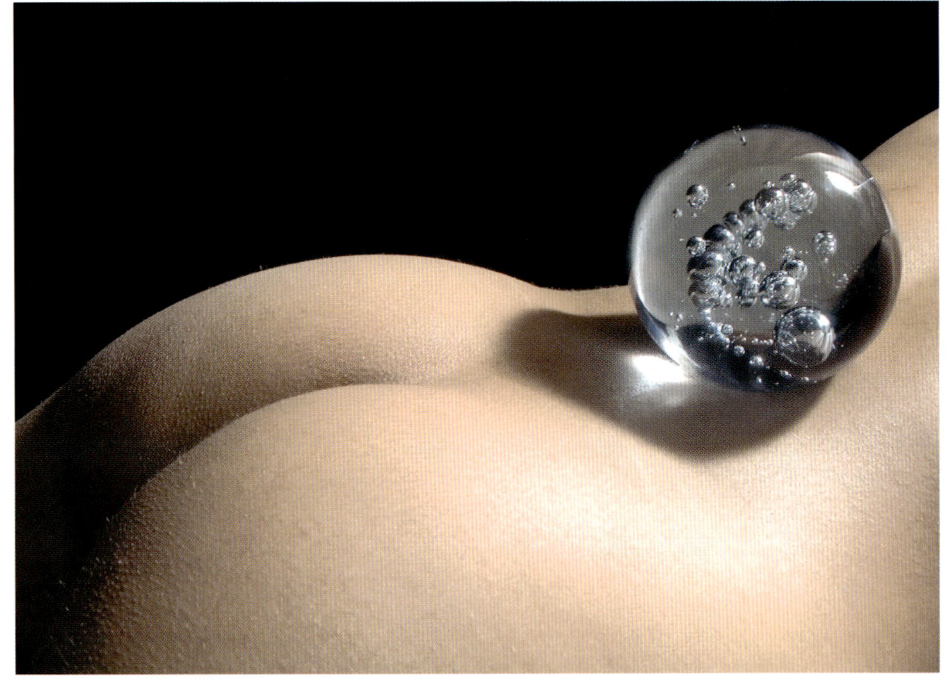

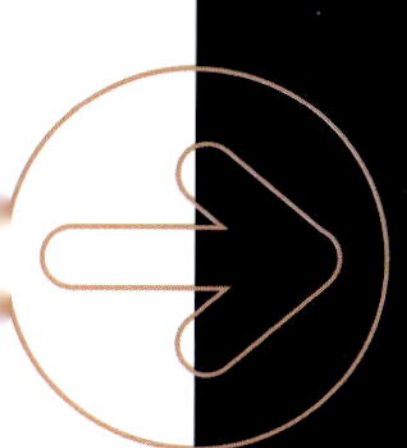

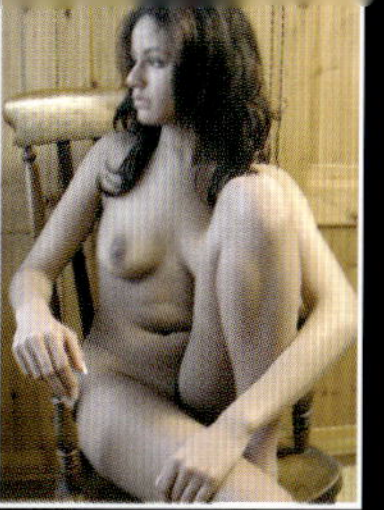

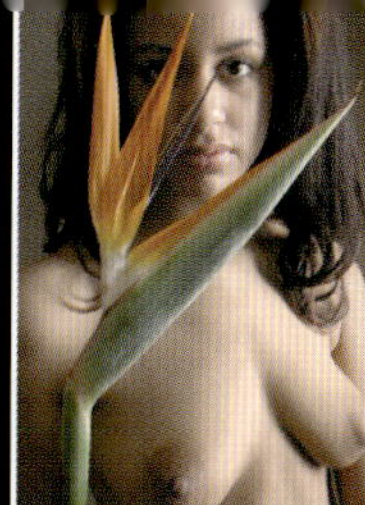

Props can be used to complement or contrast with the forms of the nude figure. Colors, textures, and reflective properties should be selected carefully to enhance the shot.

TIP

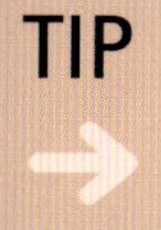

Shops may be willing to lend you stock to use as props in return for photographs. It never hurts to ask!

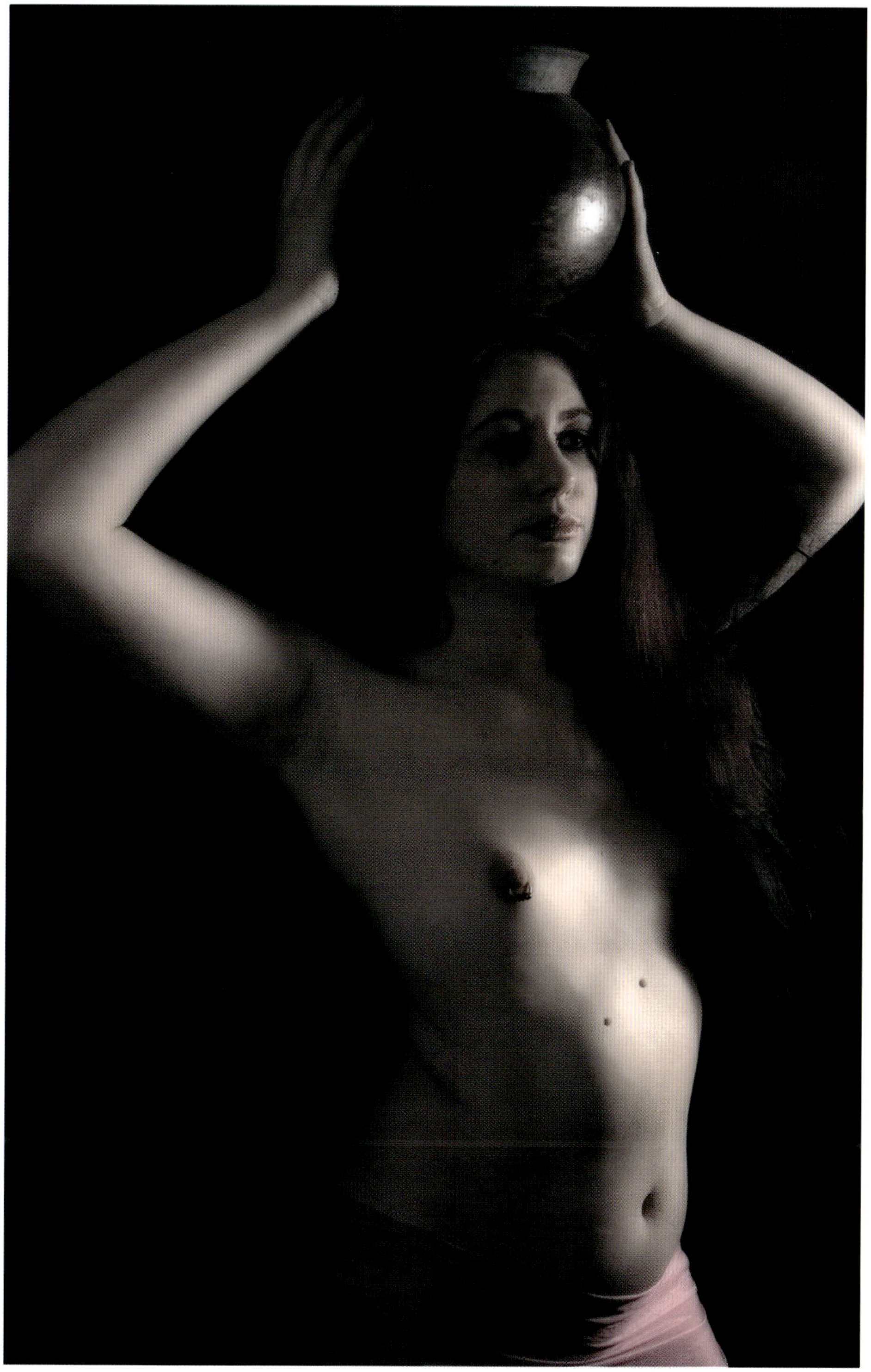

Soft oblique lighting emphasized by manipulation of the image creates a series of interlocking geometrical shapes, partly symmetrical and partly asymmetrical.

Nothing compares to the quality of light reflected off a wooden surface such as this floor. The curves of the model and the texture of her skin are set off by the parallel edges and dented surfaces of the floorboards.

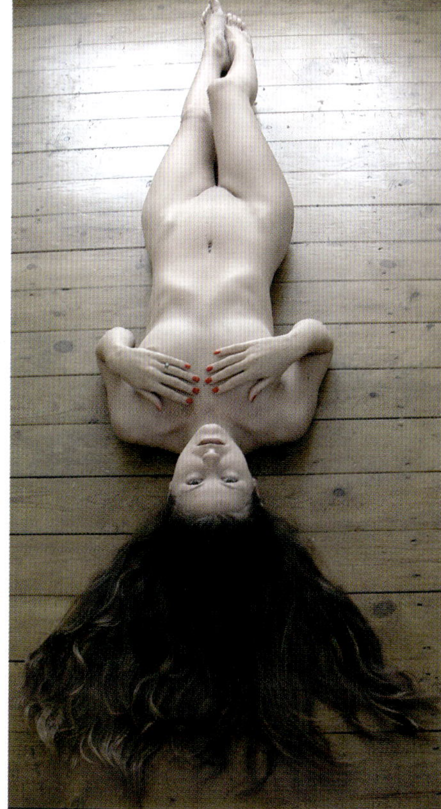

Composition

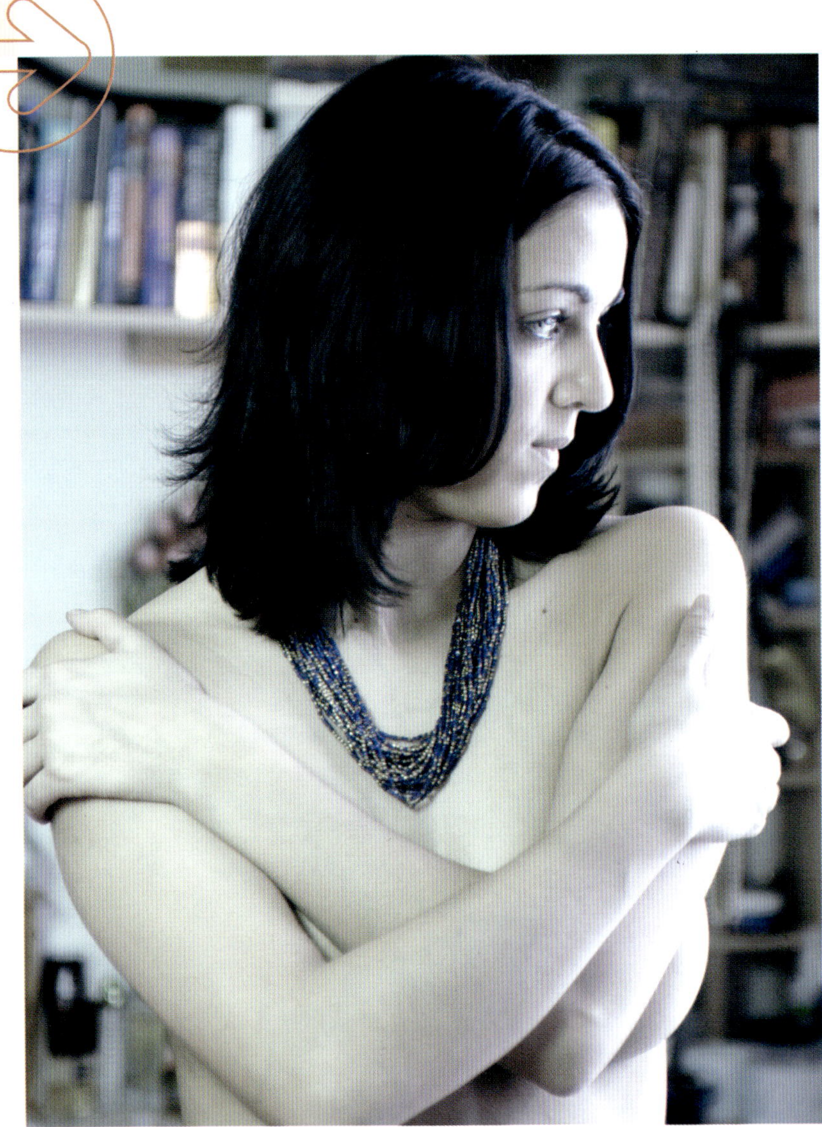

In the first picture, careful control of depth of field ensures that the background is blurred and doesn't distract from the subject. In the second shot, the cluttered dressing table and the reflection of the model's back in the ornate mirror form the focal points of the image.

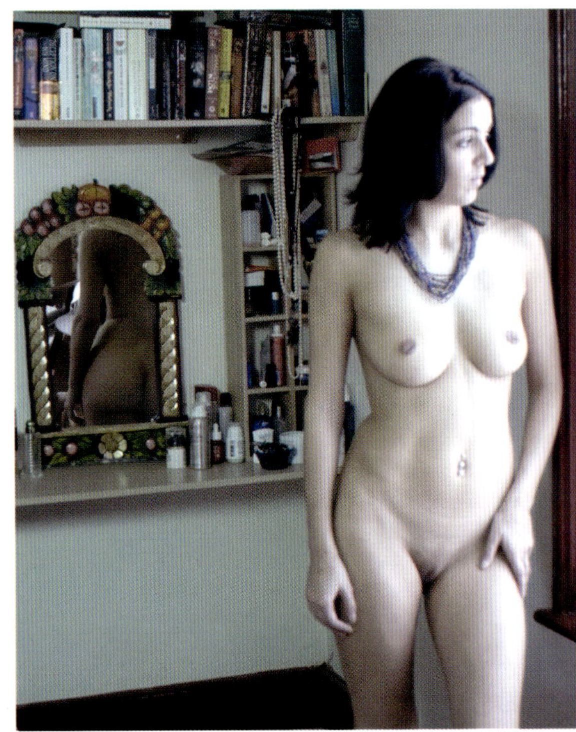

Much of the power of nude photography comes from the composition of the shot. The careful arrangement of the model within the space of the frame (or of the frame around the model) is integral to the impact of the image.

THE RULES OF COMPOSITION

Composition is about the selection and arrangement of subjects within the picture area. This may involve placing the model(s) in certain positions within the frame and within the set, studio, or location, or positioning the camera in order to achieve a particular point of view. You have two chances to determine the composition of your pictures: first when you take the shot, and then when you edit it.

There are a number of common "rules" for composition. But, like all rules applied to creativity, these are just guidelines based on the observation of what has worked in the past—so while they often work very well, you shouldn't be afraid to break them.

One guiding principle is simplicity. Of all the rules of composition, this is the most important. Simplicity means avoiding cluttering the image with elements that distract from the center of interest in the photograph, or leave the viewer uncertain as to what the center of interest is. To put it another way: everything that is in the frame should be there for a reason.

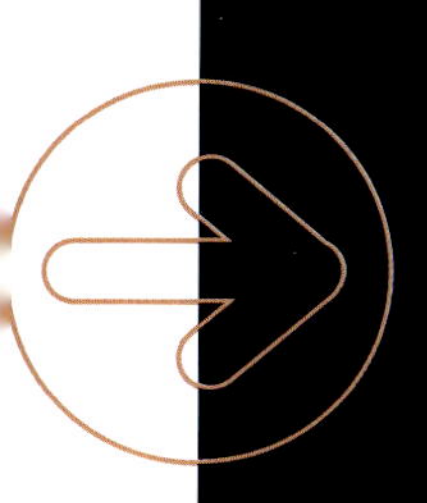

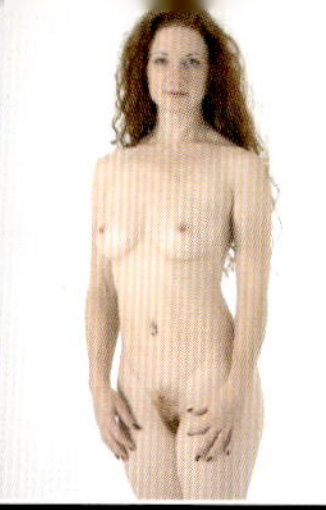

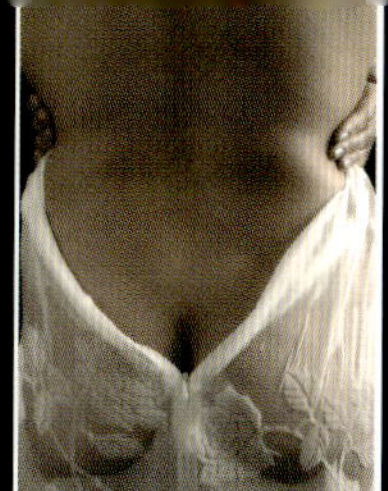

How you choose to arrange your subject within a setting is often a matter of personal taste. There are, however, a number of simple rules that can be followed that will help to improve the composition of your photographs.

TIP Shoot with a little extra space all around the frame, and you'll have room to rotate the picture in case it's not perfectly level.

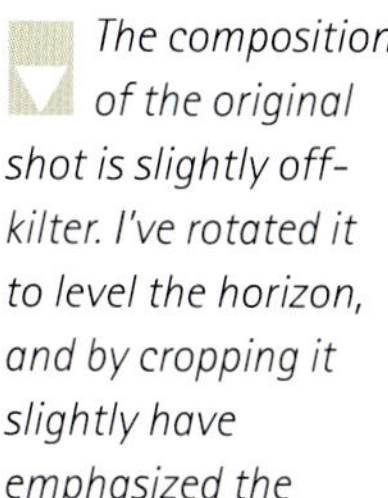

The composition of the original shot is slightly off-kilter. I've rotated it to level the horizon, and by cropping it slightly have emphasized the composition's strong contrasts, between the dark diagonals of the limbs of the tree and the pale skin of the model, who is angled on the opposite diagonal.

Color can throw a composition off-balance. In the original shot, the bright red bedhead draws the eye away from the model. When the image is made monochrome and given a more nostalgic feeling (in keeping with the objects in the room) the bedframe draws the eye in toward the model. I've also slightly cropped the picture all round to make the (arranged) jumble of objects a little less prominent.

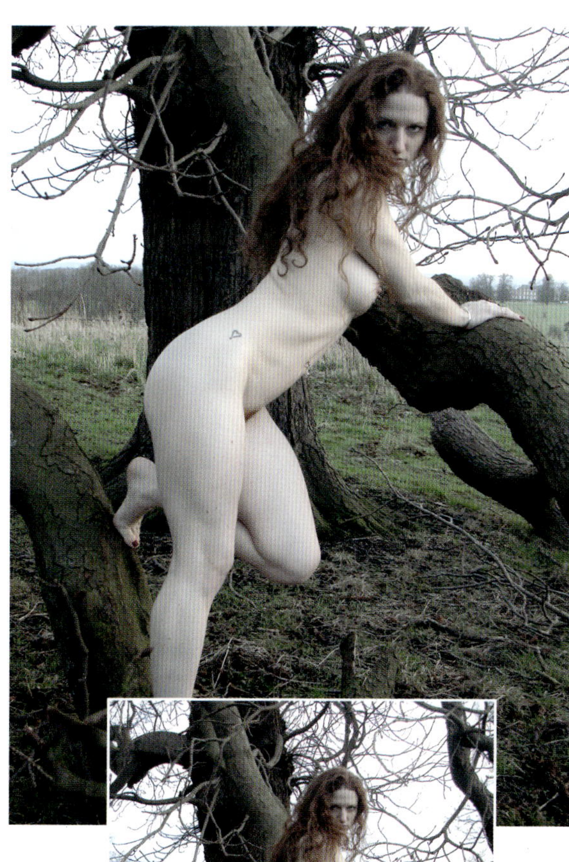

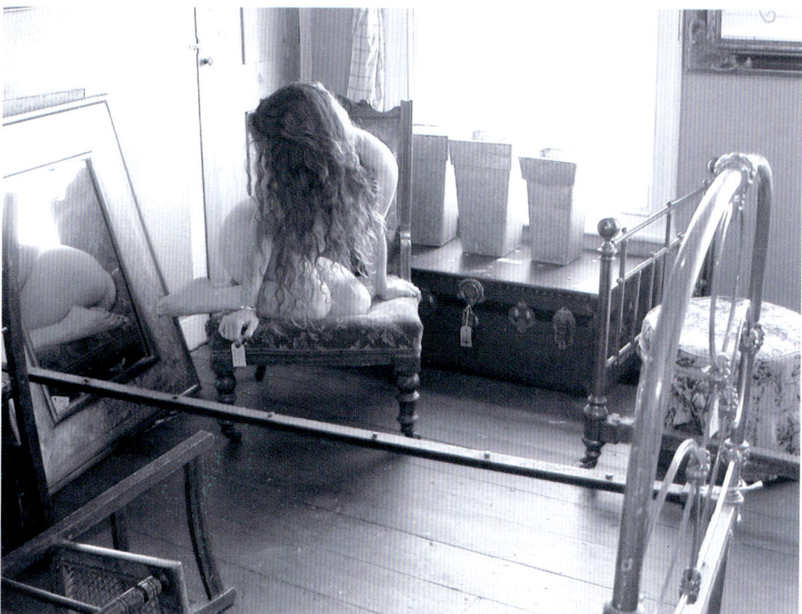

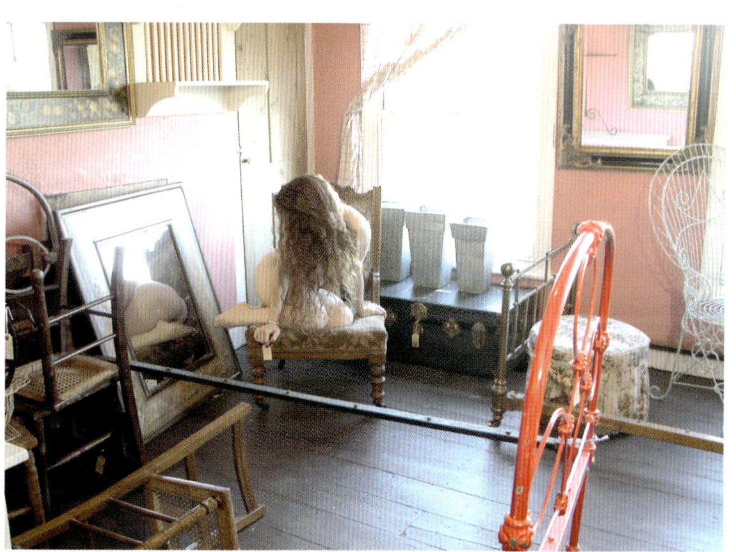

Composition

THE GOLDEN SECTION

Two related principles of composition, derived from theories of art and design that can be traced back to the ancient Greeks, are the "rule of thirds" and the "Golden Section."

To use the rule of thirds, imagine your image divided into thirds horizontally and vertically, and use those imaginary lines and their intersections to place significant elements of the composition. In the edited picture of Red Lilly in the oak tree on page 47, the skyline is one-third of the way down the frame, and the center of the trunk of the oak tree is one-third of the way across from the left-hand edge. This line also passes through the model's right leg, which is the part of her body closest to the camera.

The Golden Section divides the frame in the ratio of 1: 0.618, producing intersections where significant elements in the composition can be located. This may be easier to do when editing the picture than when taking it!

BALANCE

Balance is also important. Balance is about getting all the elements in the shot to complement each other, so that the picture doesn't seem lopsided.

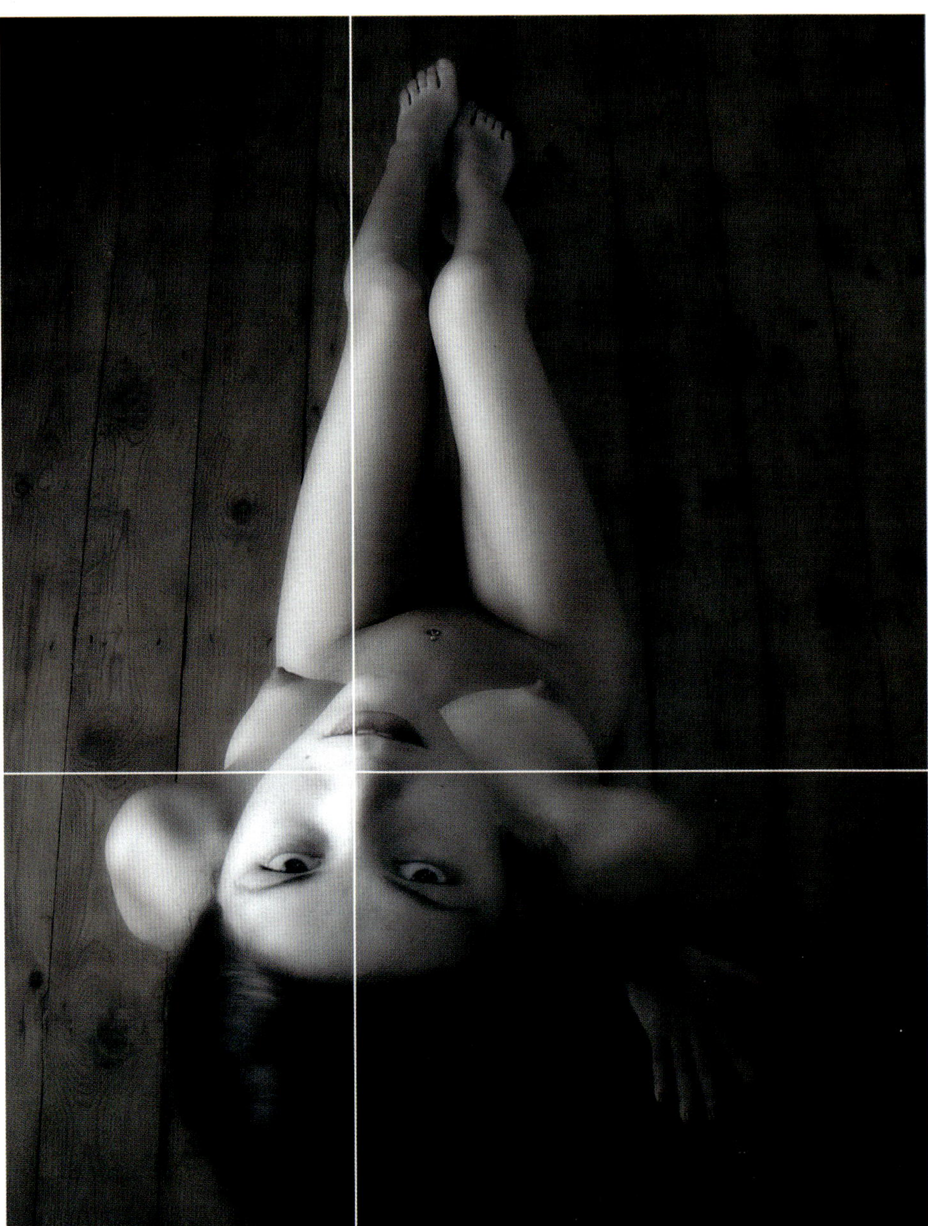

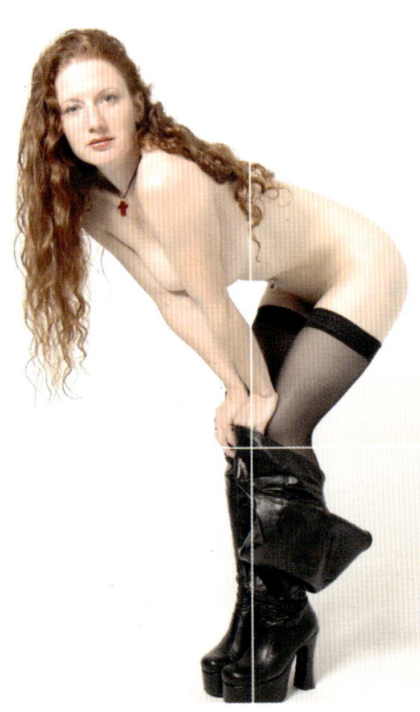

The model's hands resting on her knees are positioned in the frame at the Golden Section.

In this shot, the model's face is located at the Golden Section.

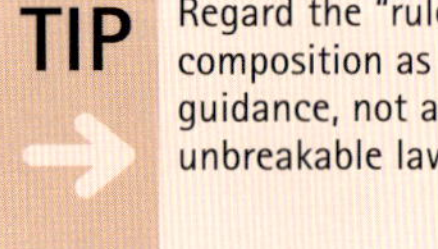

TIP Regard the "rules" of composition as guidance, not as unbreakable laws.

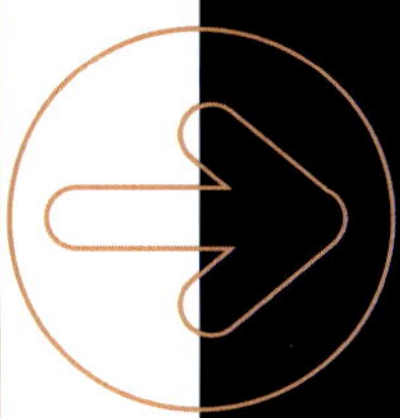

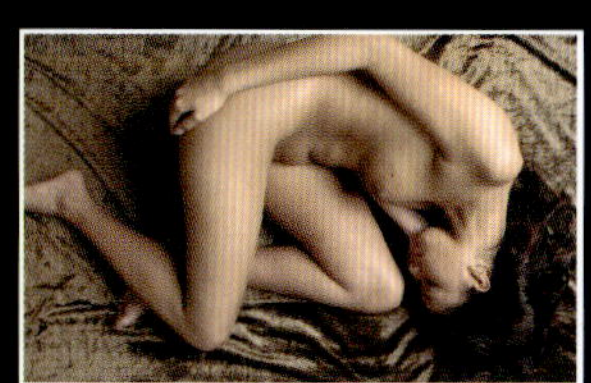

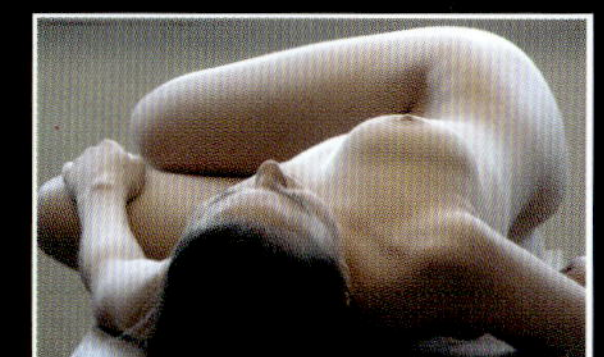

The "golden section" and the "rule of thirds" have been in use for centuries, but these theories are just as relevant today. The ideas are straightforward enough—their application, however, will greatly improve your sense of composition.

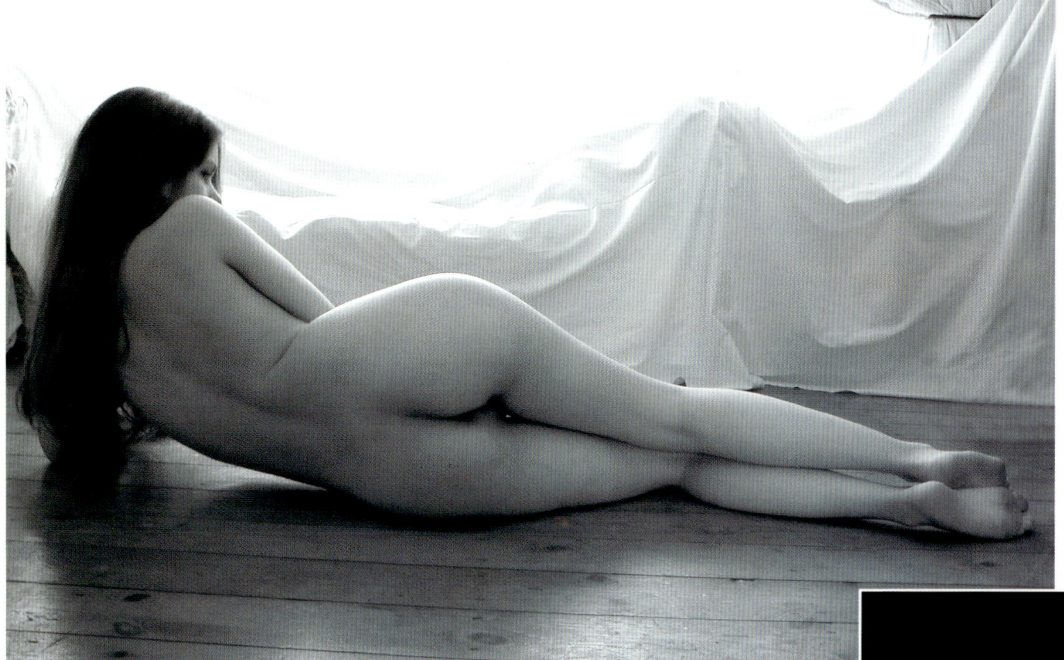

The folds in the draped cloth in the background reflect Chrissy's curves, and her dark hair balances the darker shading of the drapes on the right of the picture.

The S-curve, like that of Aylith's torso in this picture, has a pleasing balance.

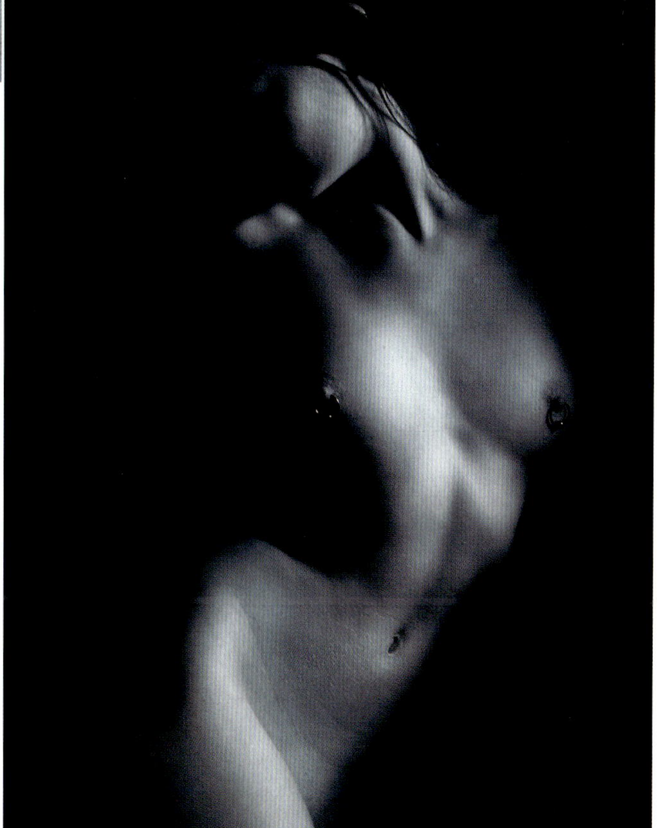

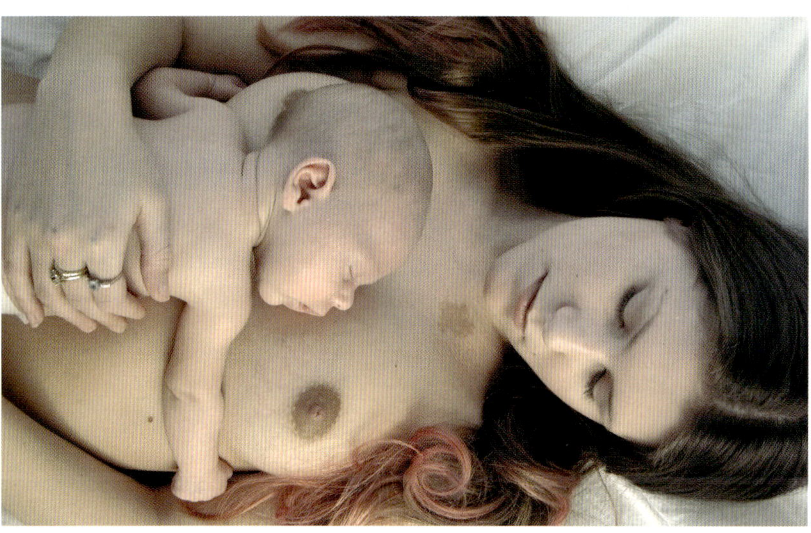

Here the sense of balance and tranquility comes from the positions of baby and breast.

Composition

ASYMMETRY

The human body has many symmetries: two arms, two legs, two breasts... Often these achieve the most impact when portrayed in an asymmetrical way: through the model's pose, through lighting, or through point of view.

Here the symmetry of the pose and camera angle is subtly offset by oblique lighting.

Here the top image works better, thanks to the curving line of the model's pose, than the bottom image, which seems too square and rigid.

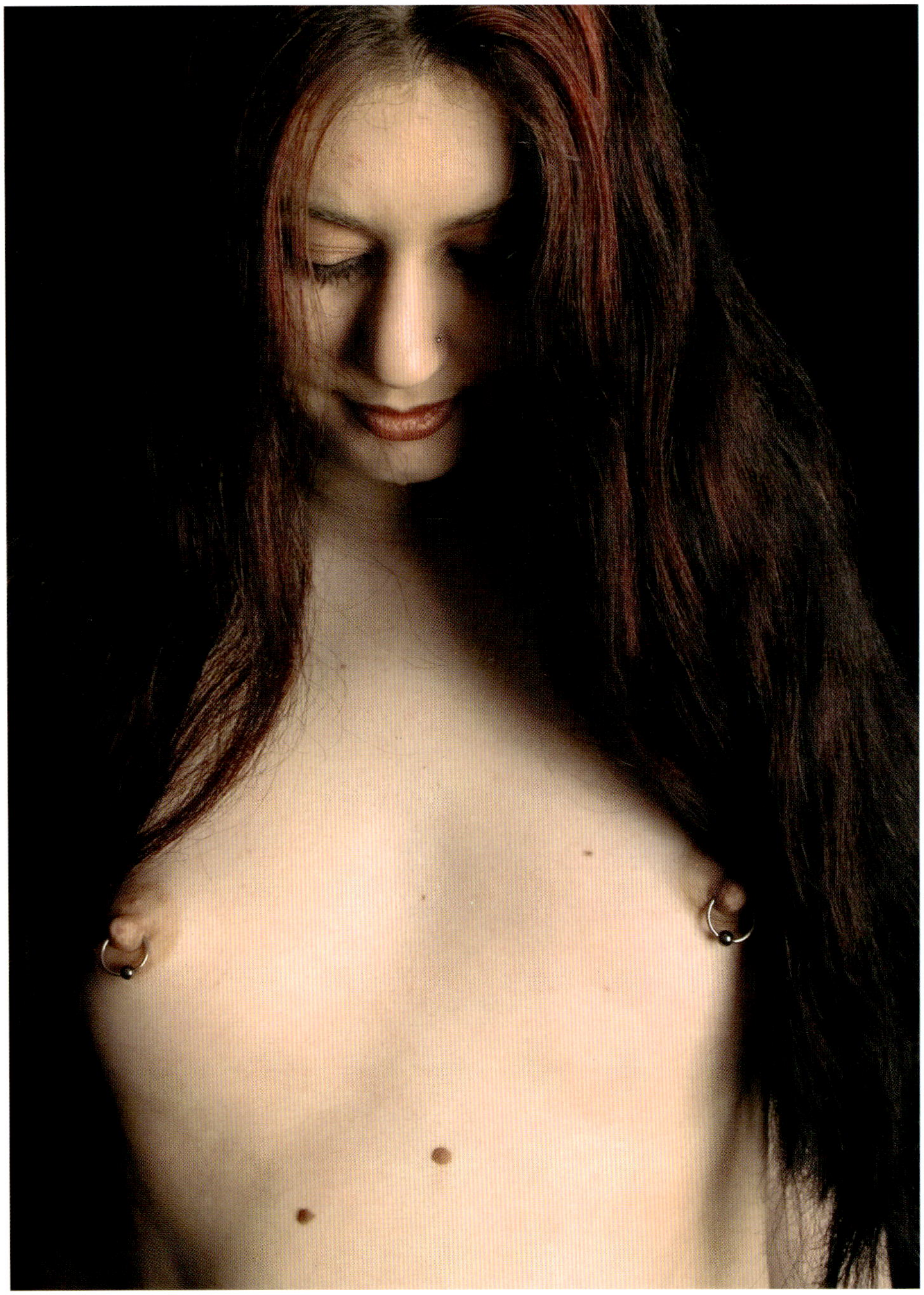

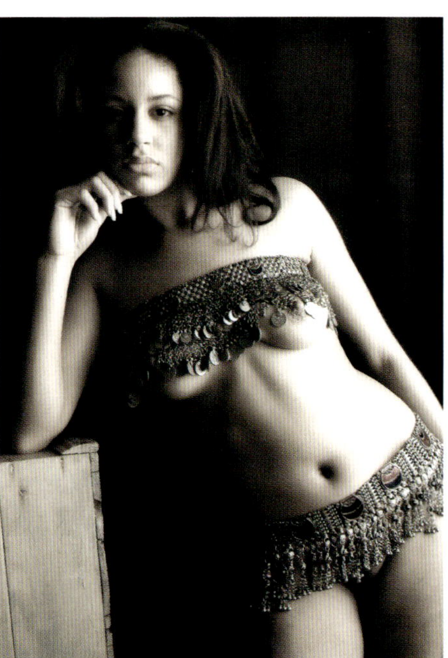

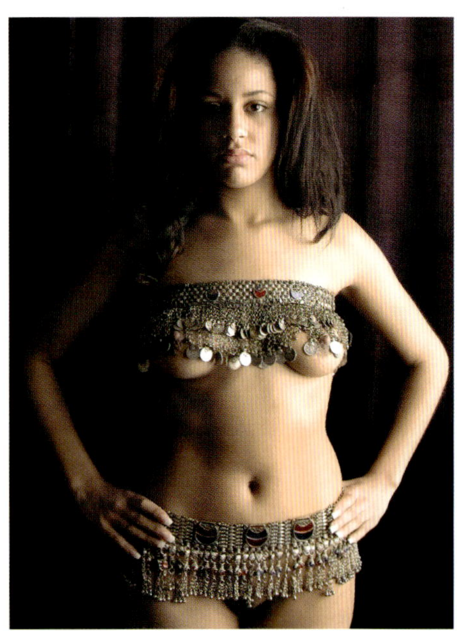

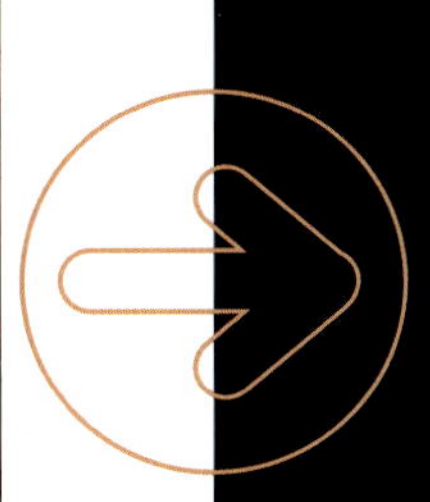

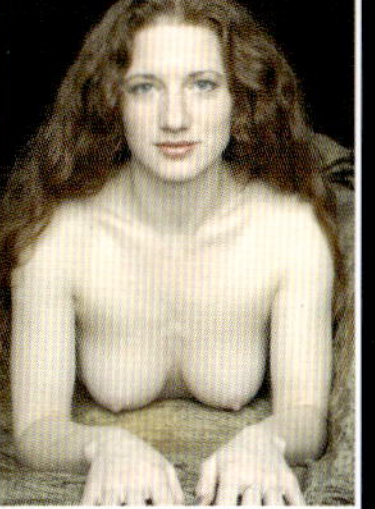

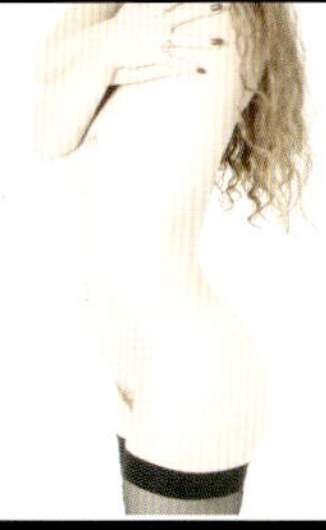

The human body is possessed of a great natural symmetry. You can use this to your advantage, working both with and against this symmetry to create arresting shapes and juxtapositions.

TIP  Experiment! To create strikingly different compositions, look for unusual camera angles, poses, and lighting setups.

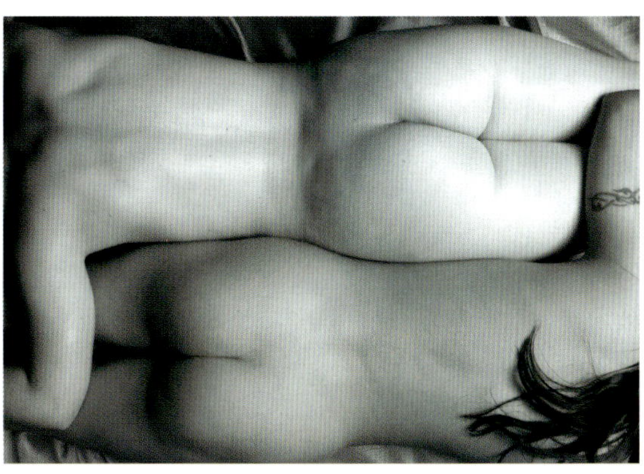

The main axis of symmetry in this picture runs horizontally through the center of the frame, resulting in an image that seems too stable and inert.

This image is much stronger. The symmetrical pose is seen from a different point of view, and the strong diagonal lines give a sense of energy to the composition.

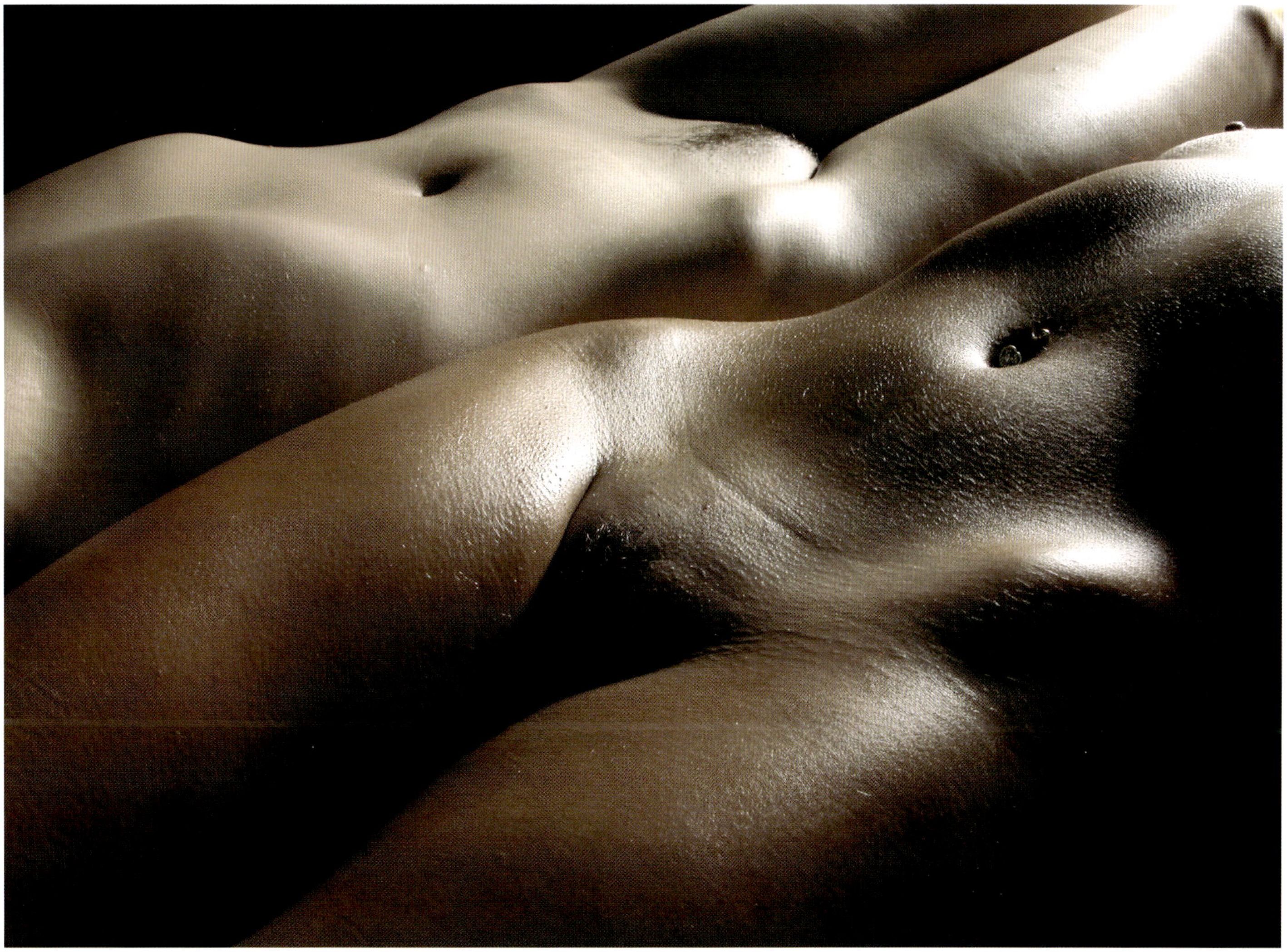

Posing the model

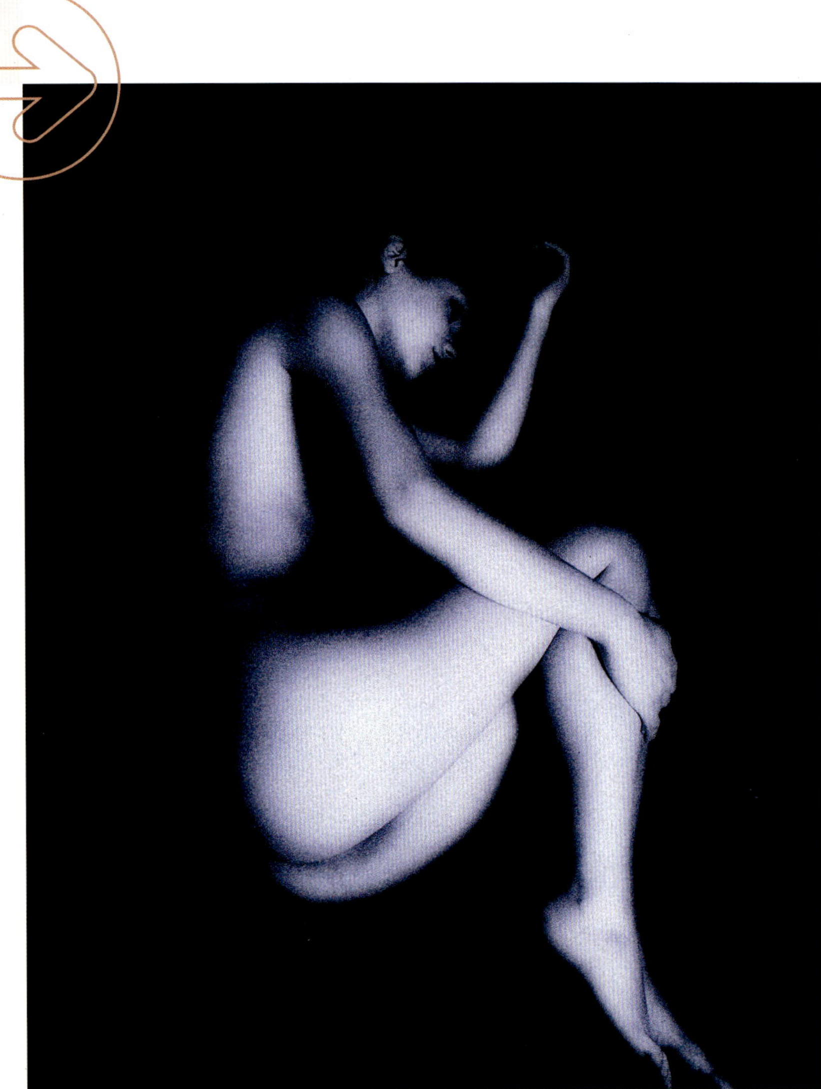

A simple idea can produce very diverse images. These shots come from sequences in which I asked the model to curl up into a ball and then slowly open out...

This pose is close to that on the left in the "opening out" sequence, but has a very different feeling, due to the altered camera position and very different lighting.

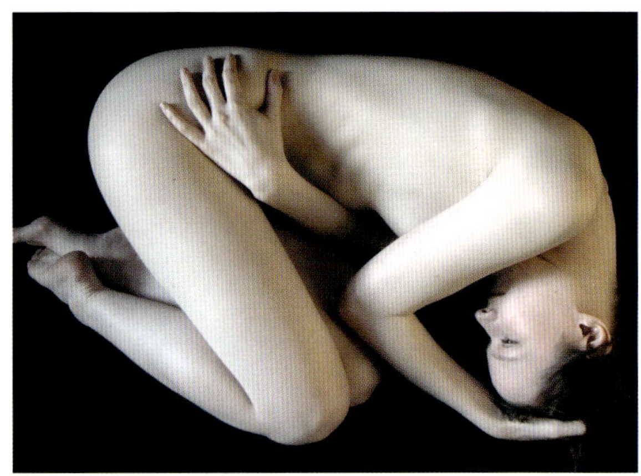

So at last here you are—in the studio, with your model standing in front of you. "How do you want me?" the model asks. Here are some tips on how to organize a shoot, particularly with a new model.

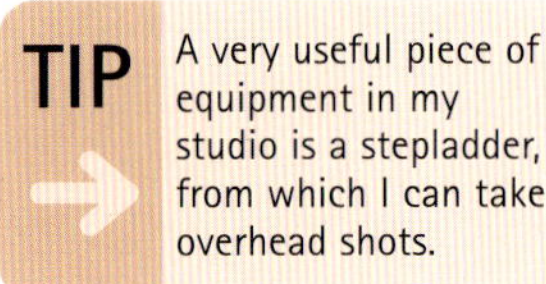

TIP A very useful piece of equipment in my studio is a stepladder, from which I can take overhead shots.

OBSERVE THE MODEL

However many images of your model you saw when you were selecting her, it's important to take a look at her before you start the shoot. For example, you could invite her to stand (nude) in the middle of your studio/working space, and to make a slow 360° turn. You don't need to photograph this: just watch the model and learn what she looks like in the flesh and from different angles. This also gives you the occasion to direct her and see how she responds. Don't be afraid to go close to her. If she has a few blemishes on her skin (as even the best models sometimes do), you need to be aware of them.

START WITH SOMETHING YOU KNOW

Another good way to get to know a new model is to shoot them in poses that you have used successfully before. Beginning with a few familiar poses makes it easier for you to experiment with lighting and camera angles and positions, while observing the model and getting a feel for their proportions, how well they take direction, and what works with them. Every model will give you something different, every time. This is also an opportunity to play back some of the images as you work, sharing them with the model to involve her in what you're trying to achieve, and using the histogram to check your lighting.

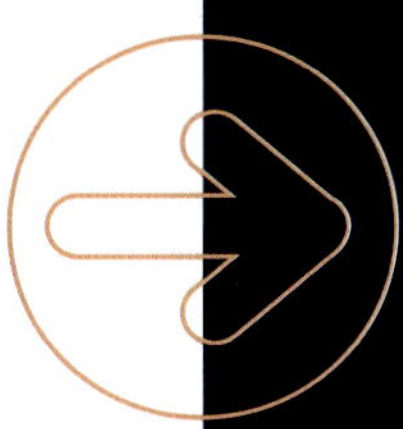

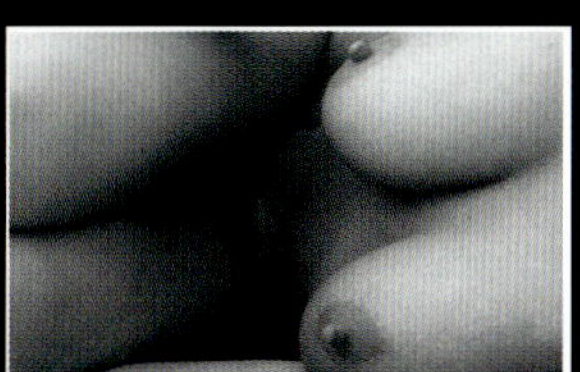

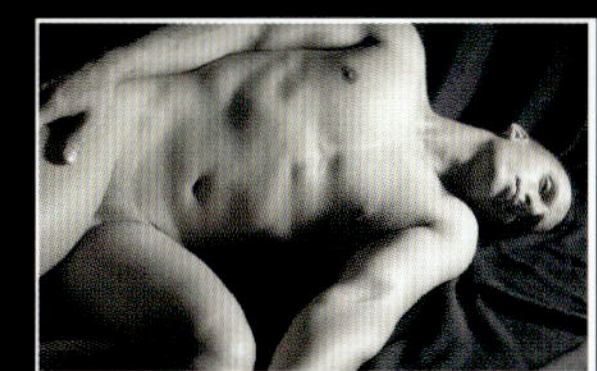

Posing the model is a key part of successful nude photography. Each model is different, and no two bodies will behave in the same way. Preparation and experimentation, as always, yield results.

COMMUNICATION AND FEEDBACK

Talk to the model as you work with her. Explain what you are doing and give her feedback and encouragement as she responds to your directions. When you need to touch her to adjust the pose, remember to ask her permission before doing so for the first time. You may also need to remind her not to anticipate your adjustments or go farther than you have moved her. You should listen to her suggestions—she knows her own capabilities—and she won't be offended if you decide not to use her ideas.

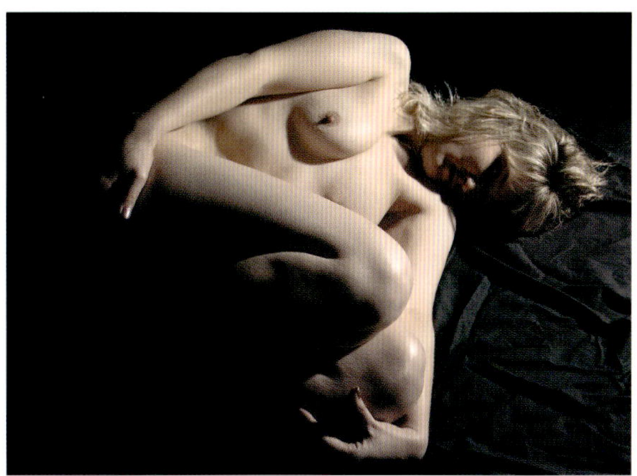

This model is seen from a lower angle, with the camera aligned on a different axis. With oblique lighting, this produces yet another different nude.

The camera is almost vertical above the model, to exploit the pattern & texture of the floor.

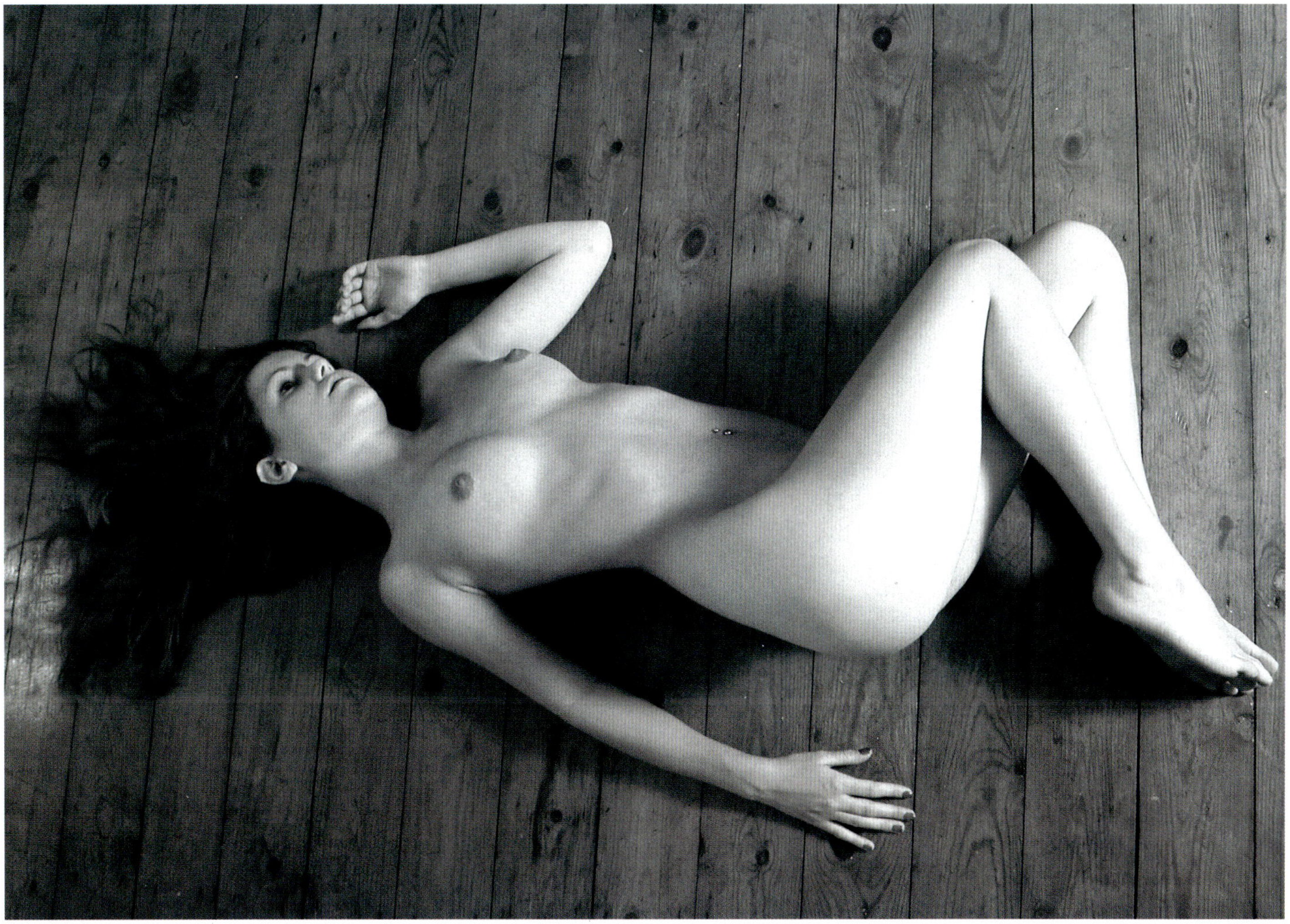

Posing the model

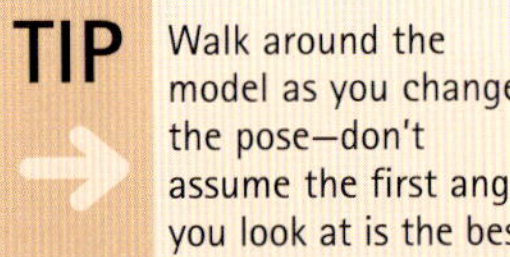

Walk around the model as you change the pose—don't assume the first angle you look at is the best.

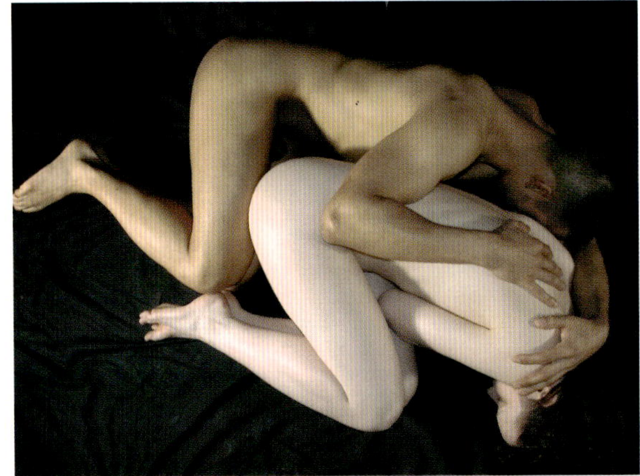

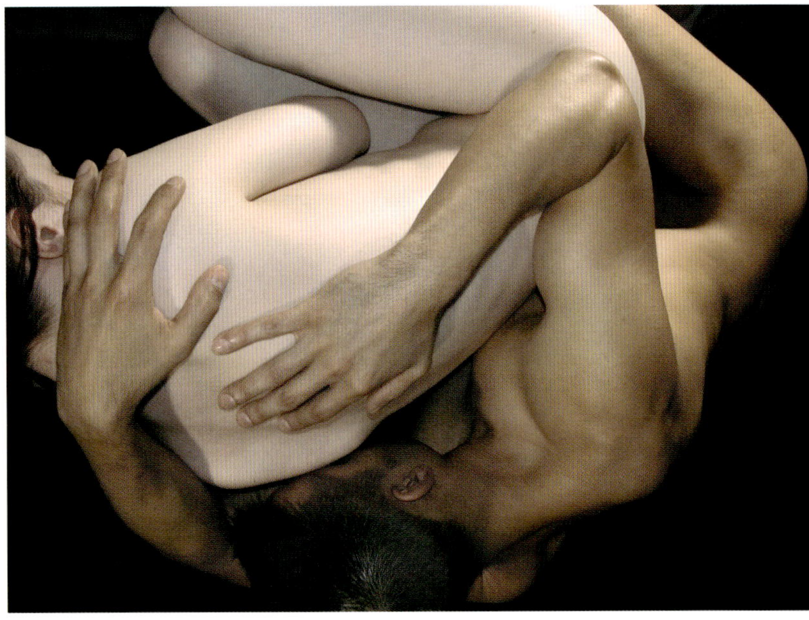

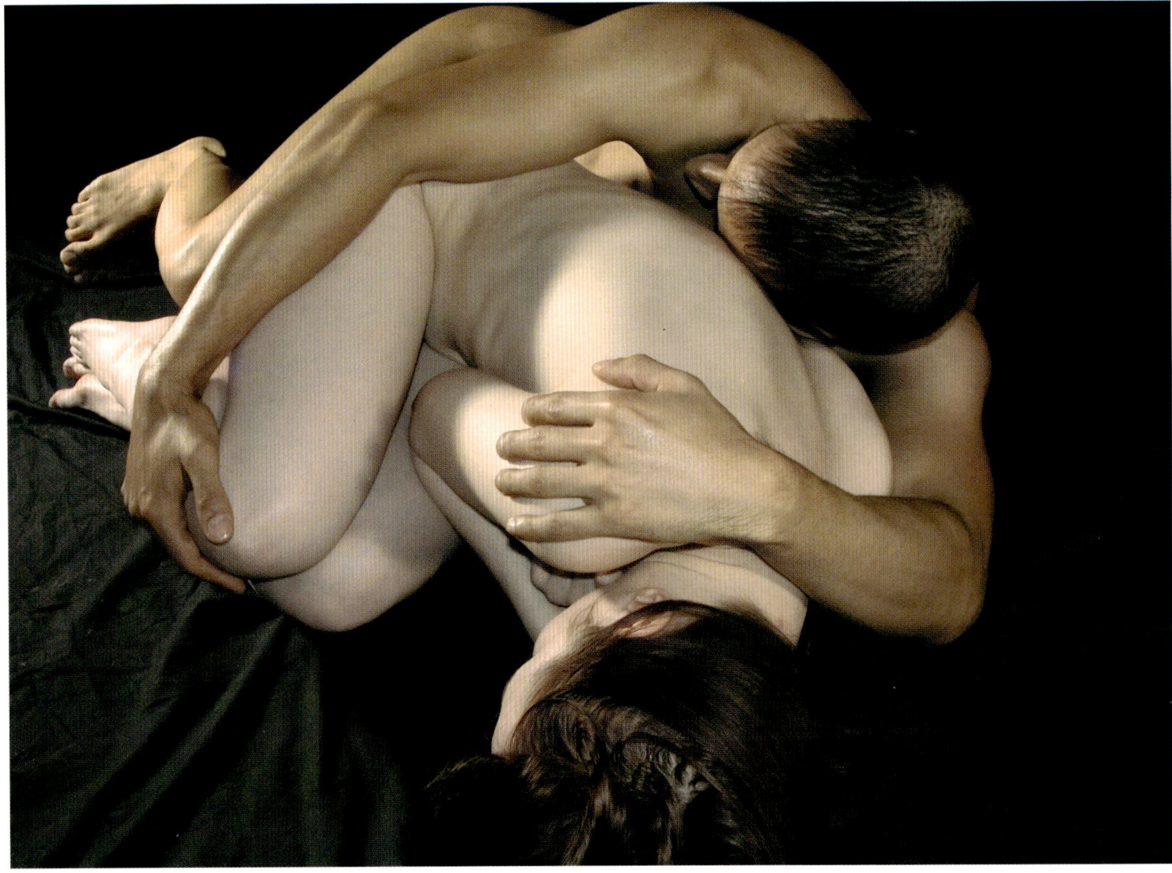

Working with two models, some poses seem to suggest themselves naturally, such as these three, shot in sequence, which all aim to use the contrasting skin tones of the models within a framework of overlapping and interlocking limbs.

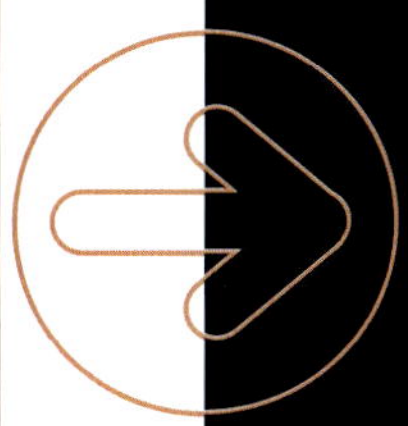

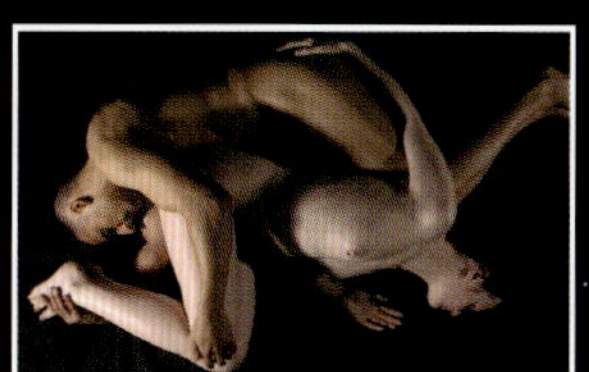

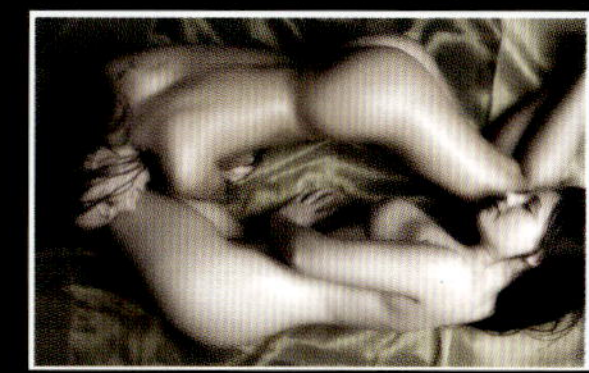

Take your shots from a wide variety of angles and viewpoints. Learn to plan ahead by making a list of the images you wish to take. Be ready at all times to experiment with your compositions.

Poses suggested by a well-known photograph by the contemporary nude photographer Bob Carlos Clarke. In the second pose the model's turned head disrupts the formality and symmetry of the original image.

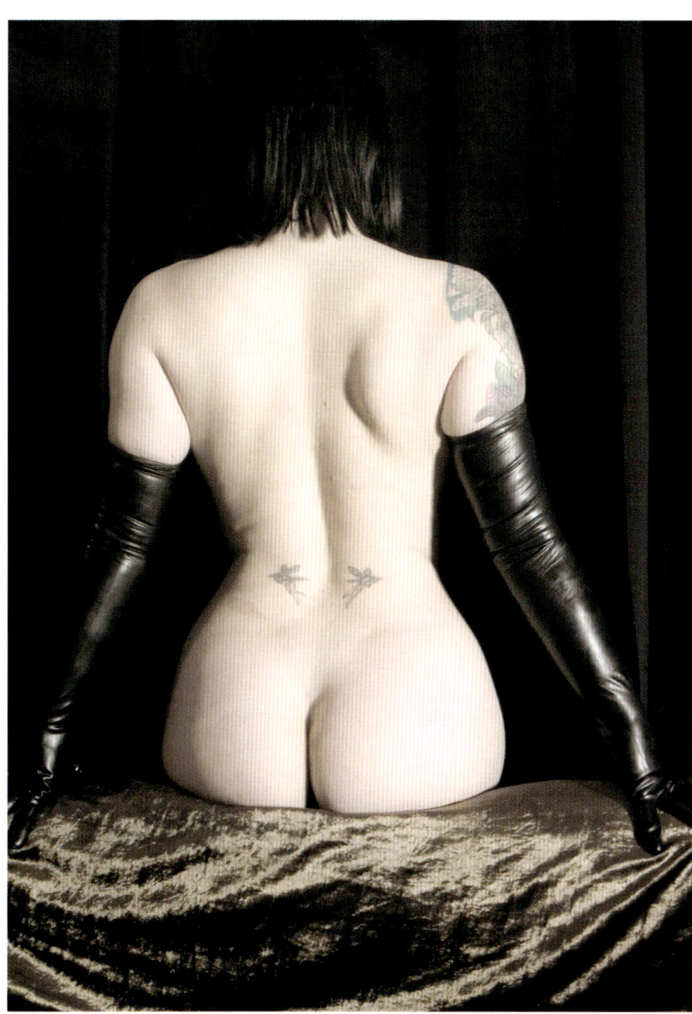

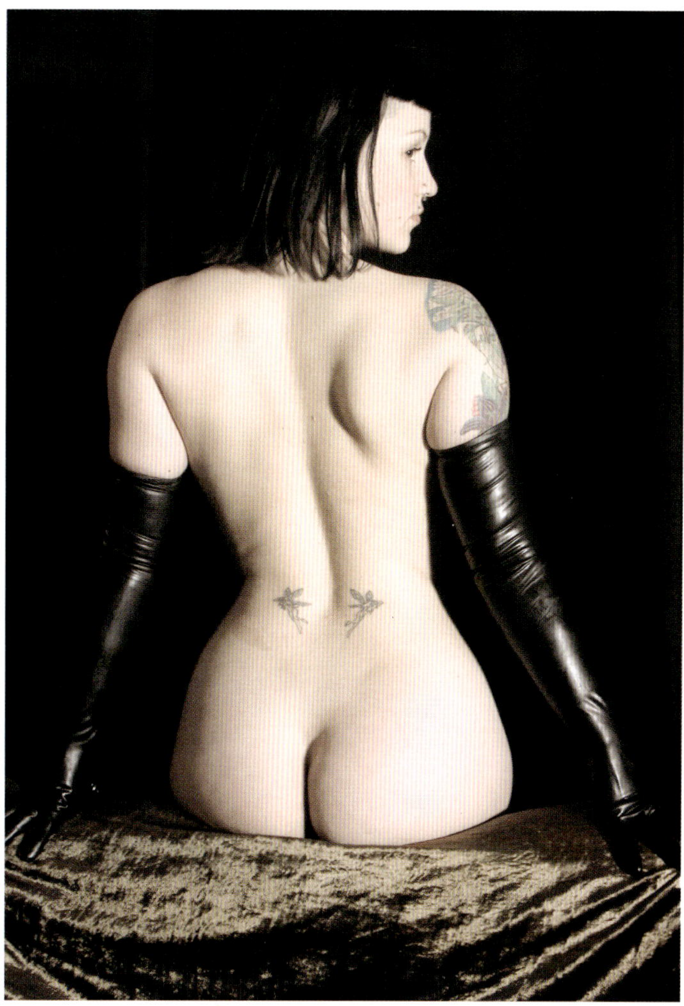

DEVELOPING THE SHOOT

It's helpful to make a list of the shots you want, and as the session develops you can move on to doing those. As you set different poses, explore their possibilities by varying them and by shooting them under different lighting conditions and from different angles.

IMITATION AND ORIGINALITY

There must be tens of thousands of beautiful nude photographs in the world. Few of us are fortunate enough to create an entirely original one, but there's a lot to learn from interpreting an existing image, adapting the pose, lighting, and camera angle to your own vision.

Experimenting with light

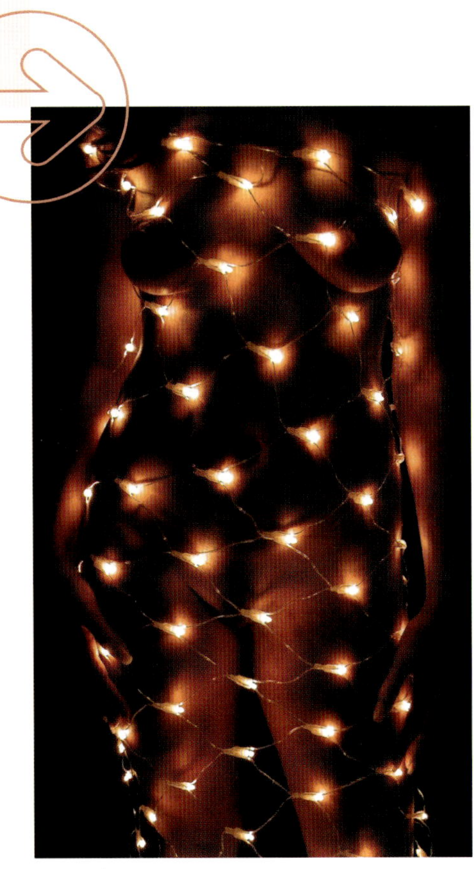

An unusual light source, a mesh of low-voltage party lights, was wrapped tightly around the model for this shot.

The softbox used here produces soft shadows with diffuse edges and little or no solid black, even at their darkest point. The most oblique lighting, starting from oblique 4, provides a strong sense of depth in the image, most clearly seen in the molding of the model's breasts and collarbones, and the shadows they cast. As the light comes round toward the camera (oblique 3 to frontal 3), this sense of depth reduces and small imperfections on the model's skin become less noticeable. The transition from oblique to frontal lighting (frontal 4) also changes the impact and emotional appeal of the image as the sense of mystery that oblique lighting imparts is gradually removed.

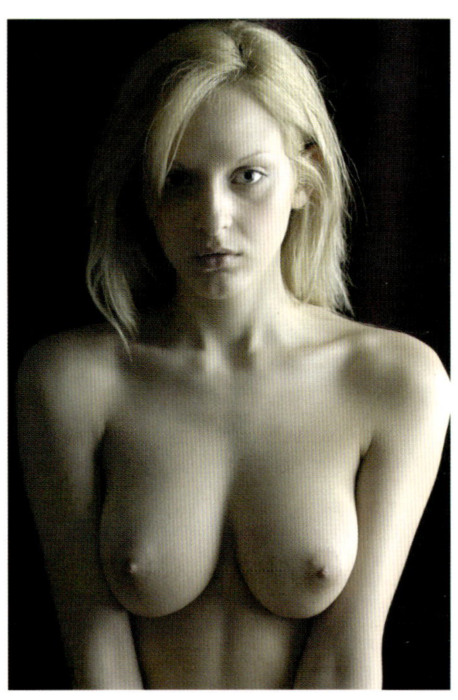

oblique 4

When we say lighting, we're talking about shadows. Here we look at the different qualities of light and shade produced by different types of lighting in different positions, and at ways of developing understanding and control over lighting. The ease with which a digital camera lets you test ideas and immediately see the results is never more valuable than when you're experimenting with light. One way to study the effects of lighting is to pose your model simply, select a light source, and take a sequence of shots while moving the light around the model.

TRYING OUT DIFFERENT LIGHT SOURCES

For the sequence shown here, I used a flash head fitted with a large softbox. For the shots shown on pages 58–59, I used a standard (60°) reflector with barndoors and some diffusion material. These different setups created quite different effects. In both setups I placed a gold reflector on the other side of the model, to bounce some light back into the shot. In each case, the center of the flash head was positioned slightly higher than the model's head. Different effects again can be achieved by varying the height of the flash head.

The camera was placed directly in front of the model, and the starting position for the light in each sequence was just behind a line running through the model's shoulders, at an angle of about 110-120° to the camera. The last shot in each sequence was taken with the camera at a different height, to avoid having both light and camera on the same alignment.

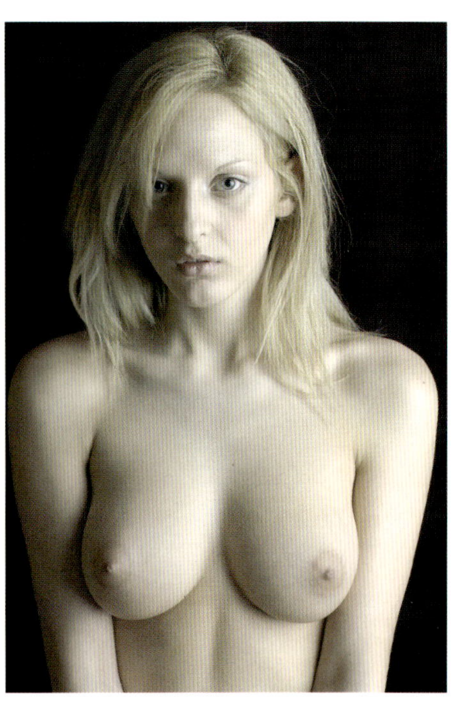

frontal 1

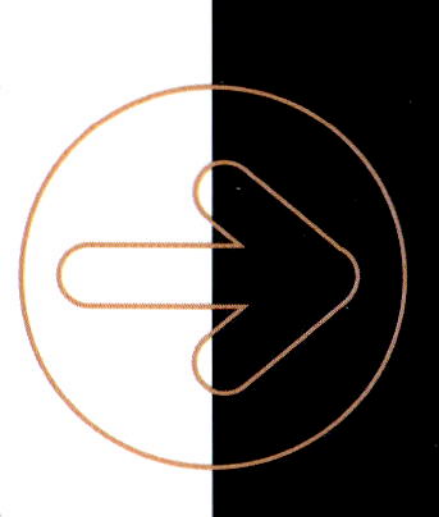

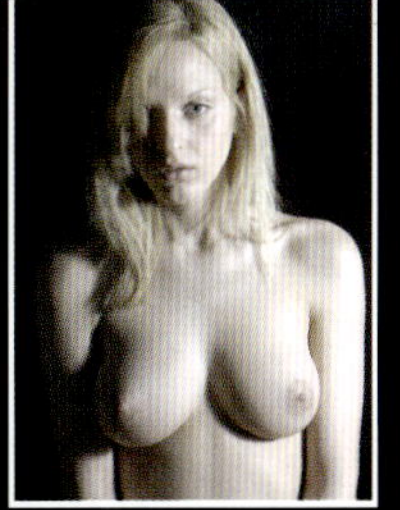

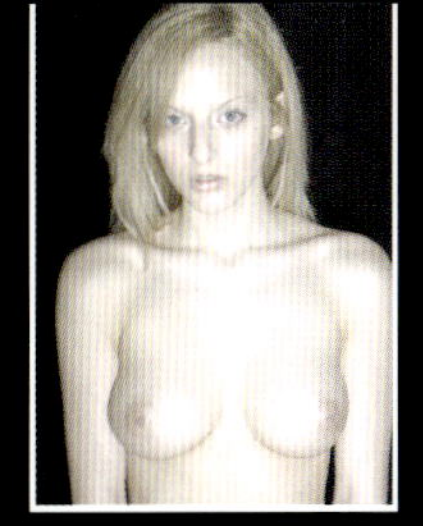

Developing an understanding of natural and artificial light will make all the difference to your nude portraits. The strength of digital photography is that it gives you scope for experimentation.

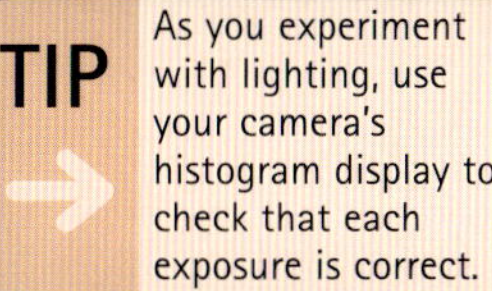

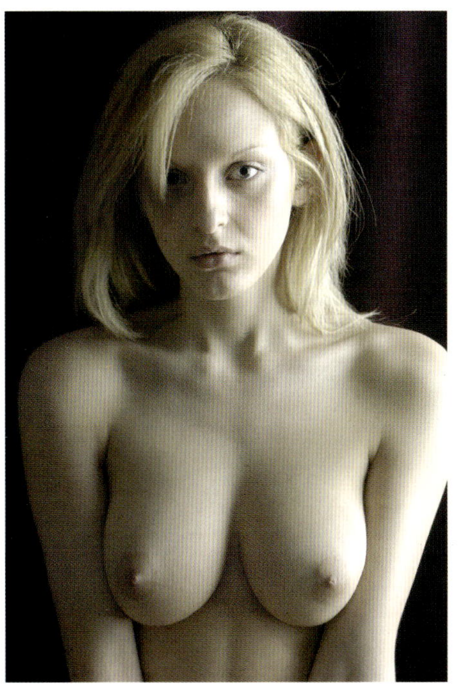

oblique 3

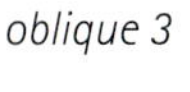

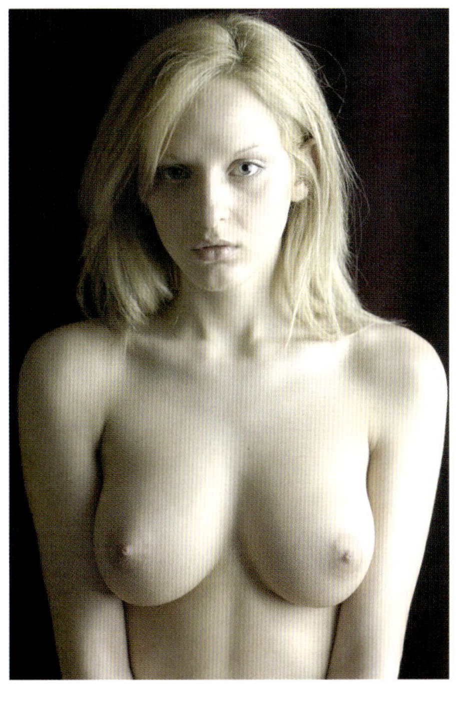

oblique 2

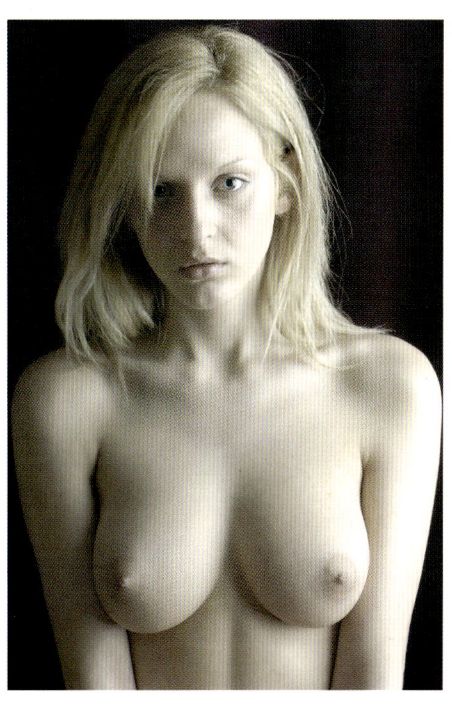

oblique 1

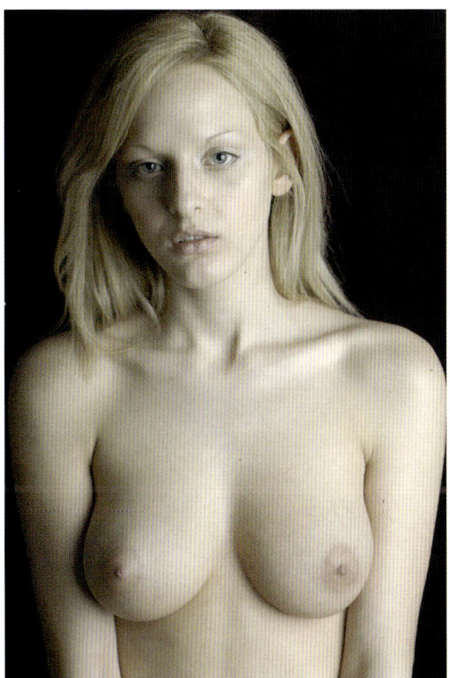

frontal 2

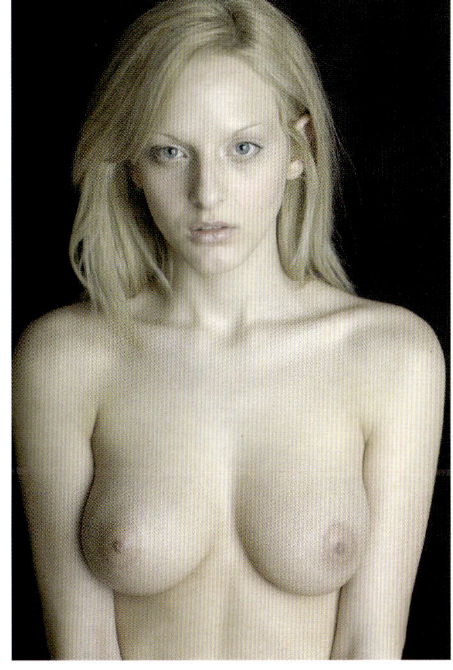

frontal 3

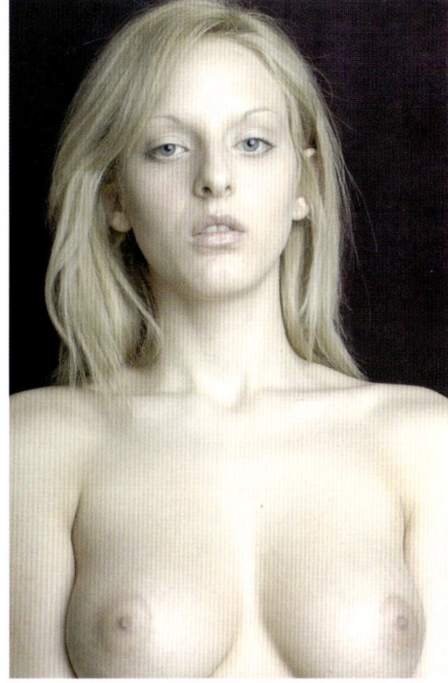

frontal 4

Experimenting with light

By itself, the reflector would produce very strong, harsh shadows, so I covered it with some diffusion material. But it still produces a narrow beam of light compared to the softbox, as this sequence makes clear. If you compare the early shots in this sequence with the corresponding images in the softbox sequence, you can see that here the shadows have more distinct edges, and are darker (if never quite solid black) at their most intense. The contrast between shadowed and lit areas is much greater than with the softbox. Again, it's instructive to consider the difference in the emotional quality of the images produced by the two different light sources.

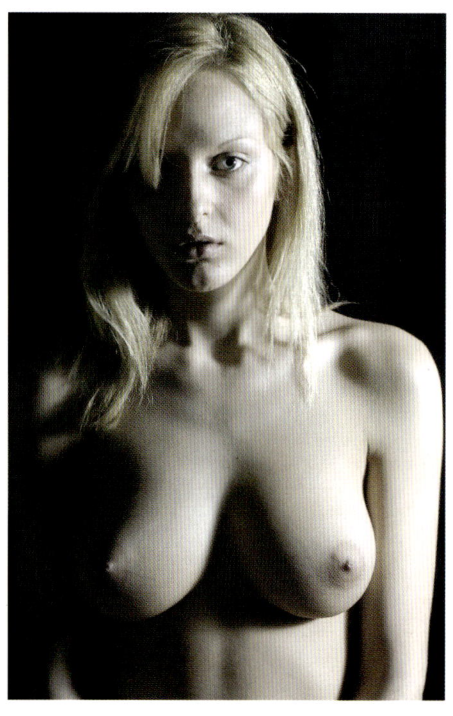

Oblique 1

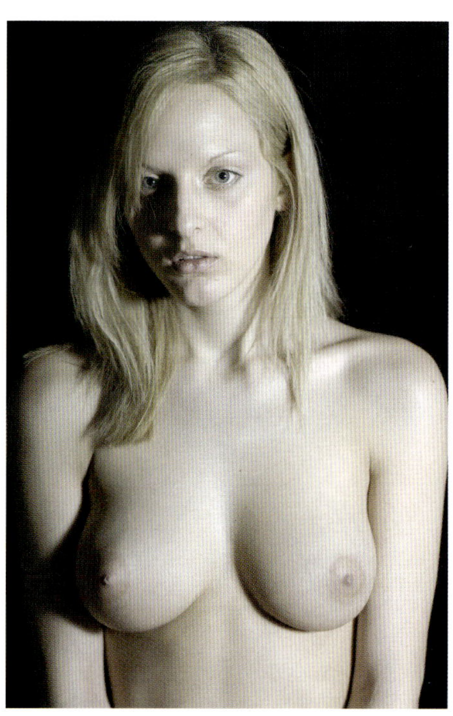

Oblique 2

MAXIMUM/MINIMUM LIGHTING

Pushing the amount of light beyond normal limits or reducing it to a minimum can also produce very striking images. You can use the histogram display on the camera, as well your eye, to assess each shot as you take it to make sure that you're achieving the dramatic effect you've set out to do without losing too much detail.

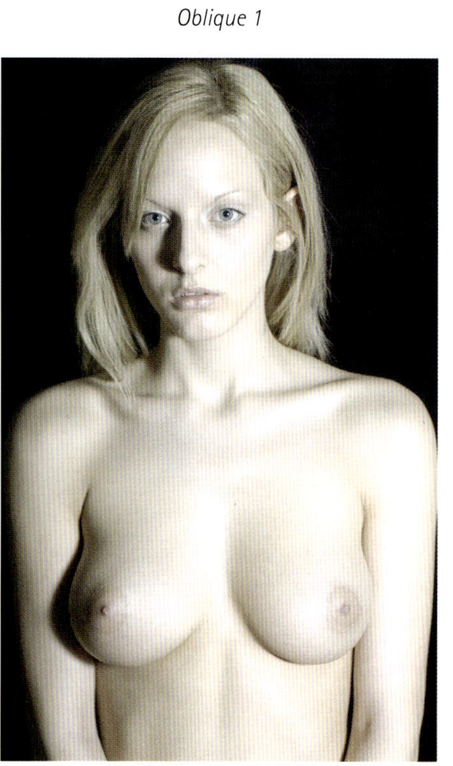

Frontal 1

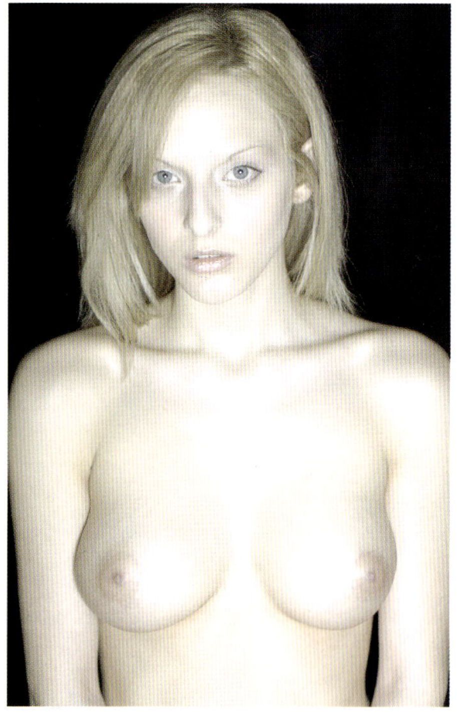

Frontal 2

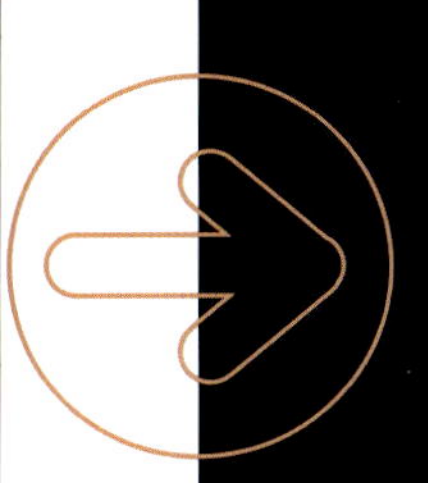

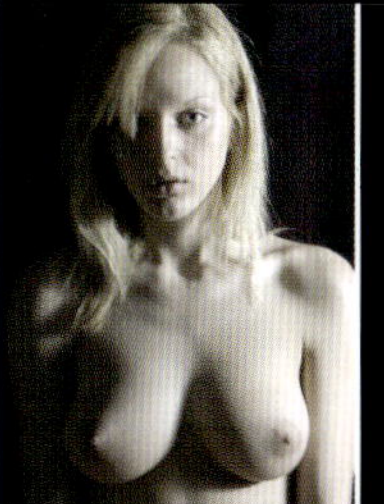

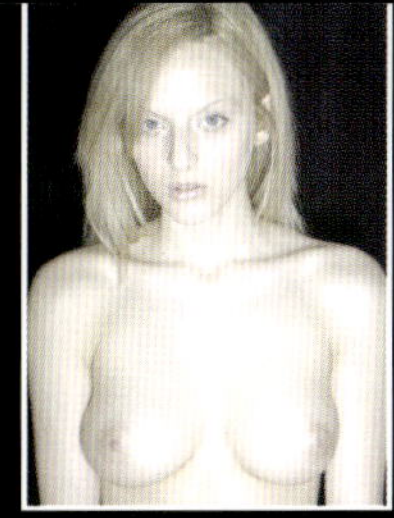

Light is much more than a simple means of illuminating your subjects. Used creatively, light is an essential tool whose effects can transform a standard nude shot into something much more exciting.

TIP

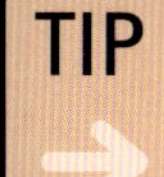

Homemade reflectors are cheap and useful for providing that crucial "bounce" from the camera side into rim-lit shots.

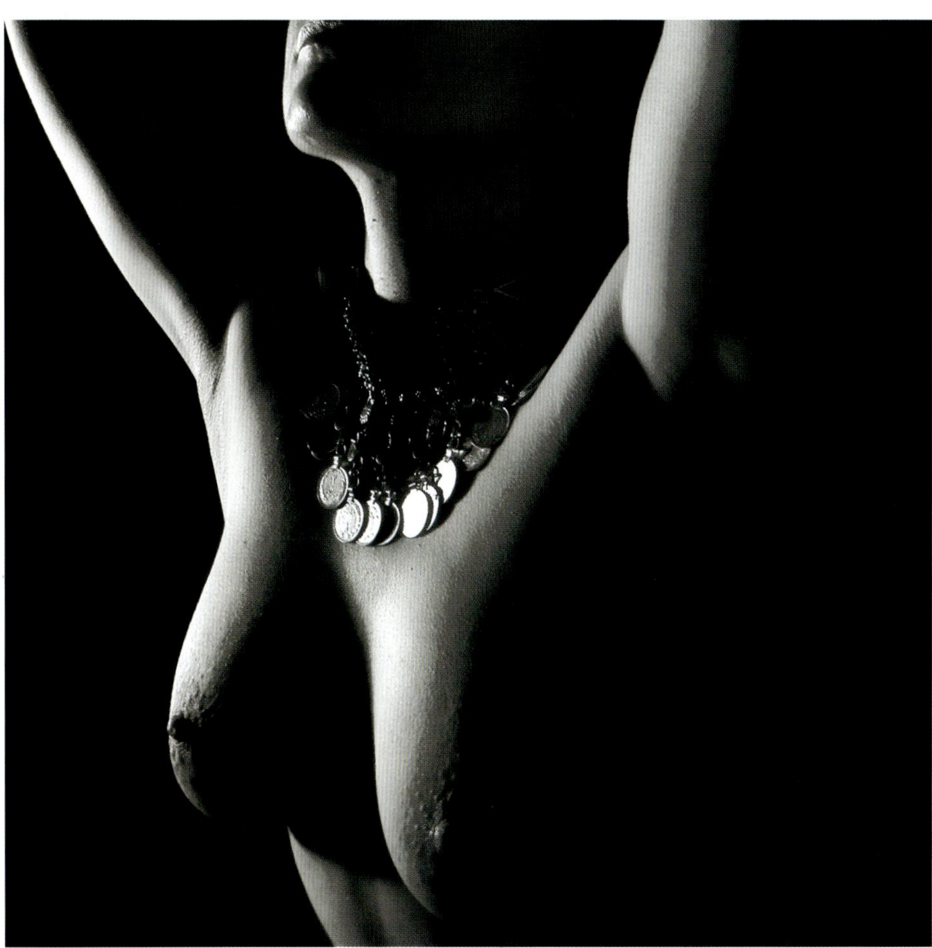

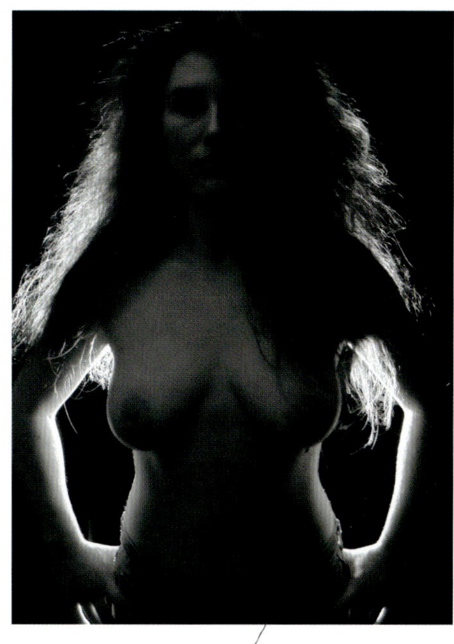

An example of high-key lighting, where deliberate overlighting and overexposure produce an image in which only key details remain, in particular the model's mouth and vivid blue eyes.

A single hard-edged light source (flash head with 60° reflector, used without any diffusing material), positioned well above the model, produces a low-key, rim-lit image.

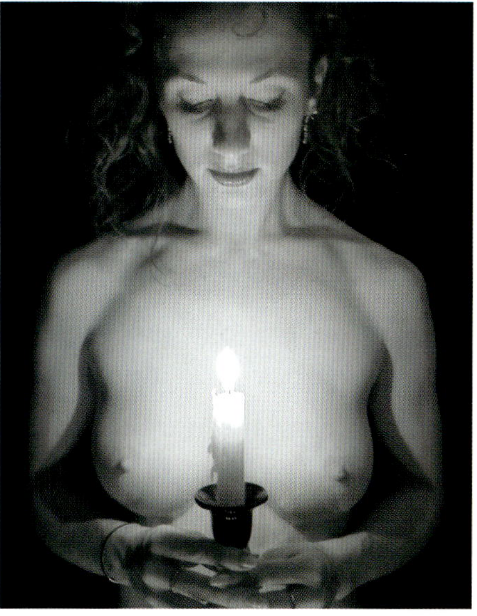

Top: A single flash head directly behind the model produces vivid effects in her long, wild hair, and gently outlines her torso.

Above: A candle can be a beautiful light source, creating weird shadows on the model. This needs a tripod and some careful exposure.

Framing the body

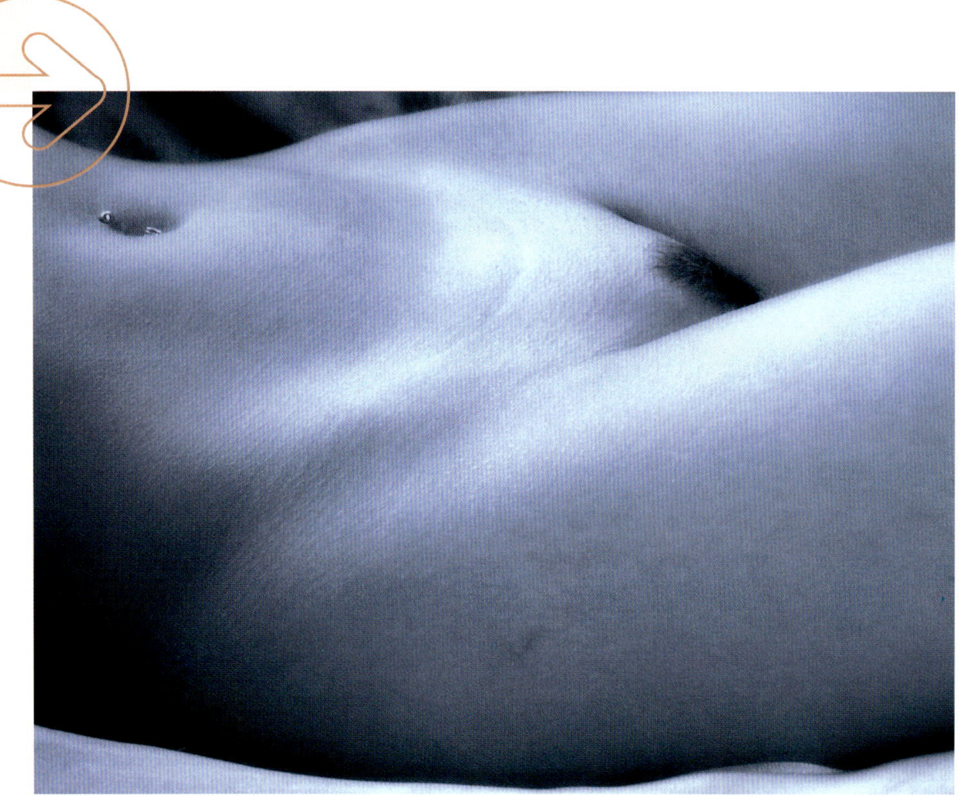

The body as landscape: the blue toning of this image creates a sense of tranquility appropriate to the model's pose.

Here the cleft between the buttocks echoes the indentation of the model's spine.

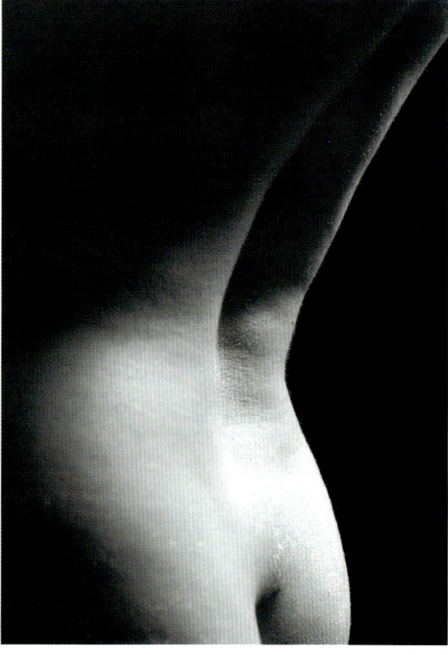

There are many themes in nude photography that concentrate on specific parts of the body—torso, back, buttocks, breasts... This is an opportunity to create evocative and almost abstract images, in which form and shape predominate. Some of these images have the quality of an artist's anatomical study.

CREATING ABSTRACT IMAGES

You can create your own version of one of these classic nude photography themes, seeking as you do so a different way of representing it, or take as your subject a less frequently visited location on the body. In effect, you're trying to make the viewer look again at the image, and wonder "What is that?" This pursuit of the abstract also explains why most of the pictures in this section are monochrome.

When shooting, you have a number of possibilities in framing the model. You can keep your lens zoomed out and work close to the model; this gives you the chance to use a shallow depth of field, and choose where to locate the focus of the shot. Alternatively, you can zoom in to frame a part of the body, with a resulting increase in depth of field. With the images shown here, rather than simply crop a section out of a wider shot, I have tried to visualize each image in the camera's viewfinder as I have shot it, so that no further adjustment to the frame of the picture is then necessary.

Lighting also plays a critical part in these abstract images, molding the body, and contributing to the sense of mystery. All the images shown here were typically shot with one soft light source, positioned at an angle of 90° or greater to the camera. In some cases I used a reflector positioned opposite the light to "bounce" a little extra illumination into the shadow areas, but in others I relied on the fabric on which the model was lying to fulfill this function.

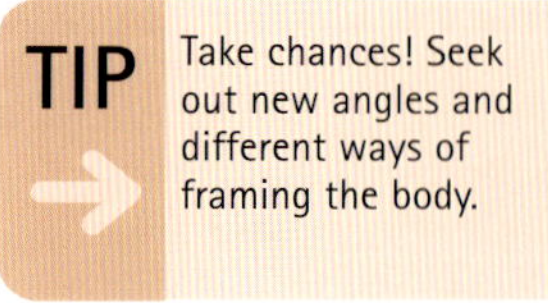

Take chances! Seek out new angles and different ways of framing the body.

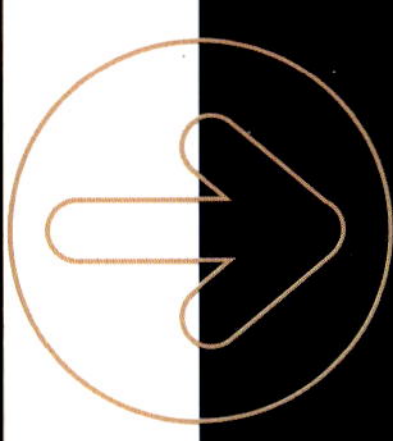

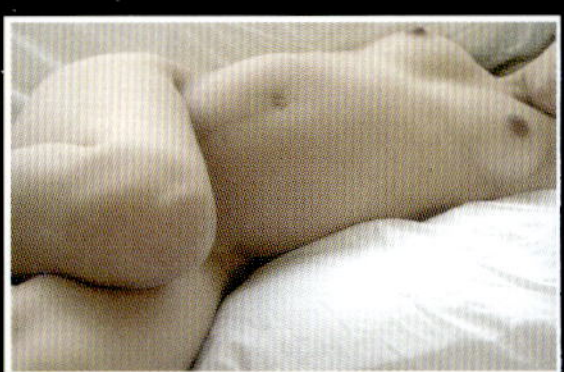

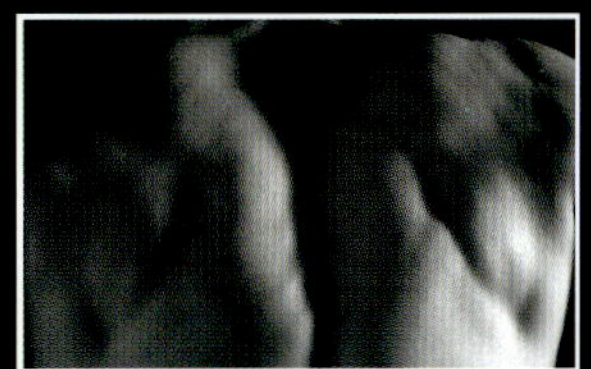

A creative approach to framing your photographs can result in powerful images. What you choose to show—or not show—can bring a different perspective to your shots that can be highly stimulating for the viewer.

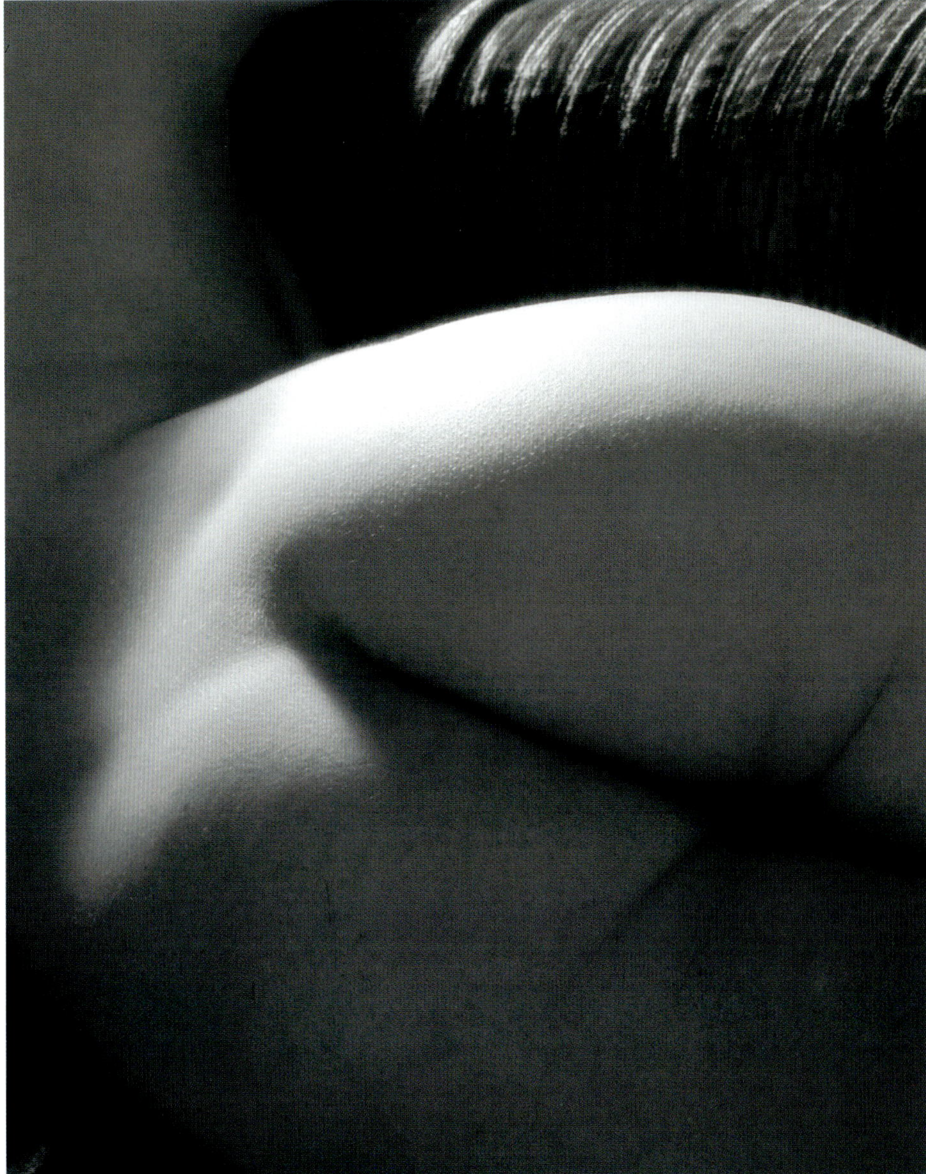

The framing of this shot brings out the sinuous curve of the body; the smooth texture of the skin contrasts with the fabric in the background.

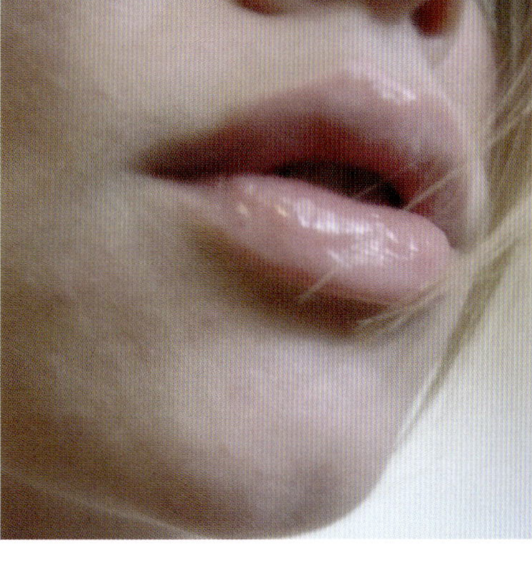

Careful framing brings out the sensuality of the face, in this self-portrait by Lyndsay Martin.

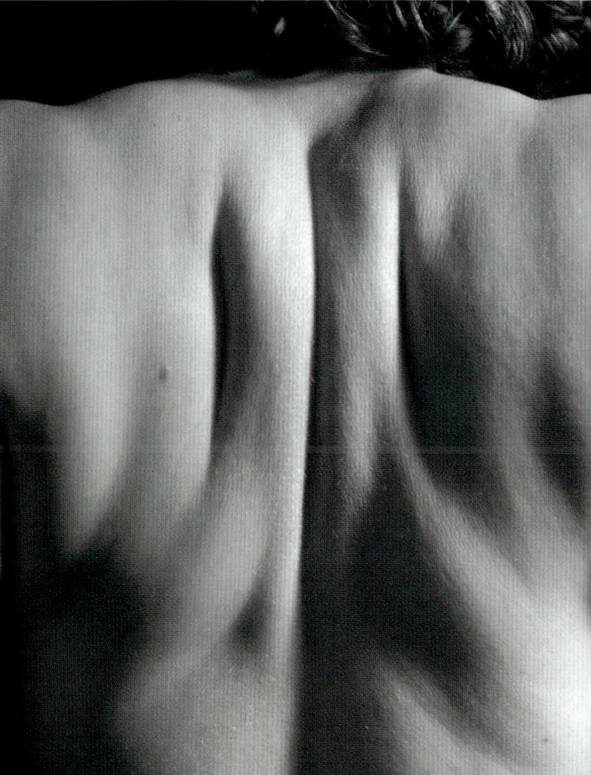

The play of light across the muscles of the model's back here produces a sense of movement and of the intricacy of human anatomy.

Framing the body

Here the wide-angle setting of the lens subtly distorts the model. This produces a heightened sense of the interlocking curves of her body.

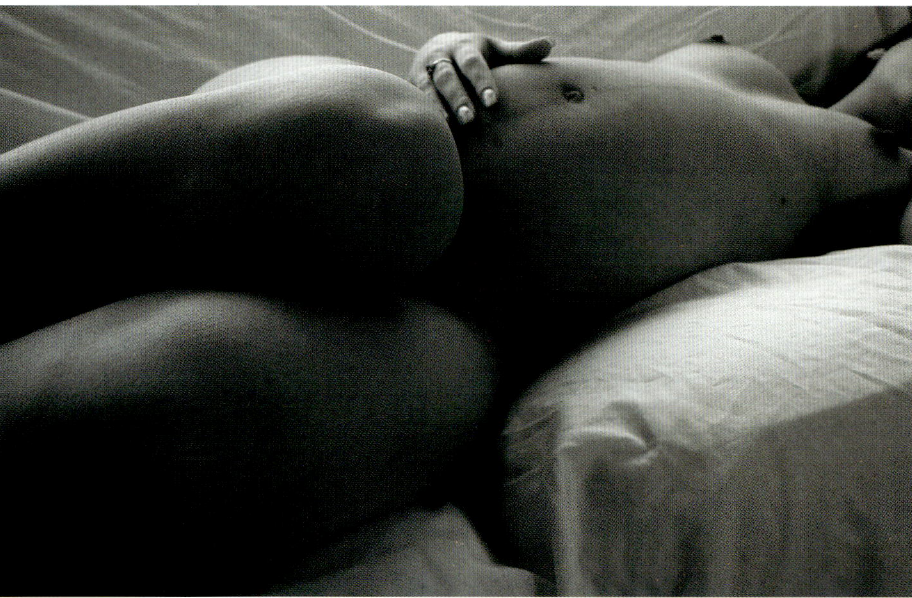

The pose, lighting, and framing in this image suggest the body's strength and power. Note the shallow depth of field and the focus on the further edge of the body.

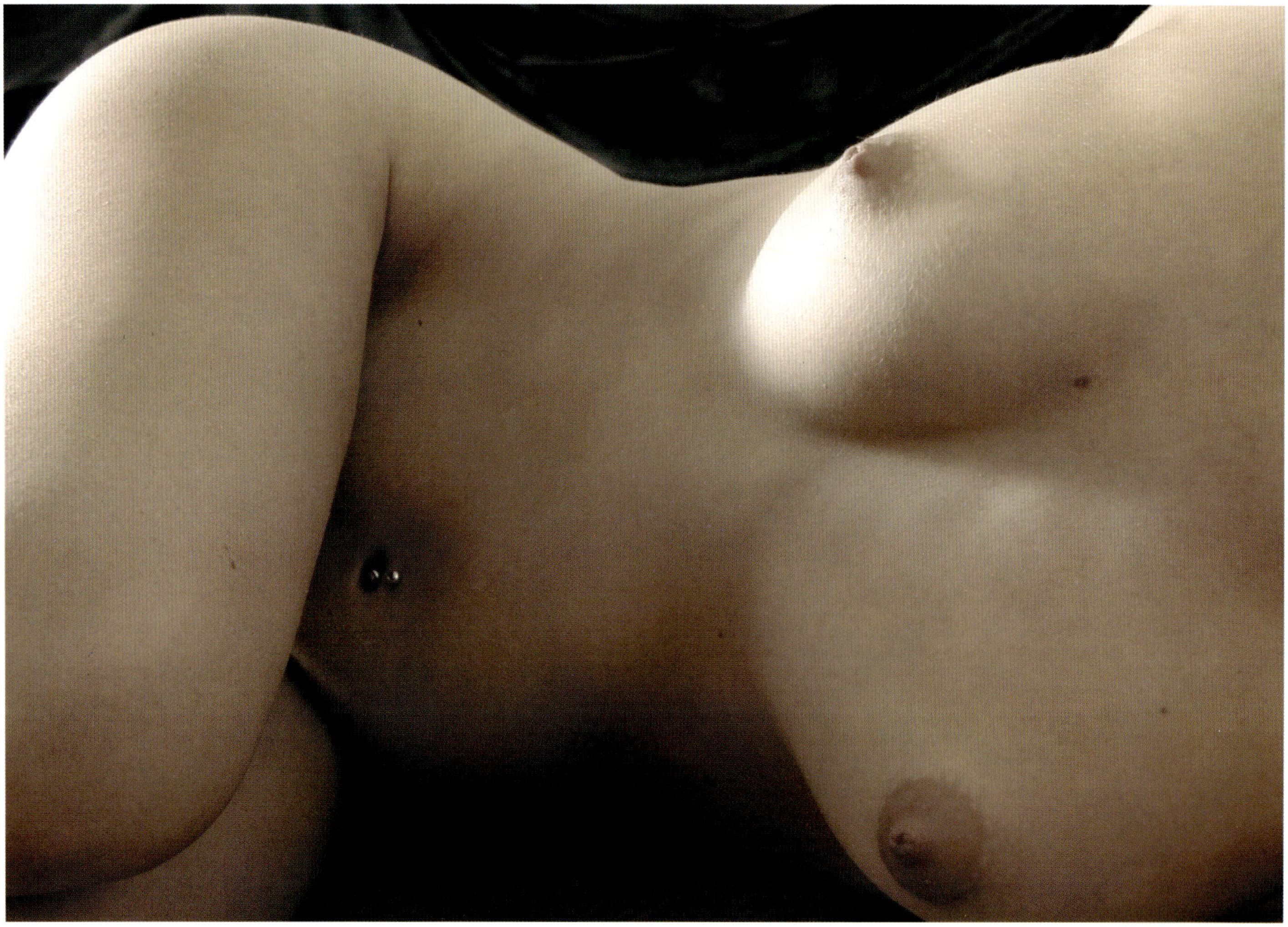

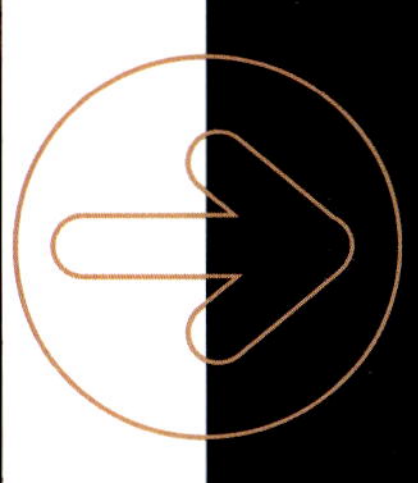

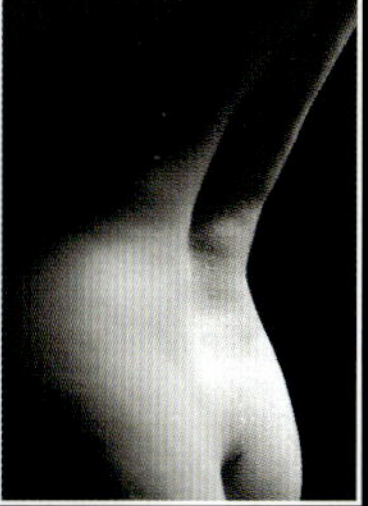

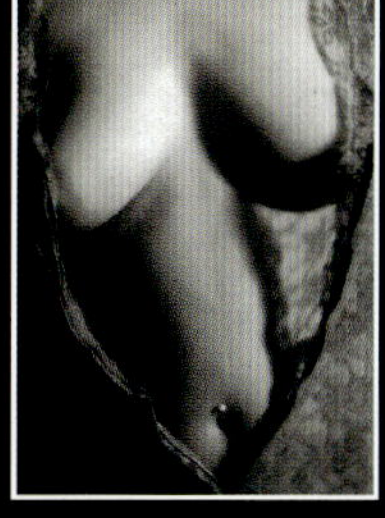

Concentrating on an individual part of the body can yield interesting results. Experimenting with depth of field and soft focus effects can help to accentuate a subject's appearance.

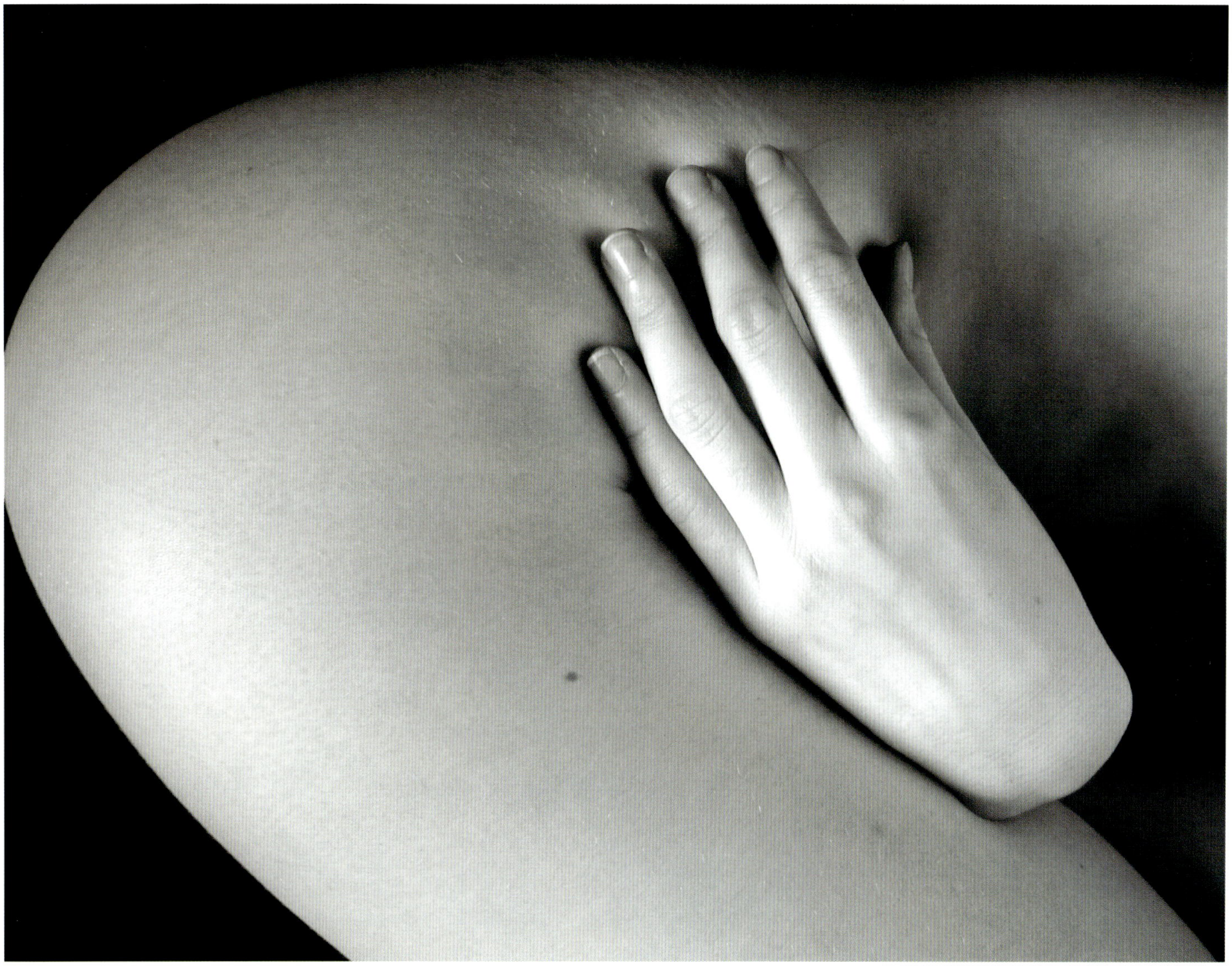

The almost geometric curve of the model's haunch is disrupted by the seemingly disconnected hand. Note the subtle difference in tone between these two elements.

The painted body

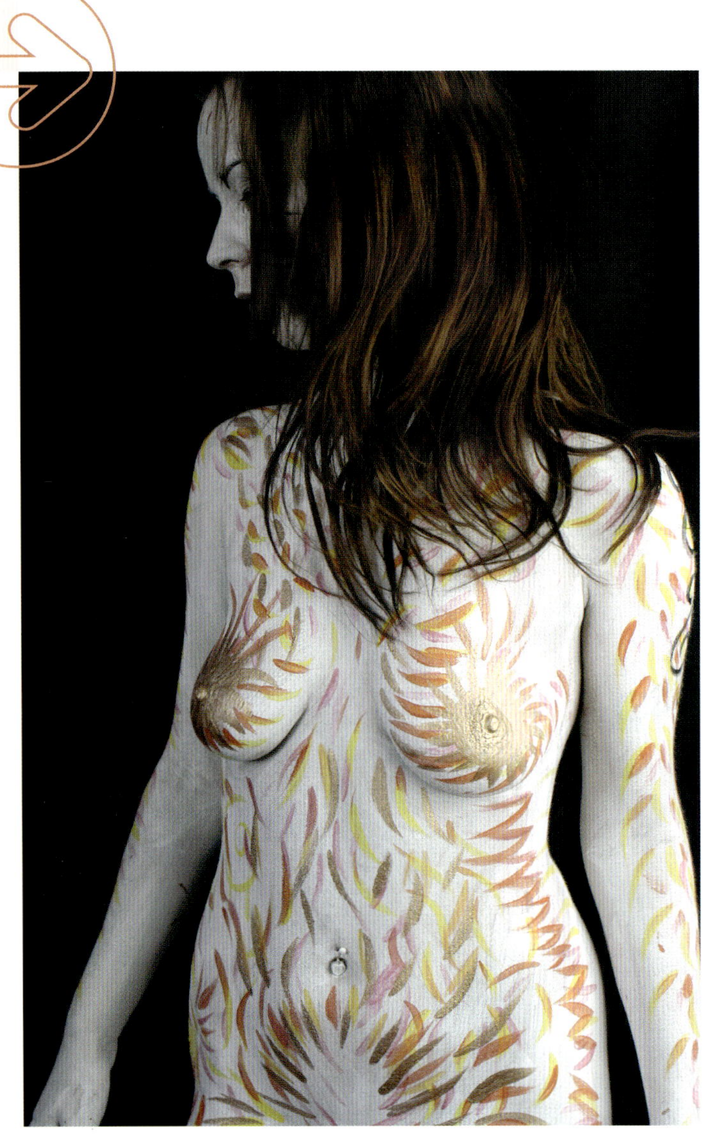

Working with two models, I had the opportunity to photograph them separately and together. The "second skins" created by the painters took us into a realm of fantasy that inspired the models as well as me.

Work in progress...one model was painted with airbrush and sponge techniques, and the other using brushes.

Here, the two methods of body painting are shown, clearly demonstrating the different possibilities that each offers.

WORKING WITH BODY PAINTERS

Body painters use two different types of paints: those that are intended to be seen by natural light, and "blacklight" materials, which fluoresce under black (ultraviolet) light. Here, we used natural-light body painting.

Some painters play with the idea of painting "clothes" onto the body; others work against a real background—say, a brick wall—and blend the model into it. Mike and Sally, the painters I worked with, prefer to explore abstract patterns and textures.

The shoot took place in my home studio. We covered the painters" work area with plastic sheeting to protect the walls and furniture from the fine particles produced by the airbrush, and we brought in extra heating so that the models wouldn't be chilled by the paint as it dried.

In recent years body painting has grown in popularity, as an artform in itself and as part of the spread of clubbing across many countries. Working with body painters offers an extra dimension of collaboration and creativity for the photographer, and it won't be difficult to find body painters who will be keen to work with you.

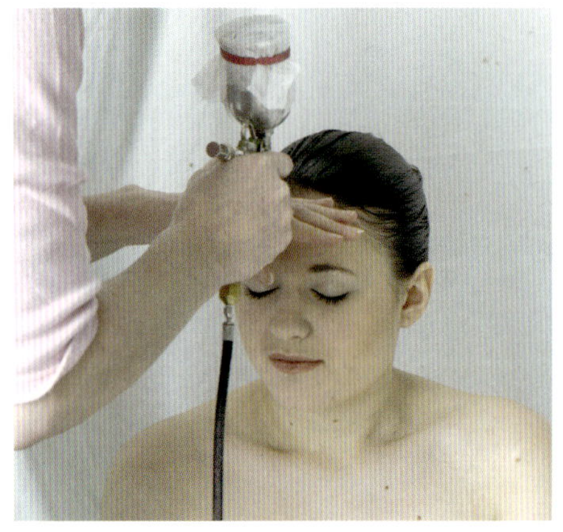

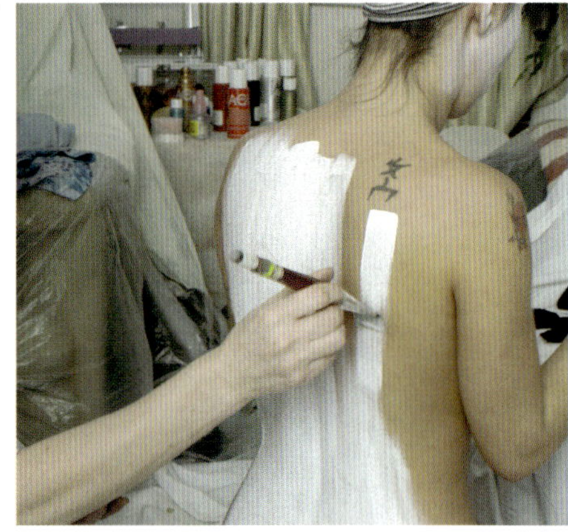

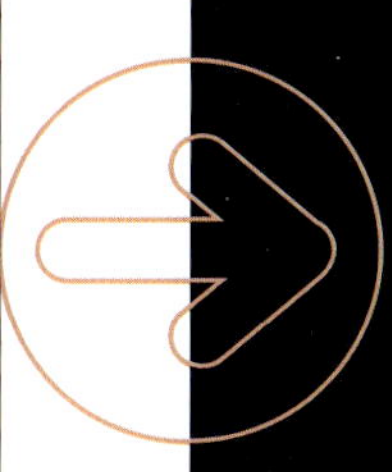

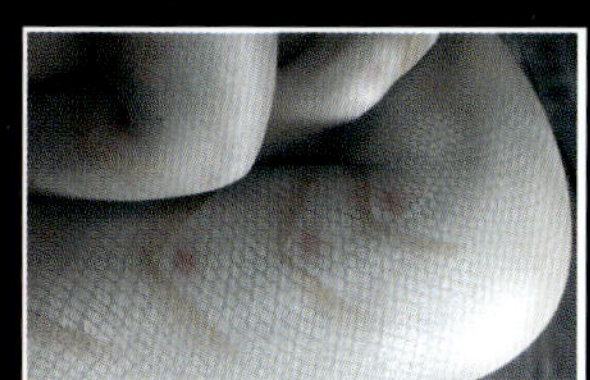

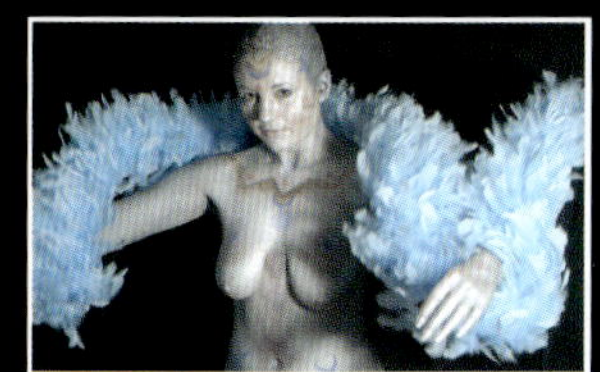

The use of bodypainting can add an extra dimension to the nude photograph. Some photographers choose to paint clothing on to the model, while others prefer to experiment by painting interesting shapes and textures on to their subjects.

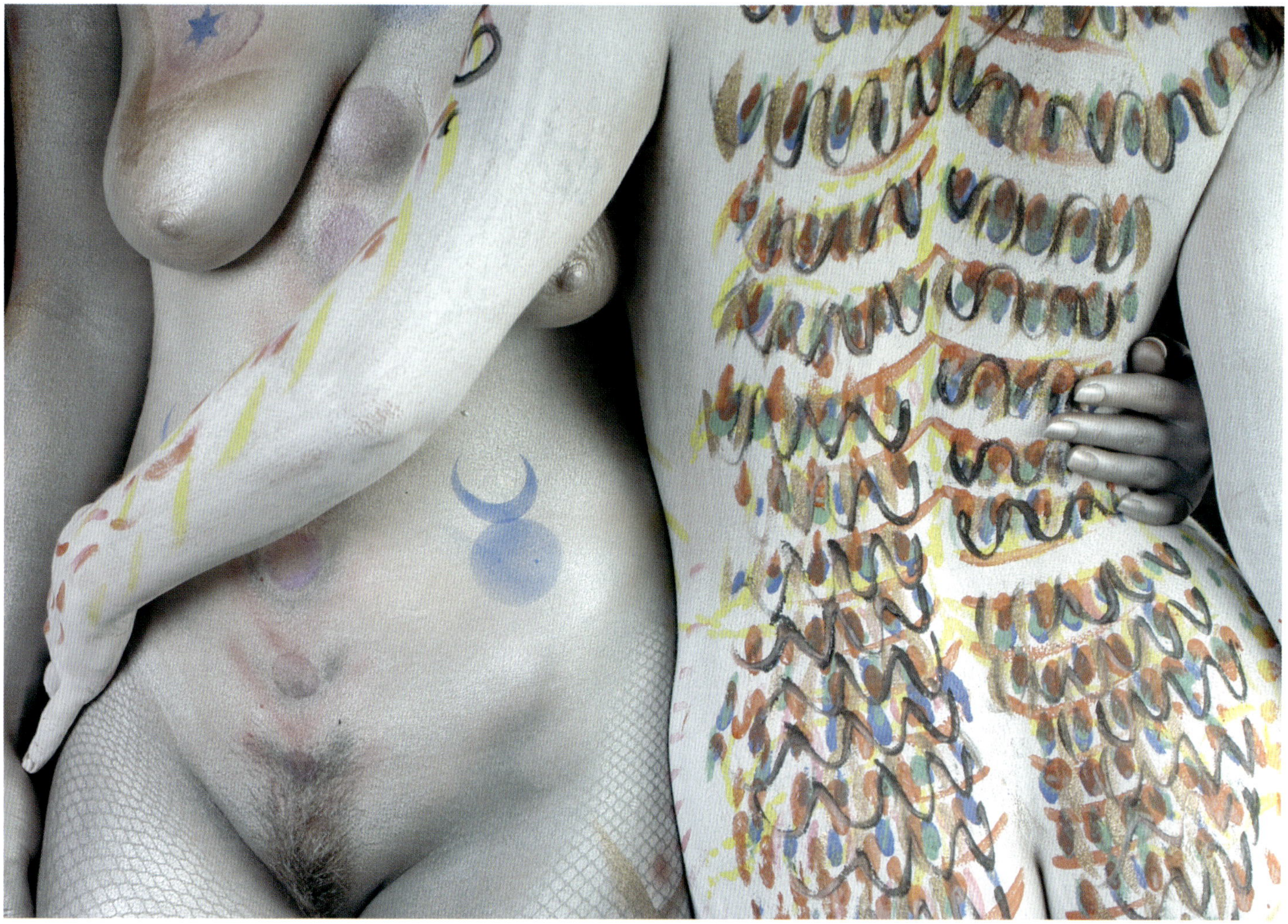

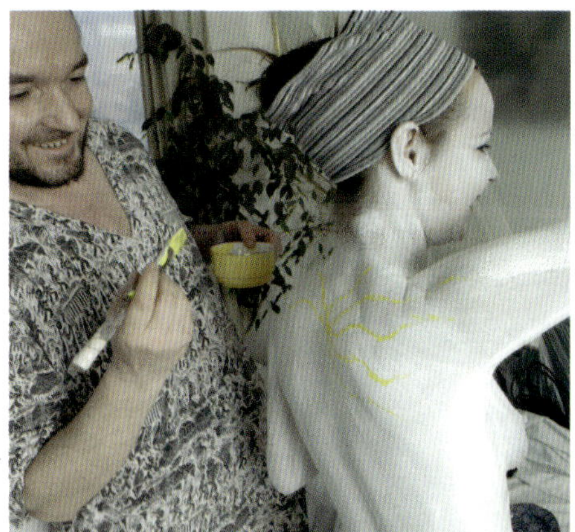

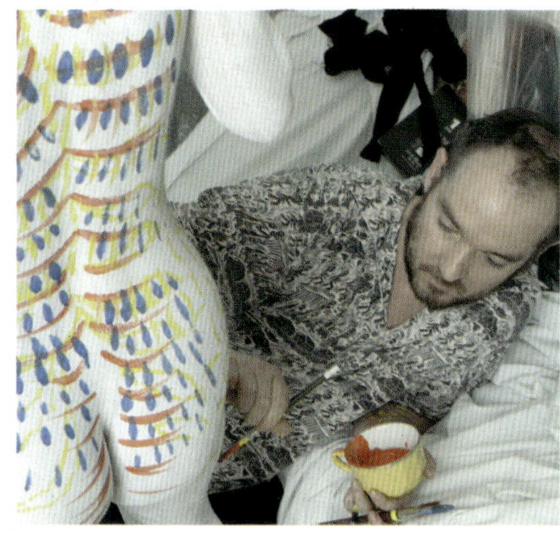

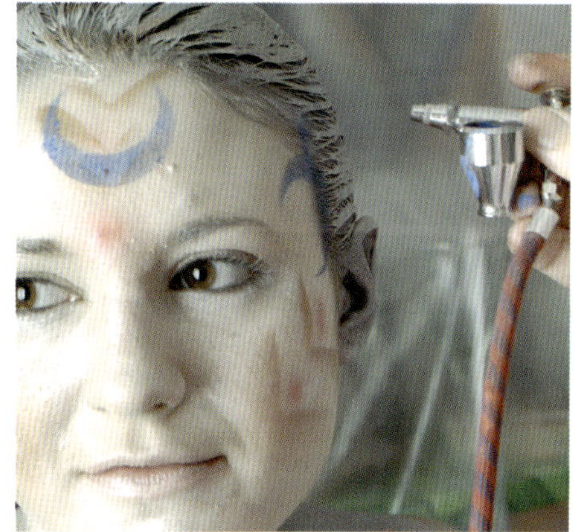

Color in photography

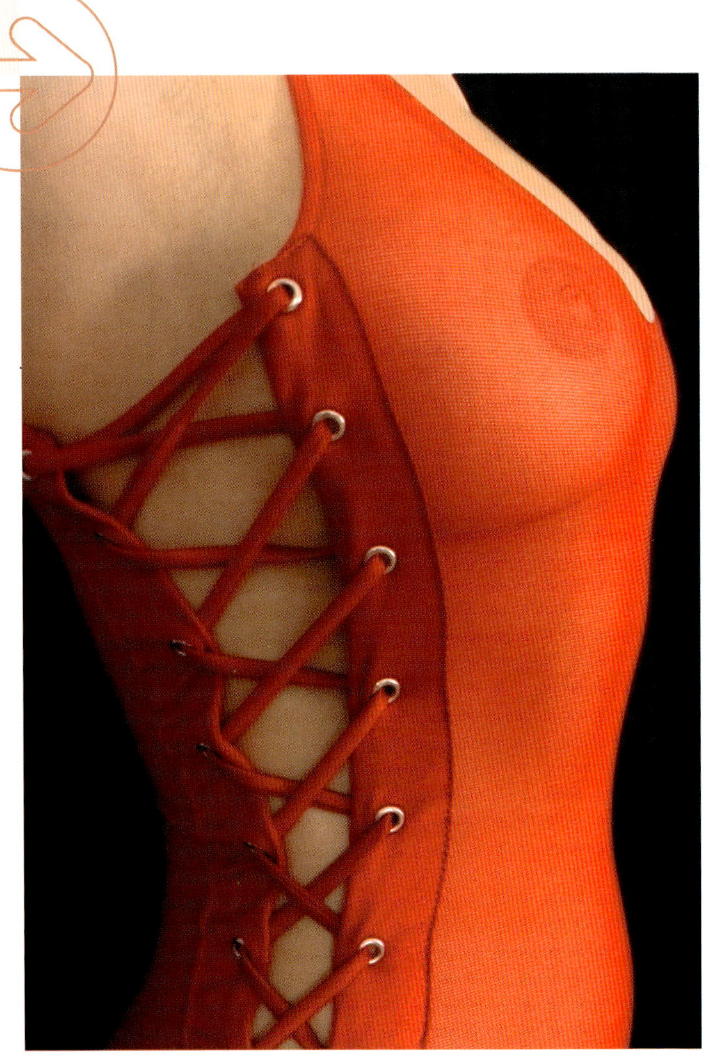

The vibrant red of the dress contrasts powerfully with the model's pale skin.

The saturated colors of the background and the model's shawl are complementary to each other.

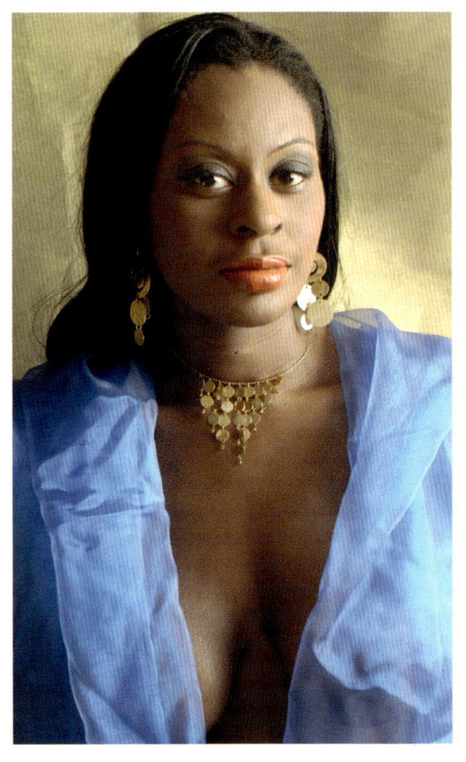

In photography of the nude, color is one element of composition that can really contribute to the impact of an image. Color is present in the model's skin tones, in garments and props, and in backgrounds.

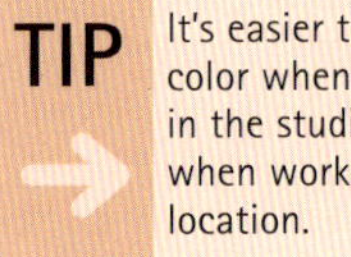

TIP It's easier to control color when shooting in the studio than when working on location.

TALKING ABOUT COLOR

Color can be described in terms of its hue, saturation, and brightness. **Hue** is the color itself—green, blue, yellow, etc. **Saturation** is the purity of the color: it represents the amount of gray mixed with the hue. The more saturated a color, the stronger and more vibrant it is. **Brightness** is the relative lightness or darkness of the color: the amount of white or black mixed with the hue.

You can use Elements' preferences to switch to the Apple color picker, which represents colors according to this model. The Apple color picker is also a "color wheel." Artists use the color wheel as a way of understanding and describing the relationships between colors.

Numerous "rules" have been devised to determine which colors work together, or harmonize. Emotional and even spiritual qualities have also been attributed to colors and combinations of colors.

One of the simplest rules of color is that complementary colors—those diametrically opposite each other on the color wheel—harmonize.

One effective use of color is to introduce a single element of color that contrasts strongly with the rest of the composition.

At the opposite extreme, you can create images where all the main colors are grouped close together, or are even monochrome.

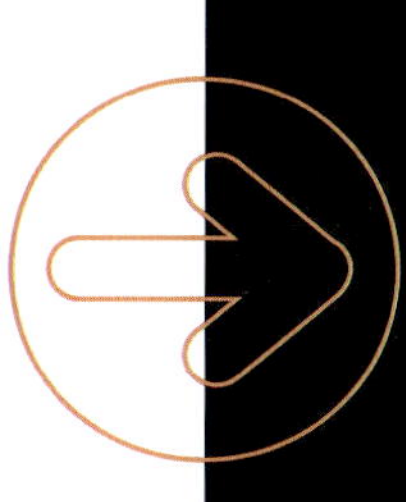

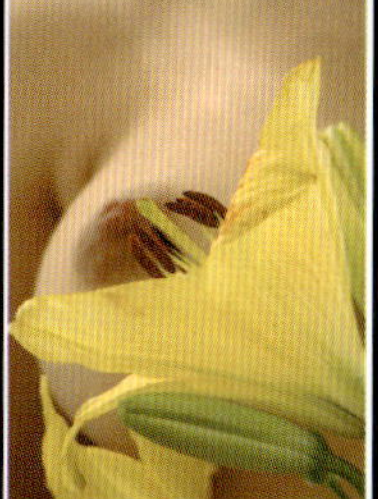

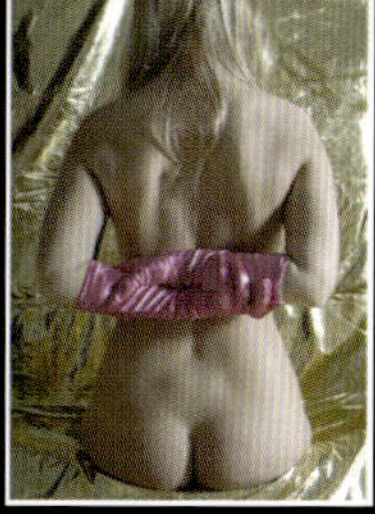

Color is a vital weapon in the digital photographer's arsenal. The use of bold, complementary colors can create striking visual imagery. Alternatively, more subtle hues can help bind an image together.

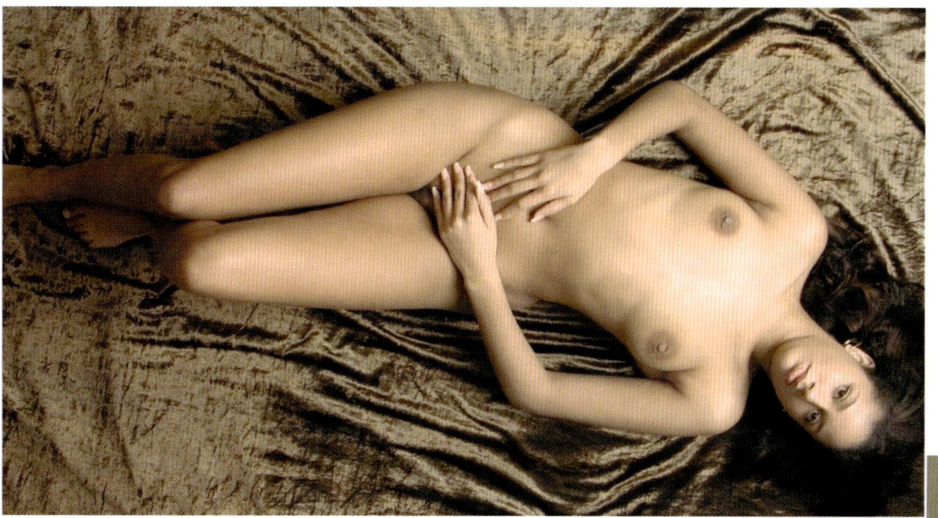

In this image, the hues of the background, the model's skin tone and hair are closely grouped together on the color wheel, the main differences being in saturation and brightness.

Here again the main colors of the image are closely grouped on the color wheel, which gives all the more impact to the bright red of the model's fingernails.

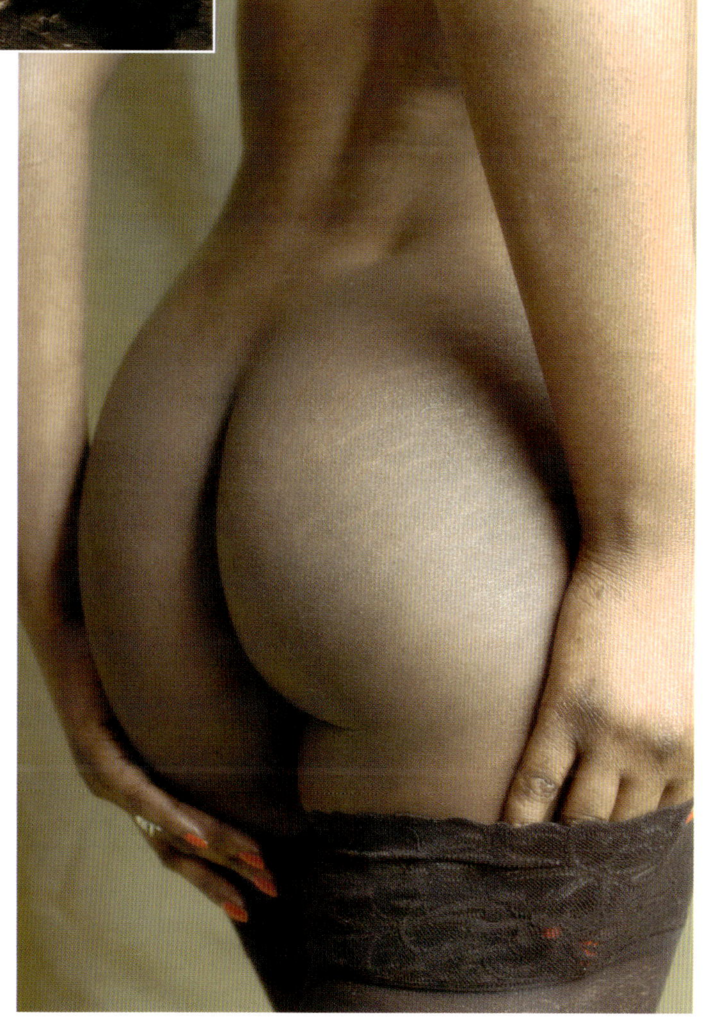

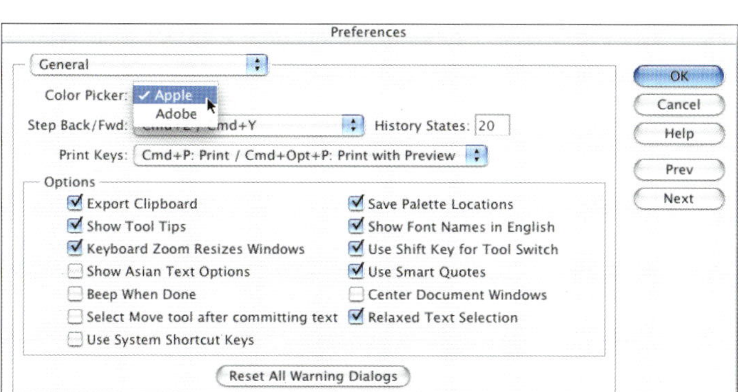

Selecting the Apple color wheel from the Photoshop Elements Preferences menu.

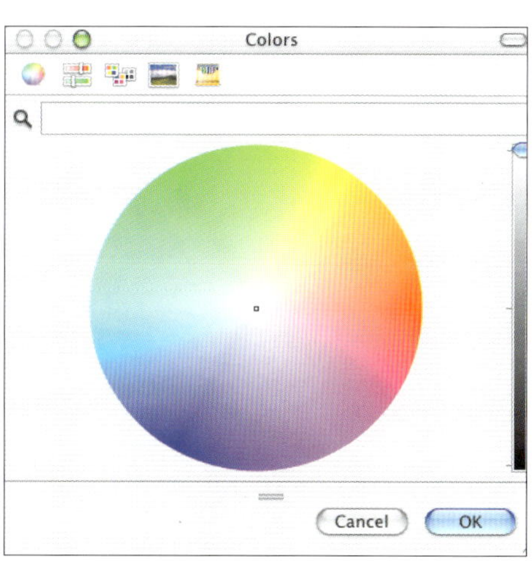

The Apple color wheel lets you adjust Hue and Saturation in the circular area, and Brightness with the fader on the right.

The covered nude

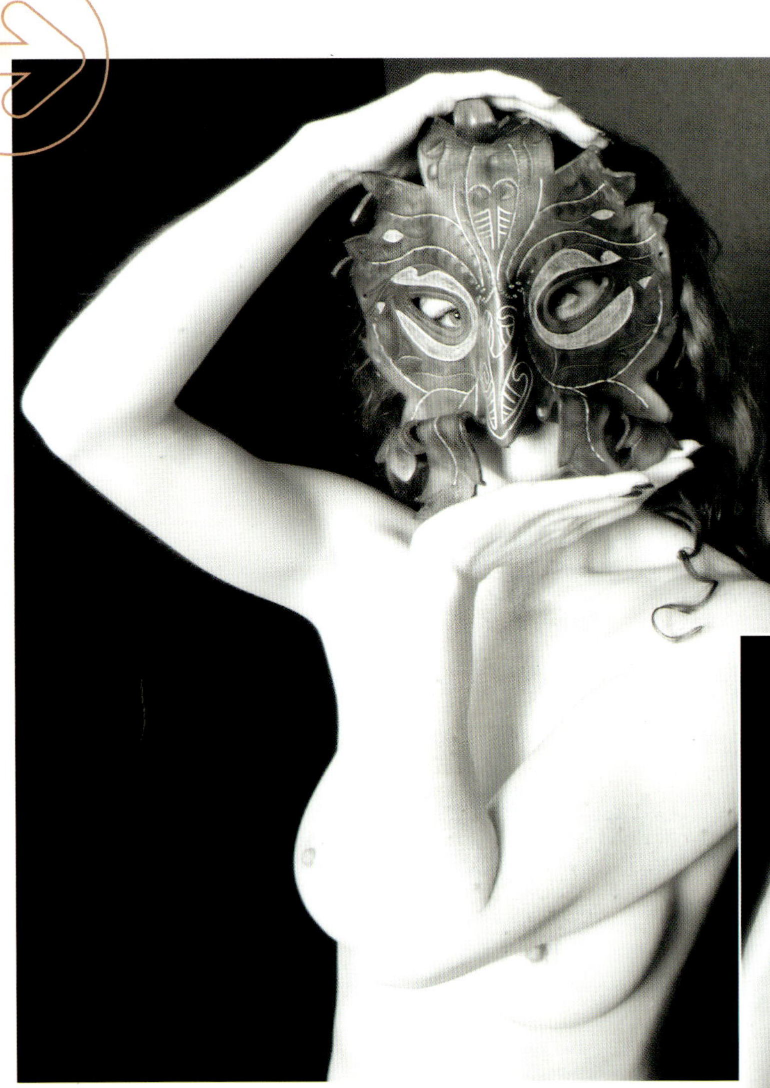

This Venetian carnival half-mask, like all masks, suggests the possibility of assuming a different character, an idea reflected here by the mirror and by the use of both color and monochrome within the image.

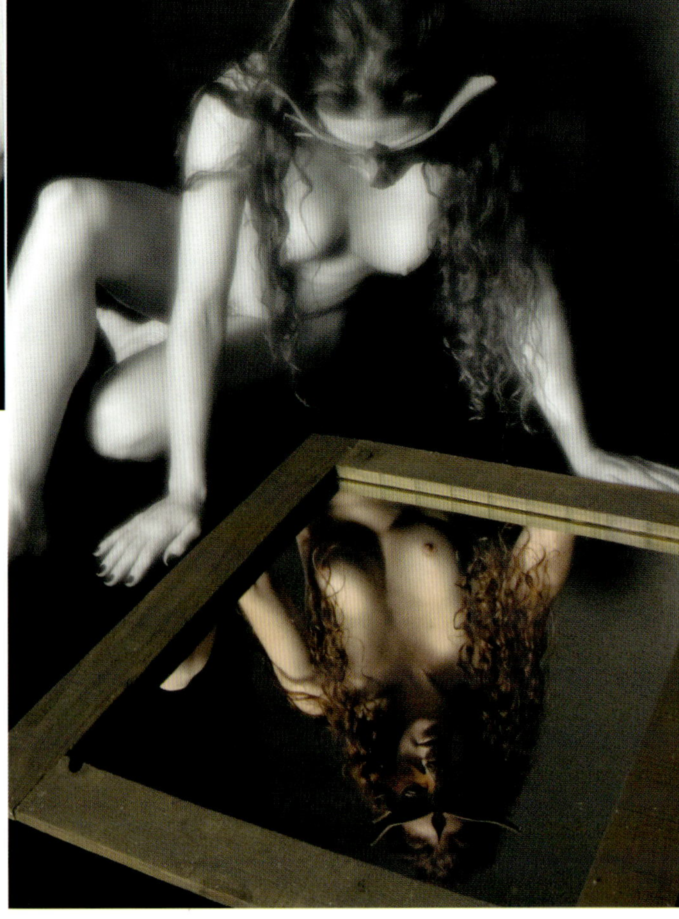

This very masculine mask (the "Green Man") makes a striking contrast with the female body, whichever way it is worn.

Not all nudes are completely naked. In partially covering the nude with anything from jewelry to a long skirt, you open up a wide range of themes, from glamor shots to fetish photography. I hope these images will form the starting point for your own explorations. Some of the garments in this sequence are the models' own, but many are mine, collected over time.

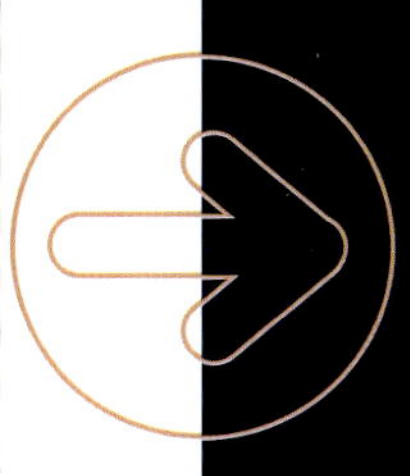

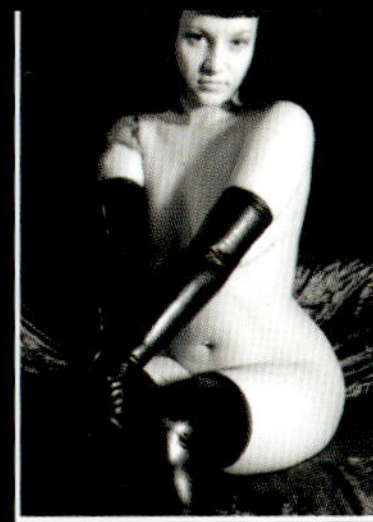

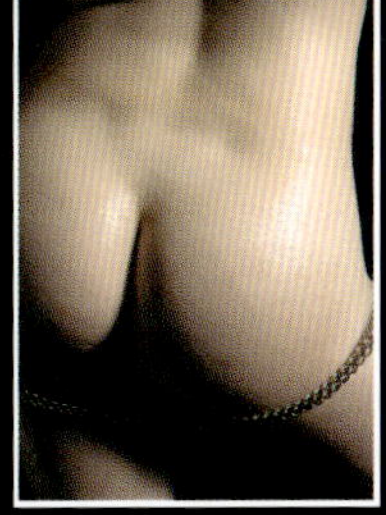

The addition of clothing can give a model an entirely different appearance. Leaving a model partially clothed can also be a means of adding tension or telling a story in a shot.

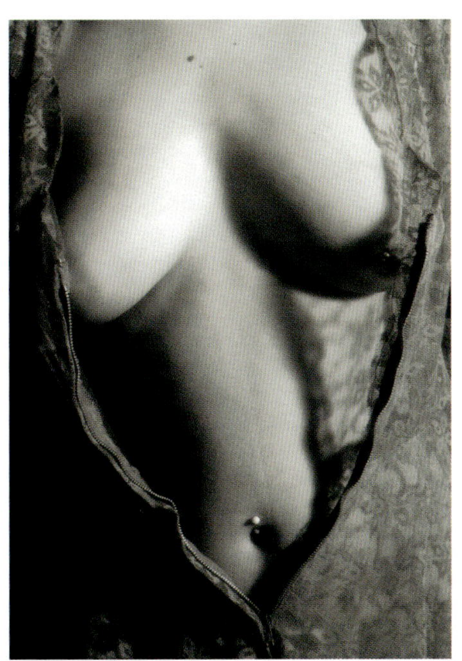

Strong side-lighting creates a shadow play through the dress.

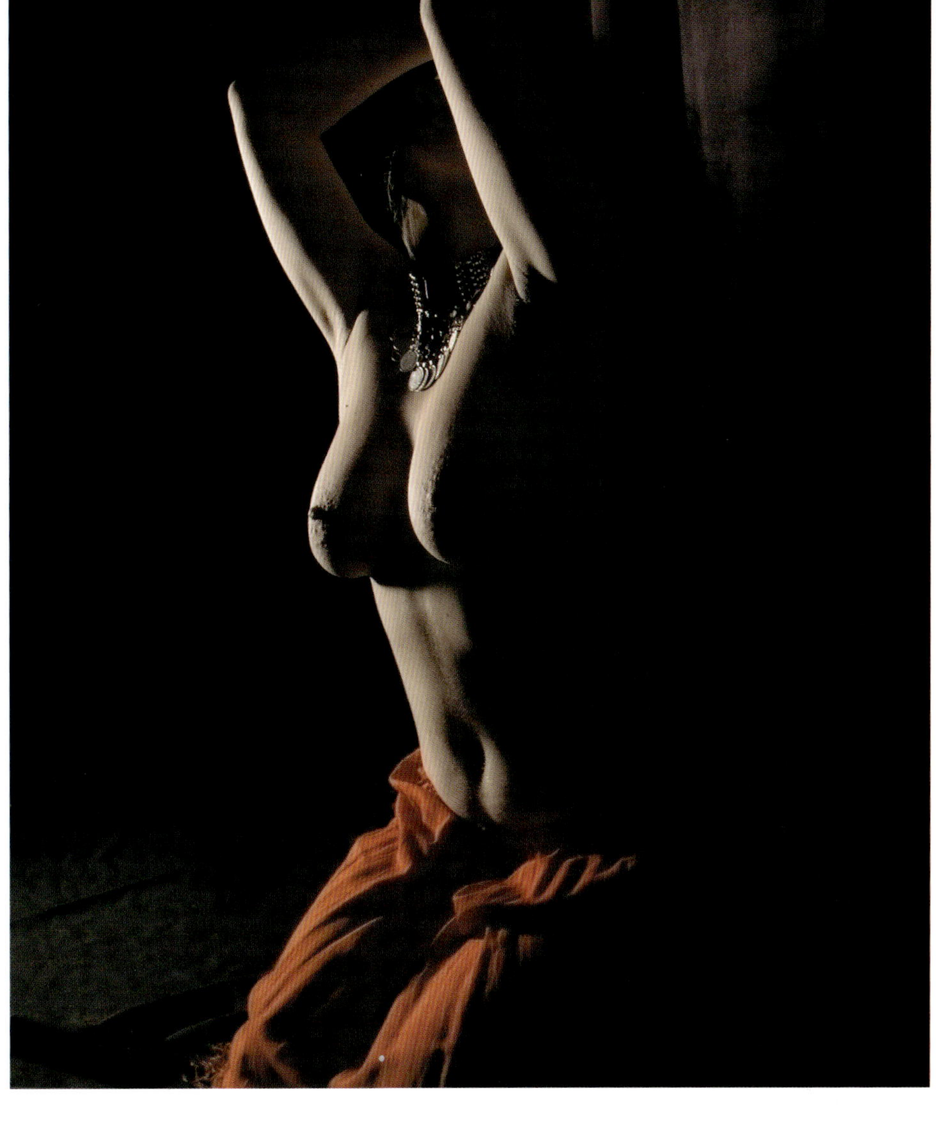

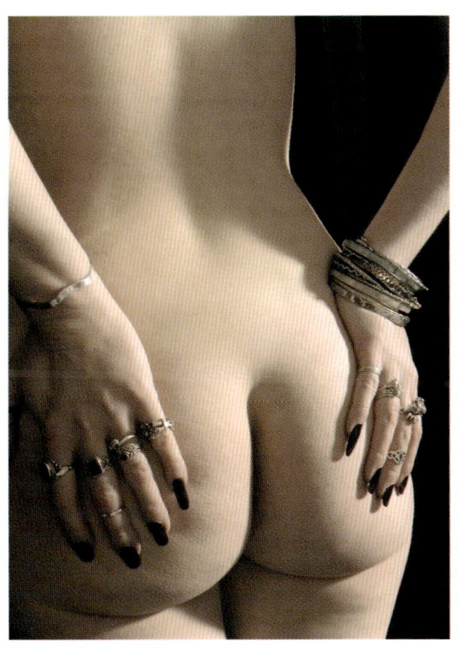

Not a "covering," perhaps, but the model's jewelry, together with her painted nails, add an erotic edge to a fairly conventional pose.

The bright red skirt with its folds and pleats contrasts well with the model's smooth skin. The necklace breaks up the shadows in the top third of the image.

The covered nude

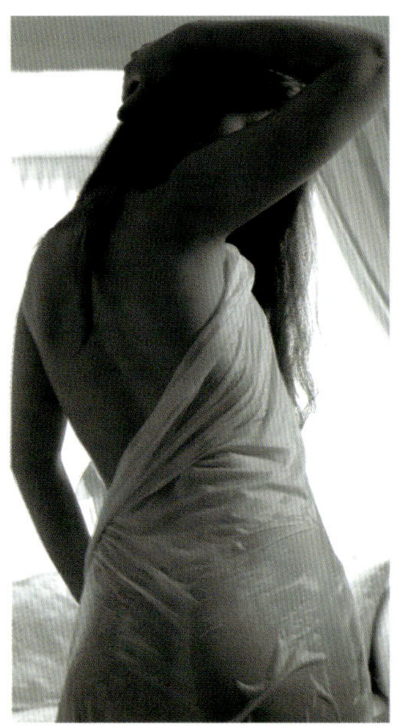

The idea of wrapping wet fabric round the body goes back to the sculptures of the ancient Greeks.

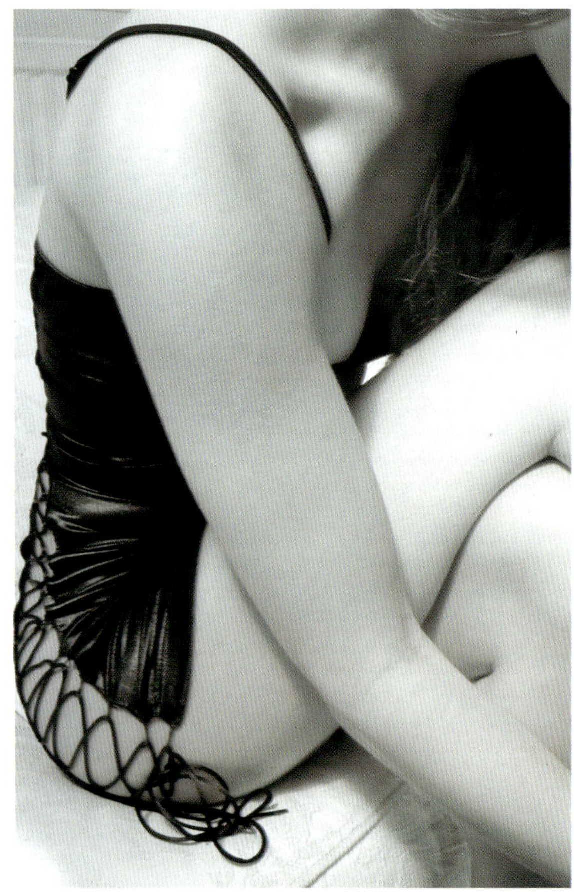

The black lace-up dress accentuates the flow of the model's limbs.

A beat-up antique lace dress, bought at a Cambridge market for a few pennies, comes into its own.

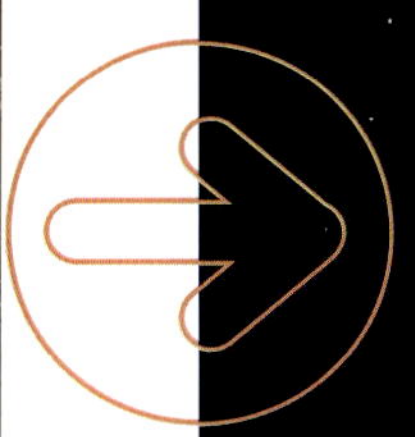

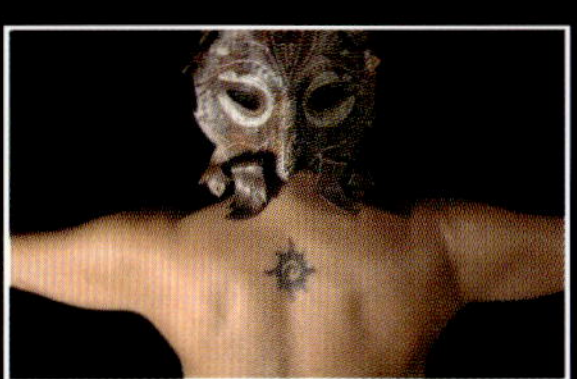

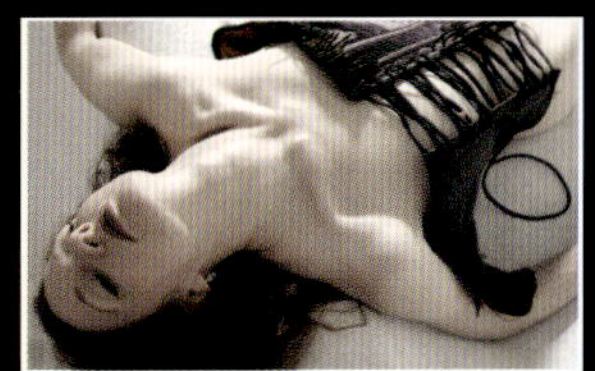

The model does not always have to be naked in a shot. Garments will sometimes adhere to the contours of the model, creating an interesting mélange of shapes and tones.

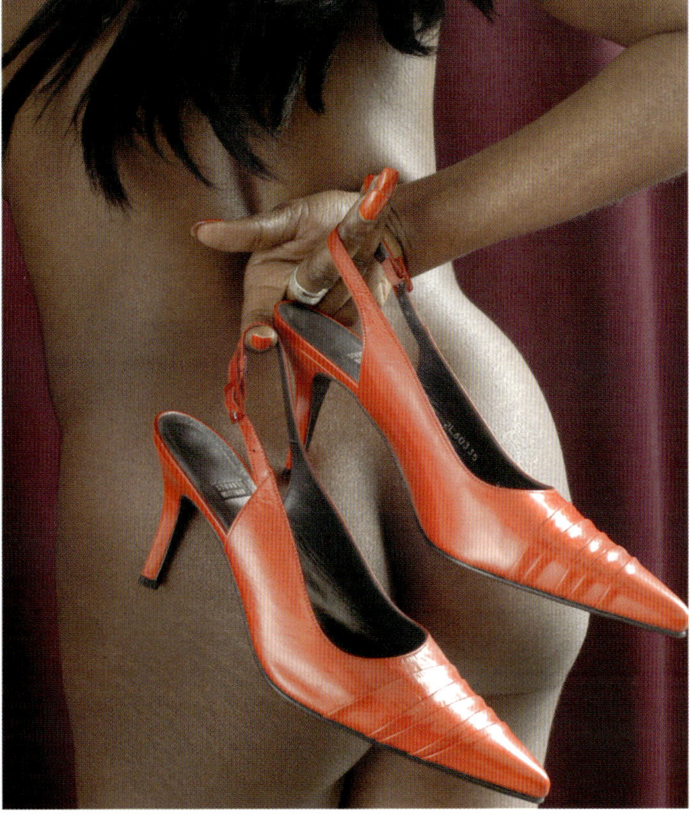

This pose is formed by having the model hold the silk scarf up with her arms outstretched. It's a theme that can be infinitely varied.

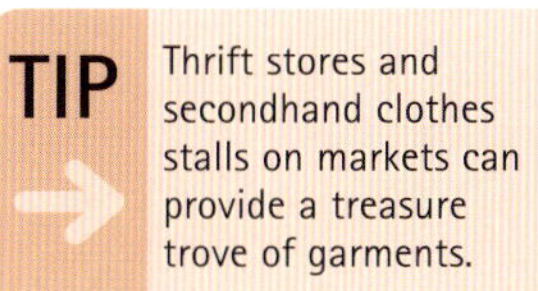

Thrift stores and secondhand clothes stalls on markets can provide a treasure trove of garments.

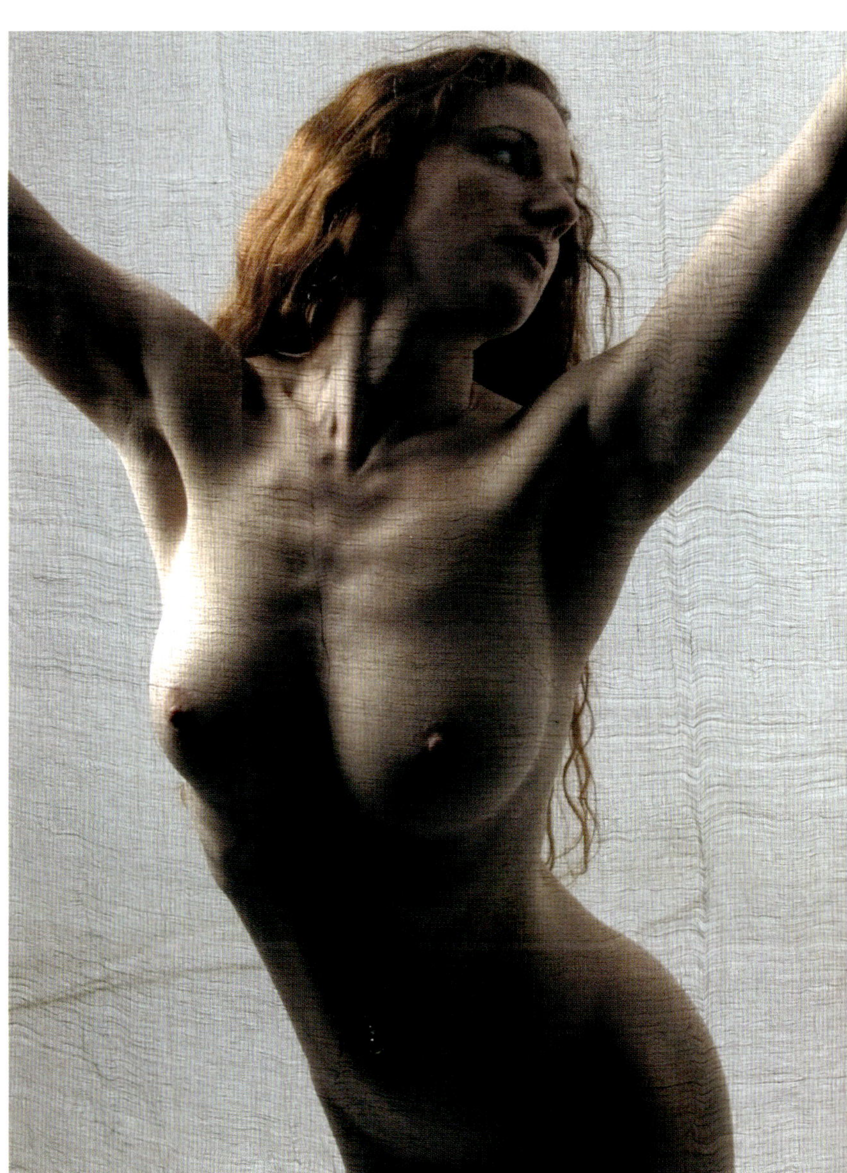

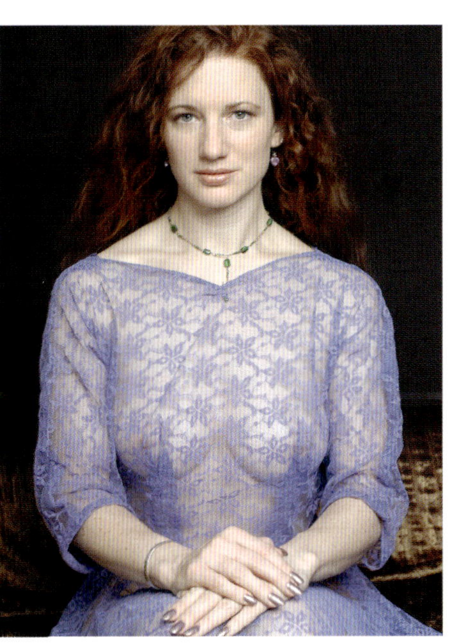

The model doesn't have to be wearing the shoes...

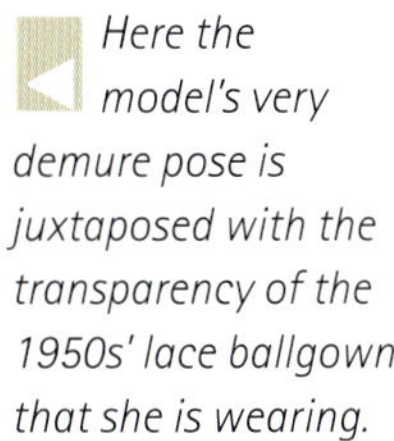

Here the model's very demure pose is juxtaposed with the transparency of the 1950s' lace ballgown that she is wearing.

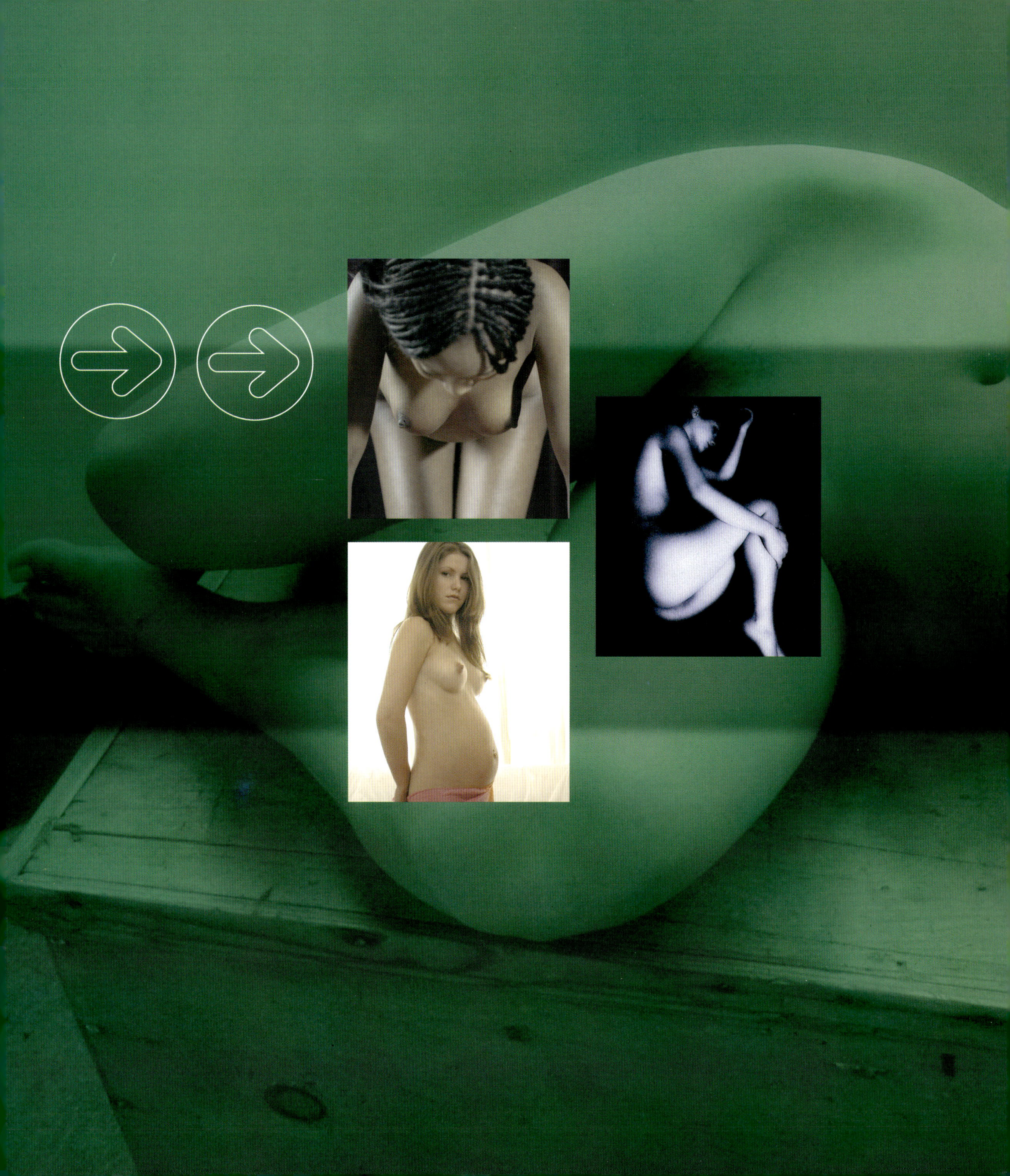

3 Digital darkroom techniques

This section explores how you can use image-editing software to enhance your digital photography. The examples are based on Adobe Photoshop Elements, but there are many similar applications with which you can produce the same results. We begin by looking at techniques for correcting images, then move on to more creative ways of manipulating images by using filters and layers. By combining these features, we can produce a rich and diverse range of visual styles.

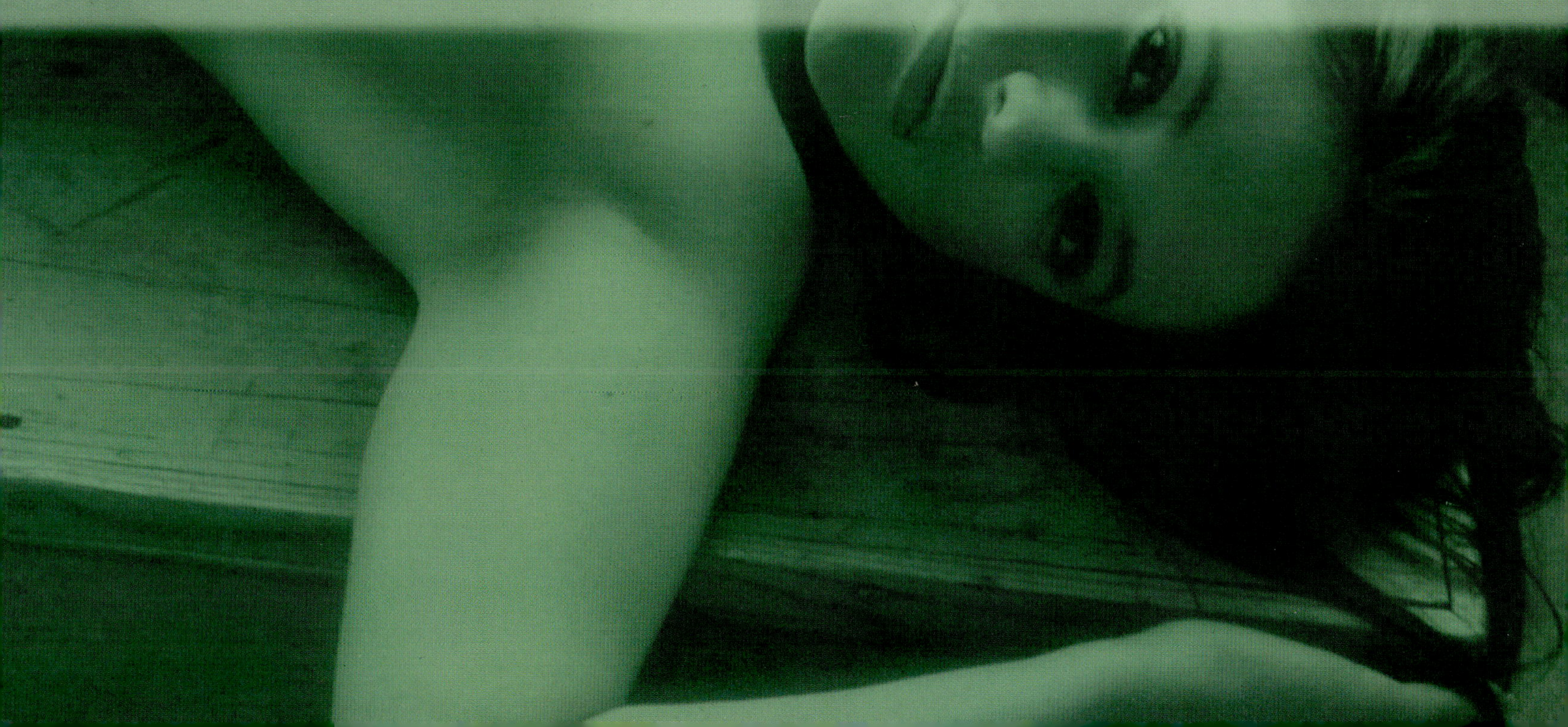

Image-editing software

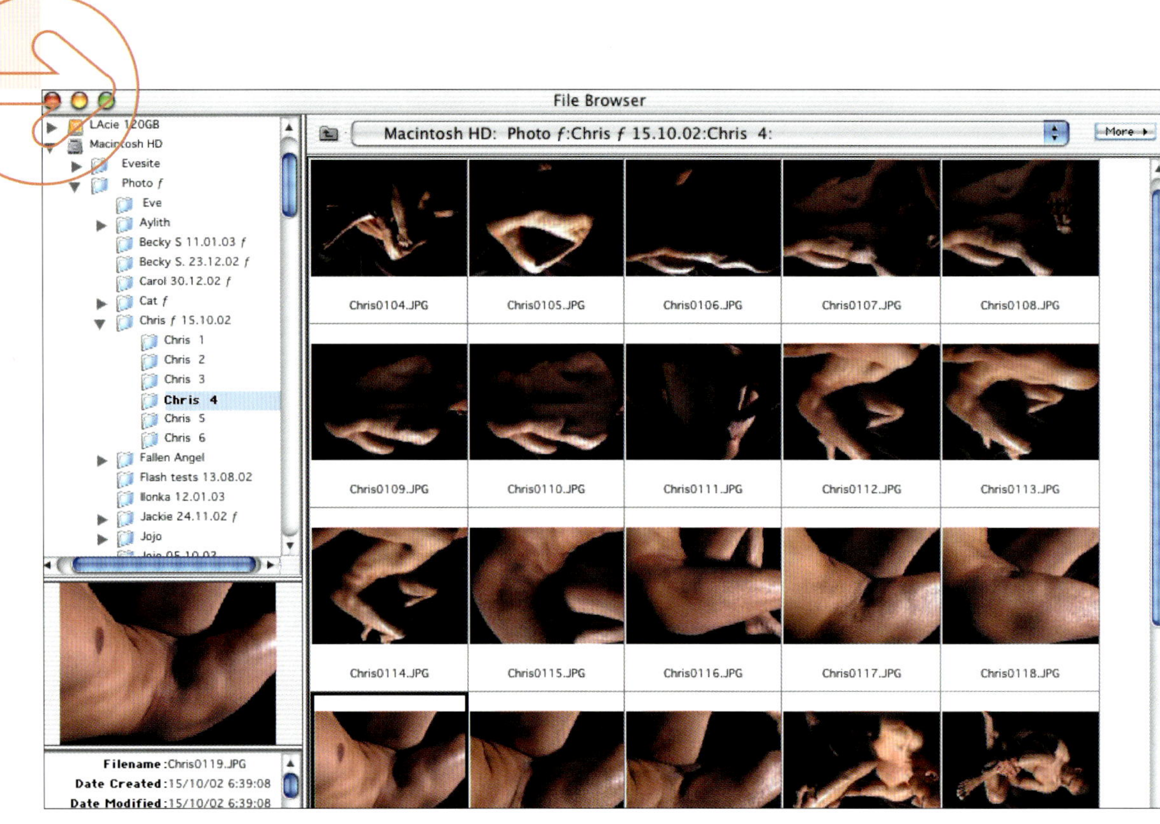

One useful feature of Photoshop Elements 2.0 is the file browser window. This lets you look through the pictures you have downloaded to decide which ones to edit.

Files are easier to recognize if named meaningfully (in this case, the model's name plus a sequence number), rather than by the file names assigned by the camera.

Once you've taken your digital pictures, the next step is to download them onto your computer in order to edit them before printing them out or uploading them to your website.

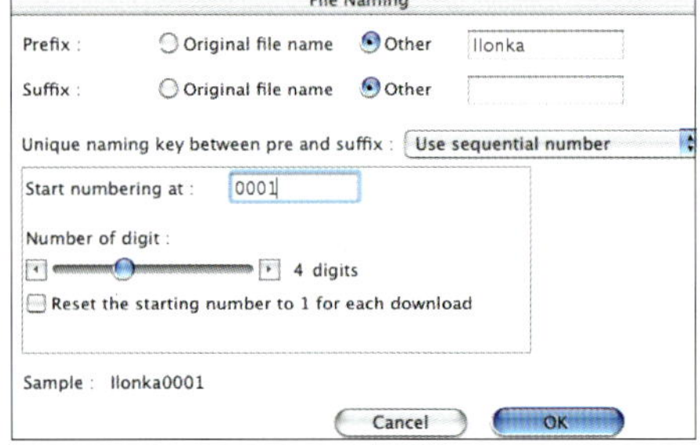

IMAGE EDITING

Image editing involves using software to make changes to the downloaded photographic image in order to enhance it. The software enables you to make the sort of changes that were traditionally carried out in the darkroom, together with a great many more. These changes might include removing blemishes on the model's skin; rotating or cropping the image; changing the background the model appears against; combining one image with one or more others; altering the coloring of the image; creatively distorting the image; or giving it the look of an old sepia print. Good image-editing software and imagination offers you endless scope and variety.

DOWNLOADING IMAGES

Download software will have been supplied with your camera; your computer may also have download software included in its operating system. It's worth checking what scope this offers for customizing the way the images are handled as they download. You may, for example, be able to specify what file names you want and alter the numbering sequence, rather than being stuck with the camera's default naming and numbering system. More usefully, you may be able to specify which application you want to use to open the files when you double-click on them.

IMAGE-EDITING SOFTWARE

Your camera may have been supplied with image-editing software, or the download software may include some editing capacity. Your computer may also have some image-editing software installed on it. There are many different packages available, but this book concentrates on Adobe Photoshop Elements 2.0. Elements is an affordable, scaled-down version of Adobe Photoshop 7.0, a very widely used but more expensive professional editing application. Other editing packages have similar features.

Although it's a reduced version of Photoshop, Elements is still a complex

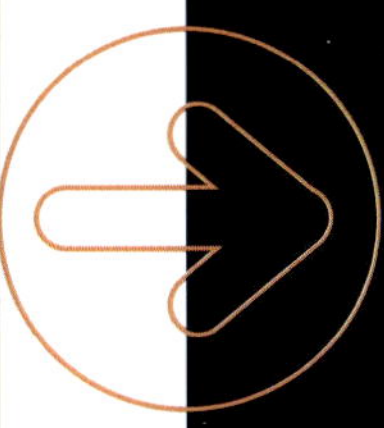

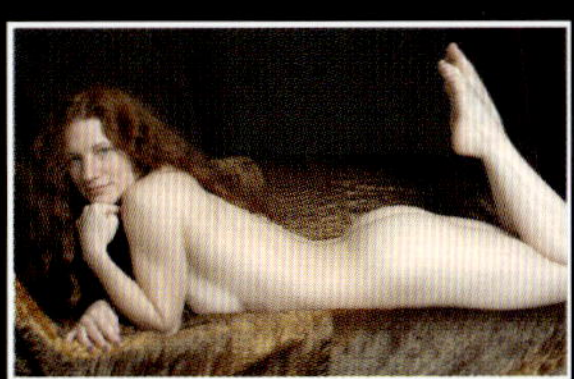

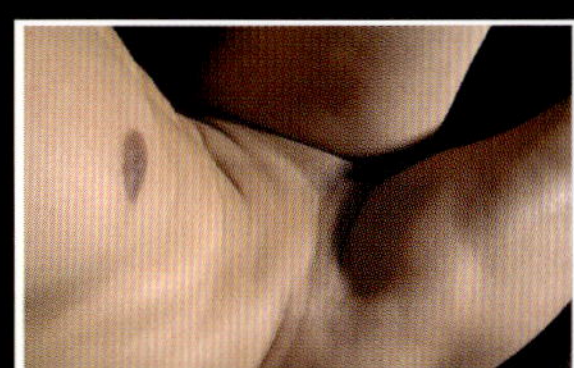

Image-editing software gives you amazing control over your images. Reasonably priced packages such as Adobe Photoshop Elements enable you to correct, embellish, distort, or recompose a shot.

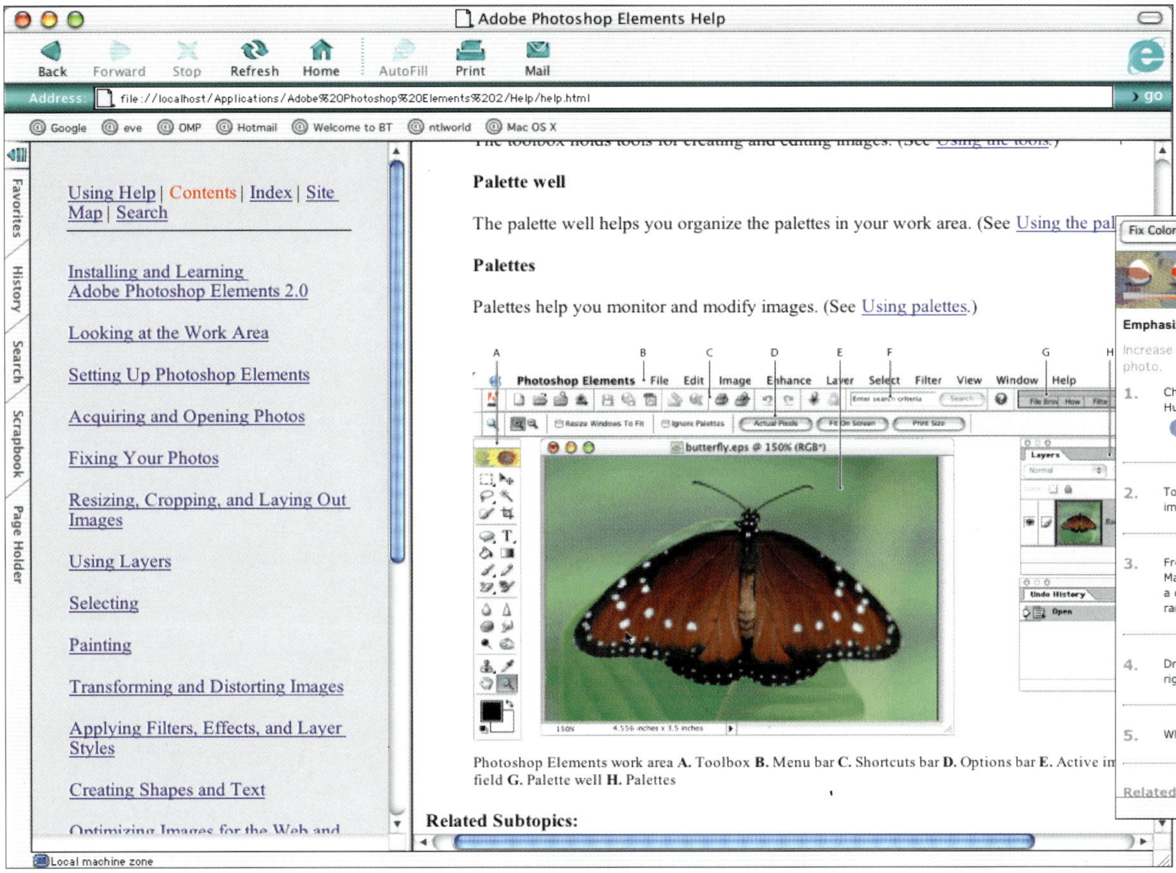

Adobe Photoshop Elements Help

Back Forward Stop Refresh Home AutoFill Print Mail

Address: file://localhost/Applications/Adobe%20Photoshop%20Elements%202/Help/help.html

Google eve OMP Hotmail Welcome to BT ntlworld Mac OS X

Using Help | Contents | Index | Site Map | Search

Installing and Learning Adobe Photoshop Elements 2.0

Looking at the Work Area

Setting Up Photoshop Elements

Acquiring and Opening Photos

Fixing Your Photos

Resizing, Cropping, and Laying Out Images

Using Layers

Selecting

Painting

Transforming and Distorting Images

Applying Filters, Effects, and Layer Styles

Creating Shapes and Text

Palette well

The palette well helps you organize the palettes in your work area. (See Using the pal

Palettes

Palettes help you monitor and modify images. (See Using palettes.)

Photoshop Elements work area **A.** Toolbox **B.** Menu bar **C.** Shortcuts bar **D.** Options bar **E.** Active in field **G.** Palette well **H.** Palettes

Related Subtopics:

Local machine zone

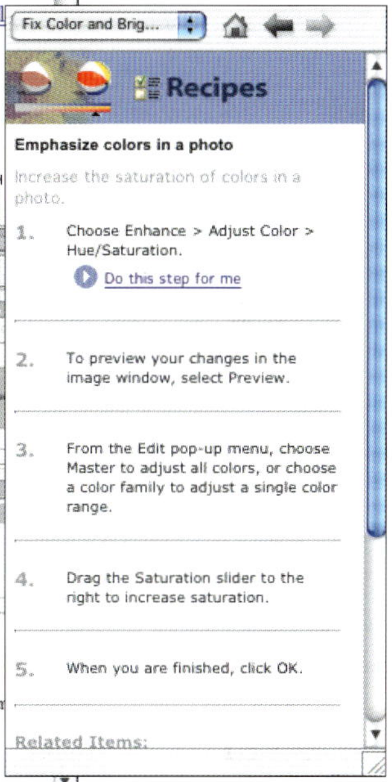

Recipes

Emphasize colors in a photo

Increase the saturation of colors in a photo.

1. Choose Enhance > Adjust Color > Hue/Saturation.
   Do this step for me
2. To preview your changes in the image window, select Preview.
3. From the Edit pop-up menu, choose Master to adjust all colors, or choose a color family to adjust a single color range.
4. Drag the Saturation slider to the right to increase saturation.
5. When you are finished, click OK.

Related Items:

One of the "recipes" included in Adobe Photoshop Elements.

Interface of the download software supplied by Nikon with its digital cameras.

A typical screen from Help. Note the contents list, which is always shown to the left of the currently displayed "page."

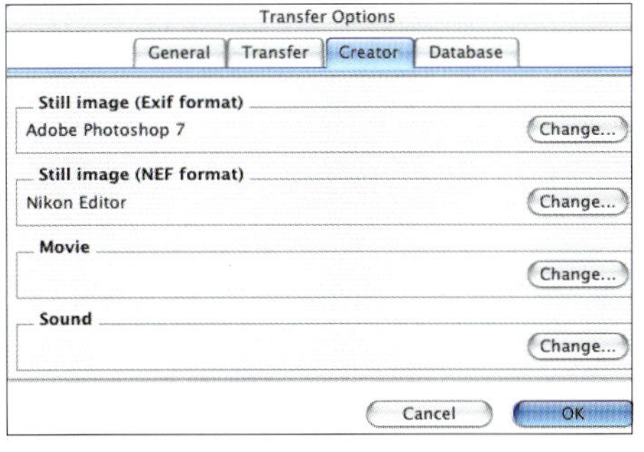

program. Rather than attempt to explain how it works in a couple of pages, we assume that you will use the User Guide and the detailed online Help and Tutorial support to familiarize yourself with the way the program works. Elements also includes some very useful "recipes"—step-by-step directions for quick and easy ways to fix your photos.

We will also occasionally use examples from Photoshop 7.0 where its additional power and features are particularly useful.

THIRD-PARTY PLUG-INS

It's also possible to buy plug-ins from other manufacturers for Photoshop 7.0 and Elements. These extend the range of filters and effects that are available with the standard programs.

FACT FILE

Direct printing

Some printers let you plug the memory card from your camera into them so that you can print your images directly without downloading them. However, this method offers only limited control over the way your pictures are printed.

Working methods

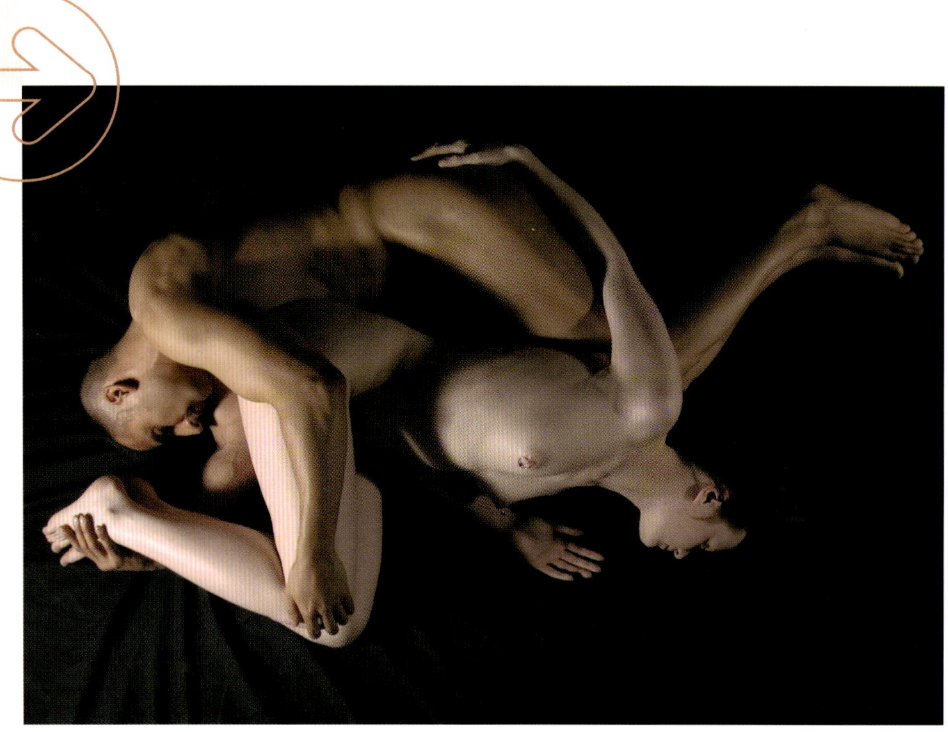

As I start to work on this image, I'll save a copy of it so that the orginal is always there for me to go back to.

Editing pictures demands closer attention to the screen and more use of the mouse than, say, browsing the Net. Ensure your chair and desk are the right height for each other and for you, and that the room has appropriate lighting for intensive computer work.

ORGANIZING YOUR WORK

One of the greatest attractions of using image-editing software is the scope that you have to experiment. You will often find yourself with several different versions of one original image, so it's important to develop a way of organizing your files and working with them methodically.

If there is one golden rule in picture editing, it has to be "Never edit the original file!" It's much safer to work on a copy. That way, if you do a lot of work on an image, but then decide that you want to try something different with it, you can go back to the original, make another copy, and try out something else. Think of the original file as the equivalent of a negative—it should be kept safe and handled with care. Therefore, as soon as you've opened a file, select *Save As* from the *File* menu, and save the file as a Photoshop format file with a different file name.

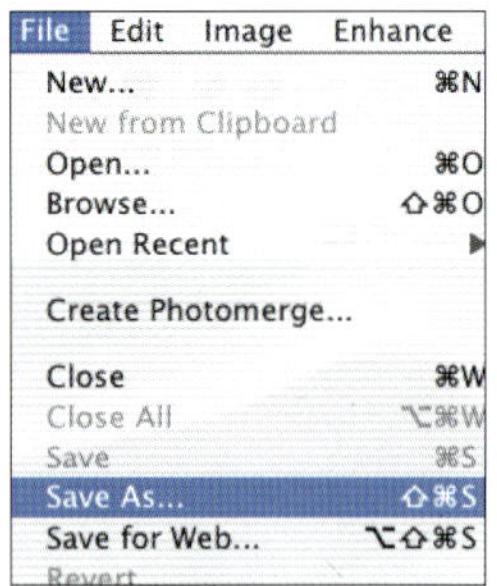

Use the Save As option to make a copy of your original file.

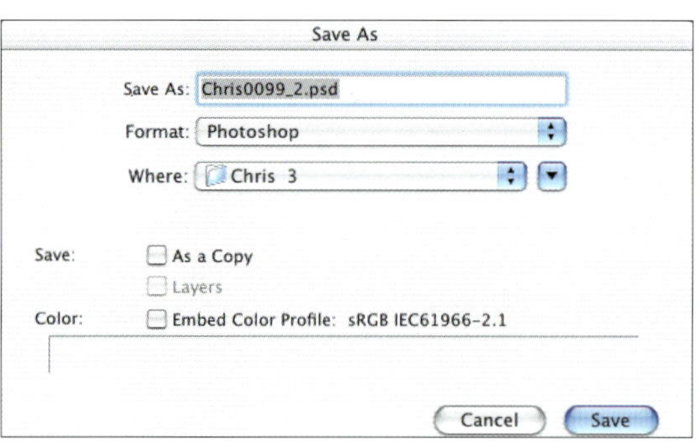

Here I've changed the file name from Chris0099 to Chris0099_2 and the file's format to Photoshop; the file extension changes from .JPG to .PSD.

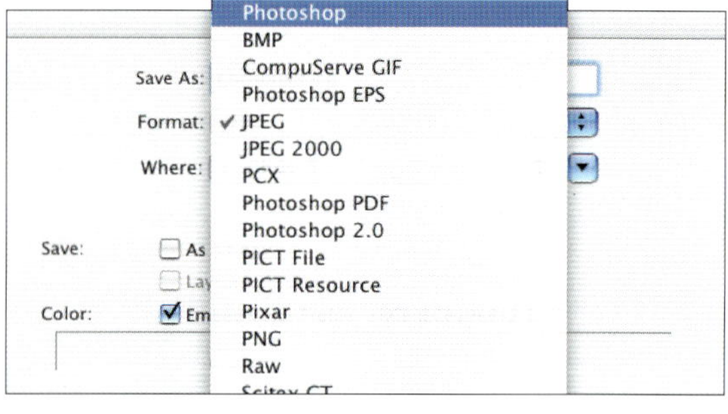

The Save As *option enables you to specify what format you want to save the copy of your file into.*

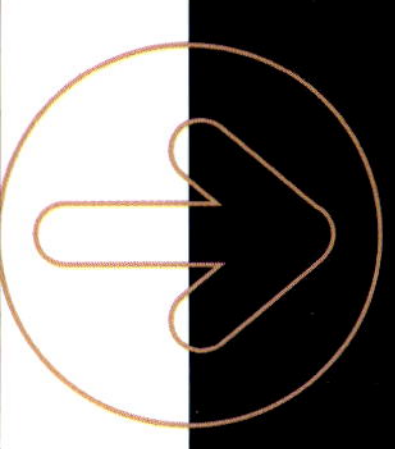

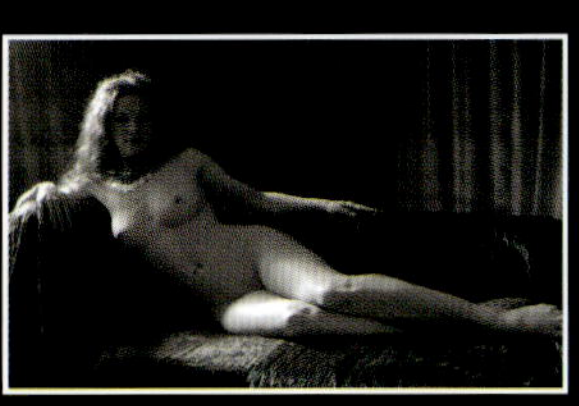

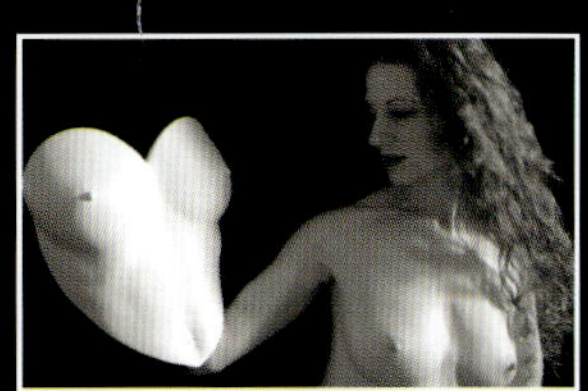

Organize the digital photographs stored on your computer. Give every photograph an individual name and store projects in separate folders. Failure to do this could result in loss of productivity and possible loss of data.

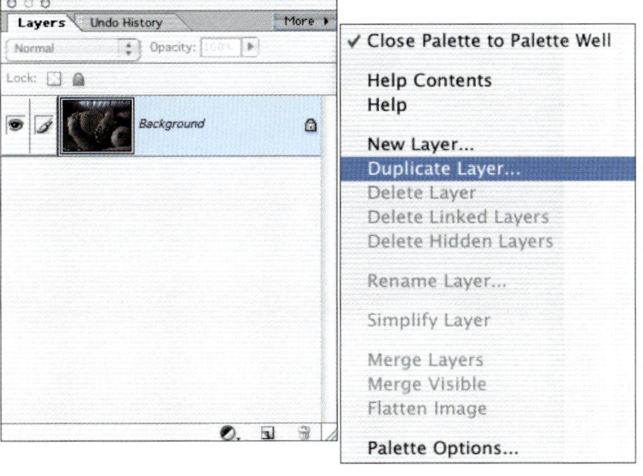

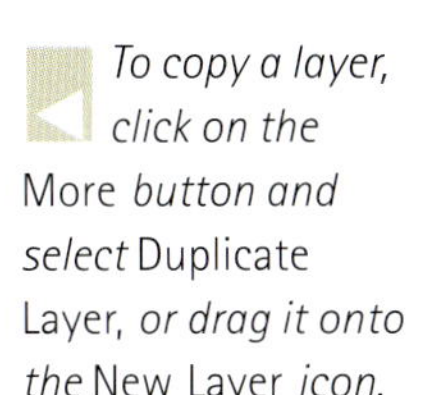

To copy a layer, click on the More *button and select* Duplicate Layer, *or drag it onto the* New Layer *icon.*

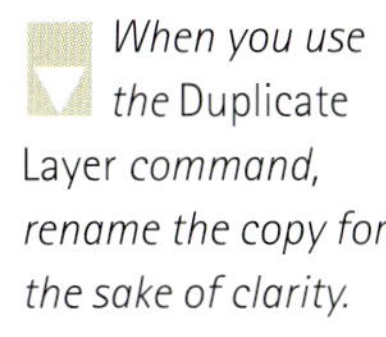

When you use the Duplicate Layer *command, rename the copy for the sake of clarity.*

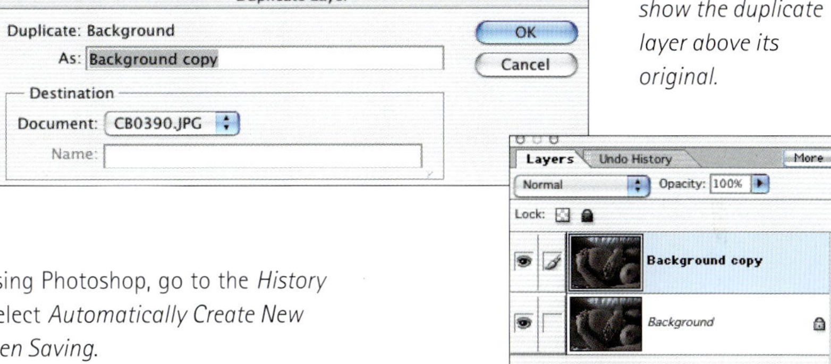

The Layers *window will show the duplicate layer above its original.*

THE PHOTOSHOP FORMAT

It's advisable to change to Photoshop format because that is the best format for image editing in Photoshop or Elements. It means that you can work on the file in uncompressed form, using the full range of layers and effects that Photoshop and Elements provide. You should never edit your images in JPEG format, as some processes, particularly repeated cropping and resizing, can produce noticeable degradation of the image. However, once you have finished editing the file, you will probably want to save it back into JPEG format, to facilitate printing or uploading the image to your website.

CHANGING THE FILE NAME

Changing the file name when you make a copy of the file helps you to distinguish your edited files from the originals. If you create more than one edited version of a file, you can name them sequentially. When you have finished editing the picture and want to save it back into JPEG format, you don't have to worry about losing the original by accidentally saving the edited version over it.

A similar principle applies when you start working on a file. It's a good idea to duplicate the layer you want to work on; if your ideas for manipulating the image don't work out, you can throw that layer away, duplicate the original layer again, and have another go.

If you're using Photoshop, go to the *History* palette and select *Automatically Create New Snapshot When Saving.*

If you get into the habit of saving your work just before you make any major changes to it, it will be easy for you to move back through the different states of the file by clicking from snapshot to snapshot in the *History* window.

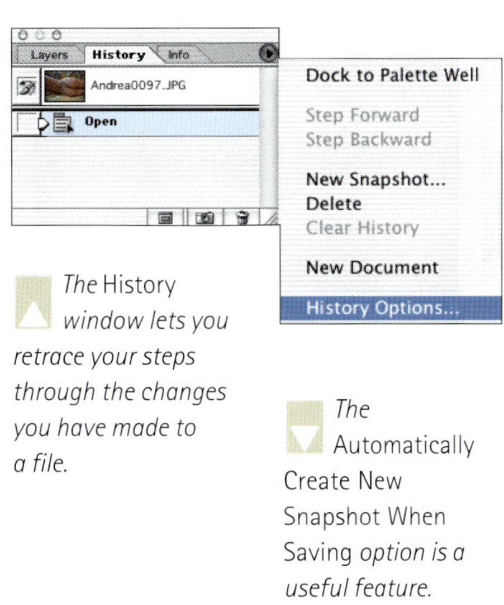

The History *window lets you retrace your steps through the changes you have made to a file.*

The Automatically Create New Snapshot When Saving *option is a useful feature.*

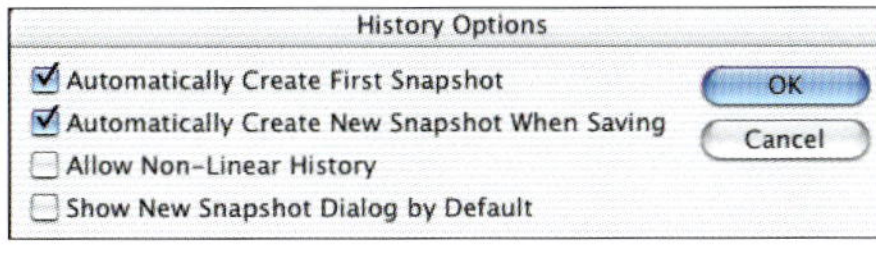

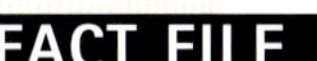

FACT FILE

Backing up your work

Even if photography is just a hobby, the thought of losing several hundred—or thousand—picture files as a result of a mechanical or other failure of your computer is pretty depressing. For additional security, you can back your work up onto recordable or rewritable CDs or DVDs. Alternatively, you can use external FireWire or USB drives. These are now relatively inexpensive and are usually supplied with proprietary backup software that keeps track of your files and regularly backs up any files which are new or which have altered since your last back-up.

Scanning

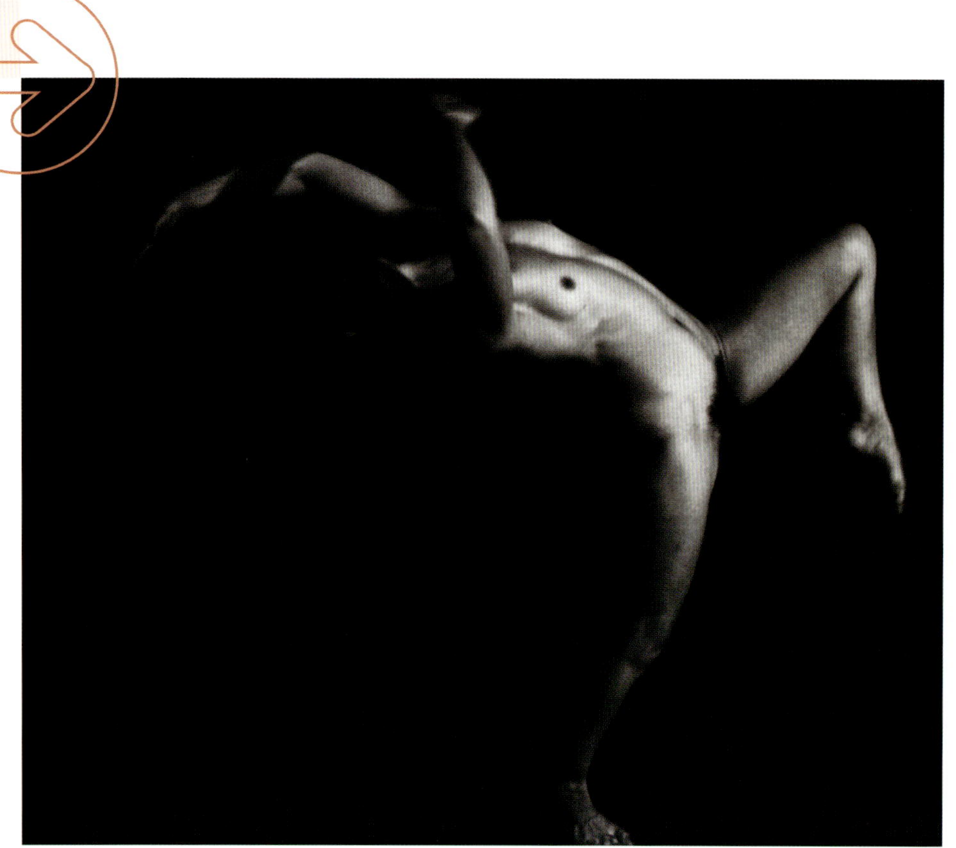

PREPARING ORIGINALS

Spend some time preparing your old material before scanning it. Use a blower brush to blow dust off negatives and transparencies, and wipe prints gently with a soft cloth. If you are using a flatbed scanner, make sure also that the platen (the glass) of the scanner is immaculately clean. These steps will reduce the imperfections that appear in your scans and thus save you time removing them later.

The main interface for one popular make of scanner. Note that the Image Type *is set to* Black & White Photo. *Scanning black-and-white pictures with the scanner set to color can produce artifacts in the scan.*

Flatbed and slide scanners let you transfer your older, film-based work into the digital domain, from negatives, color transparencies, or prints. Modern scanners are cheap (some come free when you buy a new computer); are supplied with good software; and are capable of producing very high-resolution images.

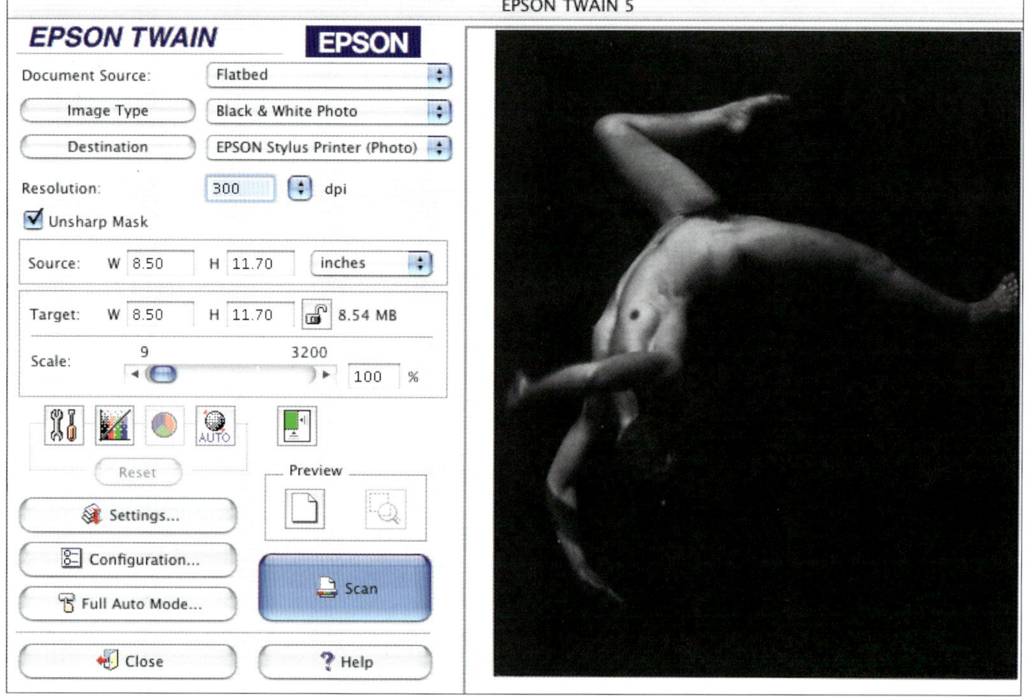

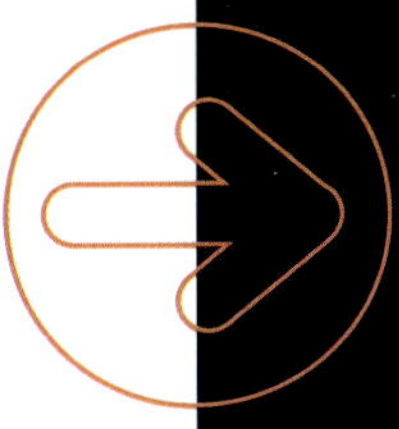

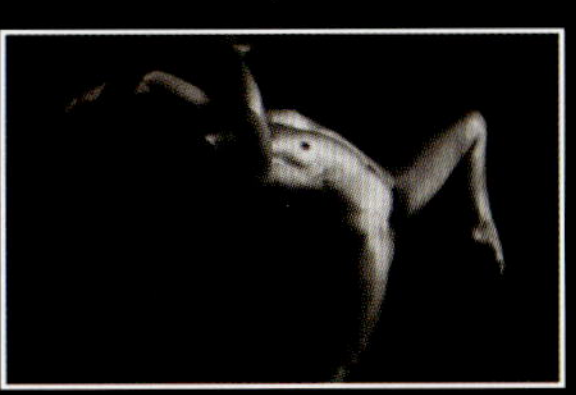

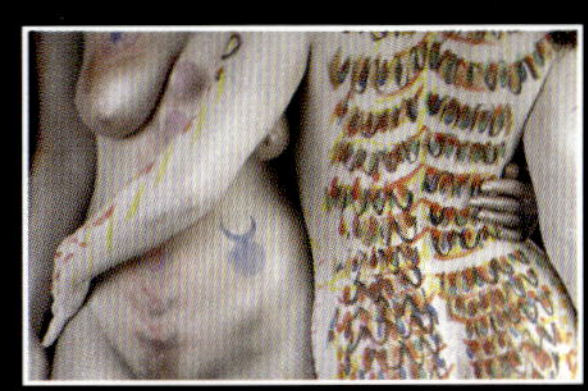

Scanners enable you to convert your old photographs and negatives into a digital format, ready to be edited. Alternatively, you may wish to scan in real objects and use them in photomontages.

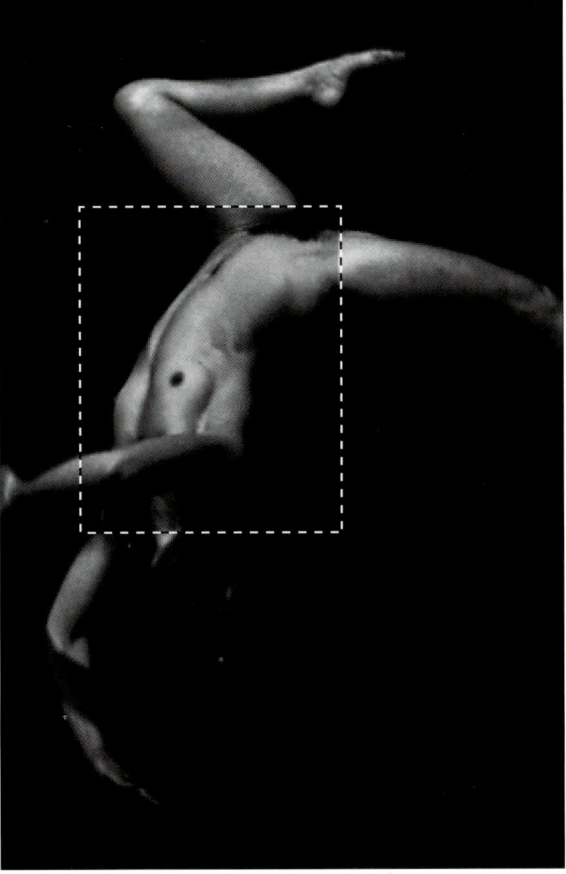

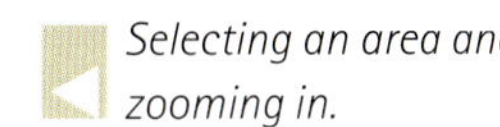

Selecting an area and zooming in.

Preview of the image using the scanner's Auto *settings after adjusting the black point and the white point.*

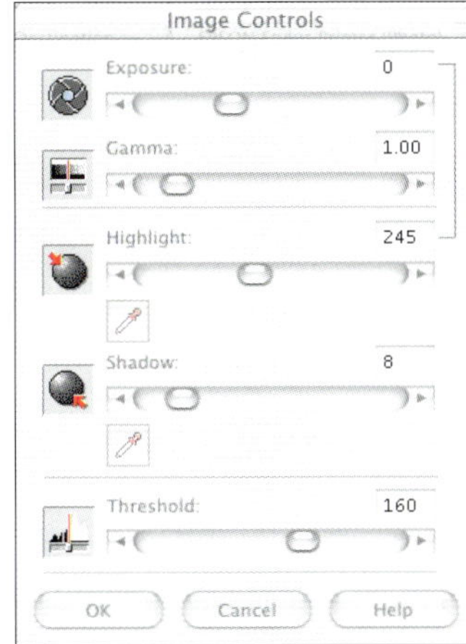

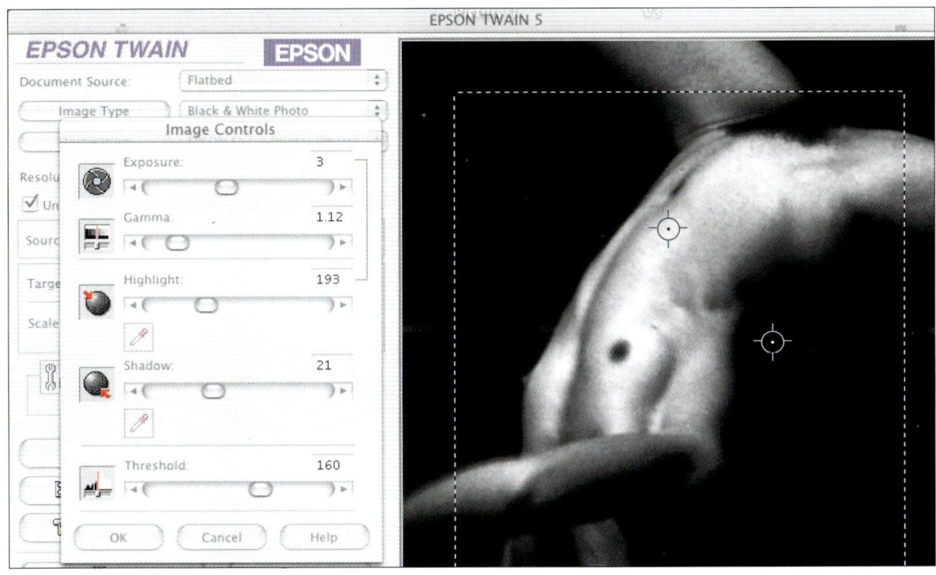

RESOLUTION

If you set the scanner's resolution to 300dpi, you will produce scans suitable for printing on your color printer. Images intended for on-screen display (for example, on the internet) can be scanned at a lower resolution (72dpi), but won't produce good results if you then decide to print them out. If you are scanning a print and want to print the scanned image larger than the original, use the scanner controls (in the example shown here, either *Target* or *Scale*) to specify what output size you require.

ADJUSTING THE SCAN

The scanner's *Auto* setting produces satisfactory results in most cases, but the interface also includes controls to adjust the scan. (You can also do further work on the image in Photoshop Elements if necessary.) The example here shows how to select an area, zoom in on it, and make adjustments to the black and the white points. Within the scanner's *Image* controls, you could use the *Eyedropper* to click on the lightest and darkest areas of the image, to ensure that the full range of tones is used. Alternatively, you could use the *Tone Correction* controls. These provide a series of tonal curves from which you can select the one that works best; otherwise you can create and save your own.

REMOVING BLEMISHES

Even the best-preserved print, negative, or transparency will have some blemishes. Once you've completed the scan, save the file, then go into Photoshop Elements, adjust the *Levels*, and use the *Clone* tool to clean the picture. Adjust the *Levels* before cleaning because changes in *Levels* may make some blemishes disappear—and others appear! *Filter > Noise > Dust and Scratches* can be helpful, but it may also remove details.

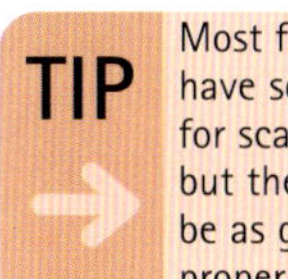

TIP Most flatbed scanners have some provision for scanning slides, but the results won't be as good as with a proper slide scanner.

Reducing noise and JPEG artifacts

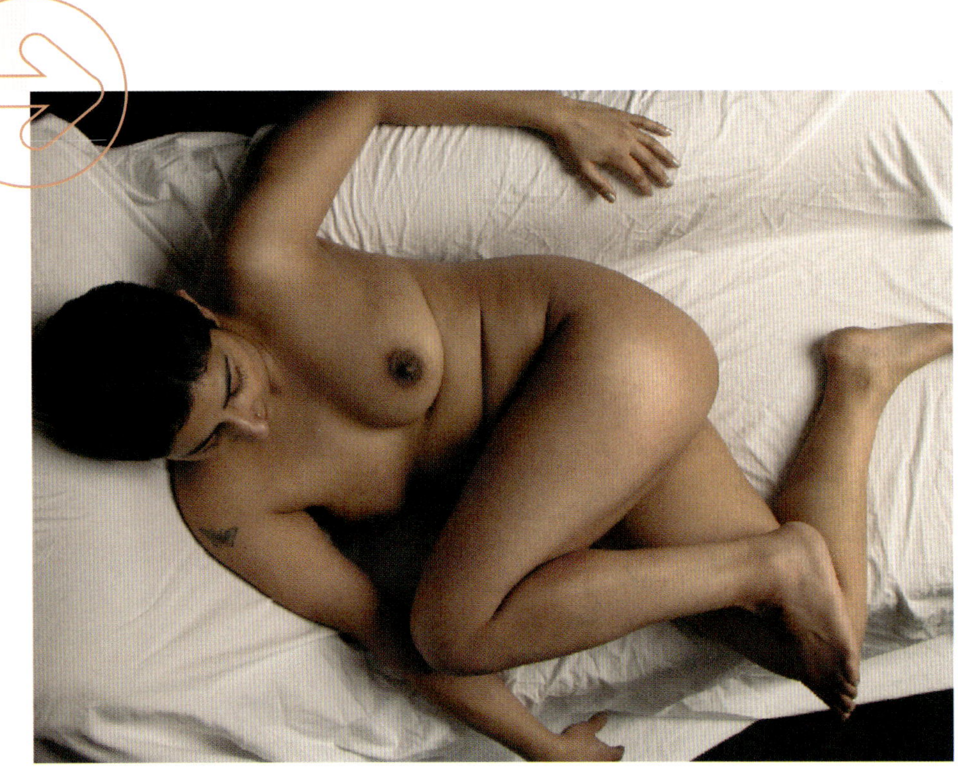

THE PROBLEM

Digital noise and artifacts are a rather unwelcome example of the way that digital cameras alter and sometimes distort what they see in order to record it.

How much of a problem noise and artifacts are depends on how you are going to use a picture. With the example left, the original measures 2560 pixels wide by 1920 deep. If you were going to put it on a website at a fairly small size (say, 700 pixels wide), then the artifacts probably wouldn't be visible. On the other hand, if you wanted to print it at 6 inches or more wide on an inkjet printer, the digital artifacts combined with the relatively low resolution of the printer would be very visible, particularly on the model's skin.

There is a simple series of steps that you can take to reduce these artifacts.

If you look closely at the areas of this image which aren't brightly lit, you will notice a red and blue mottling visible across the tone of Ja's skin. This effect is known as a digital artifact. This happens because the imaging chips and lens systems on midrange digital cameras aren't completely "clean." They generate a certain amount of random visible "noise." This is then exaggerated by the effects of JPEG compression, which connects up the individual dots of noise to produce the streaks, which are even more visible.

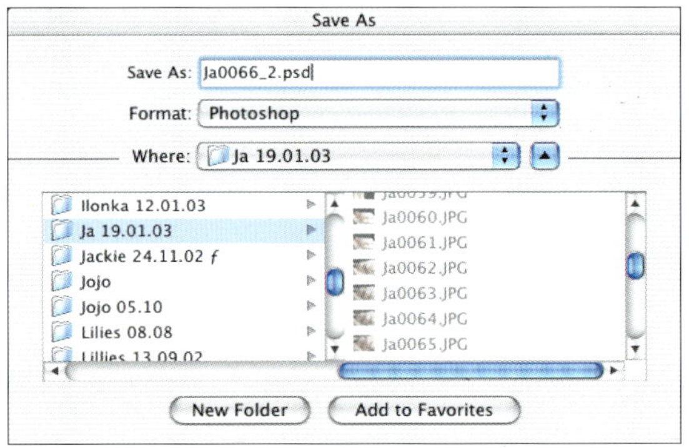

1 Save the file with a new file name in Photoshop format, as recommended on pages 76–77.

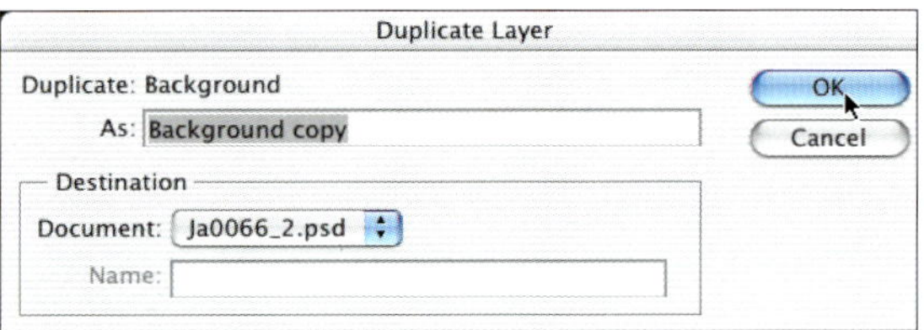

2 Duplicate the background layer.

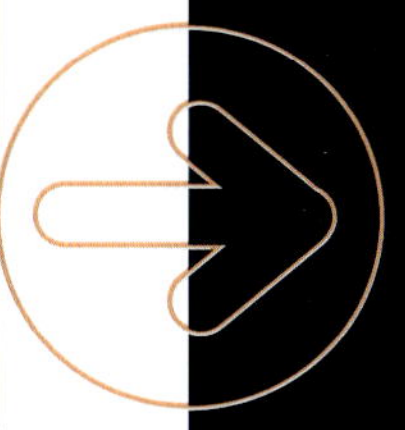

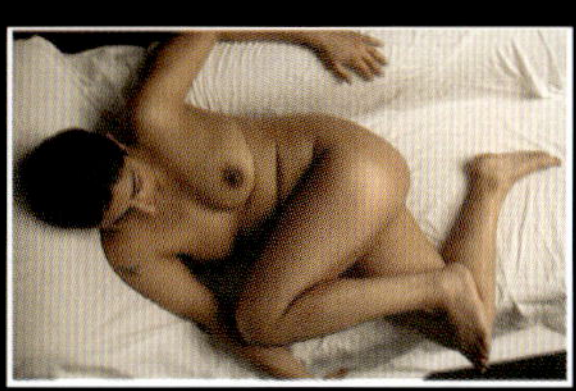

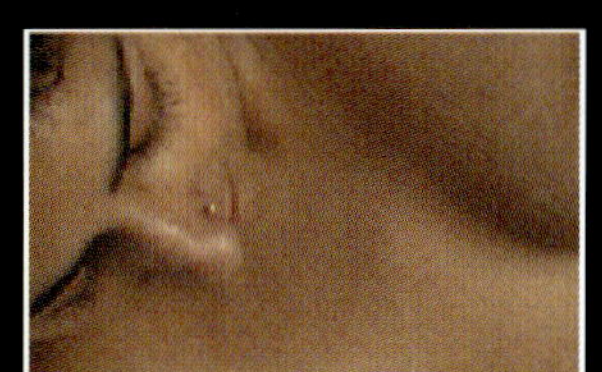

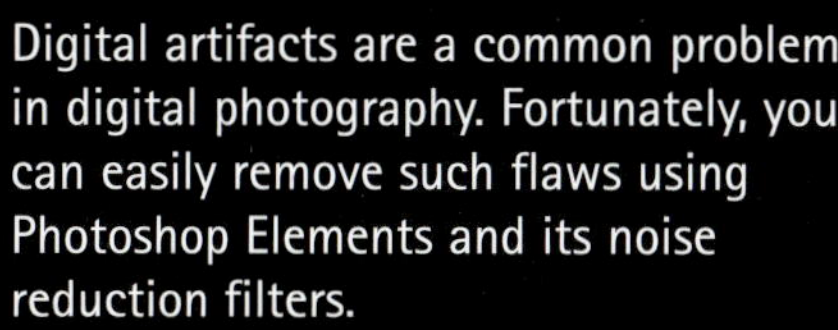

Digital artifacts are a common problem in digital photography. Fortunately, you can easily remove such flaws using Photoshop Elements and its noise reduction filters.

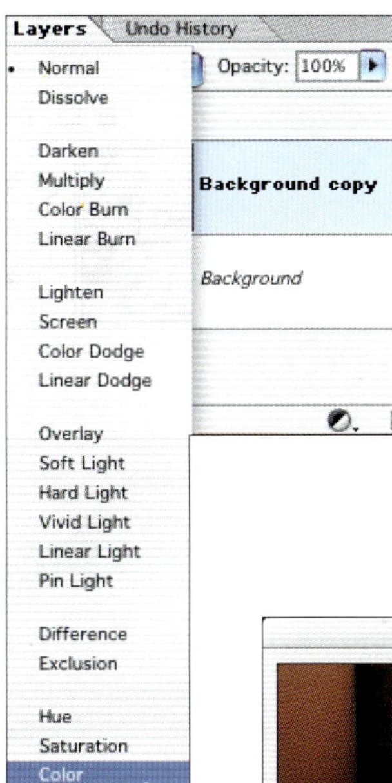

3 Set the *Blend* mode for the upper layer to *Color*.

5 Still working on the upper layer, select the filter *Noise* > *Median* and apply it with a *Radius* value of 7.

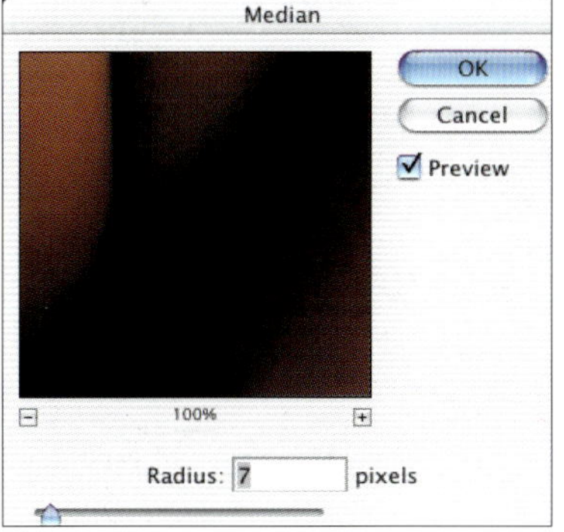

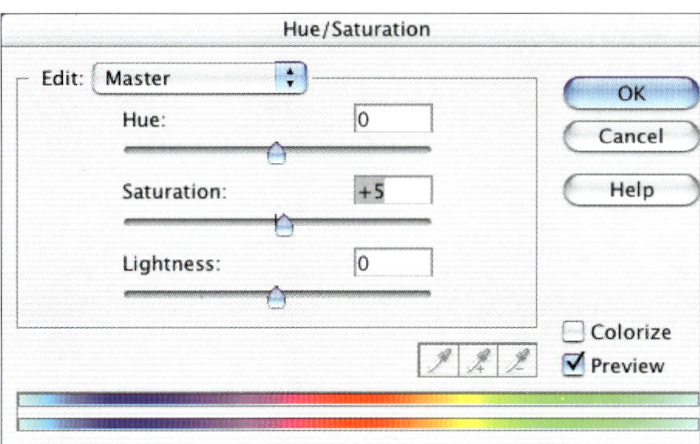

4 Increase the *Saturation* in the upper layer by about +5.

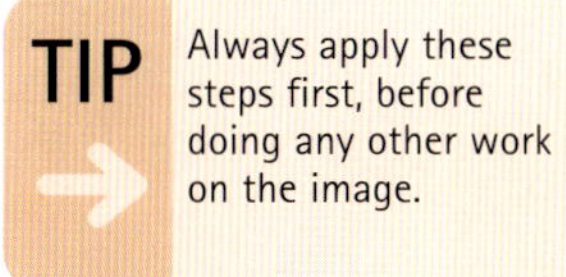

TIP Always apply these steps first, before doing any other work on the image.

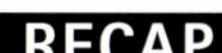

RECAP

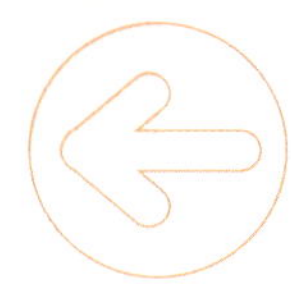

A Using the Median filter

To clean up a noisy image, duplicate the layer, set the upper layer's blend mode to *Color*, raise its saturation by about 5%, and apply *Noise* > *Median* (at about 7).

B Using the Gaussian Blur filter

Then apply *Gaussian Blur* with a radius of about 3 (experiment with this setting to see what works best).

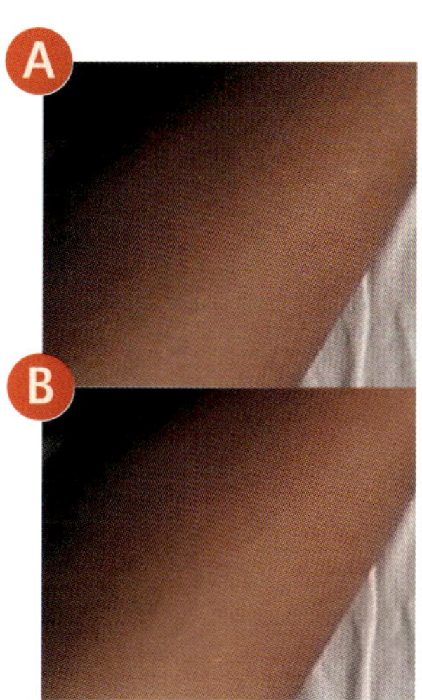

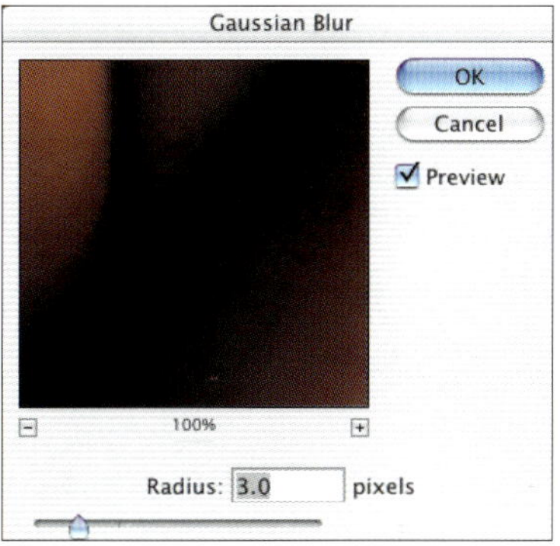

6 Still working on the upper layer, go to the *Filter* menu and select *Blur* > *Gaussian Blur.* Apply it with a *Radius* value of 3.

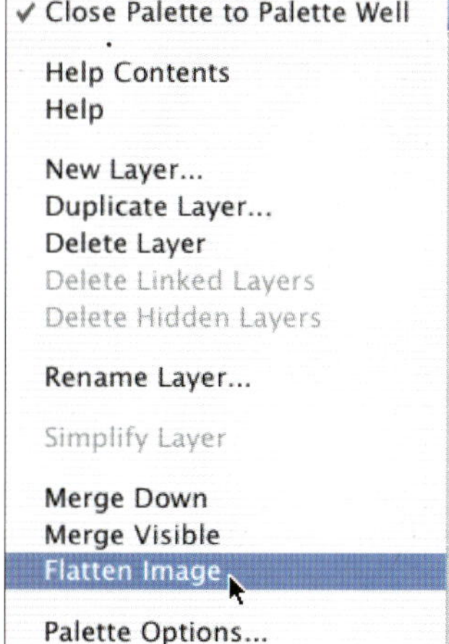

7 From *More* in the top right corner of the *Layers* window, select *Flatten Image*. Finally, save the file.

Cropping

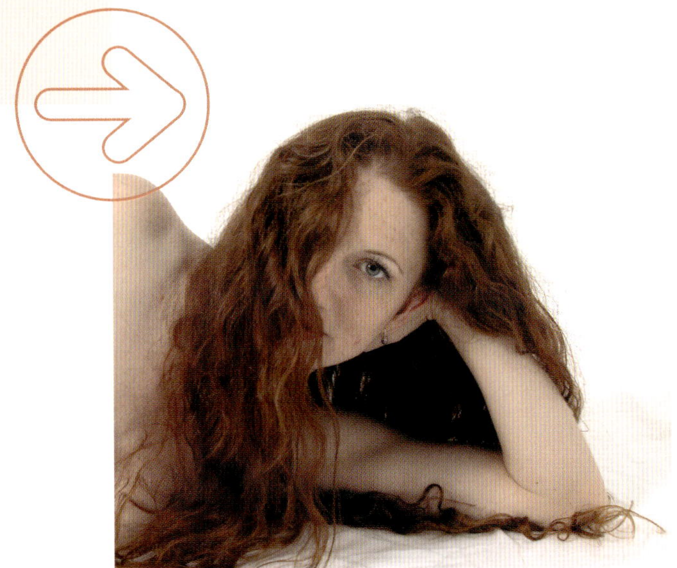

When you crop an image, you use the computer to reframe what you saw through the camera's viewfinder. Cropping may follow the original aspect ratio of the image, or may radically alter it in order to present a different emphasis from the original photograph. Cropping can simply be a way of tidying up a shot by adjusting the position of the model in relation to the edges of the frame. Alternatively, it can be a way of focussing the viewer's attention on a particular part of the body, or of creating a formal pattern in the image. Cropping is easy with Photoshop Elements. You have a choice of two tools: the *Crop* tool and the *Rectangular Marquee* tool.

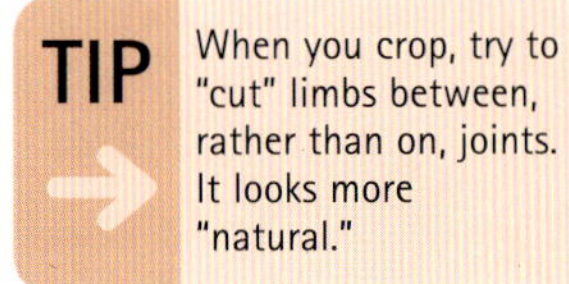

TIP When you crop, try to "cut" limbs between, rather than on, joints. It looks more "natural."

CROPPING TO THE SAME ASPECT RATIO

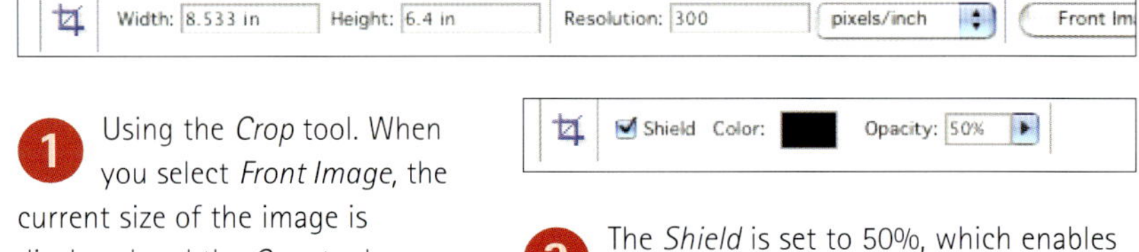

1 Using the *Crop* tool. When you select *Front Image*, the current size of the image is displayed and the *Crop* tool applies the image's aspect ratio.

2 Cropping an image while retaining the aspect ratio. Note the "shielded" area of the image.

3 The *Shield* is set to 50%, which enables you to see what you are cropping out.

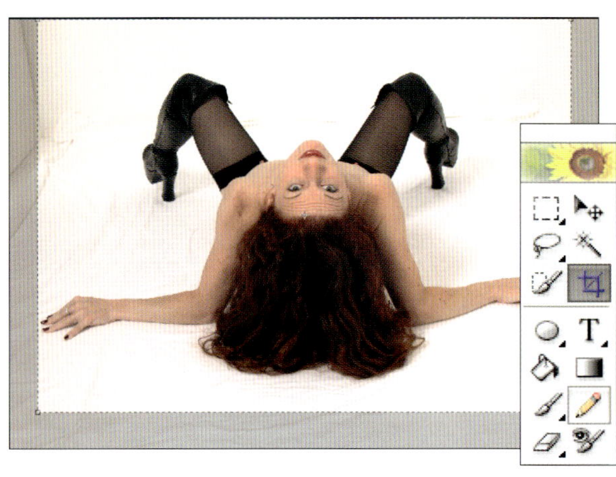

CHANGING THE ASPECT RATIO

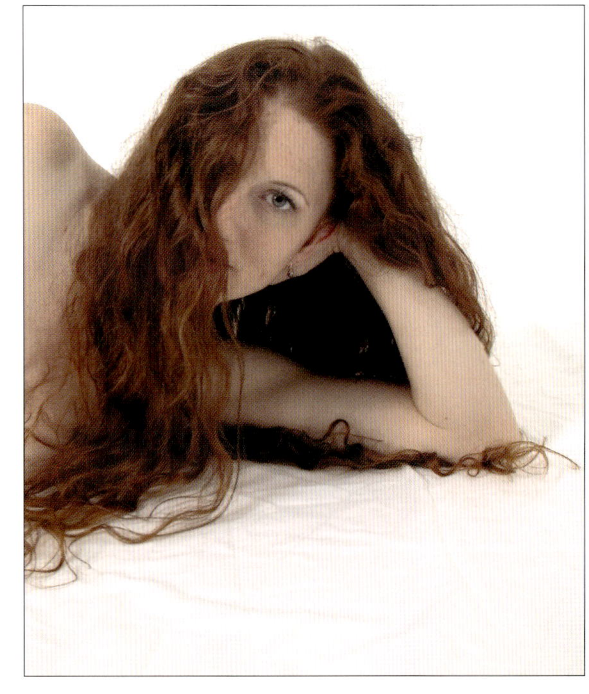

1 I shot this in portrait format when it would have been better in landscape.

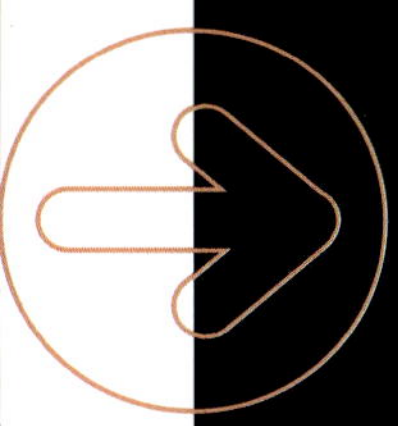

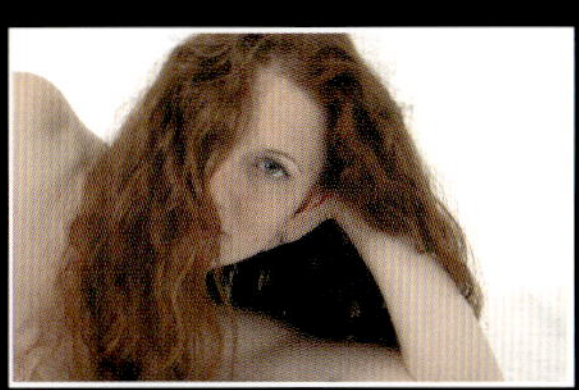

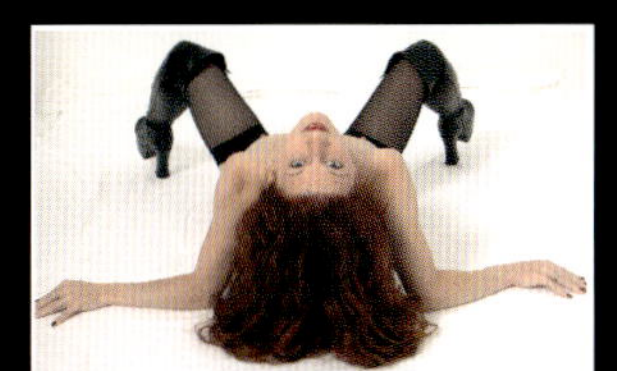

Cropping an image is easy to do in most image-editing packages. This enables you to dramatically transform a photograph. Be aware, however, that cropped images will print at a smaller size unless you can accept a lower resolution.

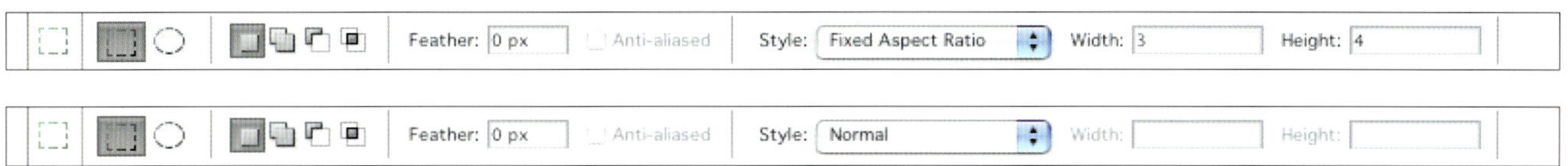

To crop to a particular aspect ratio with the Rectangular Marquee *tool, set* Feather *to 0, select* Fixed Aspect Ratio *for the* Style, *and enter the appropriate figures for* Width *and* Height. *To make a free crop, select the* Normal *style. After positioning the Marquee, select* Image > *Crop.*

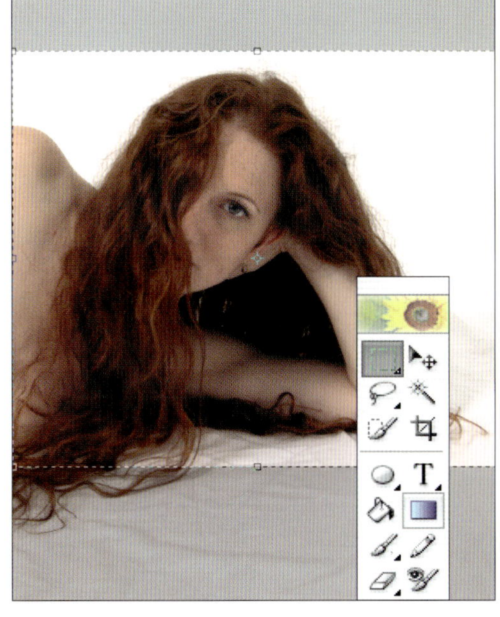

2 After selecting *Clear* in the *Crop* tool options so that I could vary the aspect ratio, I could crop the image to better proportions.

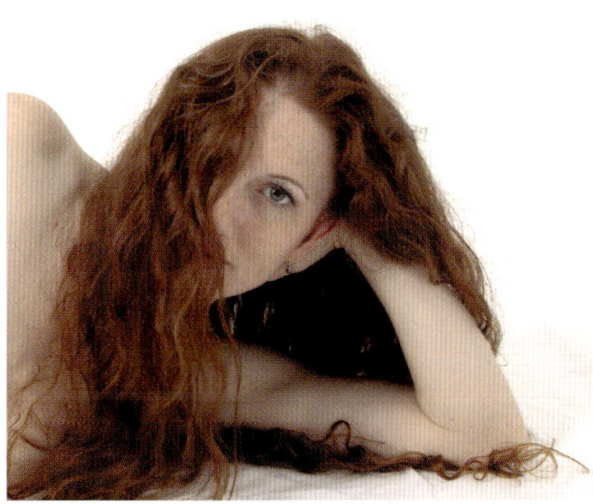

3 The result. The model now fills the frame, and the cropped image is still large enough to print satisfactorily.

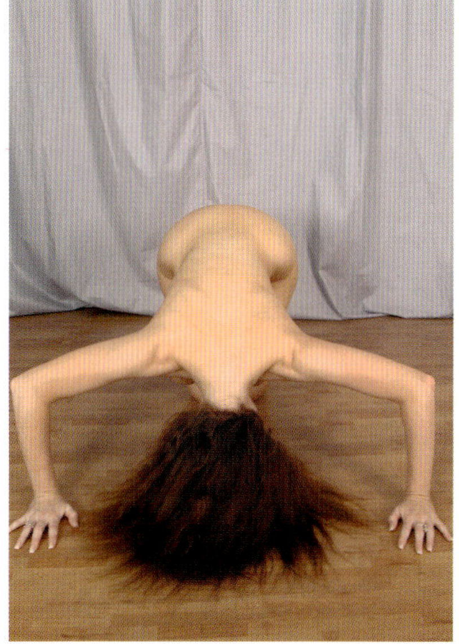

Not a satisfactory image: too much space, and too obvious a pose.

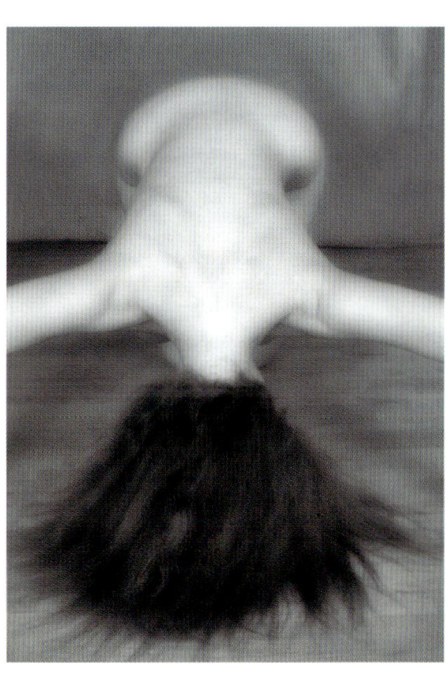

Cropping the image tightly creates a more interesting result.

FACT FILE

Blowing up cropped images

If you crop an image out of a small area of your original photograph, the result may look blurred or pixellated if you try to increase its size. When you increase the size of an image, Elements has to create extra pixels to fill in the gaps. This process, called interpolation, can produce artifacts in the image. It's wise to take more pictures during a shoot so you have more options that use the full frame.

Making selections

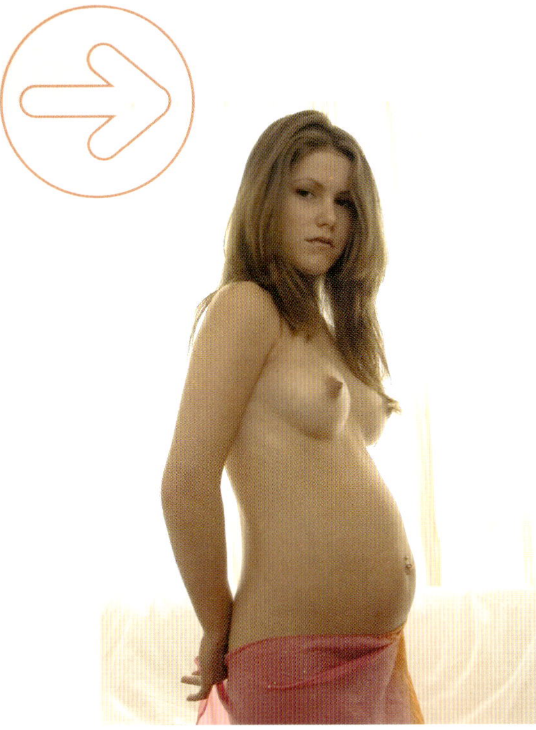

You will often want to select, or isolate, a particular part of an image, in order to alter it in some way without affecting the rest of the image. This section introduces the different tools that Elements provides for making selections: the *Magic Wand*, the *Magnetic Lasso*, the *Selection Brush*, and the *Lasso* tool. Later in the book we will look at some of the effects in which selection plays a part.

THE SELECTION TOOLS

- The *Magic Wand* selects areas of similarly colored pixels. It's particularly useful for selecting flat areas of background.
- The *Magnetic Lasso* tool "sticks" to edges, although Elements' idea of where the edge is may be different from yours.
- You can use the *Selection Brush* tool to make a selection by painting over (masking) the area you want to select.
- The *Lasso* tool can be used to draw freehand around the area you want to select.

The *Selection Brush* and the *Lasso* are useful for tidying up and making fine adjustments to areas selected with the *Magic Wand* and *Magnetic Lasso*.

TIPS ON MAKING SELECTIONS

The *Magic Wand* and *Magnetic Lasso* tools work by detecting edges: that is, areas in an image where there is a change of color from one pixel to the next. This means that they work most effectively in images where the background and foreground are distinct from each other, but less well when, for example, there is a foreground figure that melts into the shadows. The same principle applies to using the *Selection Brush* or the *Lasso*: you need to be able to see the edge clearly in order to be able to drag the *Lasso* tool along it, or to paint up to it with the *Selection Brush* tool. It has to be said that none of these tools works particularly well when it comes to selecting really intricate areas such as wisps of hair.

ANTI-ALIASING AND FEATHERING

Anti-aliasing is an option that smoothens the jagged edges of a selection by softening the color transition on the edge between selected and unselected areas. Since only the edge pixels change, no detail is lost. Anti-aliasing is useful when cutting, copying, and pasting selections to create composite images. You should always opt to switch anti-aliasing on when making selections.

Feathering blurs edges between selected and unselected areas by building a transition between the selection and surrounding pixels. This blurring can cause some loss of detail at the edge of the selection, but this often looks more realistic, since edges in photographs often are slightly blurred. Some selection tools let you specify how much feather you want before you start to make a selection. However, it's generally preferable to make your selection without any feather, then add feathering to it using *Select* > *Feather* when the selection is complete.

The steps here feature some fairly easy examples, where the models' hair and skin tones are distinct from their backgrounds.

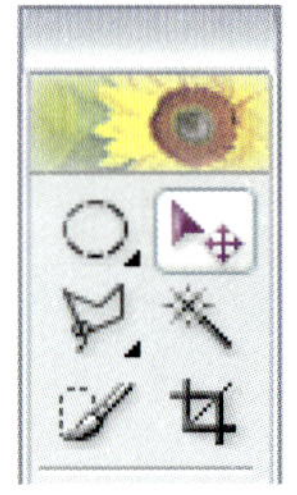

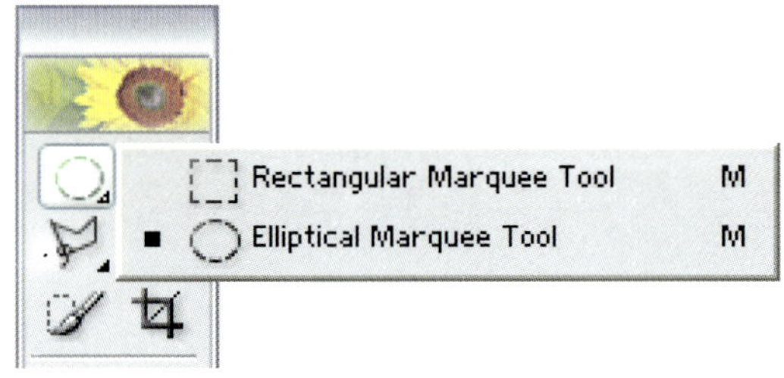

The selection tools, from top: Marquee (and Move tool), the Lasso and the Magic Wand, Selection Brush (and Crop tool). Click and hold to see variations.

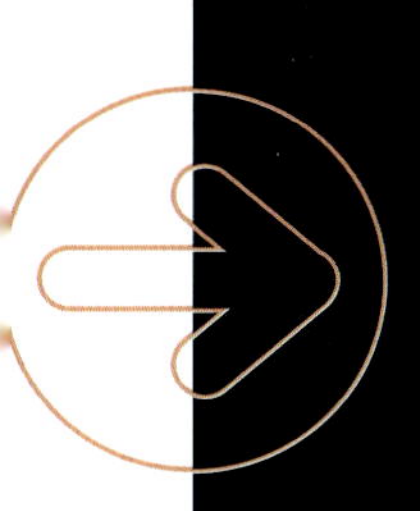

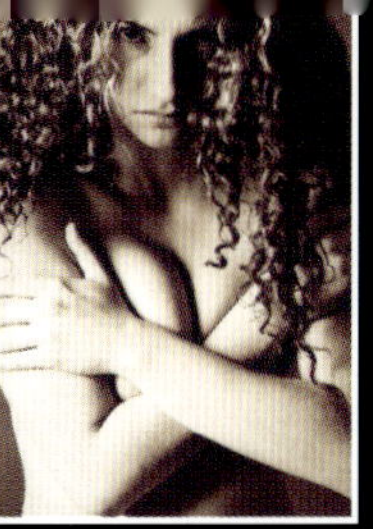

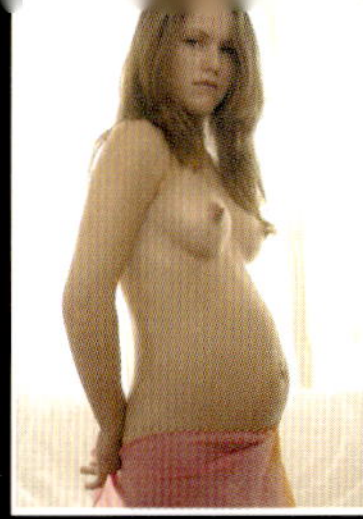

Selections let you isolate a part or section of an image so that you can edit it without affecting the rest of the photo. Selections are relatively easy to create, and Photoshop Elements has special tools that simplify the process.

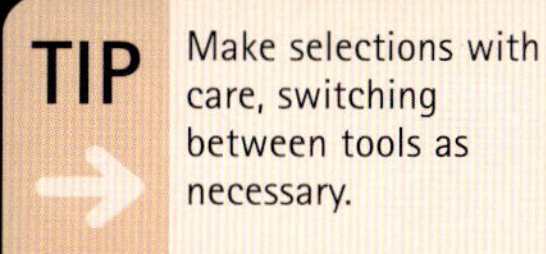

USING THE MAGIC WAND

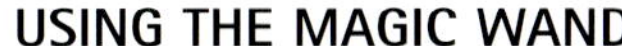

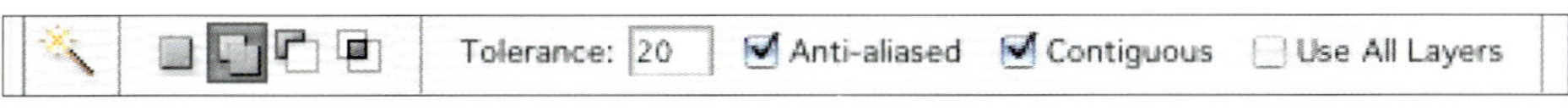

1 Begin by duplicating either the file or the layer you are working on. A low value for *Tolerance* will select only colors very similar to the pixel you click on; a higher value will select a broader range of colors. Values between 12 and 24 seem to work best most of the time. Check *Anti-aliased* so that the selection will have smooth edges, and *Contiguous* so that you select only adjacent pixels of the same color (if you uncheck *Contiguous*, you will select pixels with the same color all over the image). In the *Options* bar, specify *Add to Selection* so that with each click you gradually select more of the background.

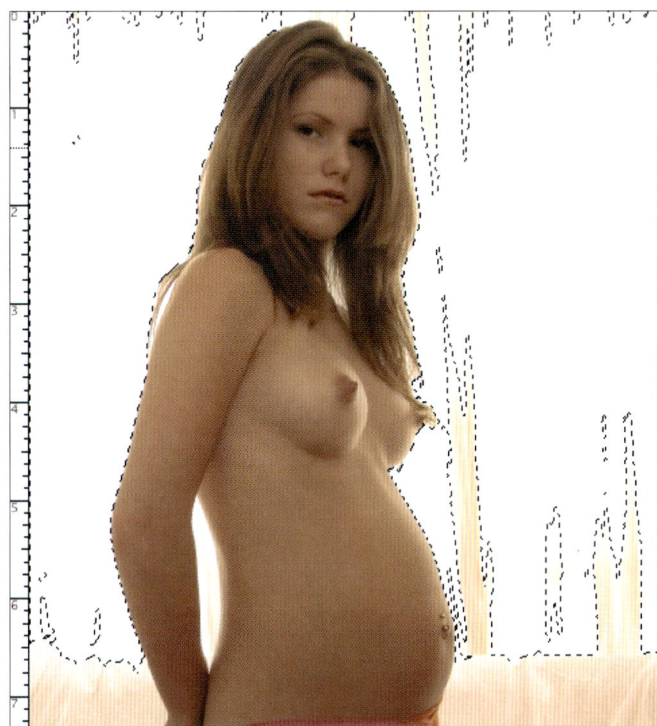

2 Now click in the background of your image. You will see selection lines appear around some areas. Click again, in an area that hasn't been selected, and keep doing this until all the background is selected. If you make a mistake and select part of the foreground, either go to *Edit* > *Undo*, or hold down the Alt key and click again in the area you wrongly selected. Note the minus sign that appears as part of the cursor when you hold down the Alt key.

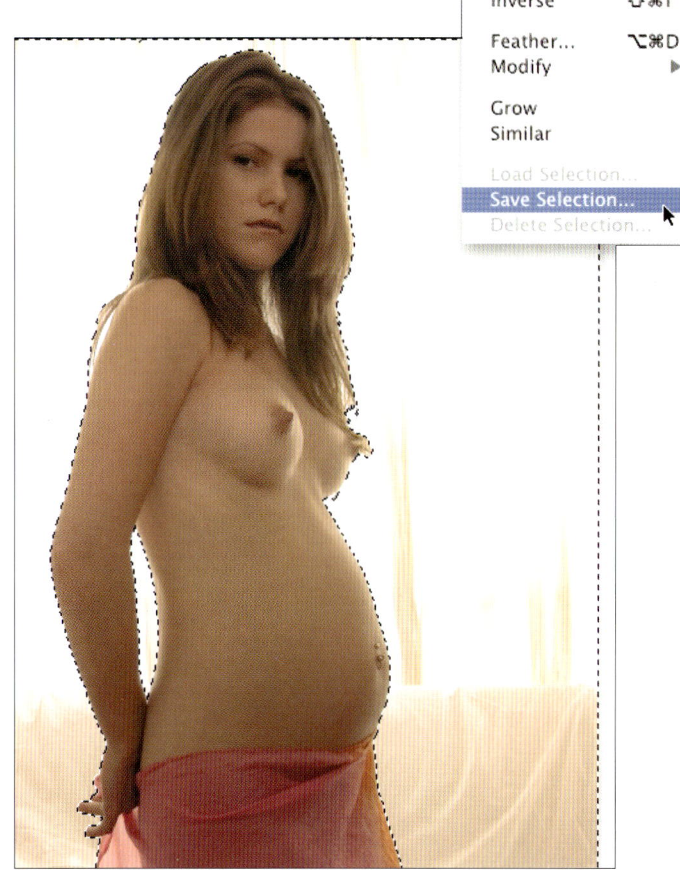

Save Selection

Selection
Selection: New
Name: outline
OK
Cancel

Operation
New Selection
Add to Selection
Subtract from Selection
Intersect with Selection

3 Now save your selection by going to *Select* > *Save Selection*. This is your first selection, so it appears as "New." Give it an appropriate name. The selection is saved as part of the file, so will still be available whenever you next open the file.

Making selections

USING THE MAGNETIC LASSO

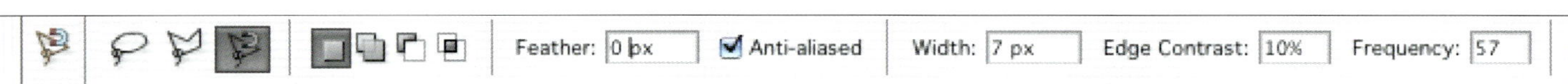

1 Select the *Magnetic Lasso* from *the Toolbar or Lasso Options Bar*. Set *Feather* to 0 and check *Anti-aliased*. Set a low value for *Width*: this is the area around the cursor within which the *Magnetic Lasso* detects edges. The higher this number, the further you can move the cursor from an edge and still have the tool detect it. A high value for *Edge Contrast* detects only high-contrast edges; a lower value detects lower-contrast edges. Try a setting of 10. *Frequency* determines how often the *Magnetic Lasso* places anchor points as you drag the tool: settings between 50 and 60 seem to work well.

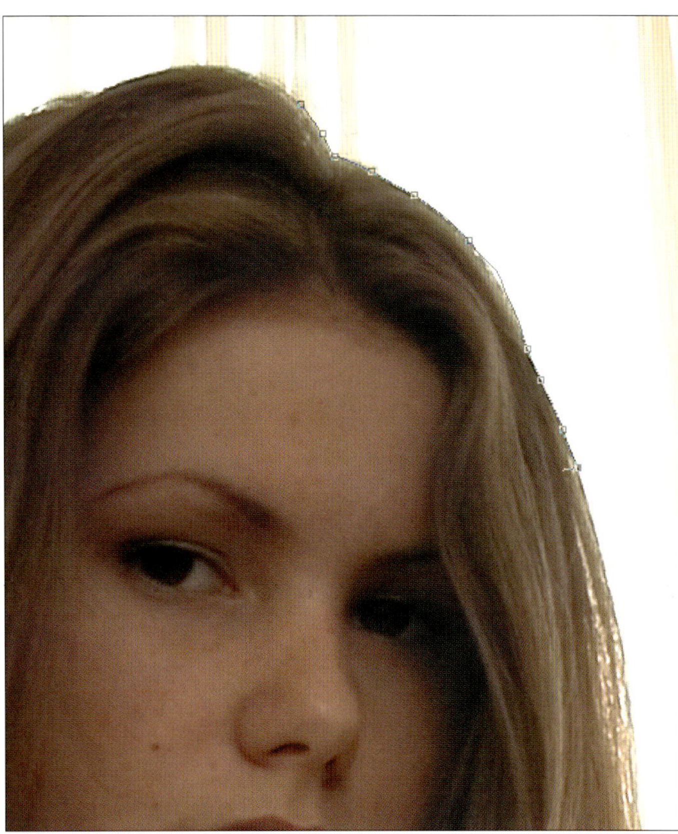

2 Now click somewhere on the edge between background and foreground and move the cursor along the edge. Go slower where the edge is more curved or complex.

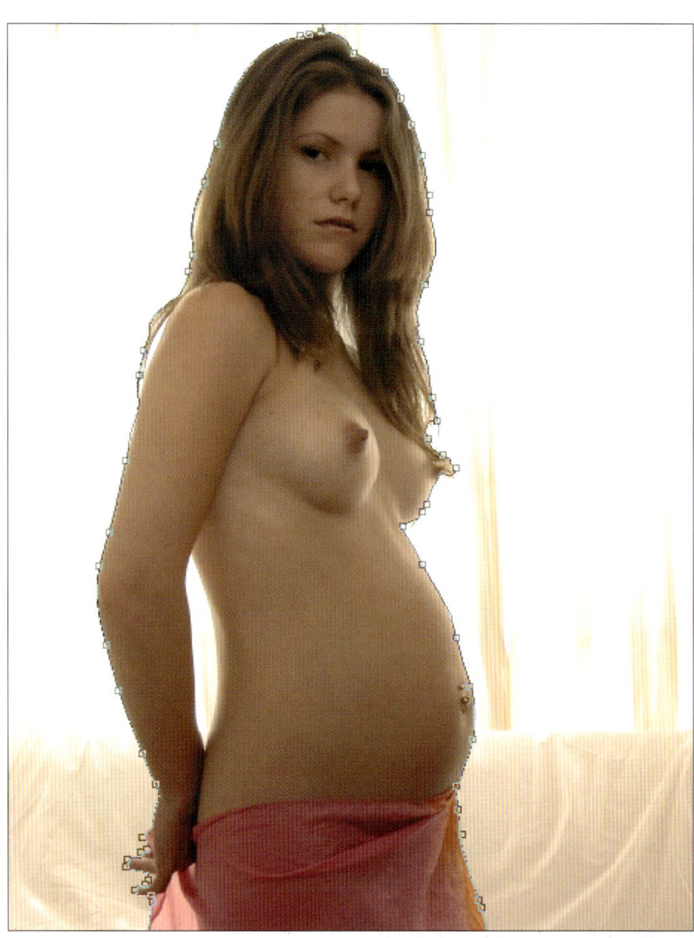

3 You see the selection line snap to the edge and place anchor points as it goes. If an anchor point goes wrong, use the Backspace key on the keyboard to delete it, then try again. In really intricate areas (such as around the fingers), you can click to place an anchor point if the *Magnetic Lasso* doesn't do it for you.

The *Magnetic Lasso* needs to end up where it began. When you come back over your start point, you'll see the cursor change: a little "o" appears in it. Click on the start point to complete the selection, and then save the selection.

If you press the Caps Lock key while the *Magnetic Lasso* is active but not being used, the cursor turns into a circle. This represents the width you've specified, with a pair of crosshairs at the center. You can adjust the width by pressing the [key to reduce it and the] key to increase it.

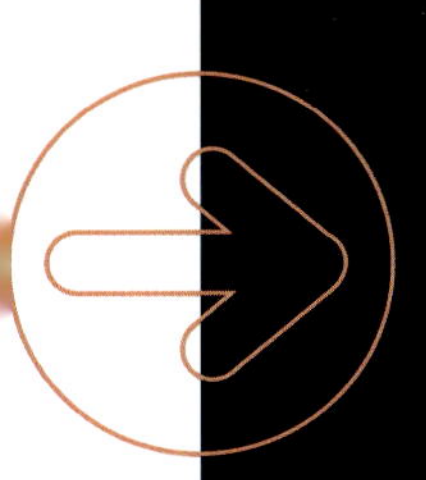

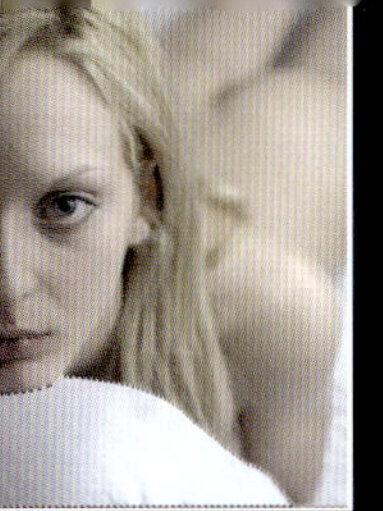

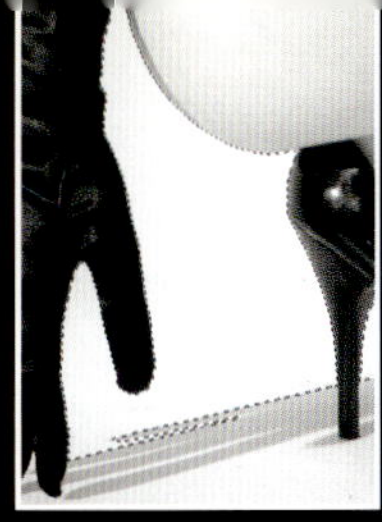

The *Magnetic Lasso* creates selections automatically by comparing the colors of pixels within a given area. It yields surprisingly accurate results and you can, if necessary, help it along or fine-tune the selection afterward.

Before starting to make a selection, consider whether the background or foreground will be easier to select.

TIDYING UP WITH THE SELECTION BRUSH

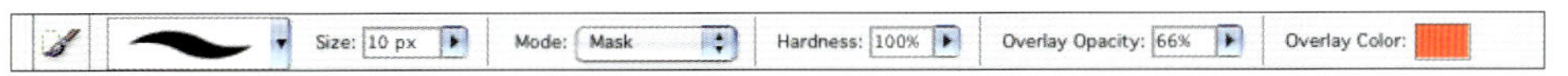

1 Start with these settings: a small hard brush, using partly opaque red to mask the selected area.

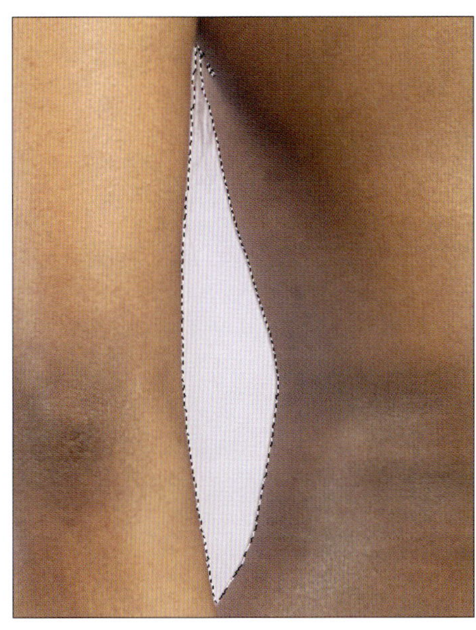

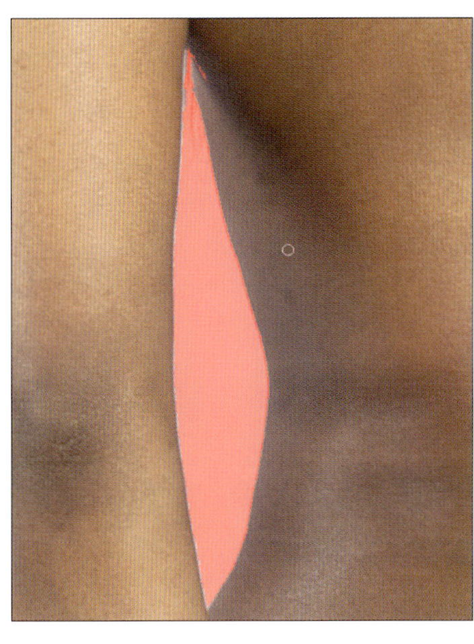

2 When we click on the *Selection Brush* tool, the appearance of the selected area changes from this (above) to this (below). The selected areas are now shown covered in a red "film," which can be added to or reduced using appropriate brushes. Then toggle to and fro between the brush and other selection tools, using whichever is best suited to the area you're trying to select.

3 Paint with the brush to extend the selected area where it doesn't go as far as it should, and paint while holding down the Alt key to erase the mask and reduce the selected area. Once more, save the selection.

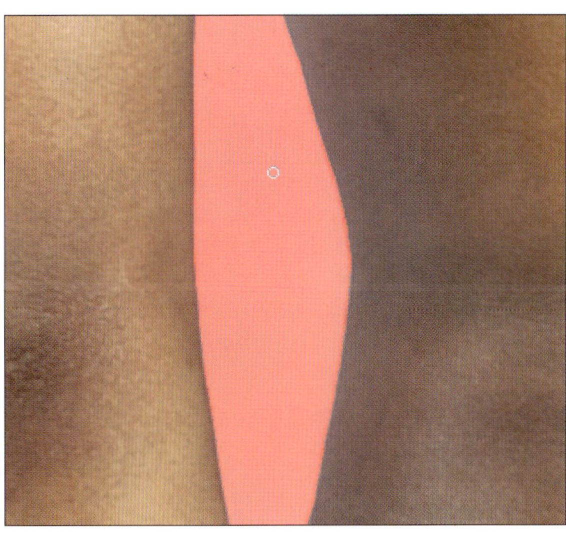

TIDYING UP WITH THE LASSO

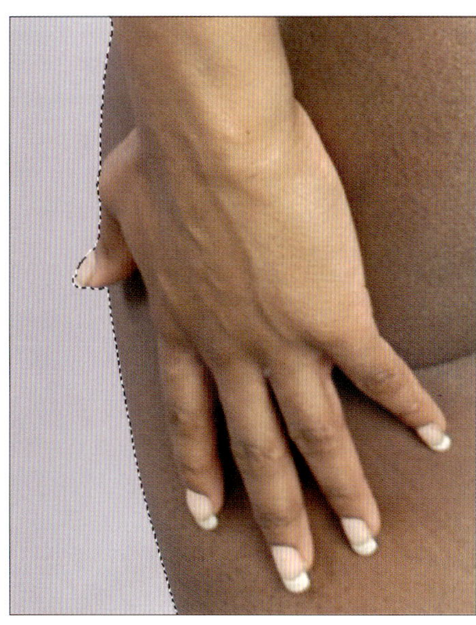

1 Try the same process with the *Lasso.* In this image, making the main selection with the *Magic Wand,* I missed a few pixels near the model's leg, and I have not quite included her thumbnail. I set the options for the *Lasso* set to *Create a New Selection*, so I needed to hold down *<Shift>* to add to the selection (a plus sign appears in the cursor) or *<Alt>* to subtract from it.

You can use the *Lasso* or the *Selection Brush* to draw or paint the whole of a selection freehand, but this usually takes far more time than using the other selection tools.

Other selection tools are the *Extract* tool, for fine detail like hair, and *Layer Masks,* which gives precise masking control .

Retouching

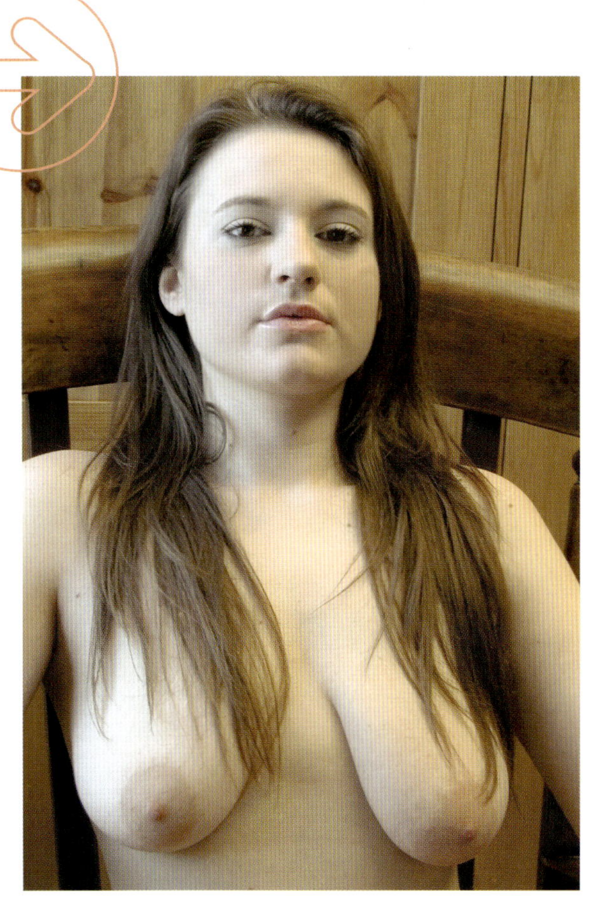

Inevitably, models sometimes arrive for a shoot with visible skin blemishes. Makeup may help to cover these, but in cases where this isn't adequate, Photoshop Elements gives you the tools to remove marks, reduce the shine on the model's nose, and generally tidy up minor flaws in the image.

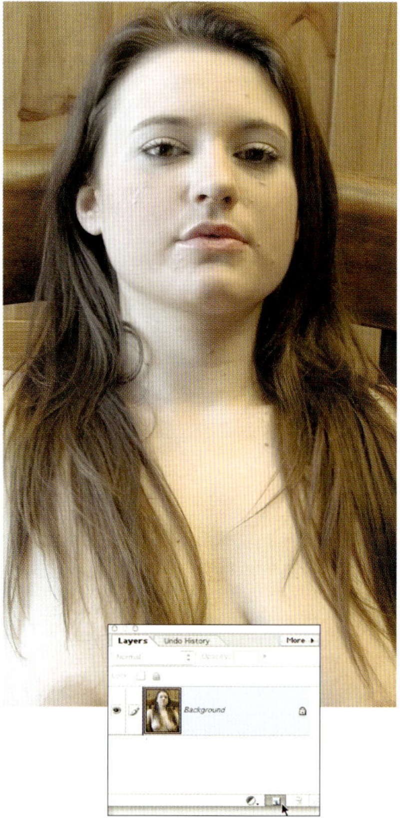

1 As an optional precaution, begin by creating a new empty layer. You will make your corrections on this layer, so that if necessary you can discard the layer and begin again without affecting the original *Background* layer.

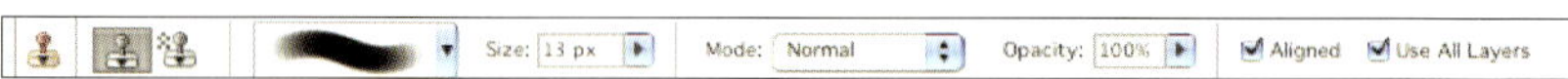

2 Select the *Clone Stamp* tool, either from the toolbar or by pressing the S key on the keyboard. Double click on the *Zoom* tool to view the picture at 100% size. Check both the *Aligned* and the *Use All Layers* boxes.

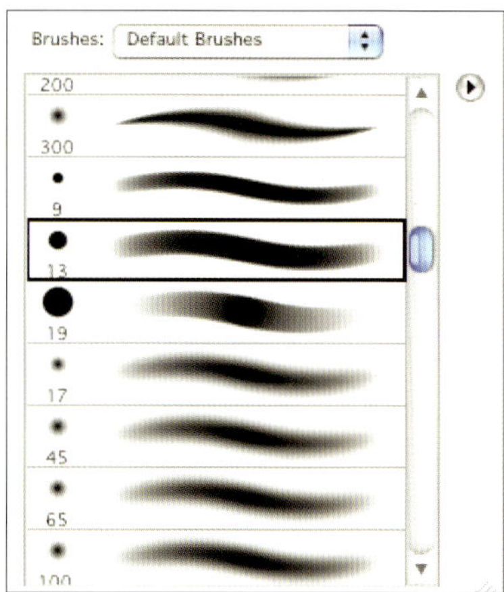

3 Select the hard round 13-pixel brush by scrolling down the display of brush thumbnails. Hard round brushes seem to give the best results.

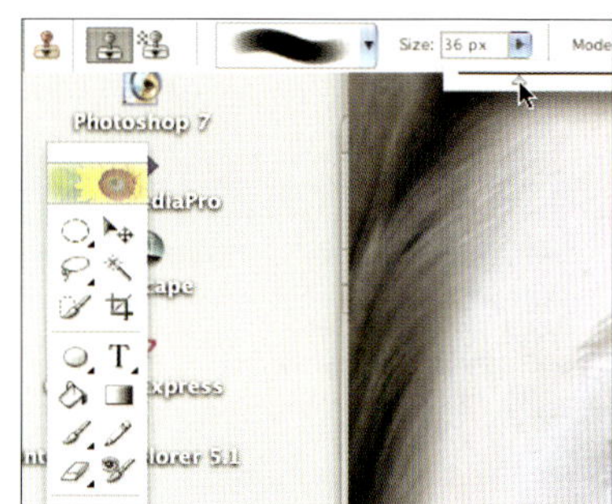

4 Increase the size of the brush, if necessary, so that it's a little wider than the blemish you wish to correct.

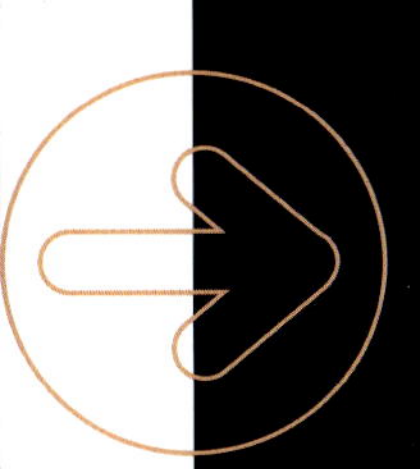
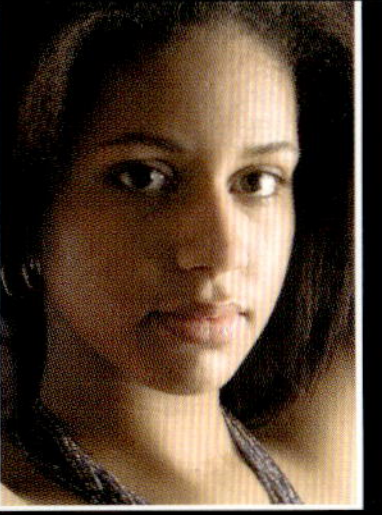
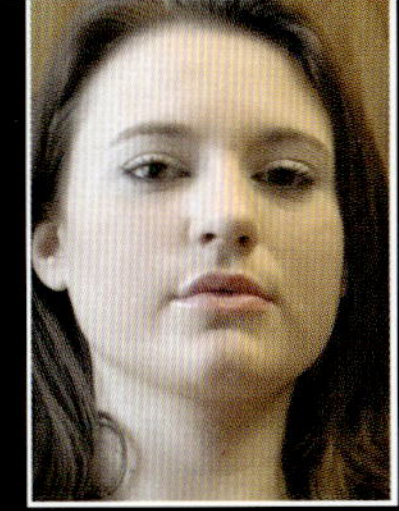

Adobe Photoshop Elements offers a variety of tools and features that can dramatically reduce visible flaws such as spots or skin blemishes. These tools are intuitive and very easy to use.

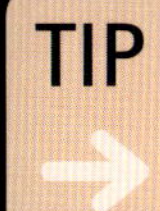

TIP If you use Photoshop 7, the *Healing Brush* and *Patch* tools are extremely useful for retouching.

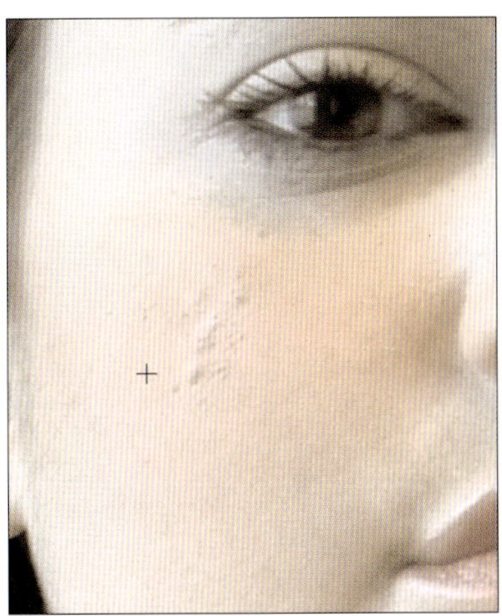

5 Now find an area (usually close to the blemish you want to correct) that has the same color and brightness. You will repair the blemish by copying ("cloning") this area over it. Alt-click (Windows) or Option-click (Mac OS) on this area to make it the source for cloning.

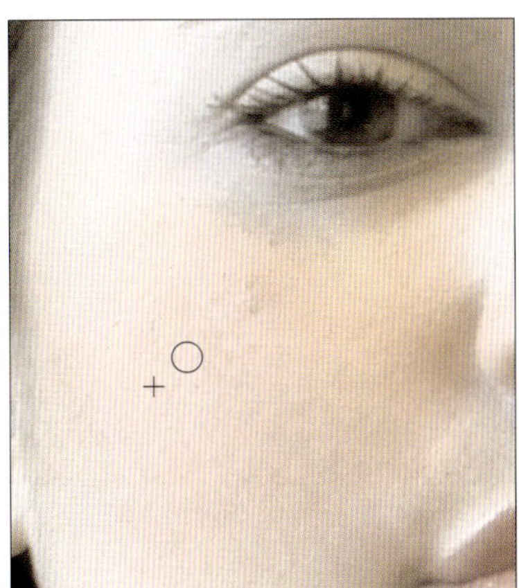

6 Use the brush to paint over the blemish. It will disappear and be replaced by a clone of the source area you selected before. A small cross appears over the source area, and moves as you paint. If the source area is smaller than the blemish, you may need to repeat Step 5 to relocate the source area where it originally was.

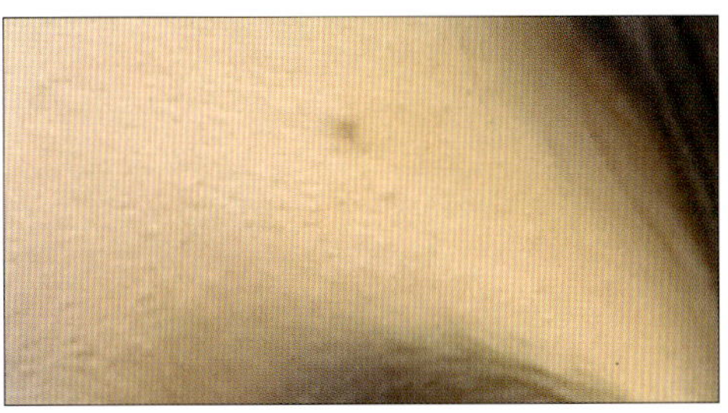

Blemish

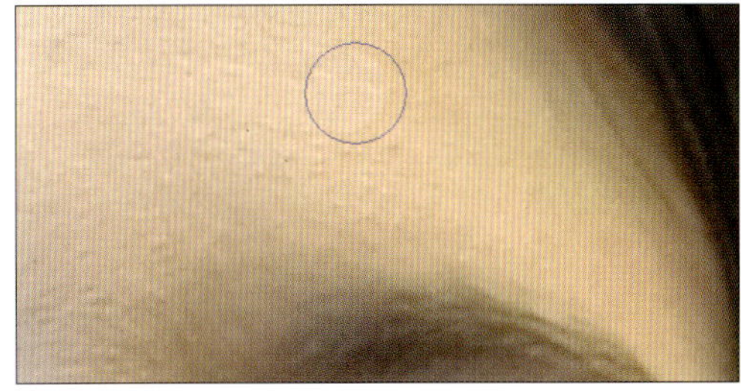

Too-light clone

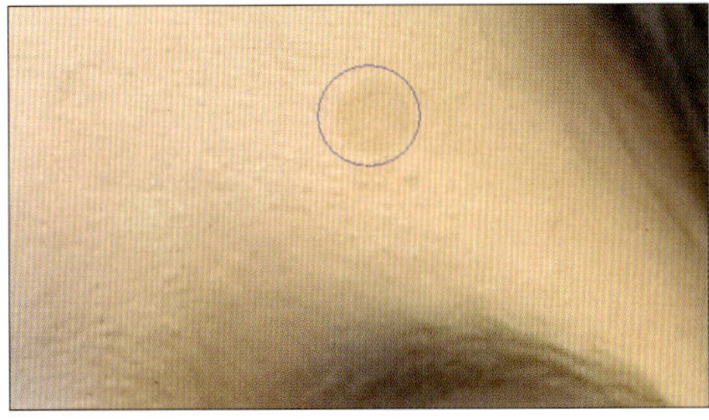

Too-dark clone

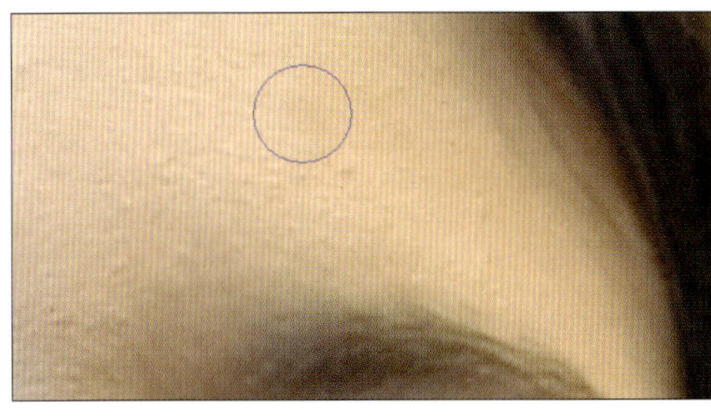

Just right

The trick with cloning is to take great care in selecting the source area. Looking at the mark on the model's forehead at 200% size, we see the effect of selecting a source that doesn't quite match the color and brightness of the area we want to repair.

REDUCING SHINE

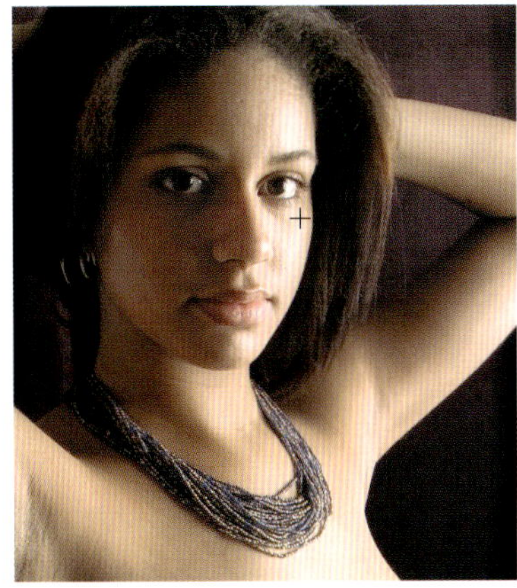

Before

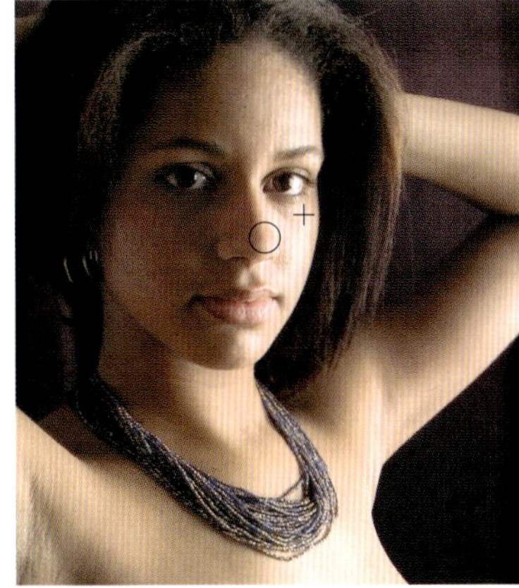

After

Another common problem is unwanted highlights on the model's nose. Again, you can use the *Clone Stamp* to solve this. Set the *Opacity* of the *Clone Stamp* quite low—10-15% usually works well. Choose a brush that is a little larger than the width of the area you are going to work on. Select as the source for the *Clone Stamp* an area with the right color and brightness to replace the highlight. Paint over the highlight, building up color until the highlight is reduced but not completely removed.

Adjusting levels

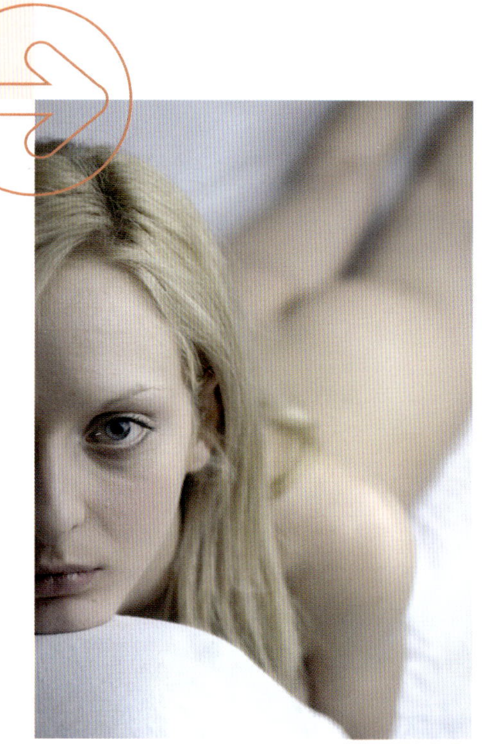

Not every photograph is perfectly exposed. It's difficult to retrieve images that are severely overexposed, but underexposed images, and images that are "flat," can be improved by using Elements' *Levels* controls. These let you expand the tonal range to the maximum possible, so that the darkest part of the image is black (RGB values 0, 0, 0) and the brightest is white (RGB values 255, 255, 255).

ADJUSTING THE TONAL RANGE

We'll begin with a pale image—one that isn't overexposed, but which still doesn't use the whole tonal range. We'll use *Levels* to extend the image's tonal range into black so that it has the maximum amount of contrast.

Before starting this process, use the *Save As* option to make a copy of the image to work on, so that you could return to the original and start again if necessary.

If you intend to print the image, try it out now, to check that what you see on your monitor is what you get from your printer. If it isn't, you may need to go back to the original image, do another *Save As*, and try again. This isn't something you'll need to do every time; you will quickly develop a feel for how far you can safely adjust levels.

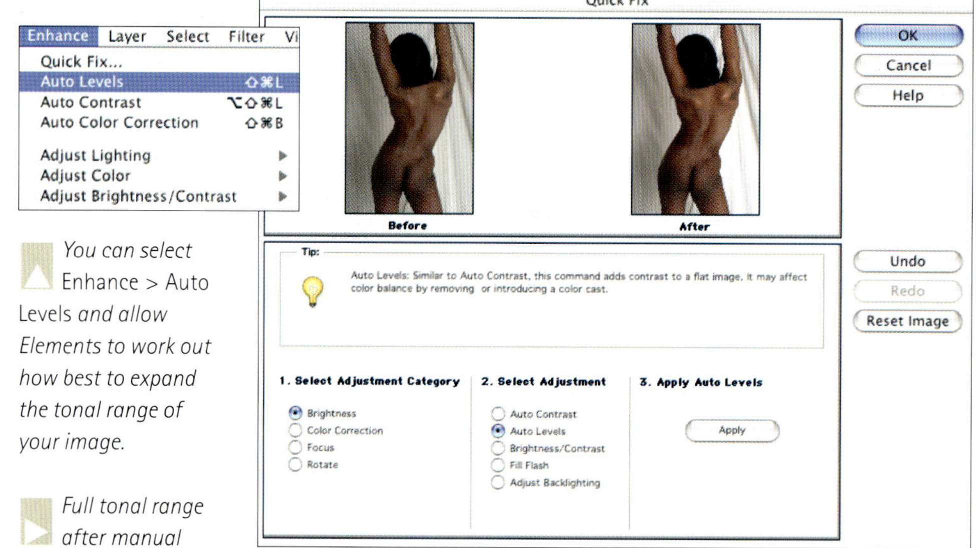

You can select Enhance > Auto Levels *and allow Elements to work out how best to expand the tonal range of your image.*

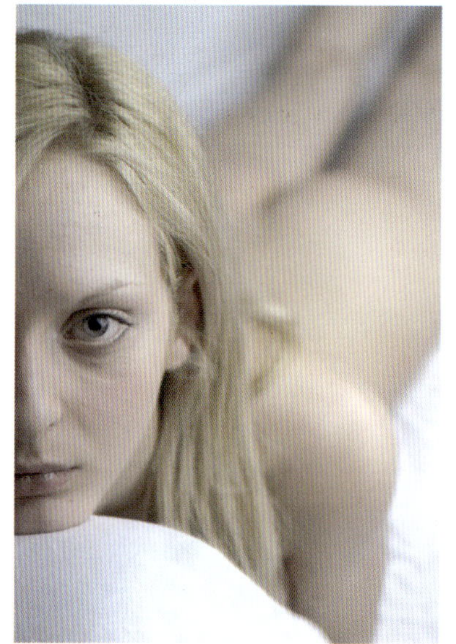

Full tonal range after manual Levels *adjustment.*

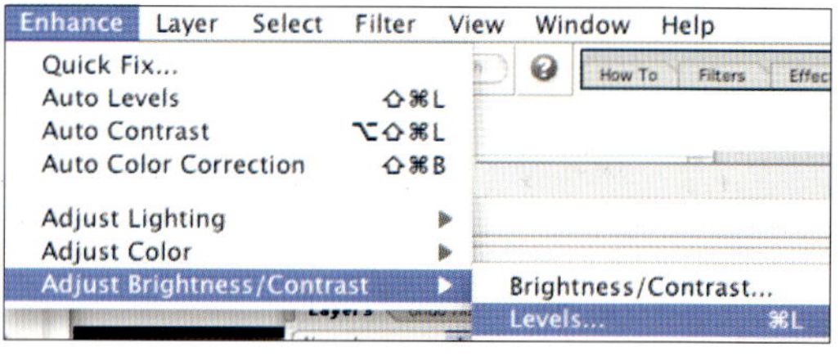

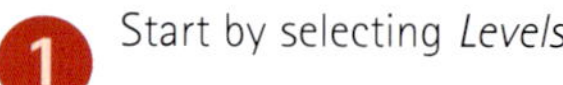

1 Start by selecting *Levels*.

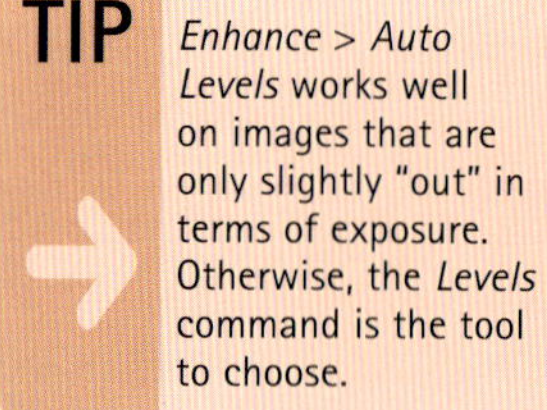

TIP *Enhance > Auto Levels* works well on images that are only slightly "out" in terms of exposure. Otherwise, the *Levels* command is the tool to choose.

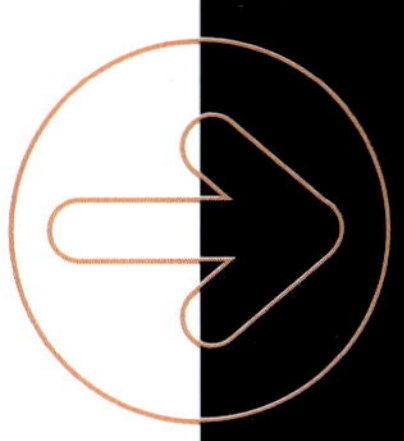

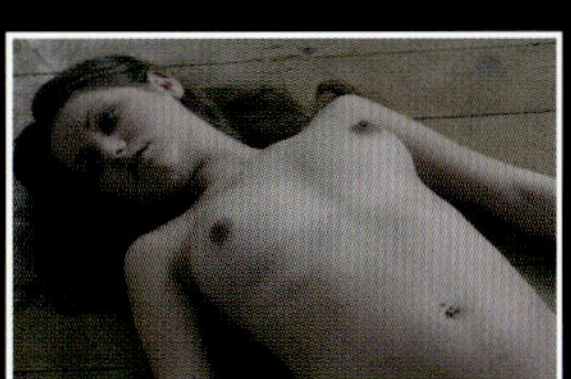

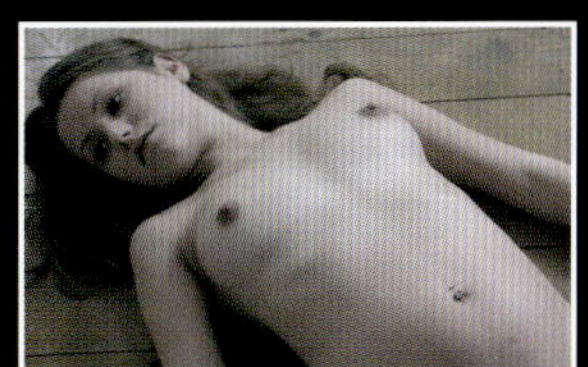

You can use *Levels* to adjust and correct images that suffer exposure problems or lack punch. When combined with selections, *Levels* can also be used to creatively edit individual colors of objects in a photograph.

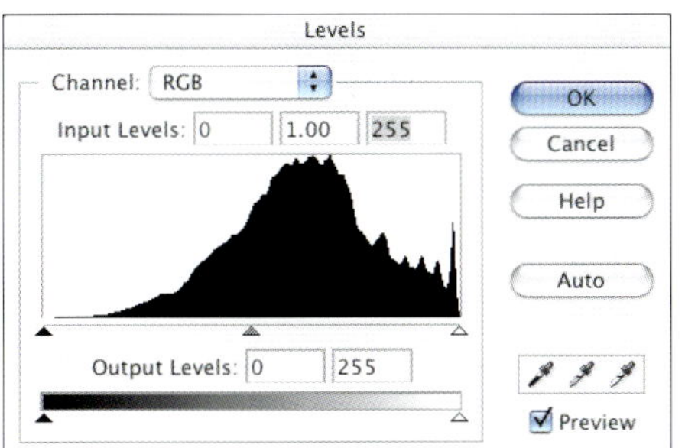

2 When the *Levels* window opens, you see the histogram that displays how the tones in the picture are distributed, from black on the left to white on the right. The higher the histogram rises, the larger the area of the picture with that tonal value. In this case, no part of the picture is black; very little of it is located in the dark gray area; but the tonal range does extend all the way up to white.

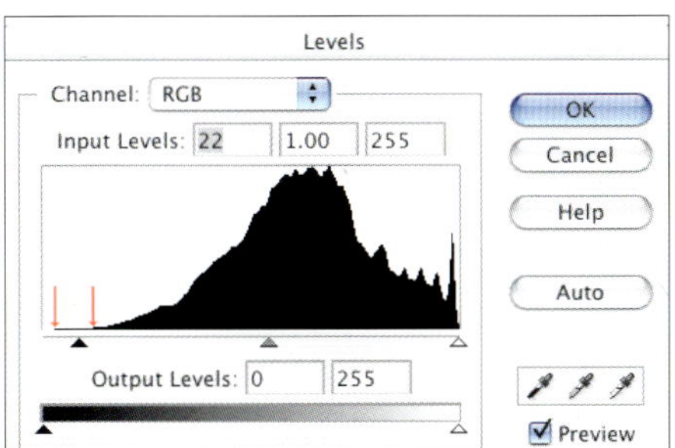

3 To adjust the black, drag the left-hand *Input Level* slider to the right. Generally the best setting will lie between the first pixels in the histogram and the point where the histogram starts to climb, as shown by the arrows here. The more you drag this slider to the right, the more contrast you add to the image. You can use the middle slider to adjust the midtones of the image without altering the shadows and highlights. When you're satisfied with your results, click *OK* and save the image.

This example has the opposite problem: it's seriously underexposed, as the histogram indicates. Here we'll make a greater adjustment with the right-hand Input Level *slider, and also adjust the midtones. As with the left-hand slider in the first example, the best setting for the right-hand slider is between the first pixels in the histogram and the point where the histogram starts to climb.*

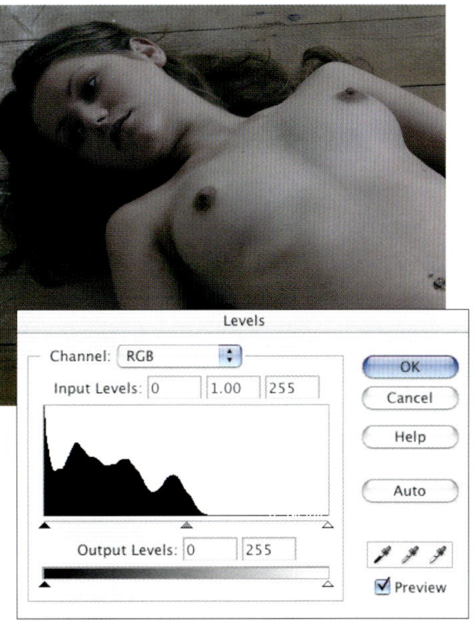

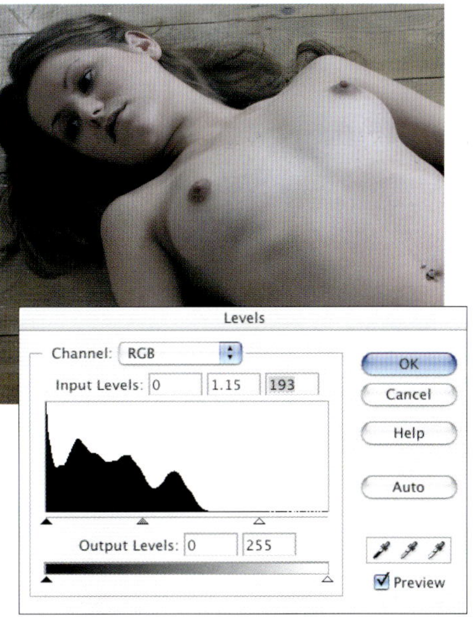

Finally, an example where minor adjustments are required at both ends of the tonal spectrum.

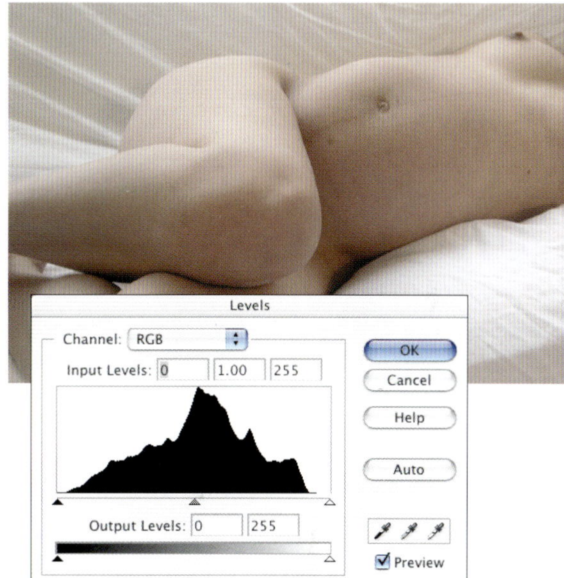

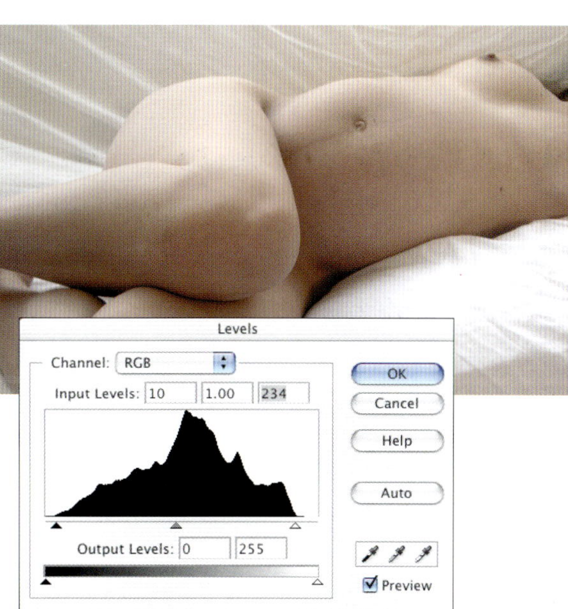

Dodging and burning

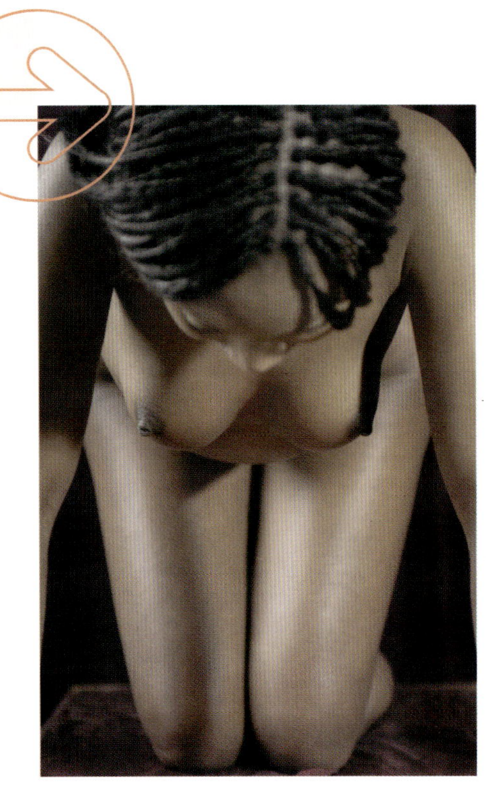

Dodging and burning are technical terms that have come across from film photography into the digital domain to describe the process of lightening (dodging) or darkening (burning) selected areas of an image. Elements has a *Dodge* tool and a *Burn* tool, although they are not always the best way to achieve the result you want. In this example, the shadow on the model's left breast is darker than I'd like it. I want to make the shadow area lighter, but without losing any of its color.

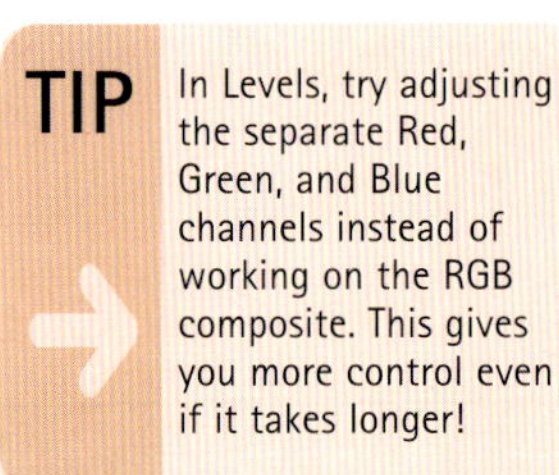

TIP In Levels, try adjusting the separate Red, Green, and Blue channels instead of working on the RGB composite. This gives you more control even if it takes longer!

THE DODGE TOOL

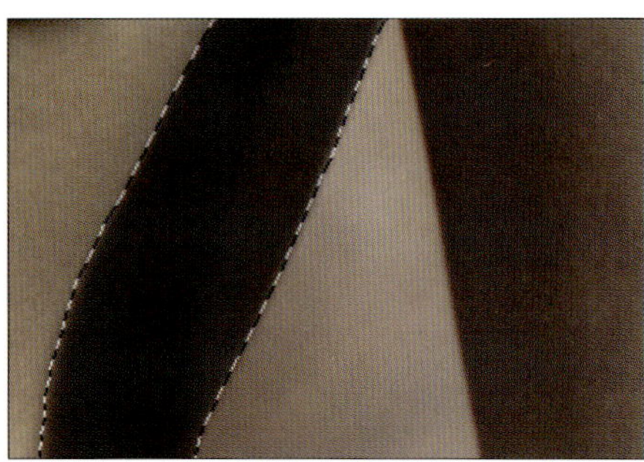

1 First, duplicate the background layer. Then double-click on the *Zoom* tool or press Z on the keyboard and click on the *Actual Pixels* button to show the image full size. Use the *Magnetic Lasso* tool to select the shadow area. Use a 3-pixel *Feather* so that, when you lighten the shadow area, the alterations blend smoothly with the surrounding area. In this example, the aureole should be darker than the model's normal skin, so should not be included in the selection.

Size: 77 px Range: Shadows Exposure: 4%

2 Save the selection, then uncheck *View* > *Selection* so that the selection line doesn't make it harder to judge the effect of what you're doing (the area is still selected; it's only the line that disappears). Now select the *Dodge* tool. Choose a soft brush, select *Shadow* for the *Range*, and a low value (in this case just 4%) for the *Exposure*.

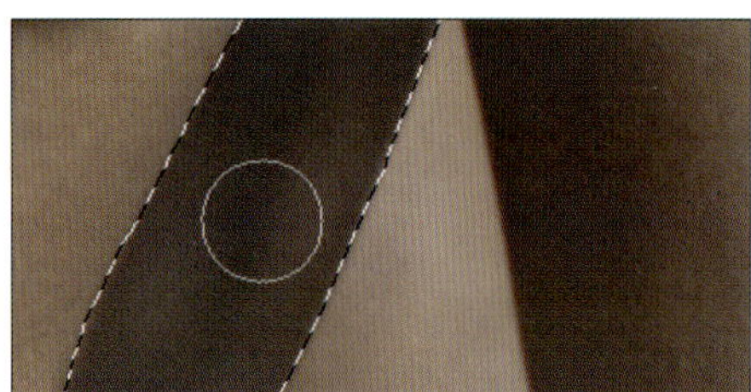

3 Paint in the selected area with the *Dodge* tool. The area becomes lighter, but it also becomes whiter—in other words, the *Dodge* tool removes some of the color information. For this reason, the *Dodge* tool is most effective on black-and-white images.

USING LEVELS FOR DODGING

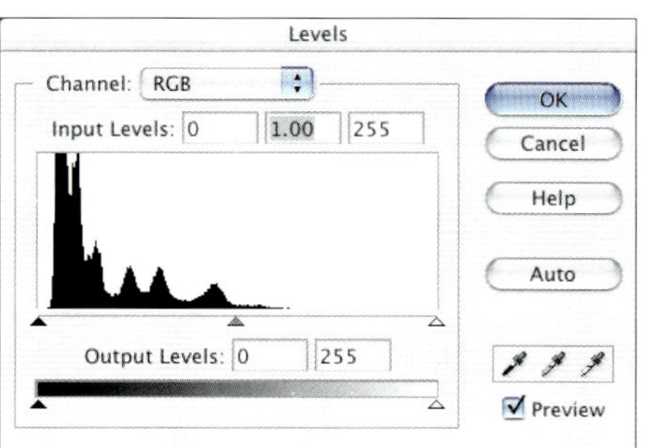

1 A better way to dodge colored images is to use *Levels*. Drag the layer you've been experimenting on into the trash, then duplicate the background layer again. The selection should still be active; use *View* > *Selection* or {Apple-H} to check. If it's not there, use *Select* > *Load Selection* to bring it back. Go to *Enhance* > *Adjust Brightness/Contrast* > *Levels* or {Apple-L}. You see the histogram of the area that you have selected.

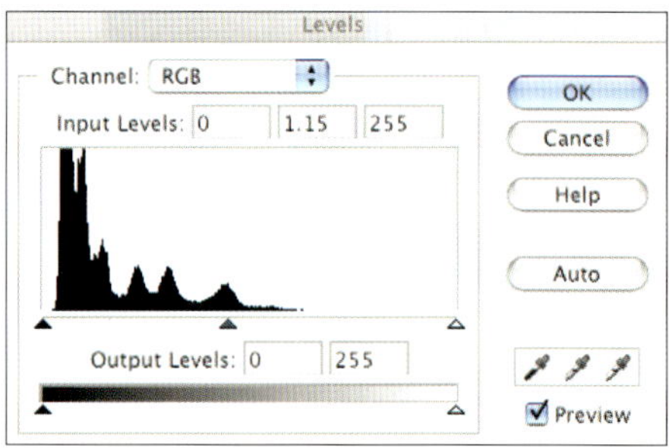

2 Move the gray (middle) *Input Level* slider to the left, observing the effect closely. The selected area becomes lighter, but the color isn't altered. When you are satisfied with the result, click *OK*. Compare the altered image with the original by clicking on and off the *Eyeball* for the layer you have been working on. If necessary, you can use the *History* tab to backtrack, or you can throw away the duplicate layer and try again.

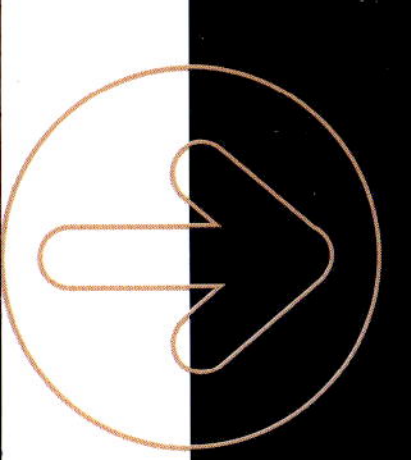

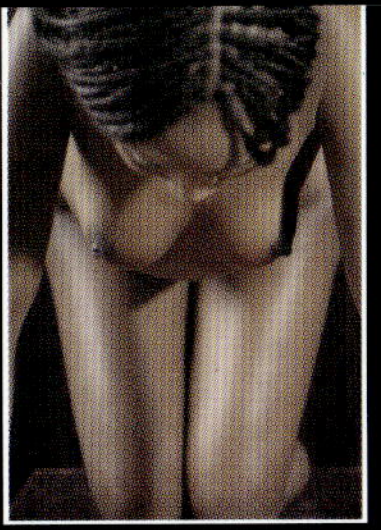

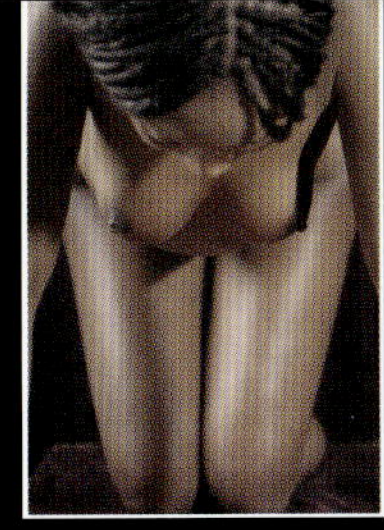

Traditional photographers will be familiar with the techniques of dodging and burning. Adobe Photoshop Elements has a range of tools that emulate these methods of selectively darkening or lightening parts of an image.

TIP

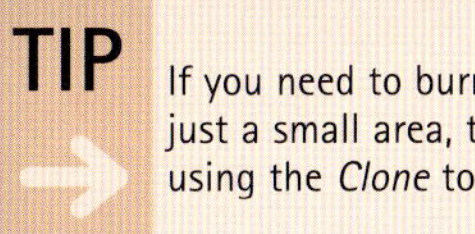

If you need to burn just a small area, try using the *Clone* tool.

THE BURN TOOL

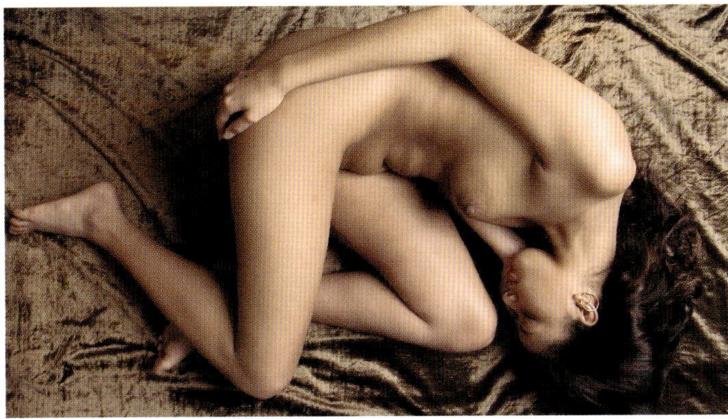

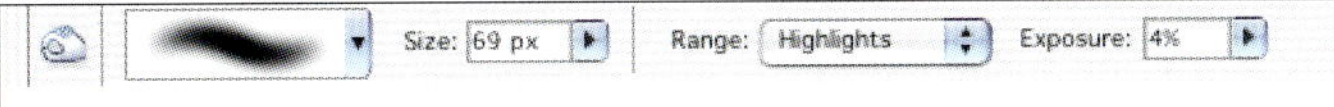

1 The *Burn* tool works well on black-and-white images, but shifts colors toward black when darkening. To lose the highlight on the model's shoulder, use the *Magic Wand* to select the area, and *Feather* it. Now select the *Burn* tool. Choose a soft brush, select *Highlight* for the *Range*, and 4% for the *Exposure*.

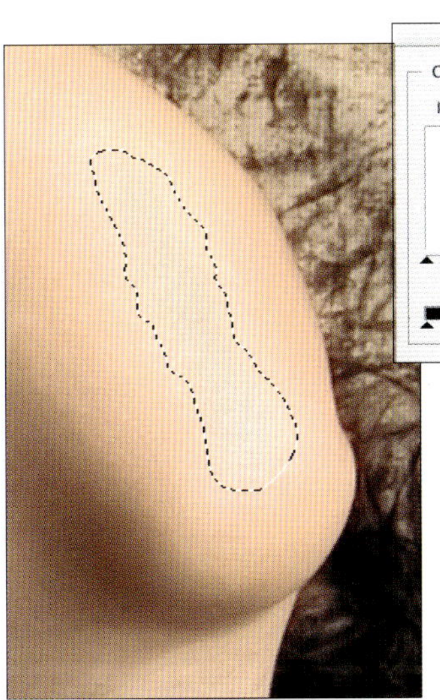

2 Paint in the selected area with the *Burn* tool. The area becomes blacker, rather than being altered to a darker version of the original color.

3 Now experiment with burning with *Levels*. Drag the layer you've been working on into the trash, and create a new duplicate layer. After checking that your selection is still active, go to *Enhance > Adjust Brightness/Contrast > Levels*. When the histogram is displayed, move the gray *Input Level* slider to the right. When you are satisfied with the result, click *OK*.

RECAP

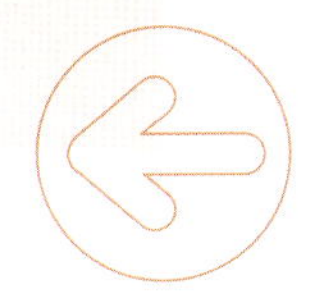

A Dodging

The *Dodge* tool works fine on black-and-white images, but to lighten dark areas of color images it's better to adjust *Levels*.

B Burning

The same applies to burning-in parts of images. *Levels* is the best way to burn-in color images, while the *Burn* tool works fine with black-and-white.

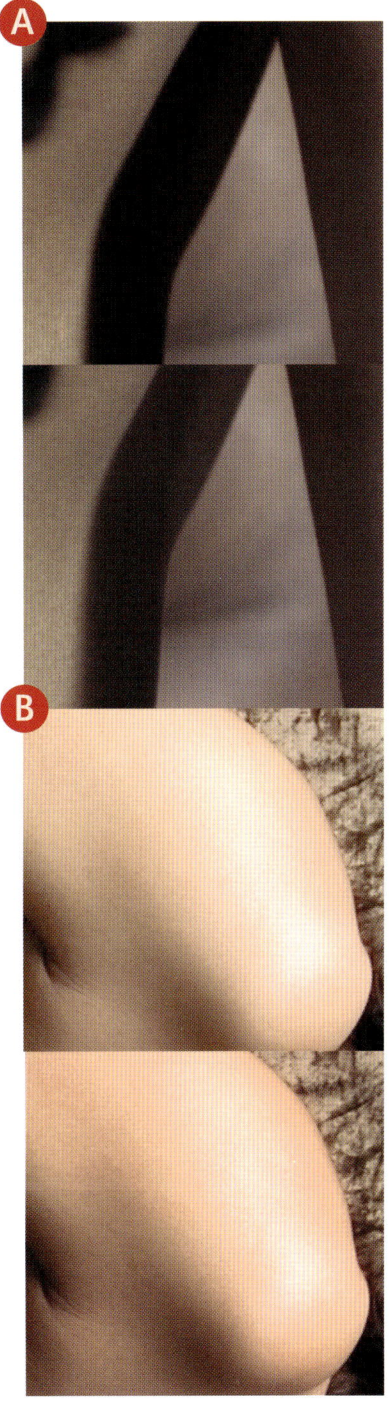

Sharpening

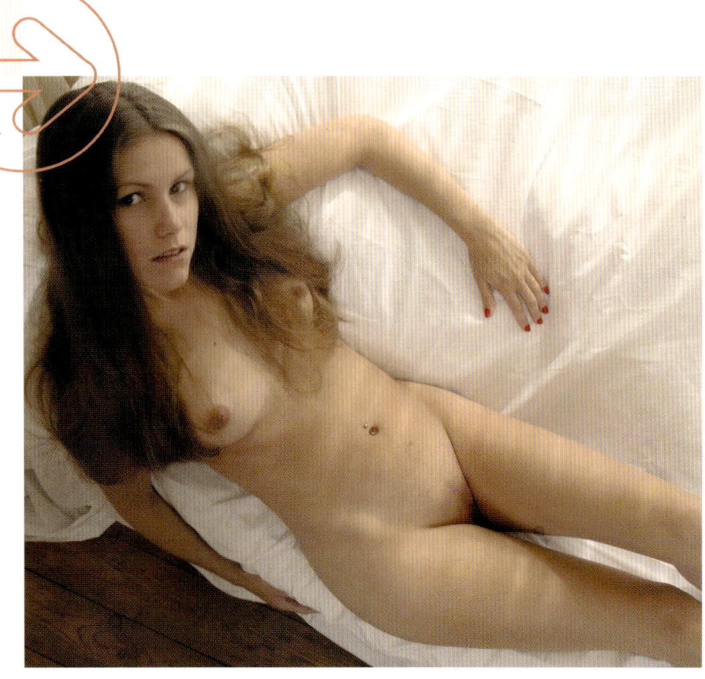

The four options for sharpening an image.

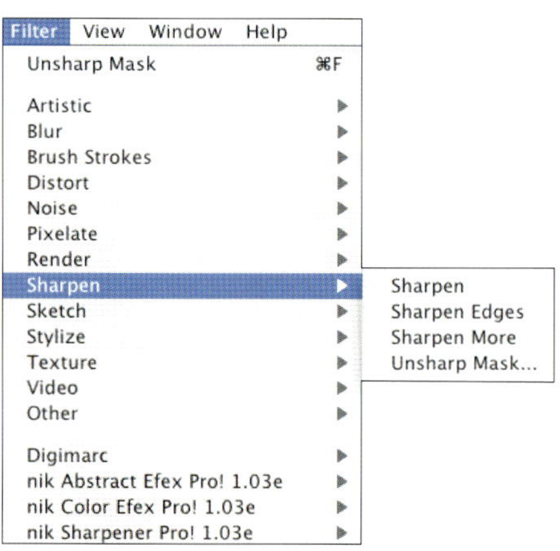

Top: the original image (left), and (right) the image with the Sharpen *filter applied once. This applies a preset amount of sharpening to the whole image, which can be repeated if it isn't enough. Bottom: the effect of the* Sharpen More *filter is stronger still. It detects and increases differences between pixels even in areas of the picture that appear flat, such as the pillow (left).*

Photoshop Elements offers a set of sharpening filters, accessible either through *Enhance > Quick Fix* or directly via the *Filter* menu. These sharpening filters can help to improve images that are slightly out of focus, or shot with a camera whose lens and imaging chip produce slightly "soft" images. The filters won't help photographs that are very out of focus. You should soon develop a feel for which images can be improved and which can't.

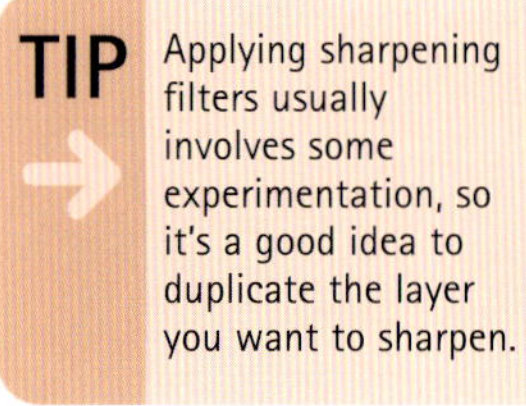

TIP Applying sharpening filters usually involves some experimentation, so it's a good idea to duplicate the layer you want to sharpen.

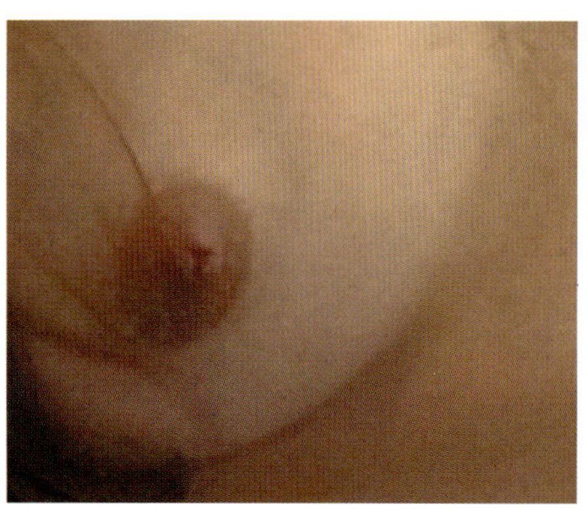

Unsharpened original (200%)

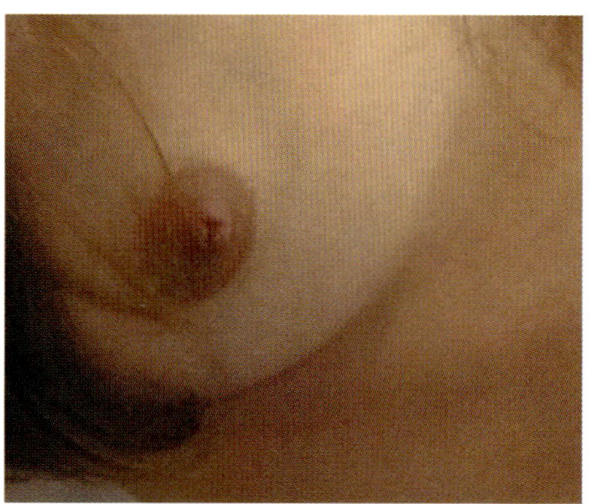

Sharpen *filter applied*

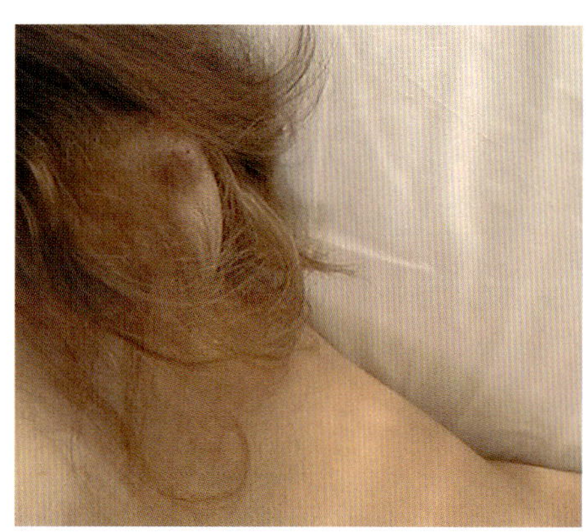

Sharpen More *filter applied (100%)*

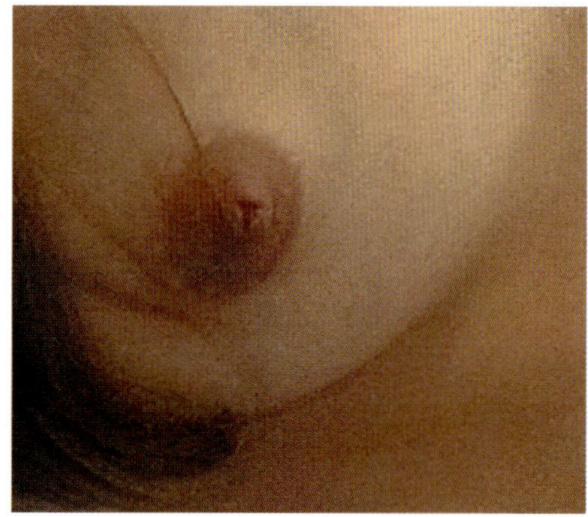

Sharpen More *filter applied (200%)*

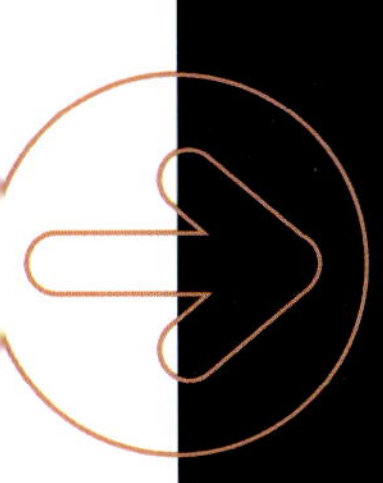

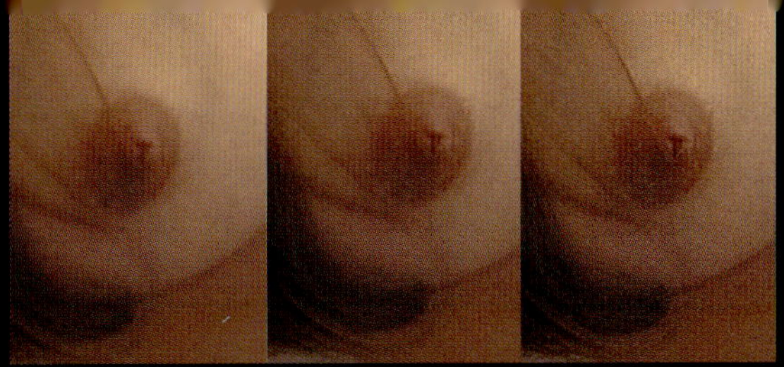

Sharpening filters do exactly as the name suggests: they sharpen an otherwise blurry image. The most powerful sharpening filter available is *Unsharp Mask*—this is used to bring definition to a low contrast image.

The most powerful and flexible of the filters is Unsharp Mask. *This offers you three sliders to control the effect of sharpening. The* Amount *slider (at 150% here) controls how much you sharpen the image (how much you increase the contrast between pixels). The* Radius *slider (1.0 here) controls how many pixels are sharpened. A low value sharpens only the edge pixels; a higher value sharpens more pixels around the edge. The* Threshold *slider (0 here) determines how different a pixel has to be from the pixels around it before it counts as an edge and is sharpened. In this example, with the* Threshold *set to 0, note the impact of* Unsharp Mask *on the flesh tones. To see the impact of the filter on the original image, uncheck and check the* Preview *checkbox.*

Raising the Threshold *to 4 reduces the noise in the flesh tones, but the edge of the model's jawline now seems overemphasized.*

*These values (*Amount *150%,* Radius *1.5, and* Threshold *9) seem to work best on screen, but it's wise to print the picture to make sure.*

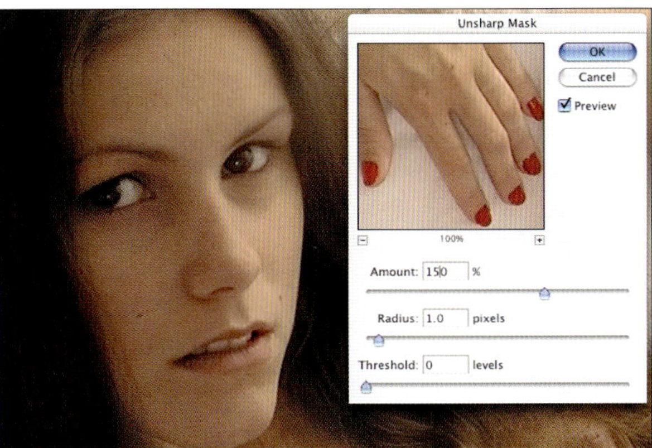

Threshold at 0

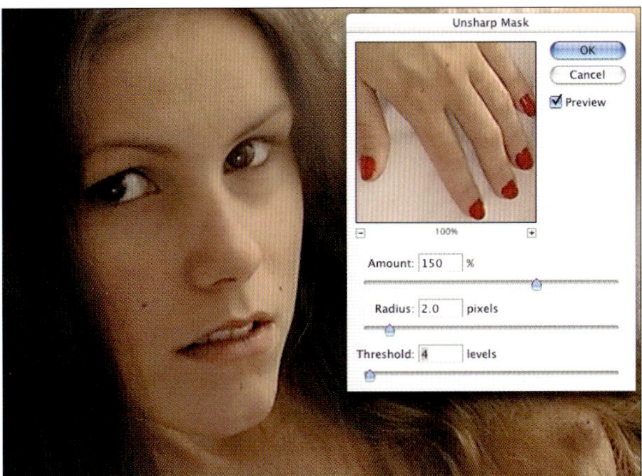

Threshold at 4

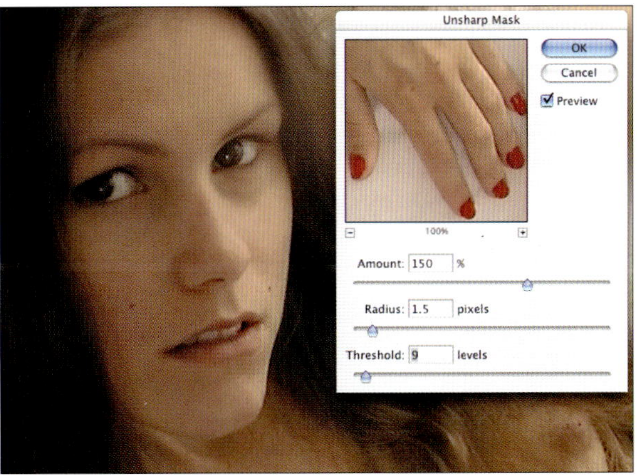

Threshold at 9

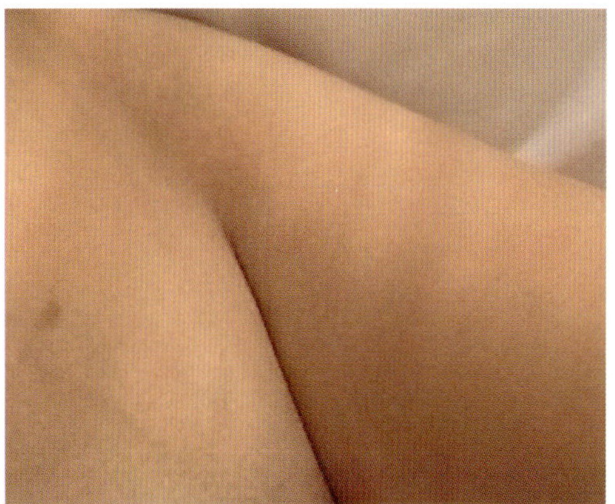

Sharpen Edges *works only on visible edges; that is, places in the image where there is a strong change in tone or brightness.*

FACT FILE

Sharpening filters

Sharpening filters work by increasing the contrast between adjacent pixels, wherever the filter detects an edge. ("Edge" here means any difference between two pixels that the computer "sees," even though it may not be visible to us.)

Sharpening should be the final stage of image correction, after you've reduced the noise in the picture and made any adjustments to levels, tone, or saturation, etc. The effect of sharpening an image may be very different on-screen from what you get if you print the image with the same sharpening applied.

Depth of field effects

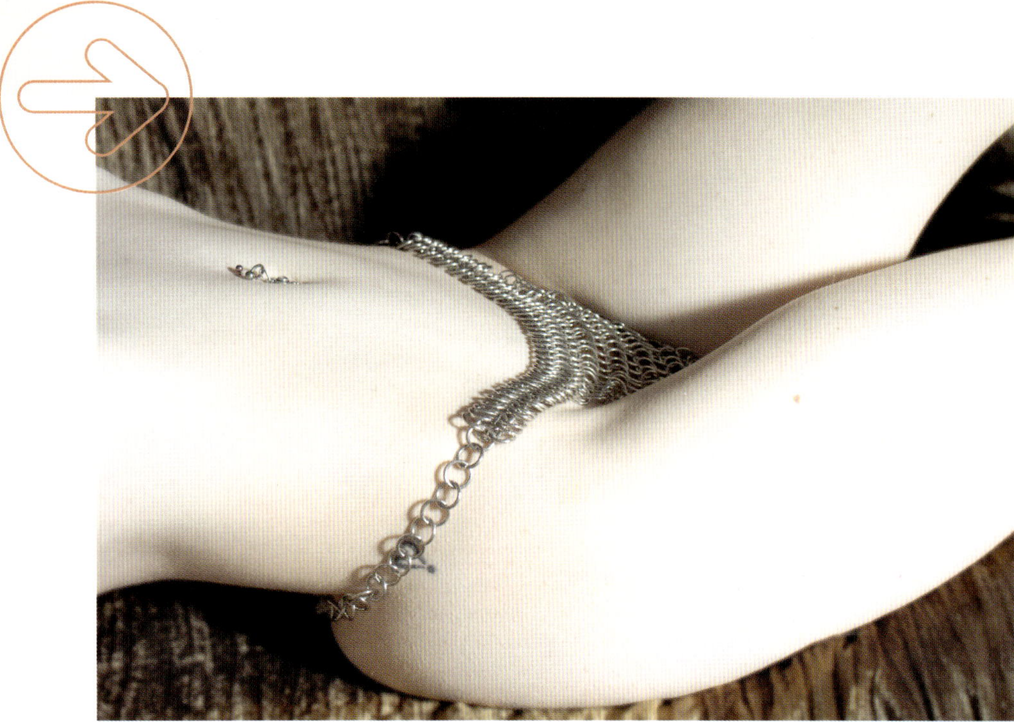

Elements' selection tools and *Blur* filters can be used to create the effect of shallow depth of field. This can be useful if your digital camera's zoom lens stops down as you zoom in, making "real" shallow depth of field difficult to achieve.

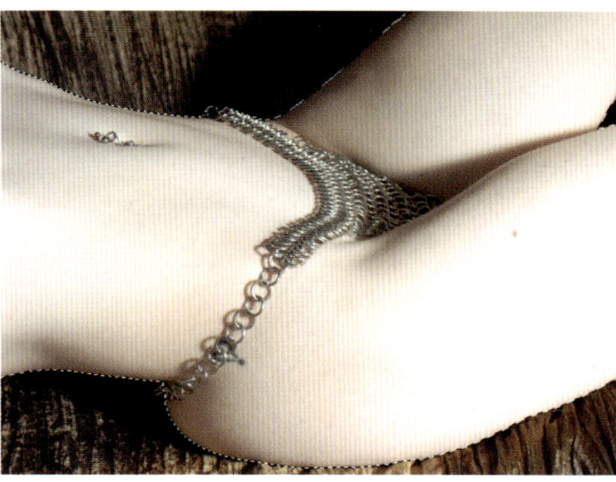

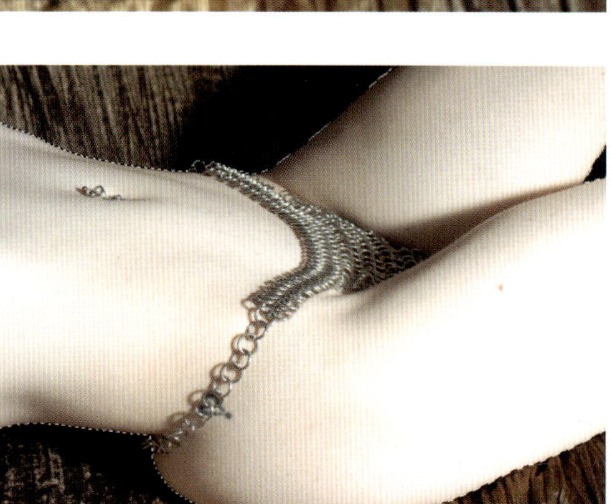

1 First duplicate either the file or the background layer. Then start by selecting the background. In this case, the easiest way is to select the model using the *Magic Wand* and tidy the selection up with the *Lasso*. Once you've selected the model, go to *Select* > *Inverse* to select the background.

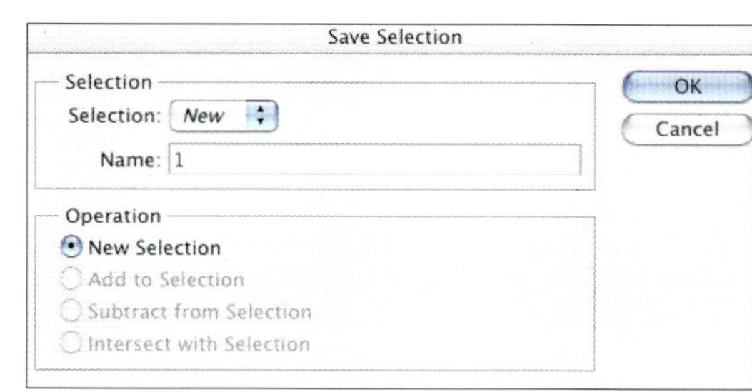

2 Now use *Select* > *Save Selection* to save your selection.

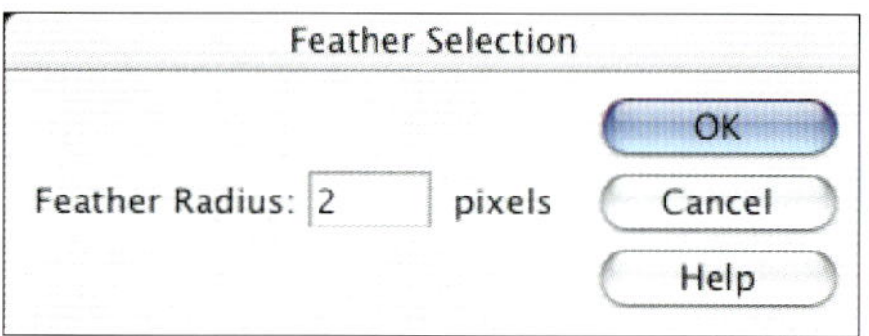

3 Next, feather the selection (*Select* > *Feather*). A 2-pixel *Feather Radius* should be enough to soften the edge between the background and the model.

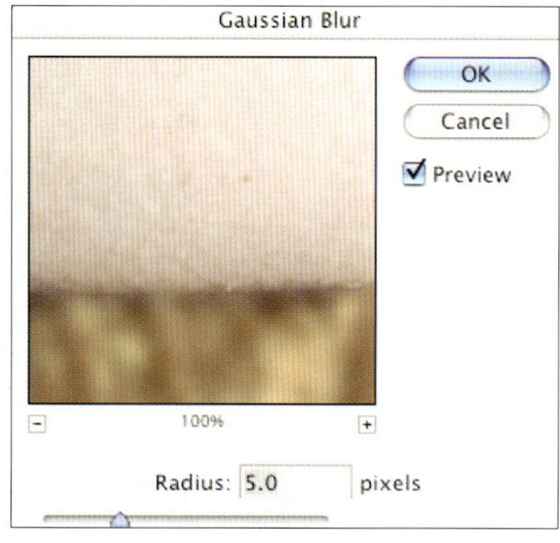

4 Apply *Gaussian Blur* to the selection (*Filter* > *Blur* > *Gaussian Blur*). A value of about 5.0 worked well with this image. When satisfied with the effect, click *OK*.

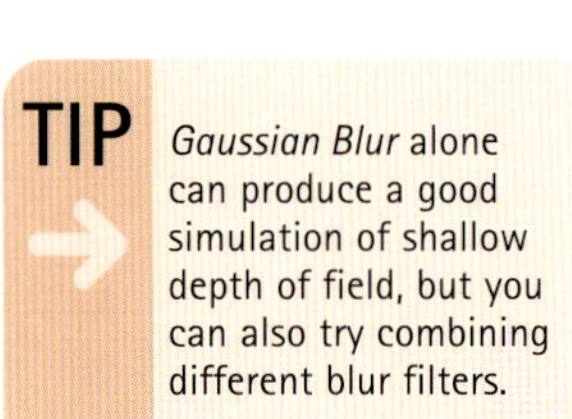

TIP *Gaussian Blur* alone can produce a good simulation of shallow depth of field, but you can also try combining different blur filters.

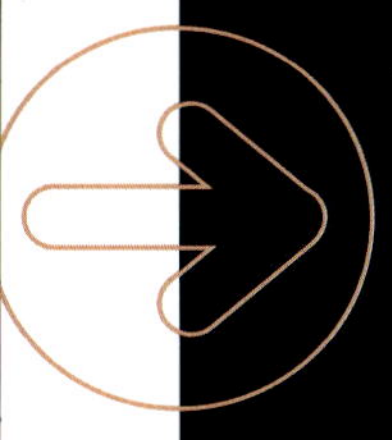

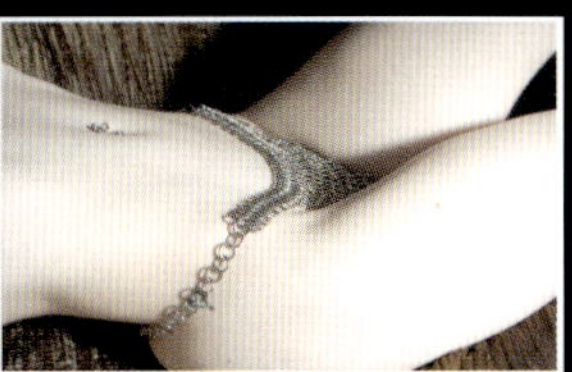

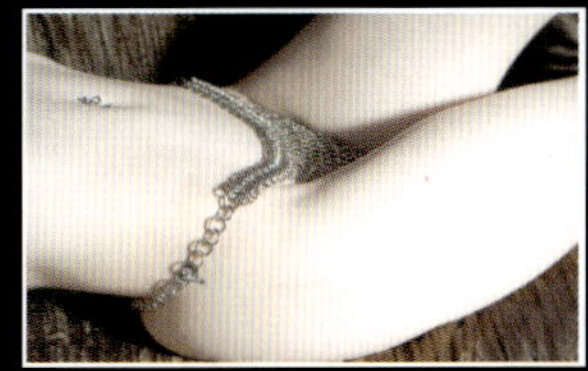

You can use selections and blur filters to increase the depth of field of your images. This enables you to create images in which the subject is in sharp focus while the background is blurred.

CREATING AN "OUT OF FOCUS" BACKGROUND

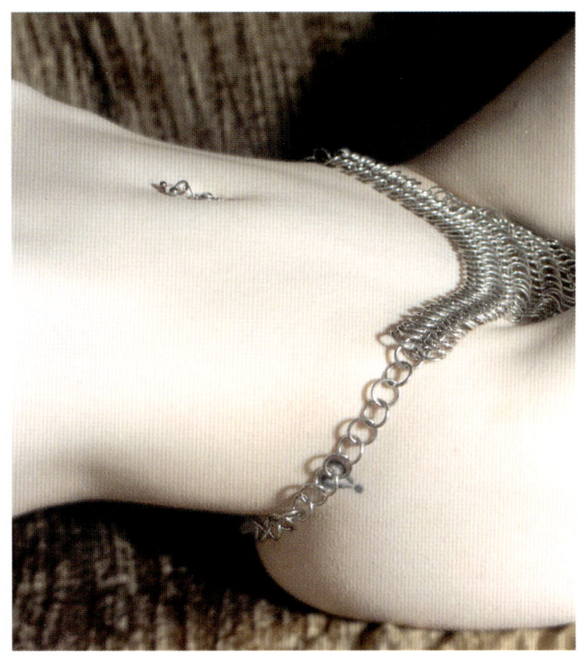

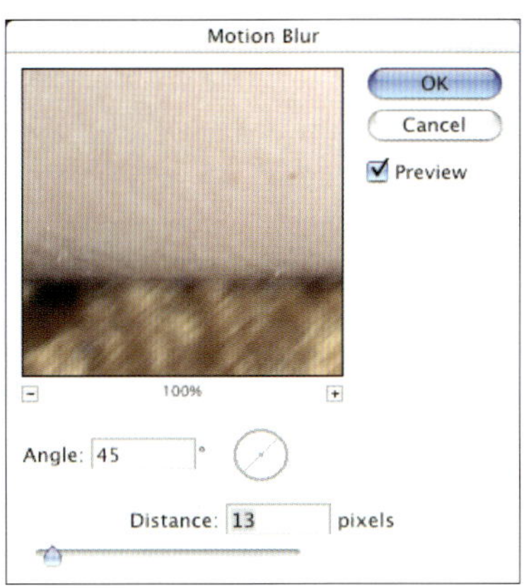

1 Go back to Step 4 and this time apply *Motion Blur* (*Filter > Blur > Motion Blur*). An *Angle* of 45° and *Distance* of 13 pixels diffuse the strong lines of the velvet covering of the chaise-longue without creating another equally distracting pattern.

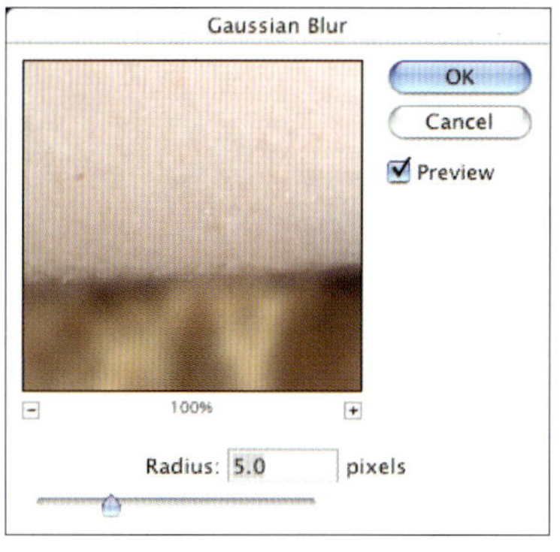

2 Now apply *Gaussian Blur* again. The effect is subtly different.

CREATING DEPTH OF FIELD IN THE FOREGROUND

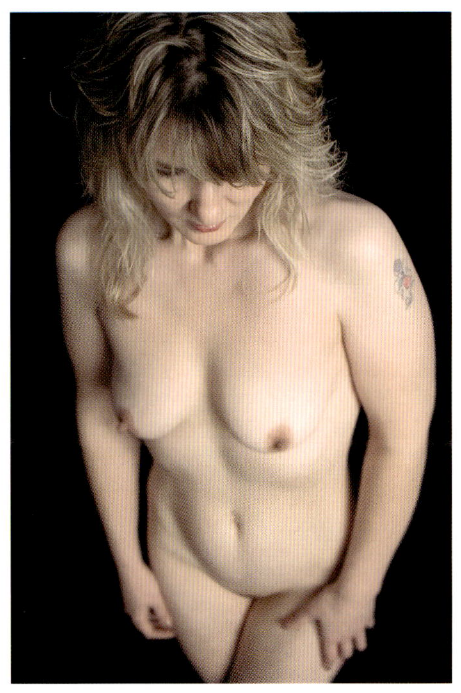

Feather: 16 px | Anti-aliased | Style: Normal | Width:

1 Here's a useful way to create a "graded" depth of field. We'll keep the top of the image in focus but make it softer toward the bottom. Click on the *Marquee* tool and set the *Feather* to around 16 pixels.

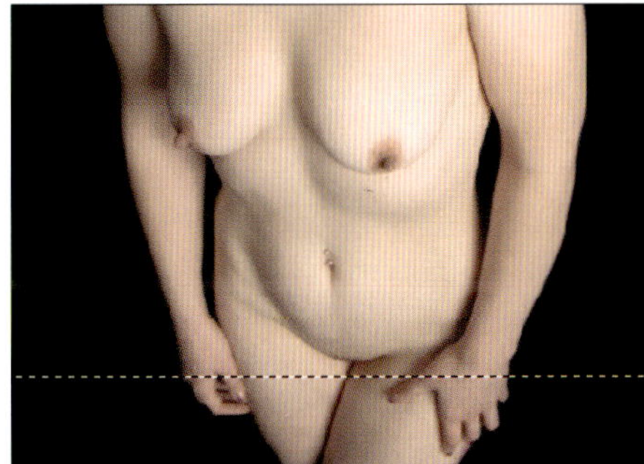

2 Now select a small section of the bottom of the image and apply a *Gaussian Blur* of 2.0.

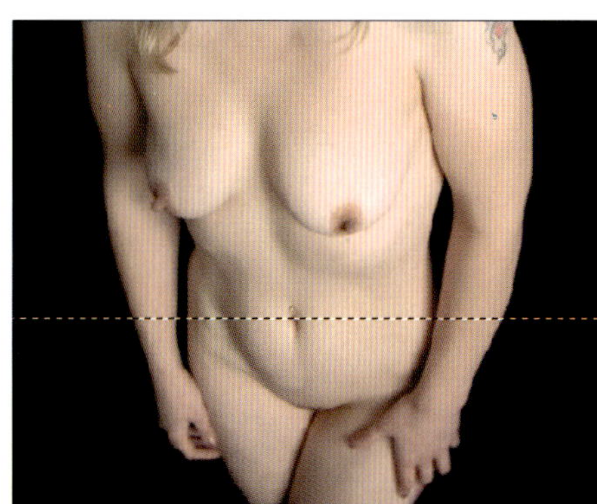

3 Select a larger area, again starting from the bottom of the image. Apply a *Gaussian Blur* of 2.0 to this larger area. Continue this process as far up the image as you require. Because each selection overlaps the previous ones, the blur effect is stronger at the bottom of the image than at the top.

Removing unwanted elements

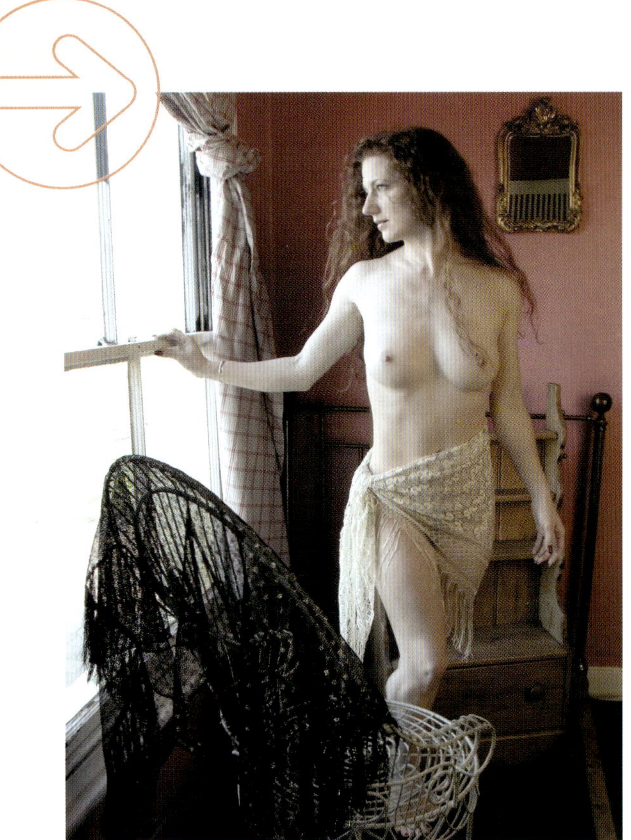

When working on location, it's easy for unwanted elements to end up in your pictures. The *Clone Stamp* tool is a way of removing such unwanted items, by copying a different part of the picture over them. In this example, a corner of the softbox on my lighting head can be seen reflected in the mirror behind the model. The top part of the softbox was in front of the wall, and was easy to fix. The bottom part was in front of a chairback, so I had a choice between trying to create the rest of the chairback, or removing that too. I chose to clone the struts of the chairback.

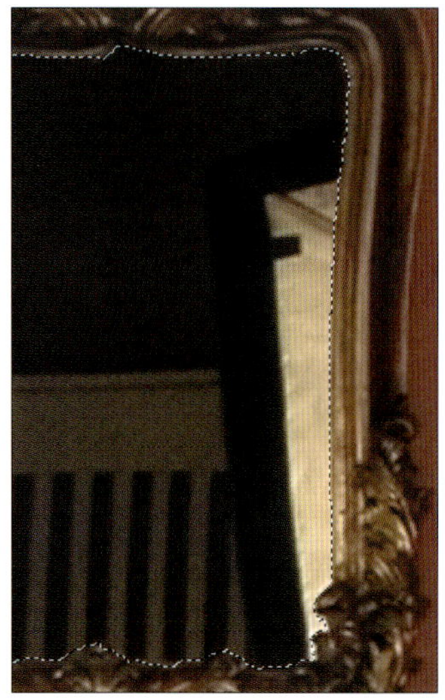

1 Zoom the image up to a scale where you have a detailed view of the area you are going to work on. Use the *Magic Wand* or the *Magnetic Lasso* to select the area that needs changing. This is a precaution against going too far with the *Clone* Stamp. Give the selection a 1-pixel *Feather* (*Select* > *Feather*) and save it.

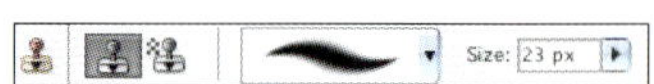

2 Create a new empty layer. You will make your alterations on this layer, and merge the layer with the background when you are satisfied with the changes. Click in the layer to make it active. Select the *Clone Stamp* tool, and choose a soft brush, then check *Aligned* and *Use all Layers*.

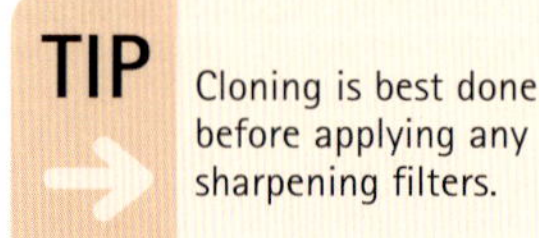

TIP Cloning is best done before applying any sharpening filters.

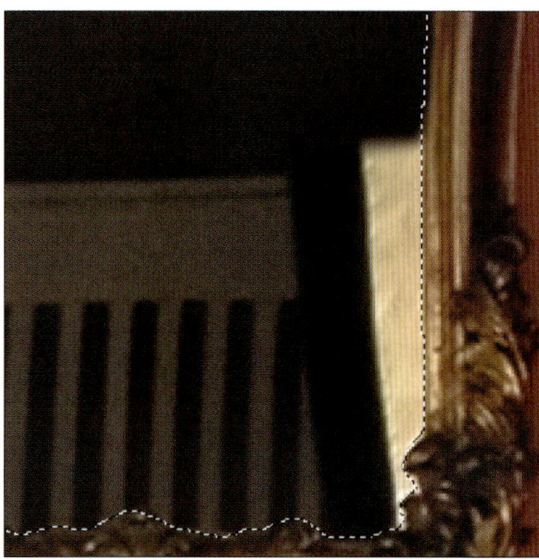

3 Alt-click in the area of flat color (the wall) just to the left of the light to set the sampling point, and paint over the light to replace it with the wall. Don't go down as far as the chairback. You can toggle the selection line from visible to invisible with **Apple-H (Ctrl-H in Windows)** to check that you have cloned the wall right up to the mirror's edge.

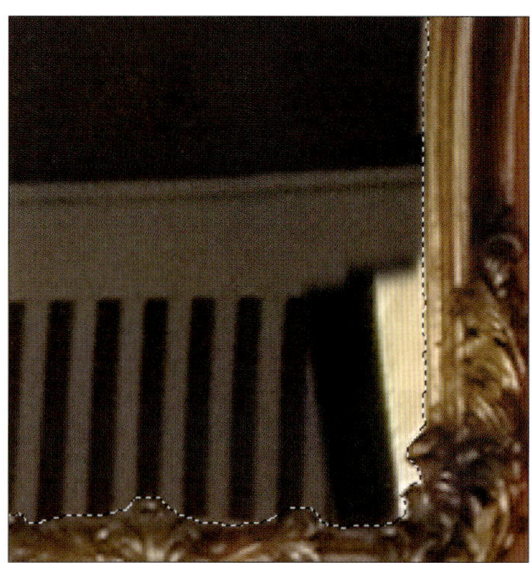

4 Now press *Caps Lock*. This will toggle the *Clone Stamp* cursor from the circle you have used so far to a pair of crosshairs, so you can see clearly where the center of the tool is. Alt-click exactly over the line that runs just below the top of the chairback, and paint with the crosshairs so that you continue the line on its correct alignment across to the edge of the mirror.

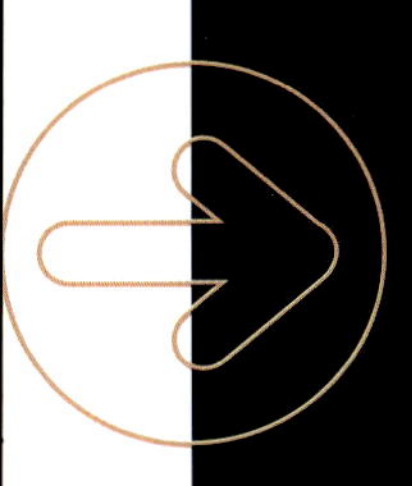

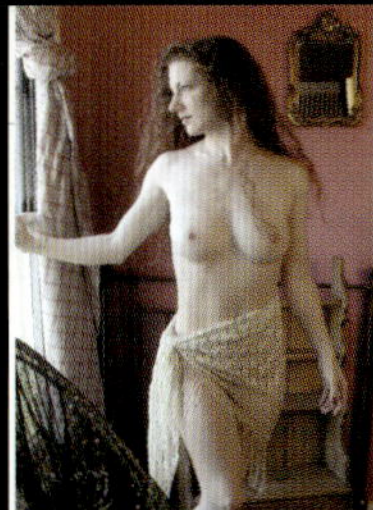

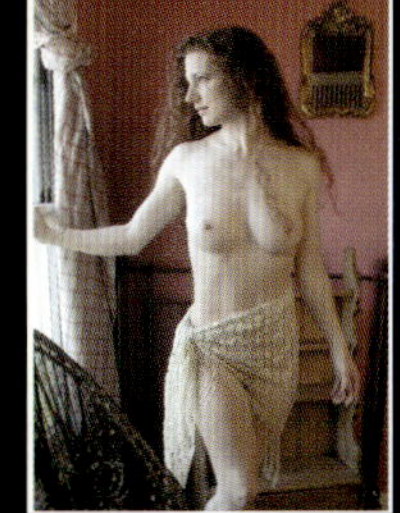

You can achieve the impossible with the *Clone Stamp*. This powerful mainstay of the digital world enables you to remove unwanted elements from photographs. Alternatively you can also use the *Clone Stamp* to replicate parts of an image.

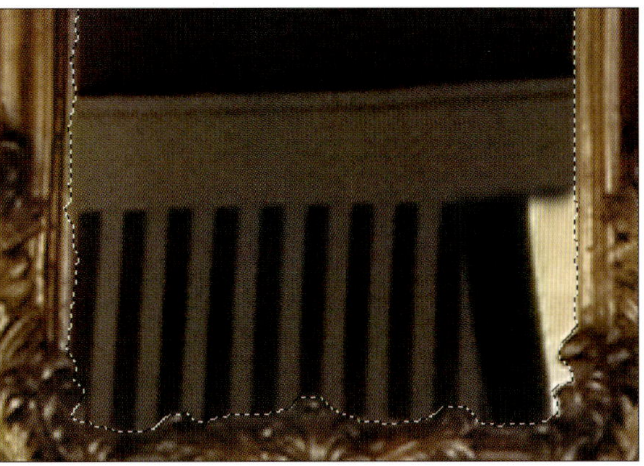

5 Continue to clone the top part of the chairback in this way until all that remains to be done is to add the extra struts.

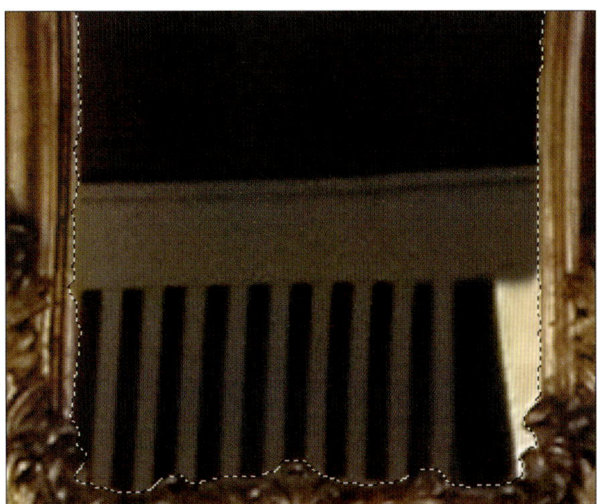

6 Now you need to create two new struts in the chair-back. Change the brush *Width* so that it's a little wider than the nearest complete strut. Alt-click low down in the nearest complete strut, and clone it over the strut that is partly hidden by the light. If part of the background spills over onto the upper part of the chairback, you can correct that by working down to it from above.

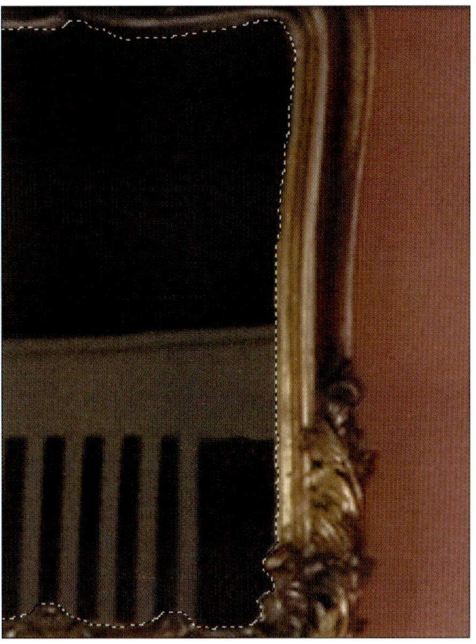

7 Next you need to clone in two more struts. This is easier if you clone out the remaining light in the bottom right-hand corner, Alt-clicking in the area above the chairback to get your sample. Clone the two final struts, taking care to space and angle them correctly. One will go right down to the bottom of the mirror frame; the other will disappear "behind" the frame in the bottom right corner. As you selected the space inside the mirror, this will happen automatically. The 1-pixel *Feather* you put on the selection should make it look natural. Finally, *Flatten* the image and save it.

RECAP

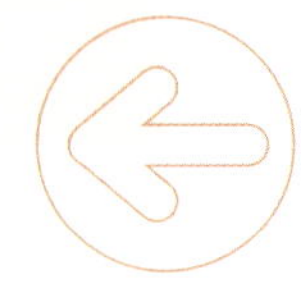

A Before
The original image contains the unwanted element of the corner of the softbox reflected in the mirror behind the model's head.

B After
The detail of the light is cloned out by using the *Clone* tool to copy struts of the chair that is also reflected in the mirror.

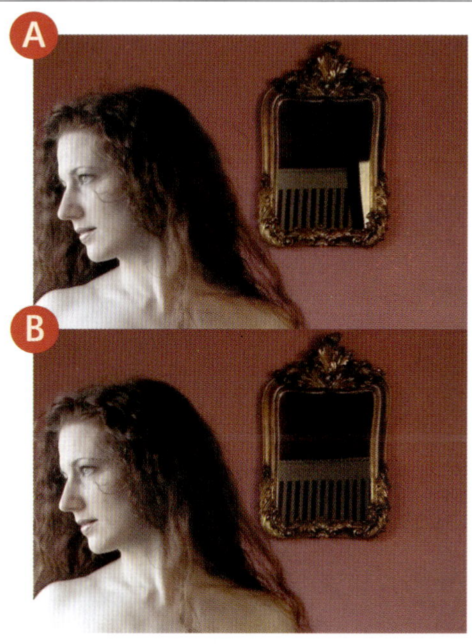

Correcting color

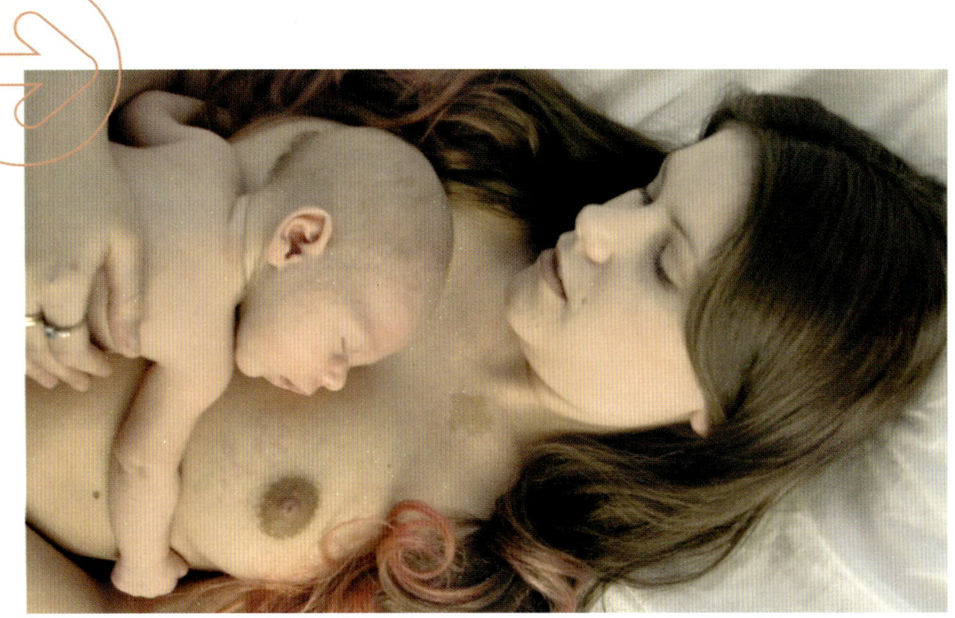

Elements provides a number of tools for fixing color casts (an overall shift of color affecting the whole of a picture) as well as for correcting color in parts of the picture. There are two ways to judge the effectiveness of color correction. You can look for what you know should be black, gray, and white areas in the image, and assess how well the color correction has rendered them as pure black, gray, and white without any other colors mixed in. Alternatively, you can look at the flesh tones in the image and decide how convincingly "real" they look. For nude photography, it's more important to get the flesh tones as you want them to be (which may not necessarily be "realistic") than to have the grayscale tones technically correct.

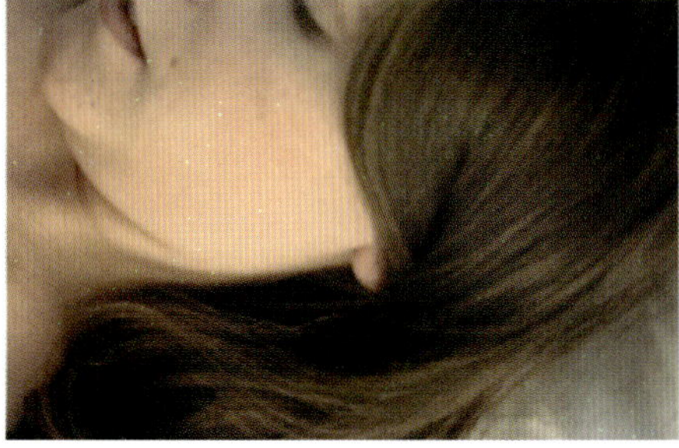

Uncorrected

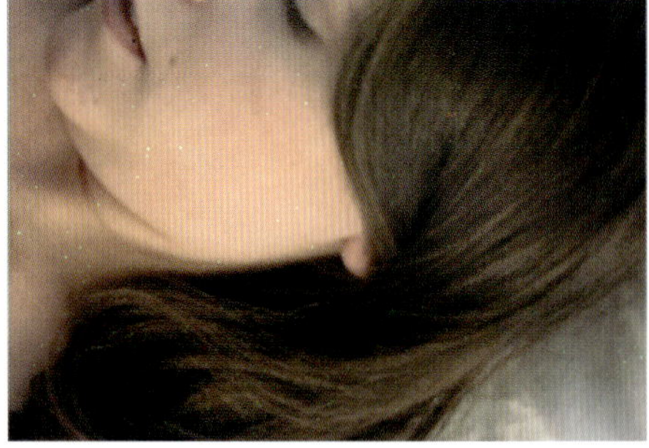

Auto corrected

1 The simplest tool for fixing color casts is *Enhance > Auto Color Correction*. The results are unpredictable: sometimes it works, sometimes it doesn't, but it takes only a moment to apply, so it's always worth trying. In this case the results are slightly too "pink."

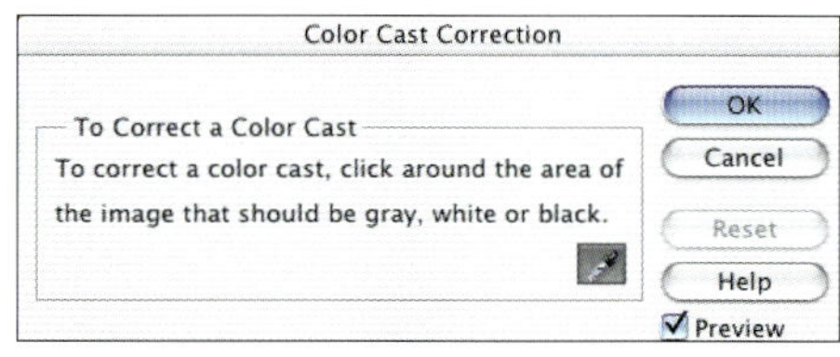

2 If you're not happy with the results of *Auto Color Correction*, try *Enhance > Adjust Color > Color Cast Correction*. Use the *Eyedropper* tool to click on an area of the image that is pure grayscale, and then adjust the image accordingly. This tool enables you to try out several different areas to find the one you prefer.

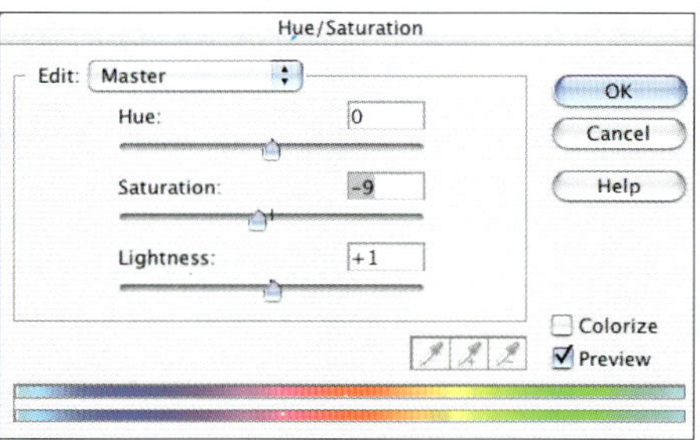

3 A more satisfactory tool is *Enhance > Adjust Color > Hue/Saturation*. You can adjust hue (color); saturation (intensity); and lightness (the amount of white mixed with the color) for the whole of the image; or, if you select part of the image, just for that part. You can toggle the *Preview* box to compare the original version of the image with the changes you want to make. Small changes in the numbers can make a great difference to the image.

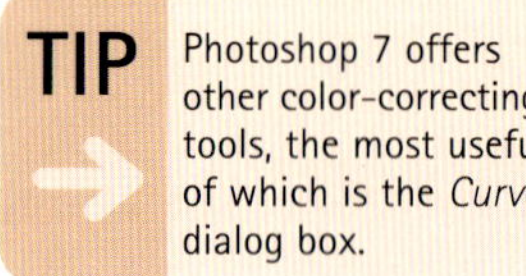

TIP Photoshop 7 offers other color-correcting tools, the most useful of which is the *Curves* dialog box.

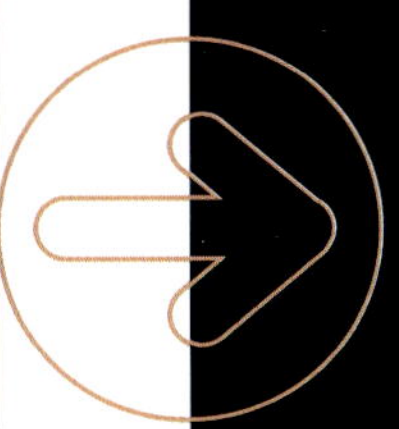

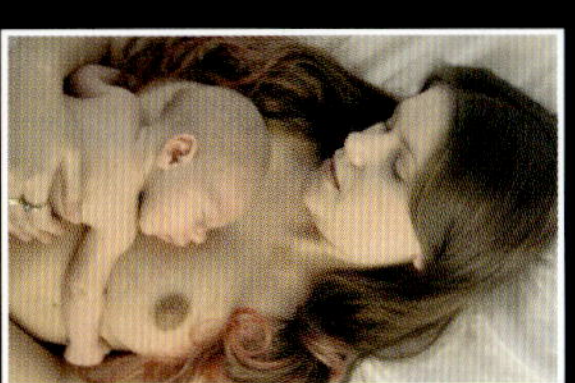

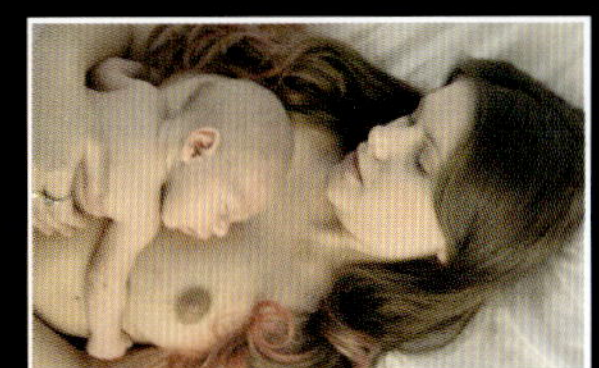

Adobe Photoshop Elements' auto correction tools make a good job of color correction at the click of a button. For more subtle corrections, you may wish to use more customizable tools such as *Hue/Saturation* or *Replace Color*.

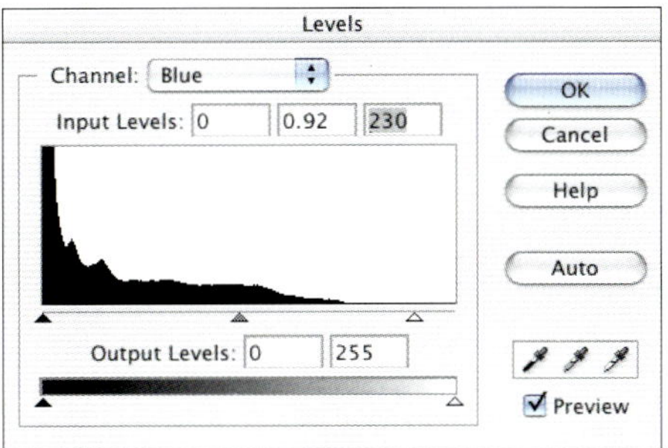

4 You can also use *Enhance > Adjust Brightness/Contrast > Levels* to make color corrections. Instead of using the composite RGB channel, you can select the color channels one at a time, and adjust them individually. Toggle the *Preview* box to see the effect of the changes you are making.

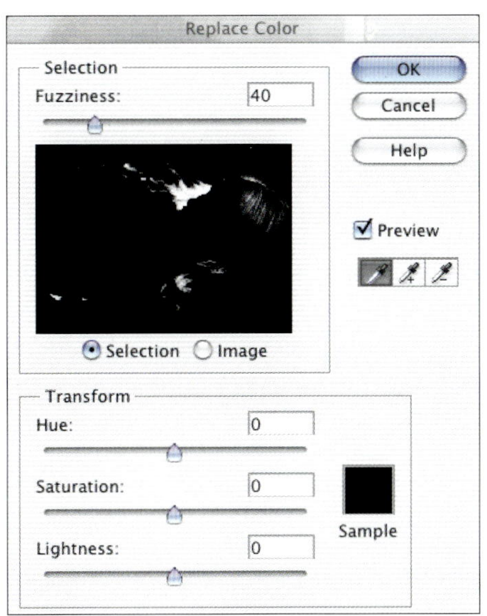

5 Another option is to go back to the original image, then select *Enhance > Adjust Color > Replace Color*. This works by enabling you to build up the range of colors you want to change by selecting them with an eyedropper tool. In this example we'll select the model and her baby, and then adjust their skintones, without altering any other colors.

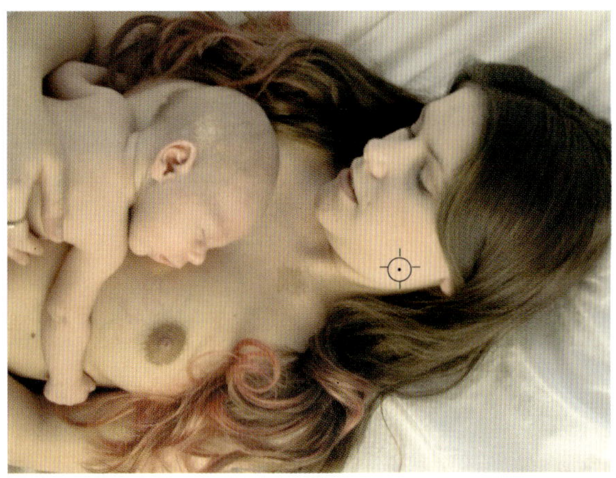

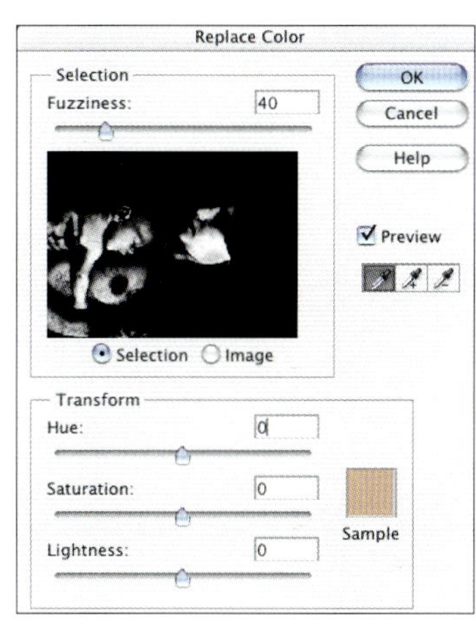

6 Click with the left-hand *Eyedropper* tool anywhere in the area you want to select.

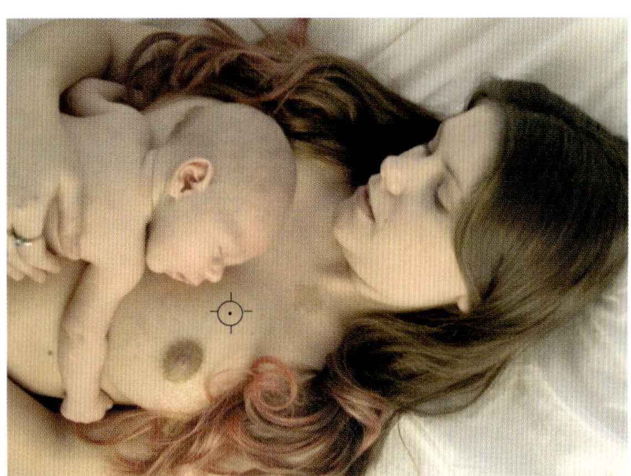

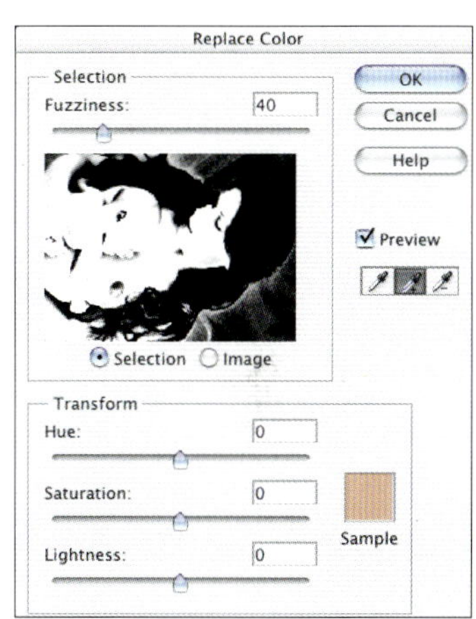

7 Now switch to the middle (*Add Color*) *Eyedropper*, and keep clicking in the area you want to select, clicking on different colors each time. The white area in the *Replace Color* window will grow.

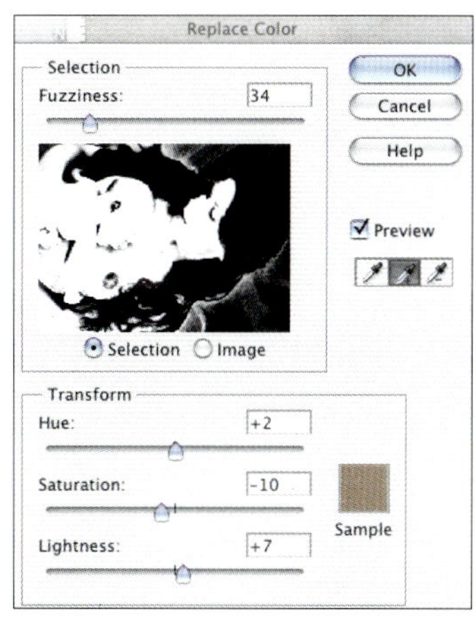

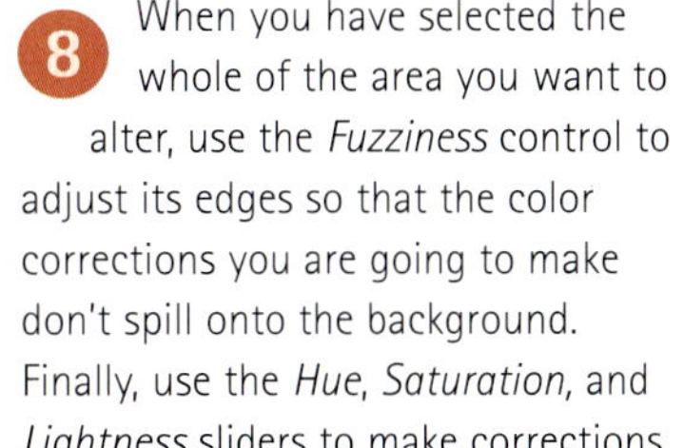

8 When you have selected the whole of the area you want to alter, use the *Fuzziness* control to adjust its edges so that the color corrections you are going to make don't spill onto the background. Finally, use the *Hue, Saturation,* and *Lightness* sliders to make corrections.

Filters and layers

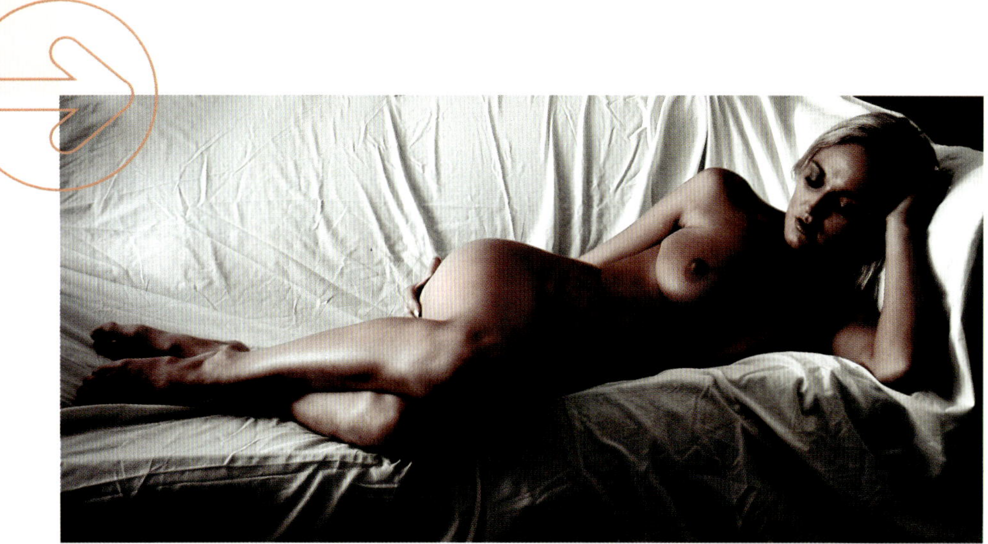

In this section and the following ones, we come to the core of digital manipulation of images. We will look at the use of layers and filters in Elements and at ways of using and combining them to produce distinctive and original images.

These are the effects that can be applied to image layers (as opposed to type layers). To use them, you click on the effect you want, and then click Apply.

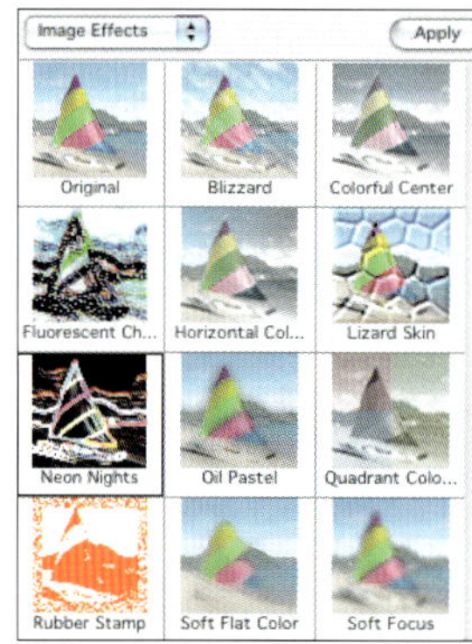

*I wanted to give this image an old-fashioned, grainy look, and reduce the color range to enhance the contrast. The final image was made up of five layers using three blends (*Multiply, Hard Light, *and* Pinlight*) to push up the contrast of the image and create the effect of a duotone. I also applied the* Noise *filter to simulate grain.*

USING LAYERS

Elements lets you place one or more images (or copies of the same image) on top of another, then adjust the upper layers so that they become partly transparent, enabling the lower layer(s) to be partly visible. Adjustments are achieved either by varying the opacity of the upper layers (that is, by making all the pixels in the upper layer become partly and equally transparent) or by changing the blend mode (that is, the way the pixels in one layer interact with those of the layer(s) beneath it).

USING FILTERS

Filters transform the layer or selection that you apply them to. They include ones that enable you to make the layer or selection look blurred, give it the texture of canvas, or make it look as if it were drawn with charcoal.

Before looking at layers and filters in more detail, let's take a brief look at Elements Effects. If you check *Windows > Shortcuts* you'll see a series of tabs at the right-hand end of the *Shortcuts* window; one of these is *Effects.*

These effects are filters with preset settings; preset combinations of more than one filter; or combinations of such filters with blended layers. You can apply them to an image, but you can't adjust them. I think they have two drawbacks: none seem to produce attractive results when used with images of the nude; and the pictures they create inevitably look very similar to those produced by other photographers using the same effects.

The skillful application of filters and layers can make your images unique, so try experimenting with your own combinations.

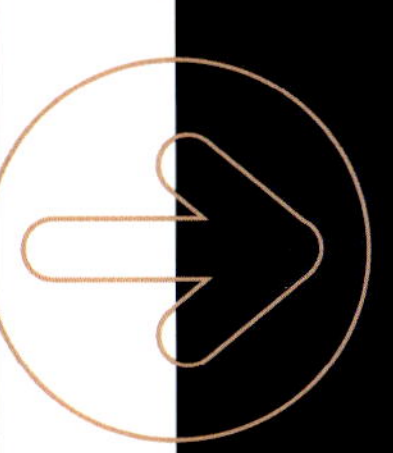

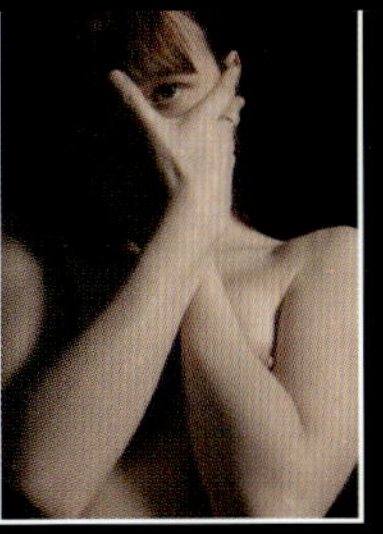

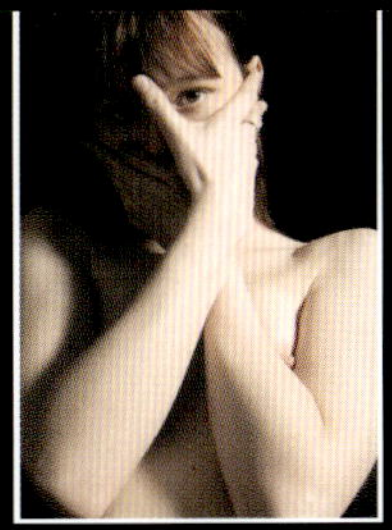

Think of layers as digital tracing paper, enabling you to place one or more images on top of each other with varying degrees of transparency. Using layers, you can control and combine selected areas without affecting others.

TIP

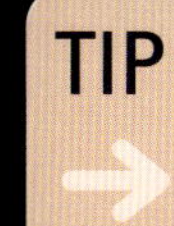

Some blend modes produce overblown results at full *Opacity*. Try lowering it before you dismiss them.

LAYERS FOR CORRECTION

Blended layers can be a useful way of correcting some images. First we'll look at the *Screen* blend mode as a way of retrieving a flat and underexposed image by improving the contrast.

1 As always, work on a copy of the original file. Duplicate the background layer by going to *Layer > **Duplicate Layer***, or by dragging the background layer onto the *Create a New Layer* icon at the bottom of the *Layers* window. Select the top layer ("Background copy"). Set the blend mode for this layer to *Screen*.

2 From the *More* drop-down menu in the *Layers* window, select *Flatten Image*. Then save the file.

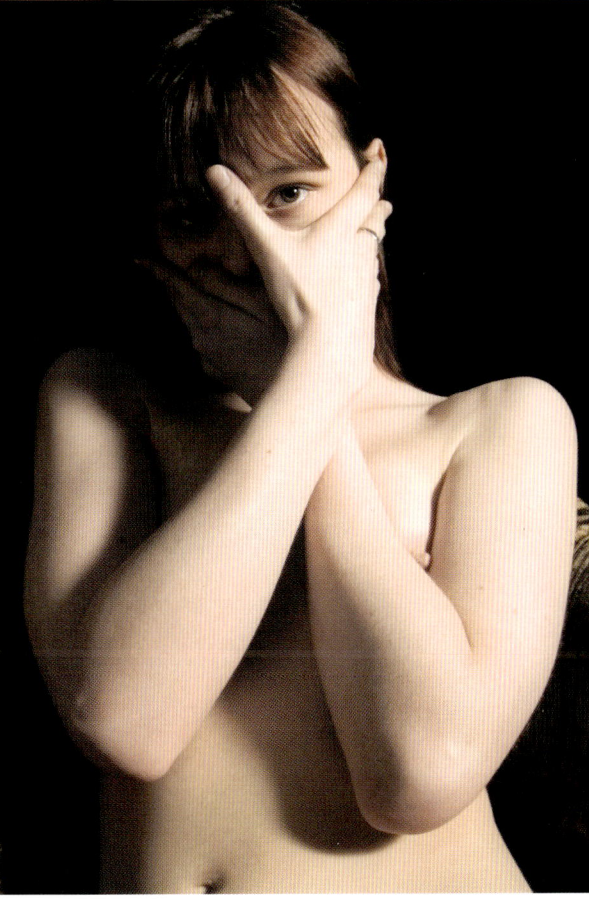

Next we'll look at the *Soft Light* blend mode as a way of intensifying color.

1 This image could benefit from increasing the saturation of the background without altering the model's skin tones. After duplicating the layer, set the blend mode on the top layer to *Soft Light*. This has more effect on saturated colors than unsaturated, so only slightly affects skin tones. By way of experiment, try varying the *Opacity* of the upper layer.

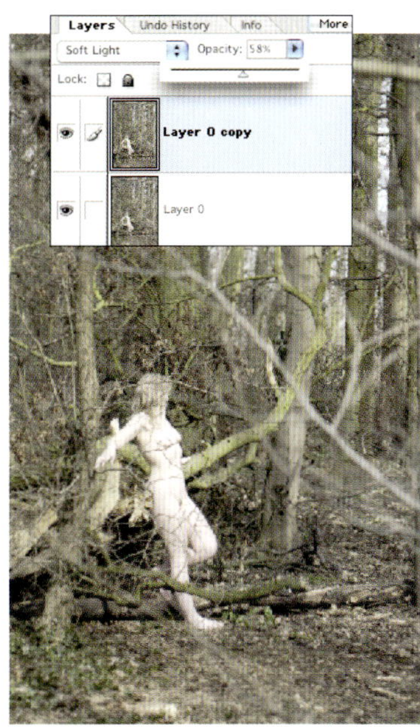

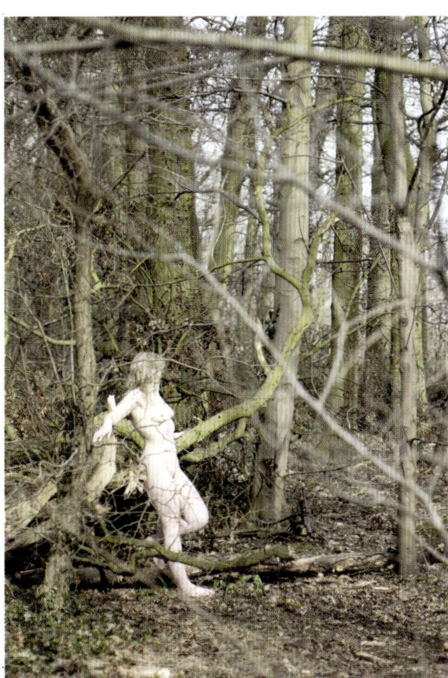

2 When you're satisfied with the *Opacity* of the blend, *Flatten* the image and save the file.

Filters and layers

EXPERIMENTING WITH FILTERS

The quickest way to get to know what the filters in Elements can do for your photography is to try them all out. Some filters take a while to render, so, if you are experimenting, try making a selection of a small part of your picture before you apply the filter. The filter will be applied only to the selected area, so you can assess it quickly.

THIRD-PARTY FILTERS

Many software companies produce extra filters to use with Elements and Photoshop 7. Try www.plugins.com/plugins/photoshop/ as a starting point. Most Photoshop plug-ins work with Elements as well. Some of the examples in the following pages use filters from Nikon's Color Efex Pro series.

ADJUSTMENT LAYERS

Many of the processes that we carry out on images involve what is sometimes referred to as "destructive" editing. This means that after you have carried out the process and saved and closed the file, you can't then reopen the file and reverse the steps to return the file to its original state. One example of this is adjusting levels. That is why there are so many reminders in this book about the importance of working on a copy of your original file and/or on a copy of the original layer. But in addition to image layers such as those we've worked with so far, Elements also enables us to carry out "non-destructive" editing through adjustment layers.

When you create an adjustment layer, it is applied to all the layers beneath it or just to the layer immediately beneath it, but those layers themselves aren't changed in any way. If you save the file (without flattening it) and then reopen it, the adjustment layer is still there and can be edited again if you decide you want to change it.

USING ADJUSTMENT LAYERS

Here is a straightforward example: this picture is more than a little underexposed, but I like the pose and lighting. I'm going to correct it and turn it into a monochrome image.

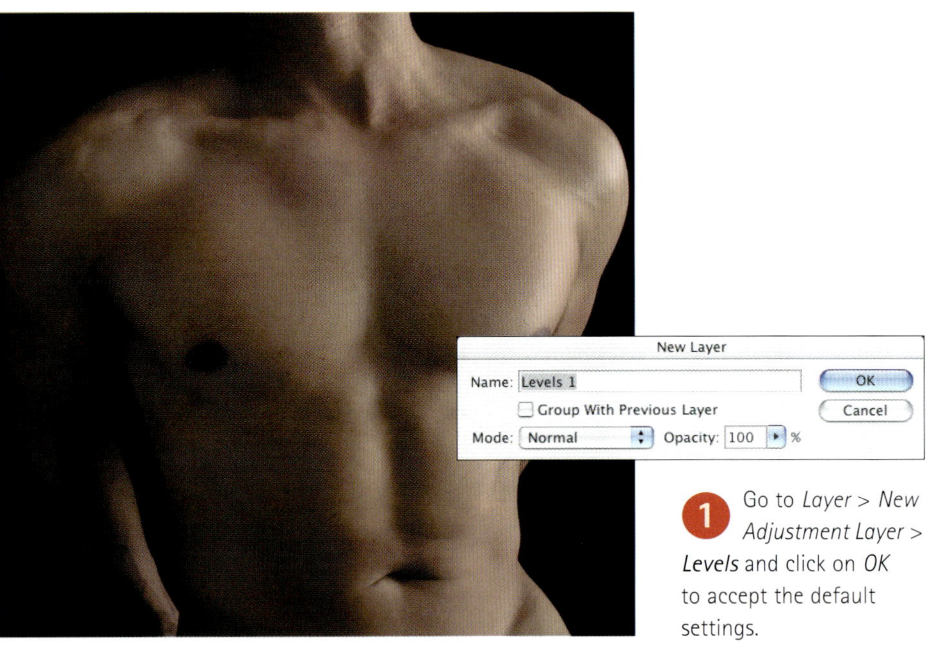

1 Go to *Layer > New Adjustment Layer > Levels* and click on *OK* to accept the default settings.

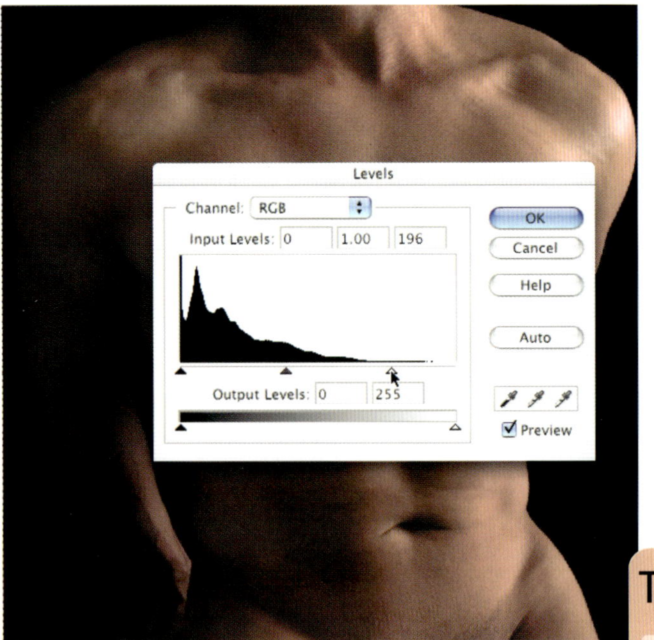

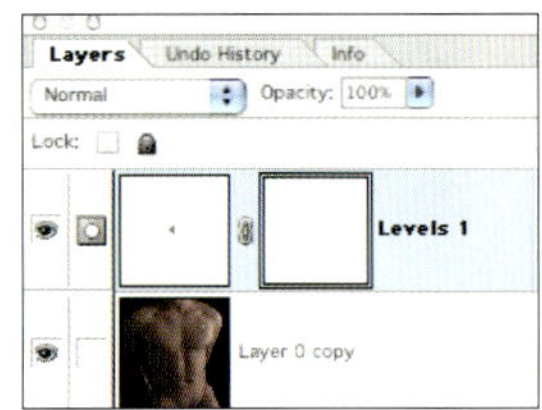

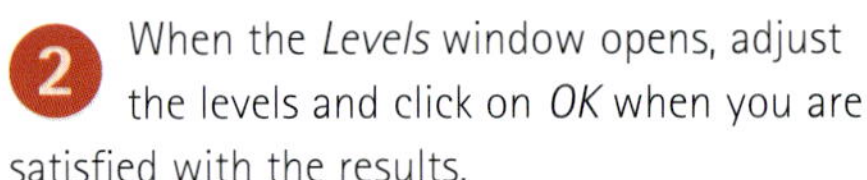

2 When the *Levels* window opens, adjust the levels and click on *OK* when you are satisfied with the results.

TIP The *Composite* blend is a useful way of improving the contrast in flat but correctly exposed or overexposed black-and-white images.

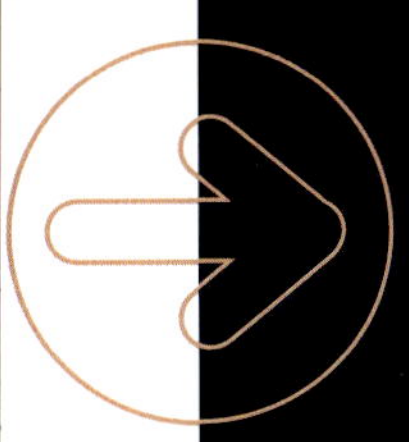

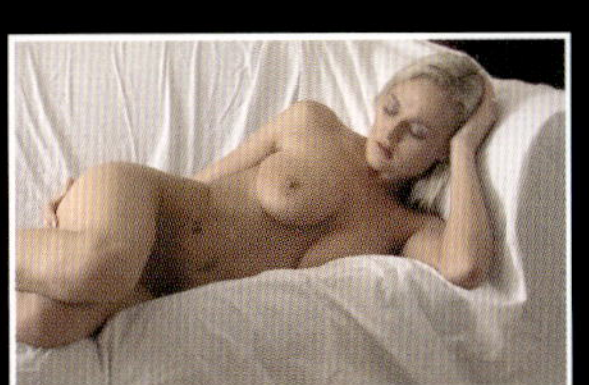

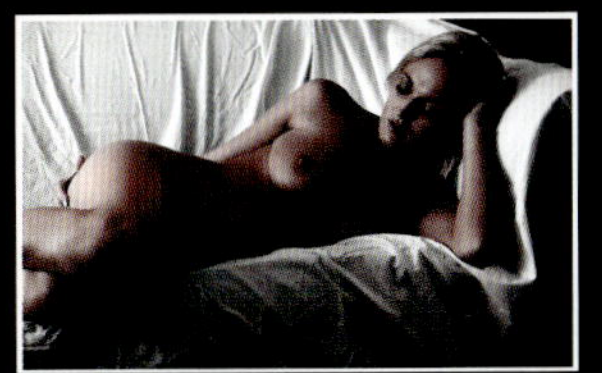

Adjustment layers interact with the layer or layers below to manipulate tones and colors or create interesting effects. Using adjustment layers makes it easy to add atmosphere or boost the contrast of an image.

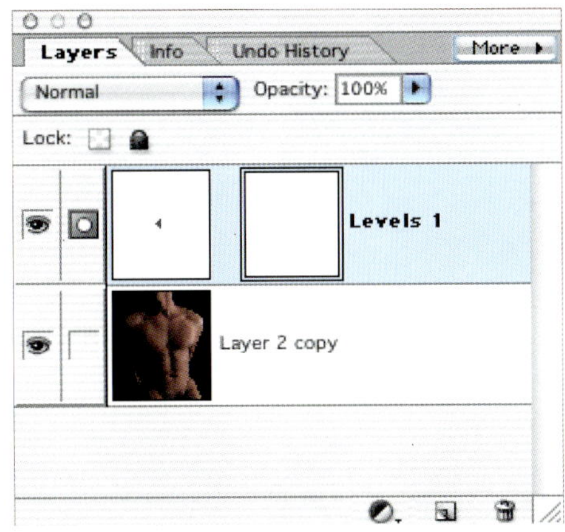

3 Note that a new layer, *Levels 1*, appears in the *Layers* window.

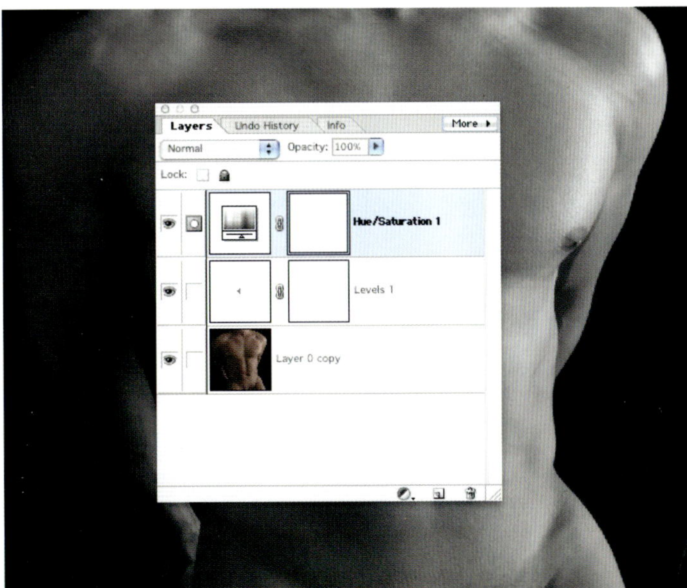

4 Now, if you double-click in the layers thumbnail for the layer *Levels 1* (that's the thumbnail above the thumbnail in the image layer), you'll see that when the *Levels* window opens, it shows the settings exactly as you left them, ready for you to adjust them again if you need to. If you save and close the file without flattening it and then reopen it, you'll be able to do the same thing. Now go to *Layer > New Adjustment Layer > Hue/Saturation*. Click *OK* to accept the default settings. In the *Hue/Saturation* window that opens, move the *Saturation* fader all the way to the left. Click *OK*. You can now go back and adjust the levels to give you an optimum monochrome image. Finally, when you are satisfied with the picture, you can *Flatten* it and save it. If you think you may want to do some more work on the image, you can save it without flattening.

RECAP

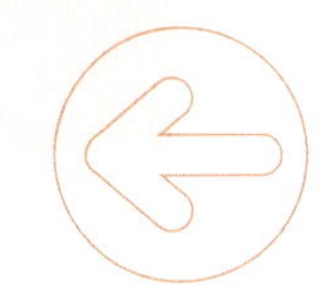

Ⓐ Multiple blends
The combined effect of three blends produces a grainy look and duotone effect.

Ⓑ Screen blend
The *Screen* blend mode can be used to boost the contrast of flat or underexposed images.

Ⓒ Soft Light blend
The *Soft Light* blend helps to enhance the saturation of colors.

Ⓓ Adjustment layers
You can use adjustment layers to correct underexposure and create atmospheric black-and-white images.

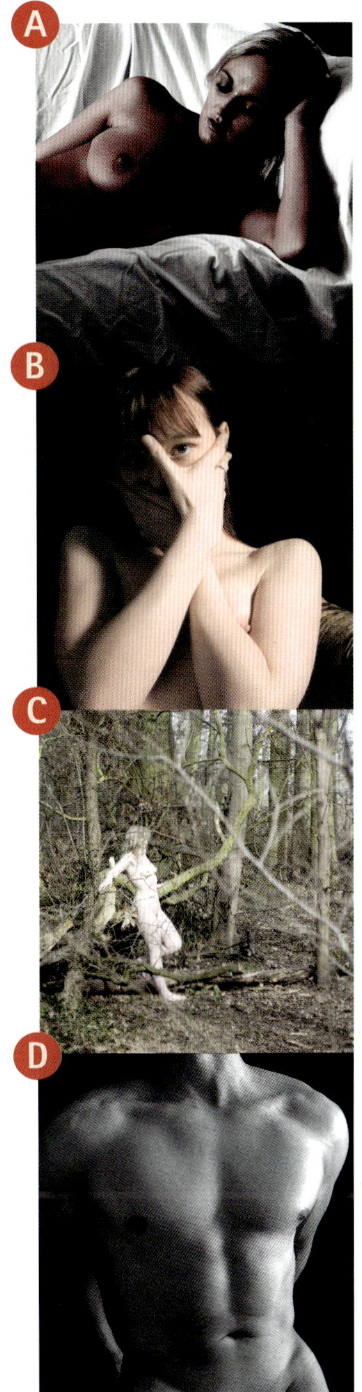

Backgrounds and filters

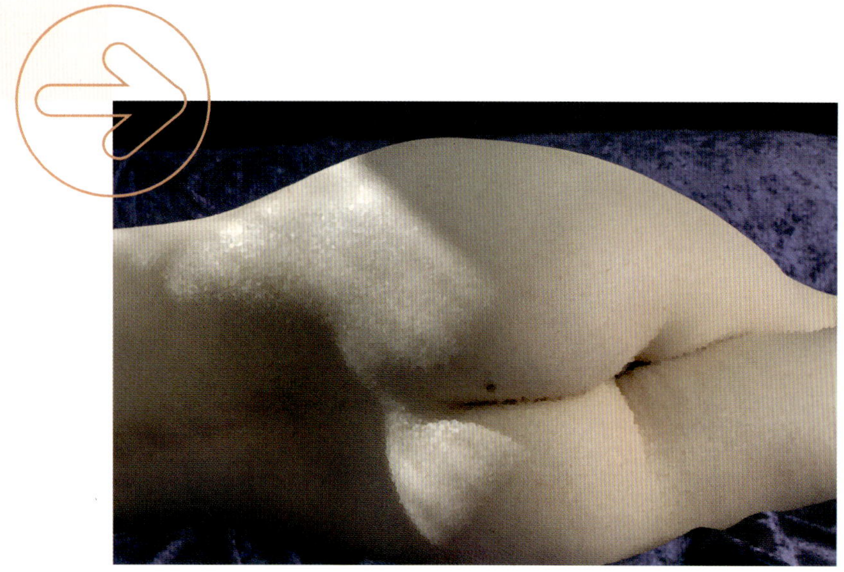

This section looks at the methods to use to apply a filter to the background but not the foreground, or different filters to each. Some filters create distracting effects on the edges of the areas they're applied to, and we look at how to handle these. We will also look at *Filter* > Pixelate > *Crystalize*, which adds a subtle, painterly effect to skin tones.

TIP Instead of using Elements filters "straight," explore ways of blending the filtered layer with another layer, or varying its opacity.

1 Make a selection of the foreground. It's often quicker to select the background and invert the selection. Where the edge of the foreground is difficult to see, as in the dark areas at the bottom of the image, use the *Lasso* tool with *Feather* set to 0. It's worth spending some time on this, because an accurate selection is important for the rest of the process.

2 Still with the foreground selected, go to *Layer* > *New* > *Layer* via *Cut*. The foreground appears in a new layer, with a corresponding hole in the background layer, and a narrow white edge around parts of the selection. Switch off the top (foreground) layer and duplicate the Background layer. Apply *Filter* > *Pixelate* > *Crystalize* to the new layer, with a setting of about 20. Then go to *Select* > *Deselect*. Use the *Clone Stamp* to extend the inner edge of the layer you created previously, so that the hole where the foreground used to be gets smaller. This ensures that the layers join smoothly.

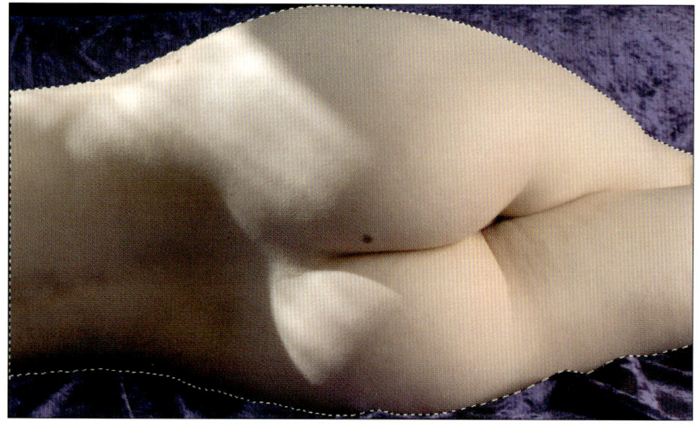

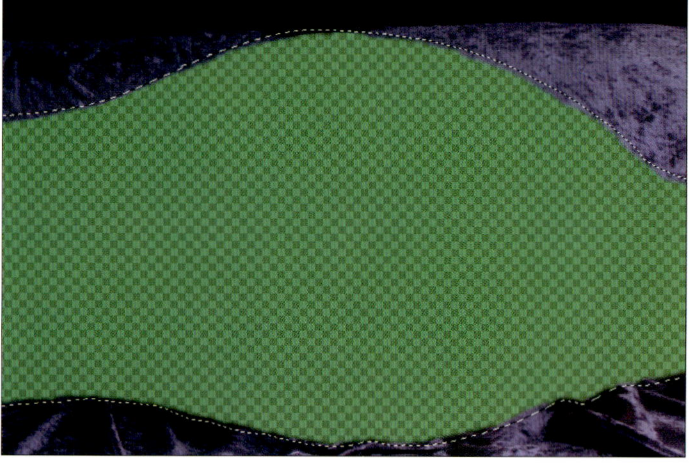

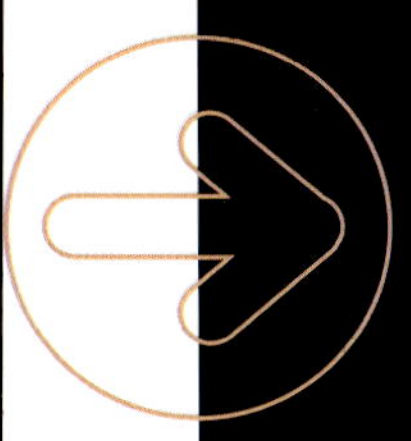

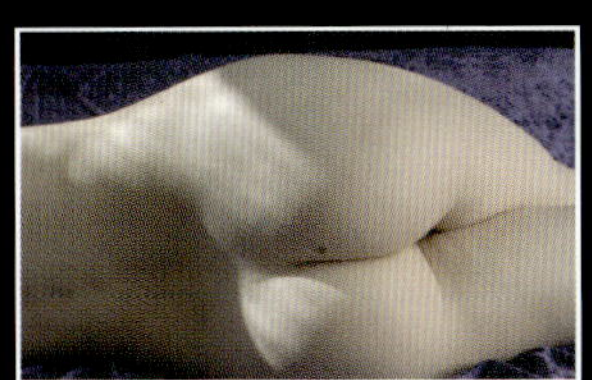

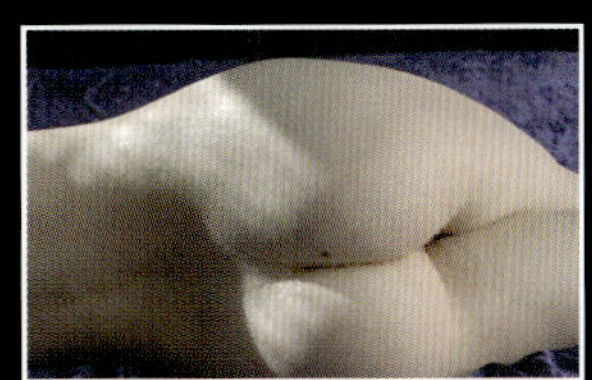

Isolating a subject from the background of an image increases your creative scope. Using Adobe Photoshop Elements, you can add effects such as the *Crystalize* filter to your backgrounds and give them a more painterly appearance.

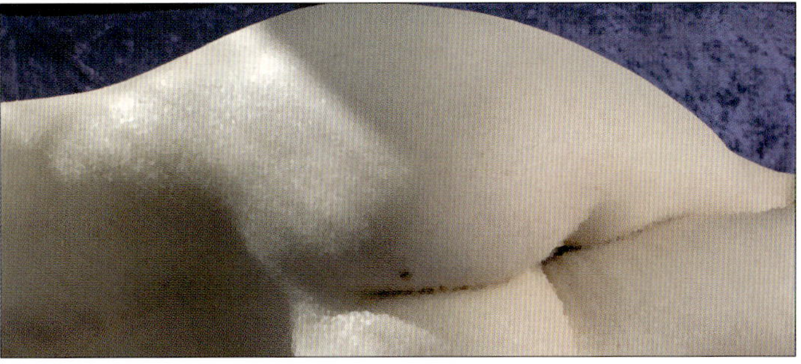

3 Set the blend mode for this layer to *Dissolve*, and reduce its *Opacity* so that the edges produced by the *Crystalize* filter are softened. Now switch the top layer back on. If the white edges are still there, remove them carefully with the *Eraser* tool set to a small soft brush (about 9 pixels) and 50% *Opacity*. Select the foreground by Command-clicking on the top layer in the *Layers* window, and go to *Select* > *Save Selection* to save the selection. Then go to *Select* > *Deselect*. Duplicate the foreground layer, and apply *Filter* > *Pixelate* > *Crystalize* to this new layer, with a setting of about 20. The filter will be applied, but with some unwelcome effects around the edge.

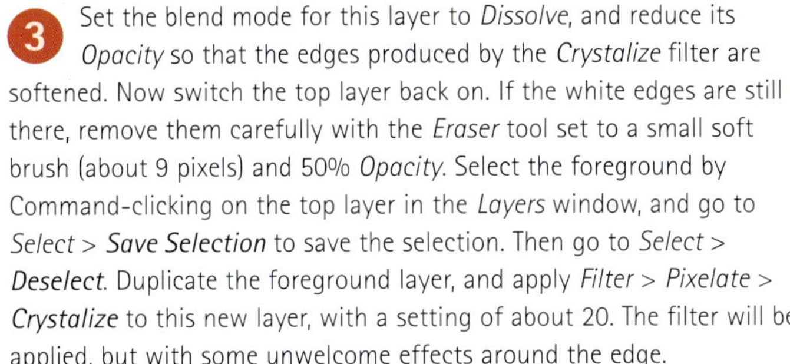

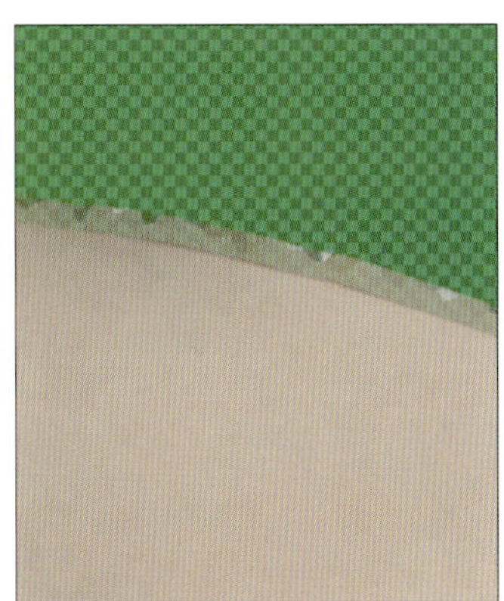

4 Switch off the two bottom layers. Still with the top layer active, set its *Opacity* to about 50% (so you can see the original layer below). Then go to *Image* > *Resize* > *Scale* and increase the scale of the layer until you can see that the edge effects created by the *Crystalize* filter have moved beyond the edges of the layer below.

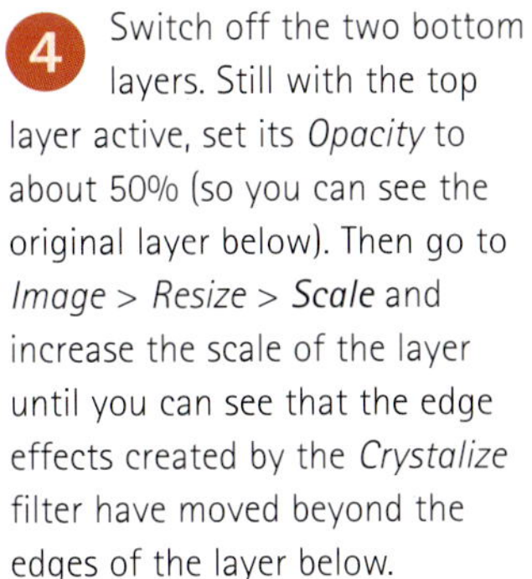

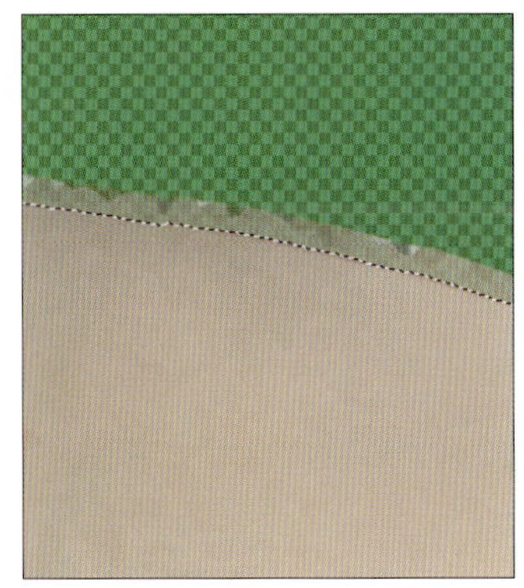

5 Still with the top layer active, go to *Select* > *Load Selection*, and load the selection you saved previously. Invert the selection, and hit the backspace key. The edge effects created by the *Crystalize* filter will disappear. Now switch the two bottom layers back on. Adjust the *Opacity* of the top layer so that the edges produced by the *Crystalize* filter are softened.

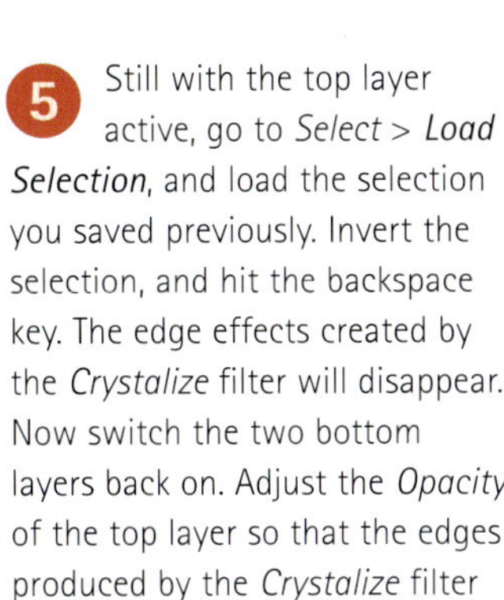

6 Finally, slightly darken the foreground to match the background, which has become darker through manipulation. Make the top layer active, then merge it with the layer below it using *More* > *Merge Down* in the *Layers* window. Then use *Enhance* > *Adjust Brightness/Contrast* > *Brightness/Contrast* on the merged foreground layer.

RECAP

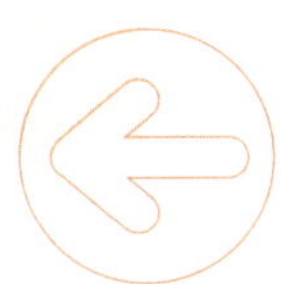

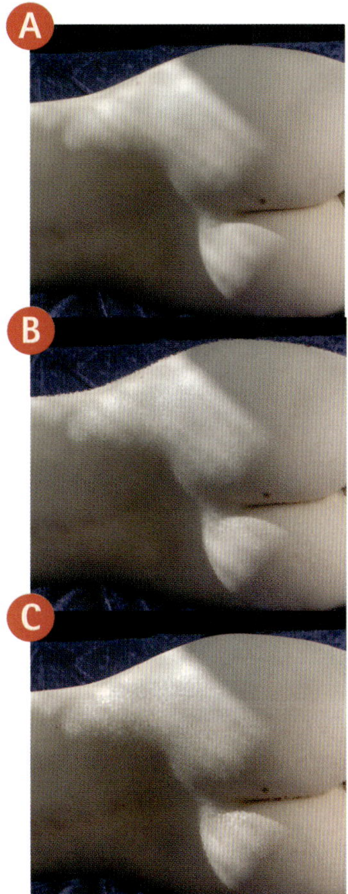

A Isolate the foreground
Carefully select the foreground and make it a separate layer. Apply the filter(s) you want to use to a duplicate of this layer.

B Adjust the background
Apply the filters you want to the background, again duplicating the layer to give more control over the strength of the filter.

C Assemble the elements
Expand the top layer to eliminate the filter's edge effects. Adjust brightness and contrast and/or those of the background layer(s) to get the right balance between them.

Black-and-white images

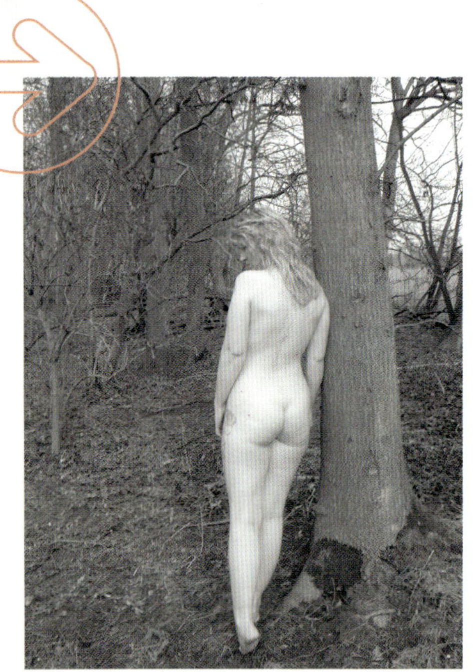

Camera set to black-and-white

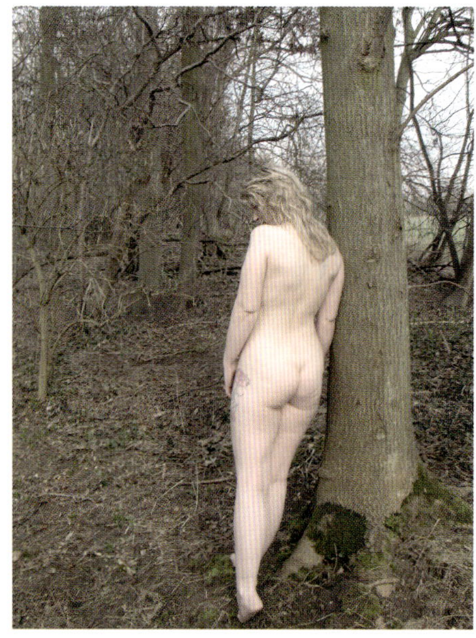

Camera set to color

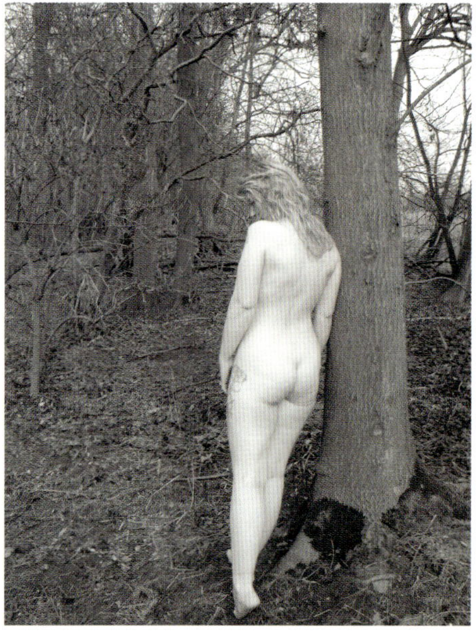

Black-and-white version of color picture

Black-and-white photography has traditionally been the preferred medium for serious nude photography. In this section, we explore a choice of different routes to achieving strong black-and-white pictures with good contrast, starting with the camera settings.

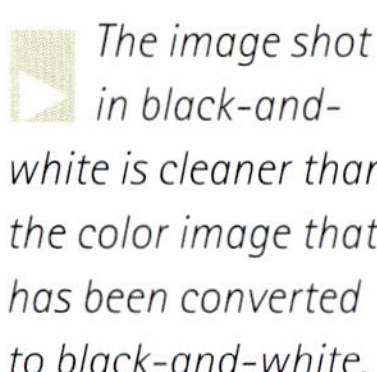

Top left: image taken with the camera set to black-and-white. Top middle: color picture taken under the same conditions. Top right: version made by selecting Enhance > Adjust Color > *Remove Color.*

The image shot in black-and-white is cleaner than the color image that has been converted to black-and-white.

SHOOTING IN BLACK-AND-WHITE

Many digital cameras can be switched to taking black-and-white ("b/w") photographs. There is a certain amount of confusion about this. You may read that you'll get better results if you don't switch your camera to b/w, but work in color and use Elements to convert the images to b/w. In fact, shooting in b/w may produce slightly cleaner pictures with less digital noise. It won't produce inferior images.

On the other hand, if you do shoot in b/w, you can't, of course, put the color back in! So unless you are absolutely certain that you will only ever want a particular image in b/w, it may make sense to shoot in color. Alternatively, if you're a well-organized digital photographer, you could cover your options by taking every shot twice: once in color, and once in b/w.

Detail from black-and-white original

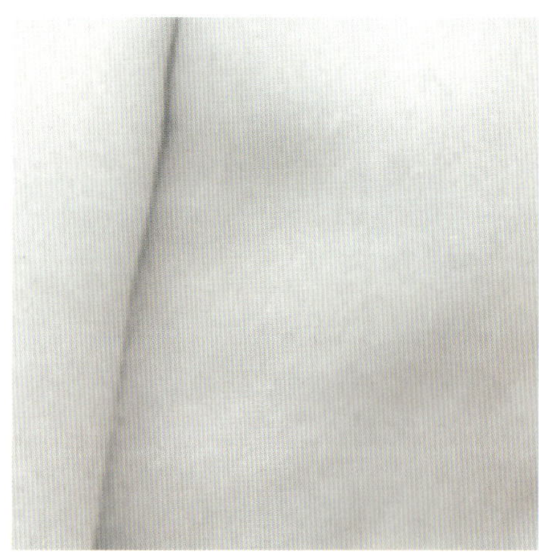

Detail from color changed to black-and-white

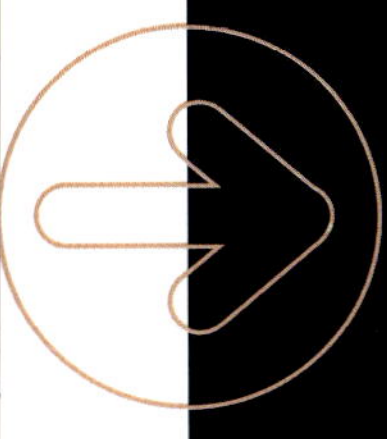

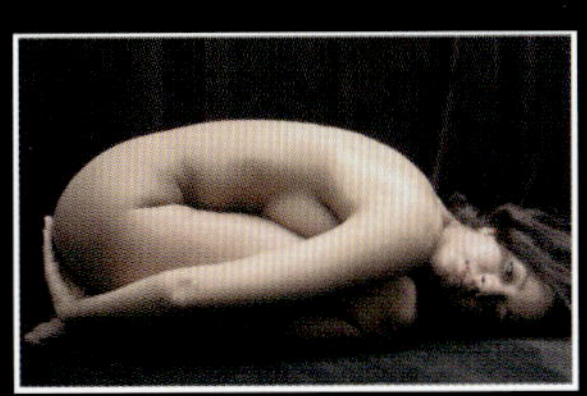

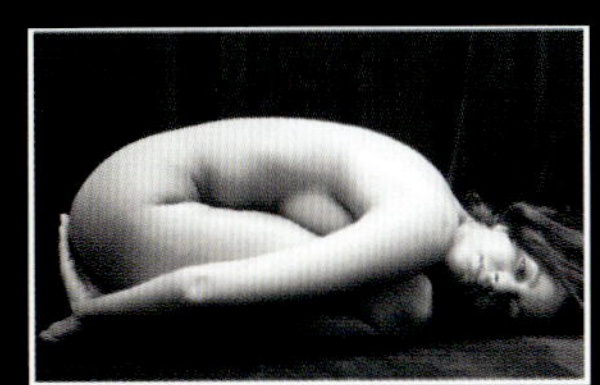

Digital photography offers you two ways of creating black-and-white images: you can either shoot the photograph in your camera's black-and-white mode or remove the color later in an image-editing program.

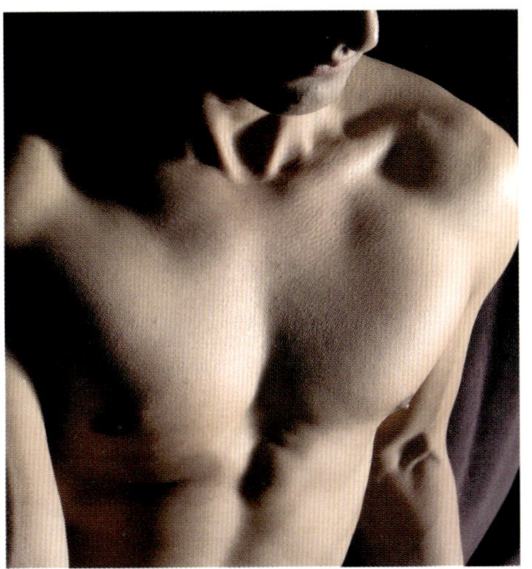

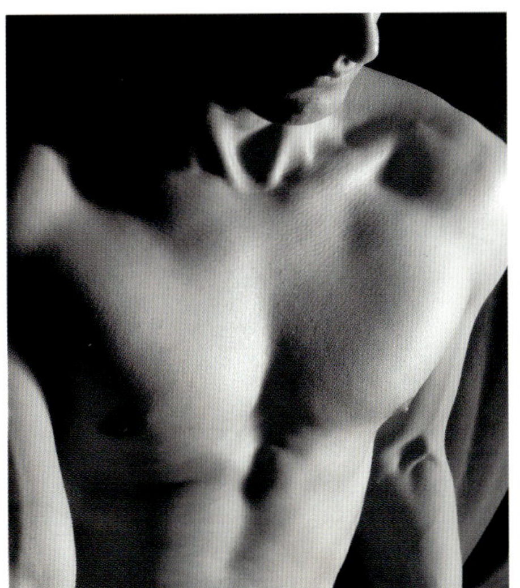

Using Enhance > Adjust Color > Remove Color to make a black-and-white image.

CONVERTING COLOR IMAGES TO BLACK-AND-WHITE

The simplest way to do this is to go to *Enhance > Adjust Color > Remove Color.*

If the b/w image is noisy, go to *Edit > Undo* to return to the original image, and follow the steps on pages 80–81 to reduce noise. Then try removing the color again. This method often produces a slightly flat image, but you can improve the contrast using adjustment layers.

IMPROVING CONTRAST WITH ADJUSTMENT LAYERS

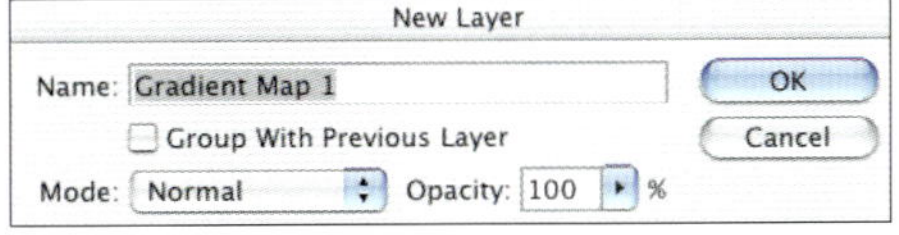

1 Starting with a color image, go to *Layer > New Adjustment Layer > Gradient Map.* Click on *OK* to accept the default settings for the layer.

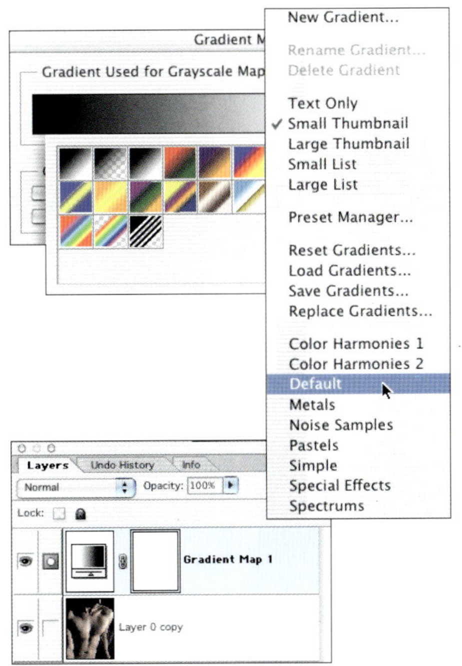

2 Choose the *Black-to-White* gradient, which is the third in the default menu (the first sample will use the colors that are currently in the foreground and background color boxes, which will often be black-and-white, but these won't produce the right effect).

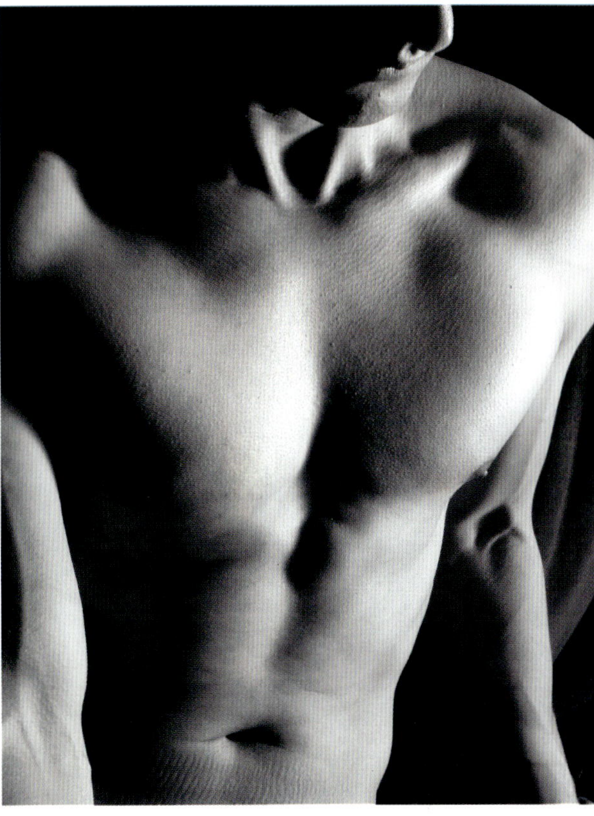

3 The image changes from color to black-and-white, with a little more contrast than was present using just *Enhance > Adjust Color > Remove Color.* Now duplicate the adjustment layer by dragging it onto the *Create a New Layer* icon at the bottom of the *Layer* window. The contrast will increase again.

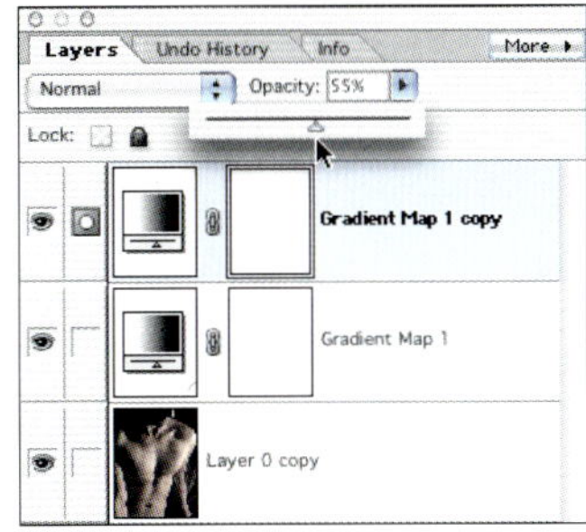

4 You can experiment with the *Opacity* of either of the adjustment layers to vary the contrast in the image. To increase the contrast further, you could try adding a third adjustment layer.

Black-and-white images

BLENDING ADJUSTMENT LAYERS TO BOOST CONTRAST

You can also experiment with blends of the adjustment layers. This image is rather dark, as well as flat, and would benefit from a boost in contrast.

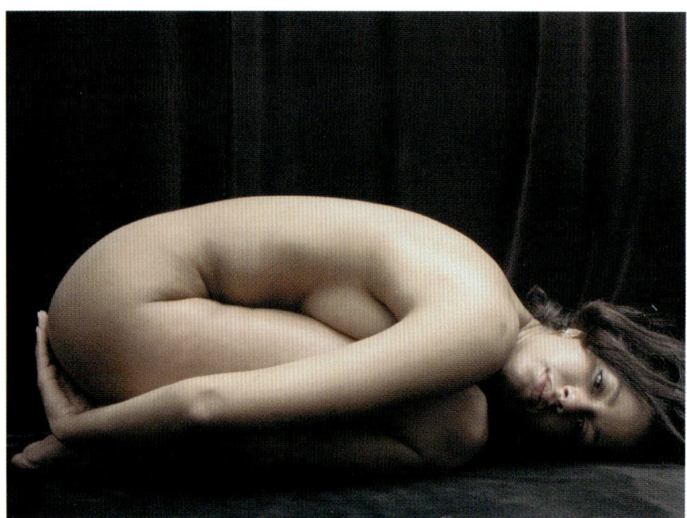

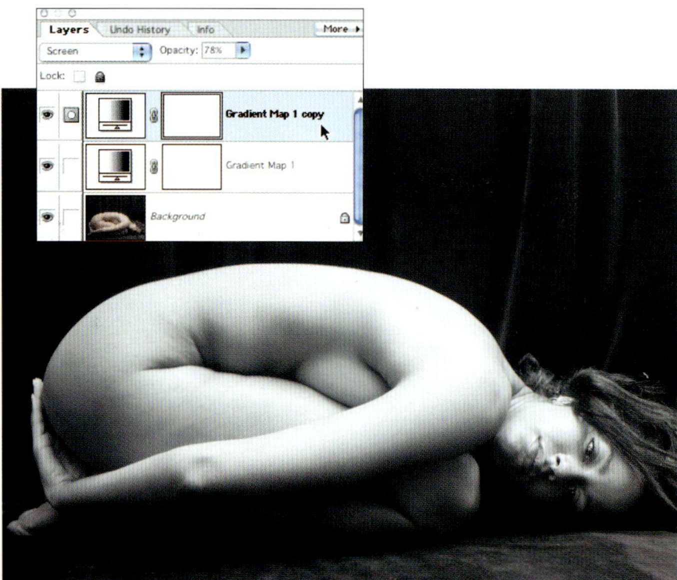

1 Follow the same steps to create two *Gradient Map* adjustment layers. Then set the blend of the top layer to *Screen*. Experiment with the *Opacity* of the layer to achieve the tonal balance you require.

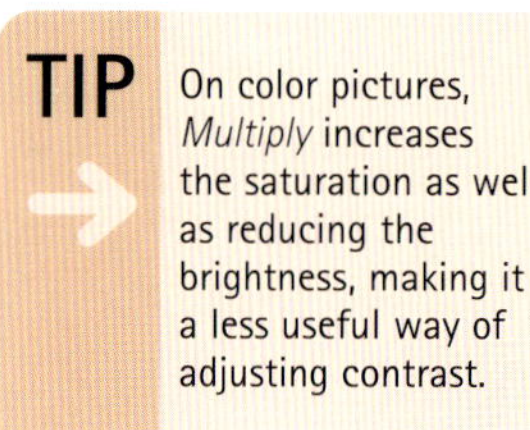

TIP On color pictures, *Multiply* increases the saturation as well as reducing the brightness, making it a less useful way of adjusting contrast.

INCREASING CONTRAST USING MULTIPLY

The effect of the *Multiply* blend on b/w images is to darken areas that are already dark, while making little alteration to light areas.

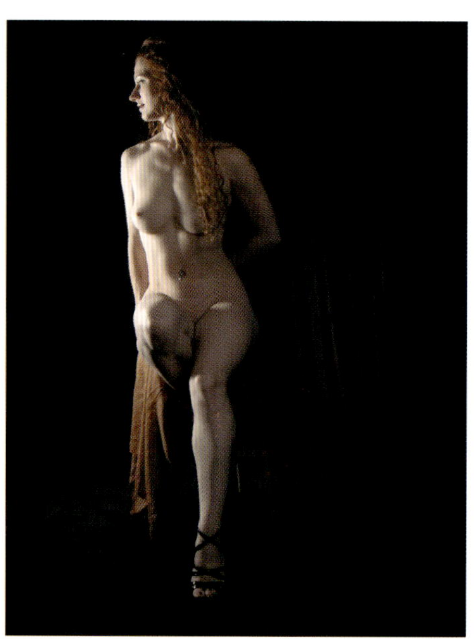

1 Make a b/w image by using *Enhance > Adjust Color > Remove Color*.

2 Duplicate the layer and set the blend for the top layer to *Multiply*. The image will become more contrasty but also darker. Adjust the *Opacity* of either layer until you achieve the desired effect. Often a low *Opacity* setting is all that's necessary.

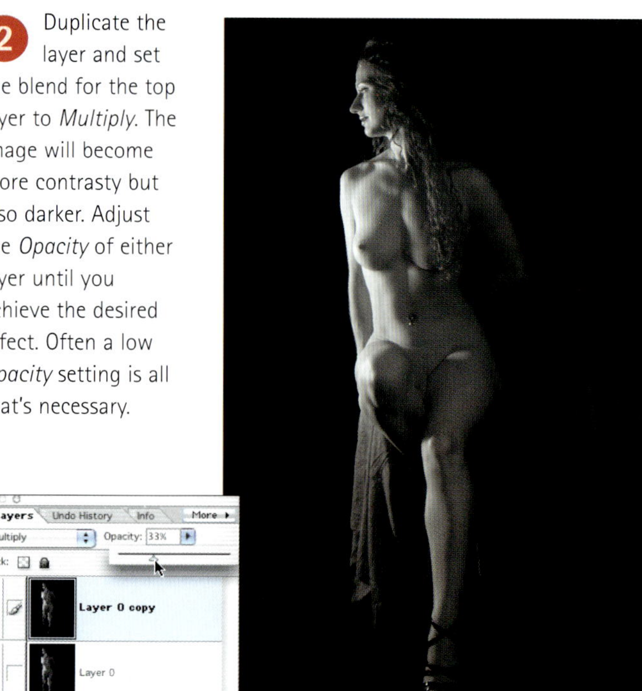

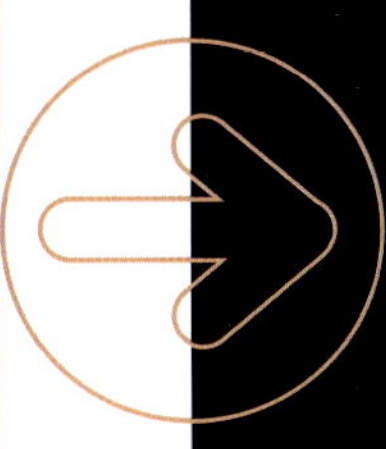

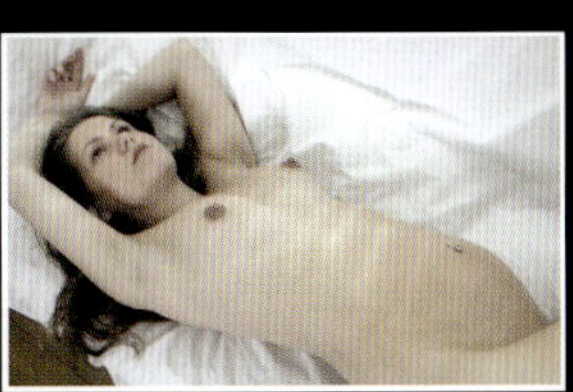

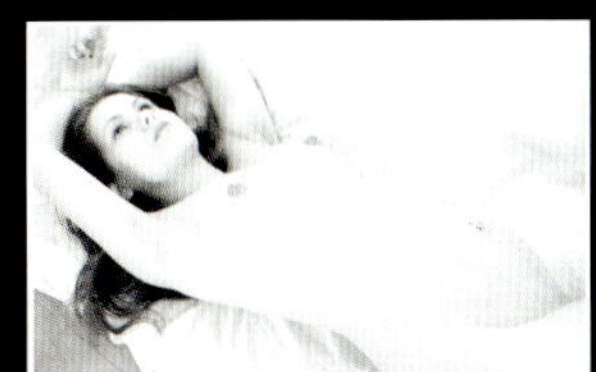

Adjustment layers can be applied to black-and-white images to dramatically add to their impact. You can also create similar effects using special software such as Nik Efex Pro.

USING NIKON EFEX PRO

Finally, we'll look at the black-and-white conversion filter available in Nik Efex Pro.

1 Go to *Filter > Nik Color Efex Pro > B/W Conversion.*

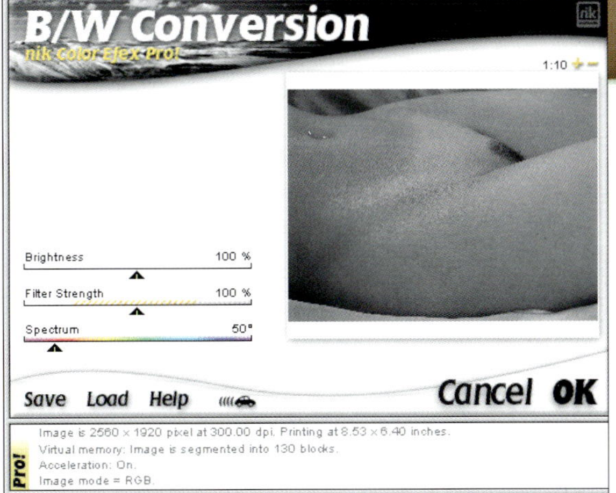

2 In the *B/W Conversion* window, try settings of 100% *Brightness*, 100% *Filter Strength*, and 50° *Spectrum*. *Spectrum* is the control that has the greatest effect on the filter. Click *OK*.

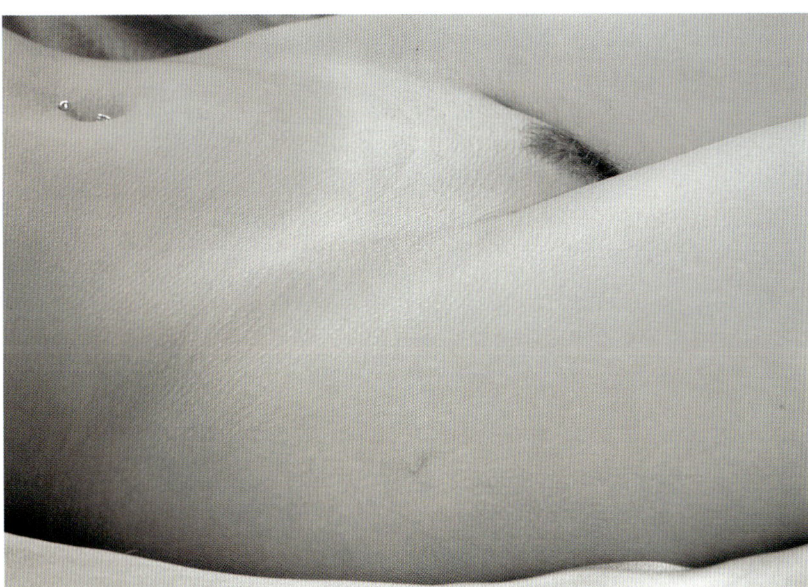

You can also use the *Screen* blend mode, with the Nikon Efex Pro b/w conversion filter, to produce a high-key image.

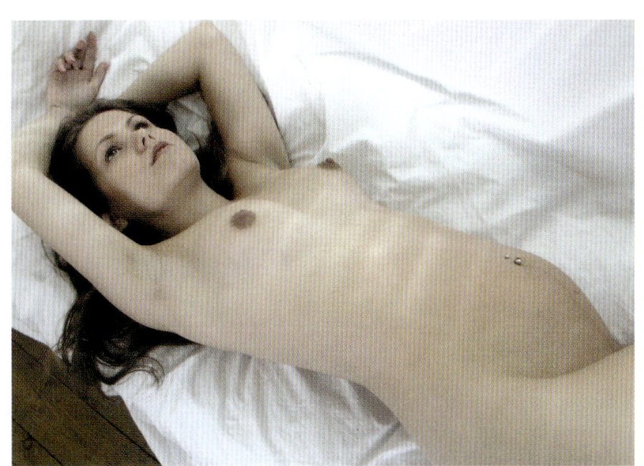

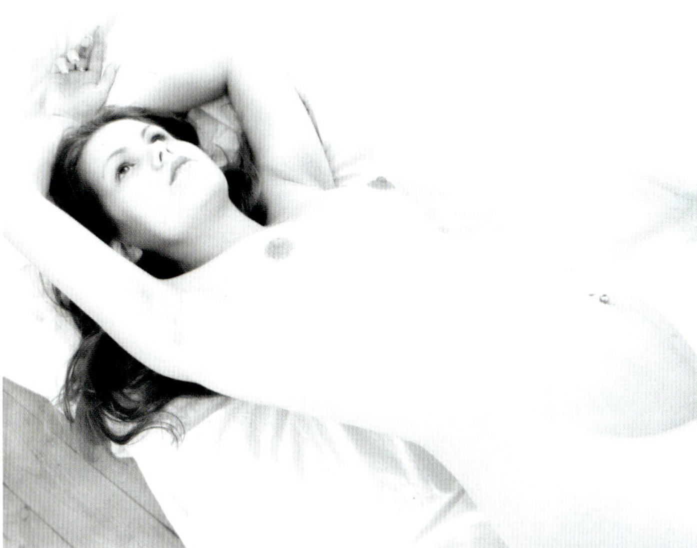

1 Convert the image to b/w and then duplicate the background layer. Set the blend of the top layer to *Screen*. Adjust the *Opacity* of the top layer as necessary.

TIP

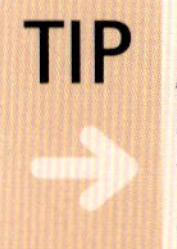

Adjustment layers also make it easy to try out images that are monochrome but not necessarily black-and-white.

Negative and solarized images

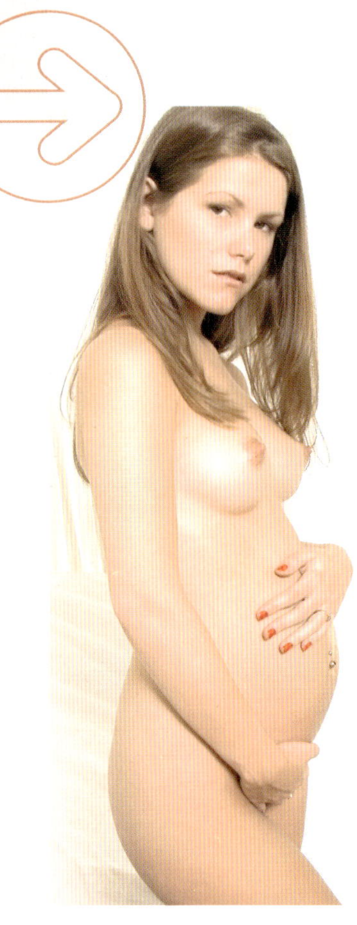

Elements can be used to produce negative (inverted) and solarized images. We'll look at ways of using these processes, and also consider what kinds of images make the best negatives.

NEGATIVE IMAGES

You can make a negative version of an image via *Image > Adjustments > **Invert***. Slightly flat images seem to make better negative images than contrasty ones, as deep shadows turn into distracting highlights.

SOLARIZATION

In film photography, solarization involves exposing a partially developed sheet of photographic paper to light, then continuing its development to completion. This renders part of the positive image as a negative. The *Solarization* filter in Elements creates a similar effect. However, the result isn't very attractive on color images, and, when applied to b/w pictures, is almost the same as making it negative.

Monochrome solarized images from film photography have two attractive qualities: an almost metallic finish in the solarized areas, and strong, distinct edges. You can simulate these effects in Elements; the results will depend on the tonal range and contrast of the original.

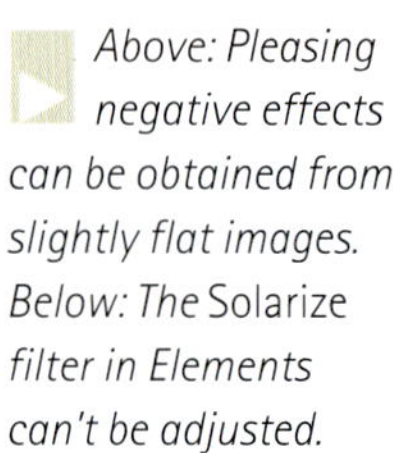

Above: Pleasing negative effects can be obtained from slightly flat images. Below: The Solarize *filter in Elements can't be adjusted.*

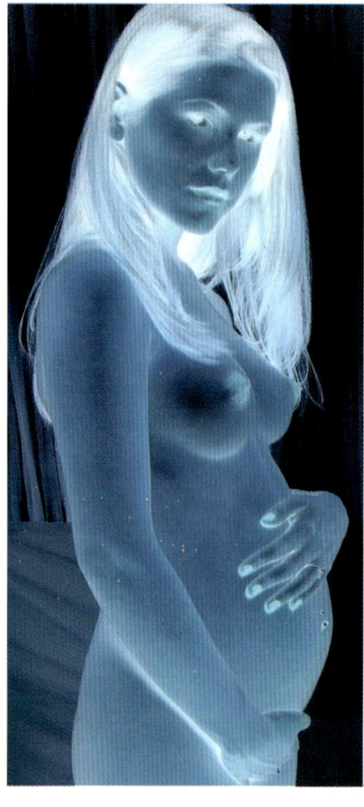

Color negative

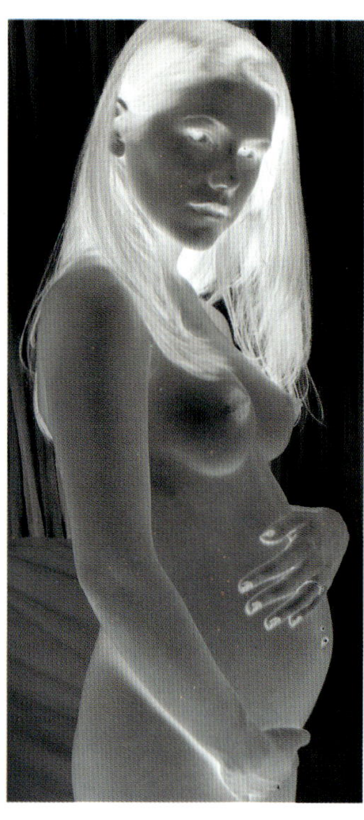

Black-and-white negative

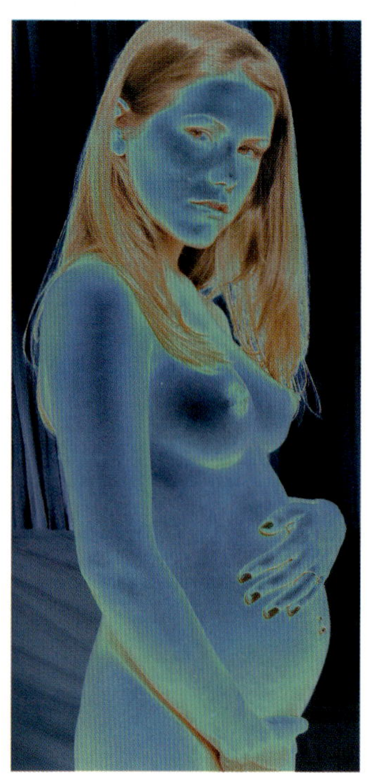

Solarize filter on color image

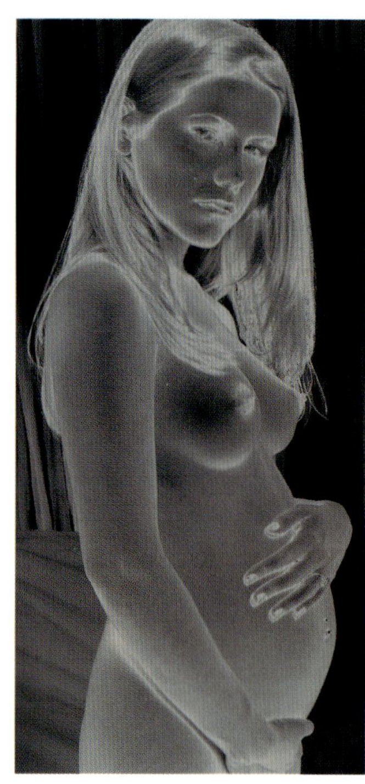

Solarize filter on b/w image

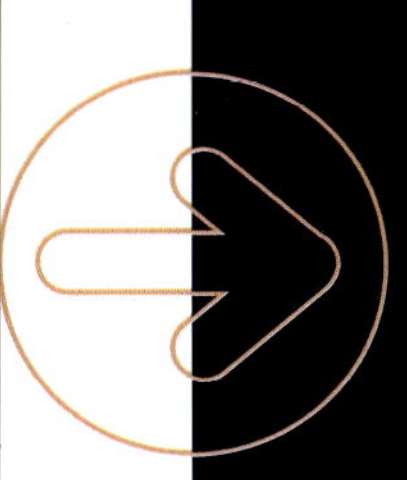

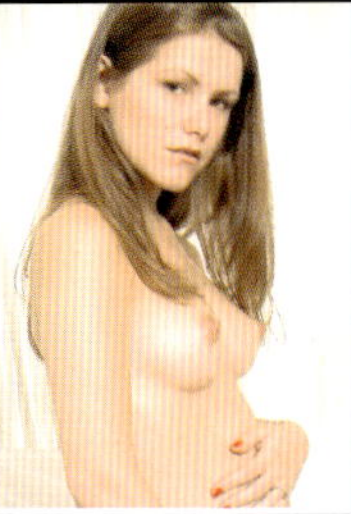

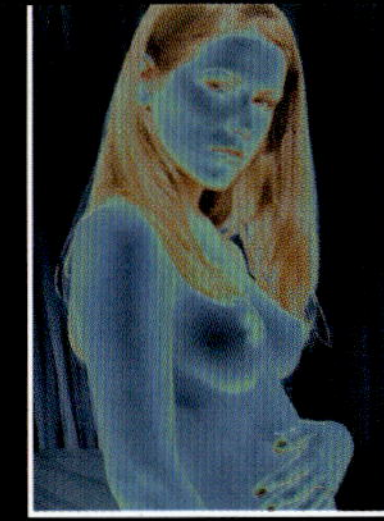

While solarization effects are often pigeonholed with Sixties psychedelia, they can be used in more subtle ways to add a deeper mood to an image.

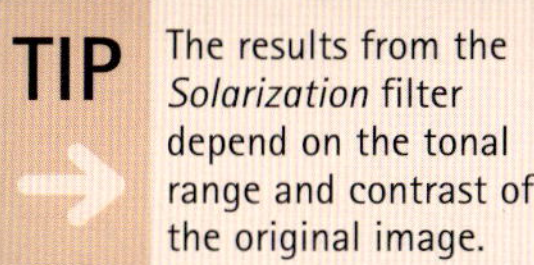

TIP The results from the *Solarization* filter depend on the tonal range and contrast of the original image.

METALLIC TEXTURES

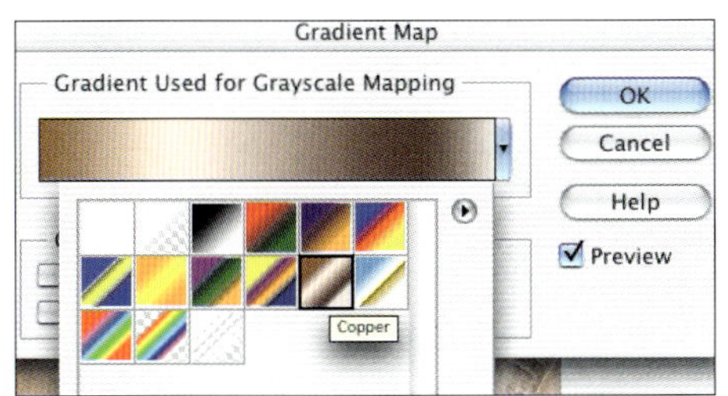

1 You can try these steps with either the original color image or a b/w version. If the image is noisy or grainy, clean it up first. Duplicate the background layer, and go to *Enhance > Adjust Color > Remove Color* to make the duplicate copy b/w. Next, go to *Layer > New Adjustment Layer > Gradient Map* and select the *Copper* gradient sample from the *Default* set.

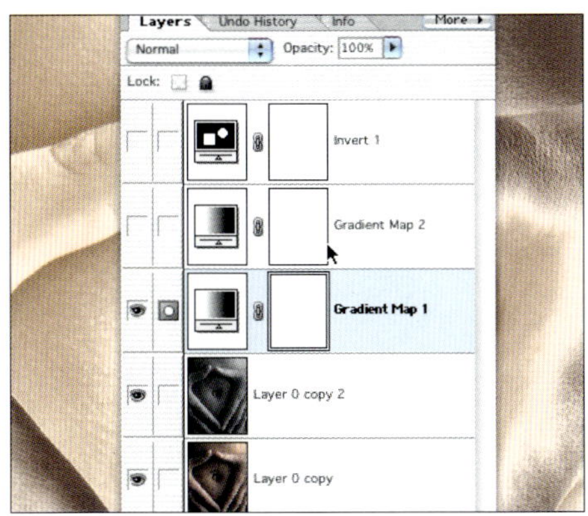

2 Click in this new layer to select it, and select *Gradient Map* again. This time select the *Black-to-White* gradient (the third in the *Default* menu). The new adjustment layer appears above the previous one. Click in this layer and go to *Layer > New Adjustment Layer > Invert*. You now have two image layers and three adjustment layers.

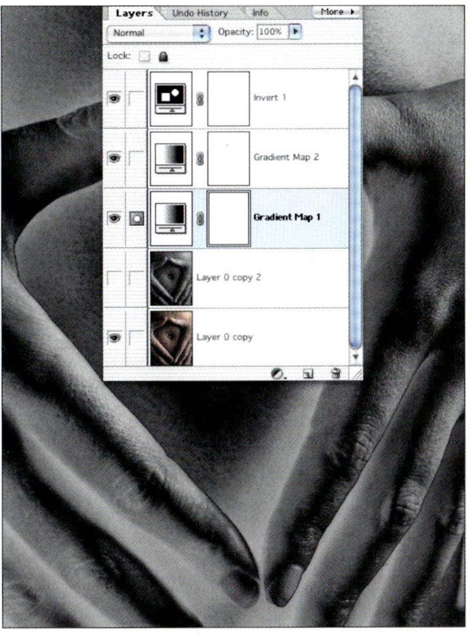

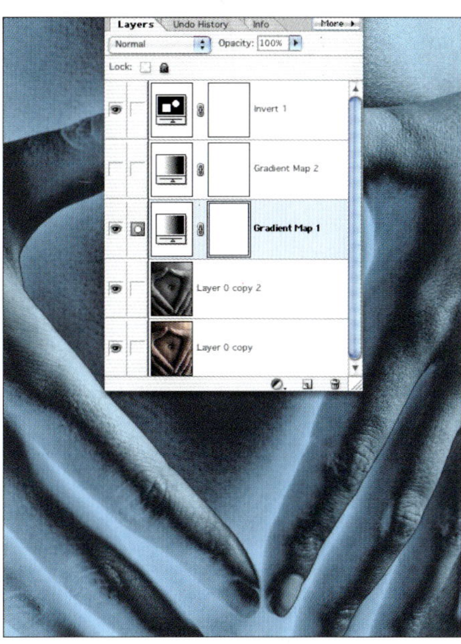

3 Experiment by switching the three layers on and off in different combinations. You can produce different effects by selecting different gradients in the lower *Gradient Map* layer. When you find a combination you like, use *Save As* to save a copy of the file. Flatten that copy of the file and save it, then reopen the original file to explore further possibilities.

EDGES

Edges are easiest to produce from less contrasty images.

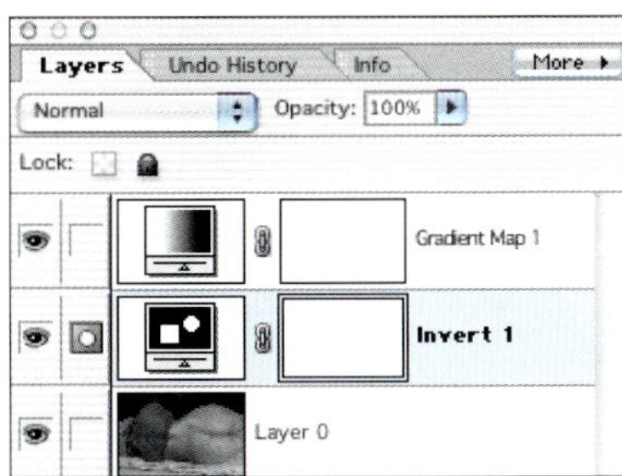

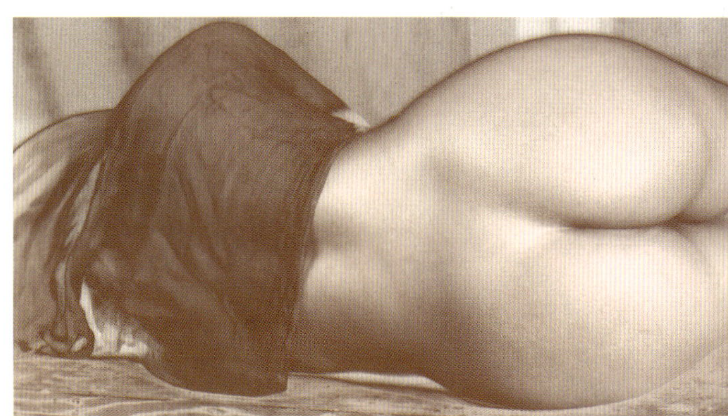

1 Again, you can experiment with using either a color or b/w image as the basis for this. This example uses a b/w version. Add an *Invert* adjustment layer and then a *Gradient* adjustment layer above it, once more selecting the *Copper* gradient sample from the *Default* set.

2 The image needs to be tidied a little. With the *Clone Stamp* tool, remove the deep crease in the background drapes. Then select the box in the foreground and invert it (in the image layer itself, not with an adjustment layer) to make it darker. Finally, apply Nikon Efex's *Classic Blur* to soften the edges within the image (Elements' *Gaussian Blur* filter would also be effective).

Creative manipulation

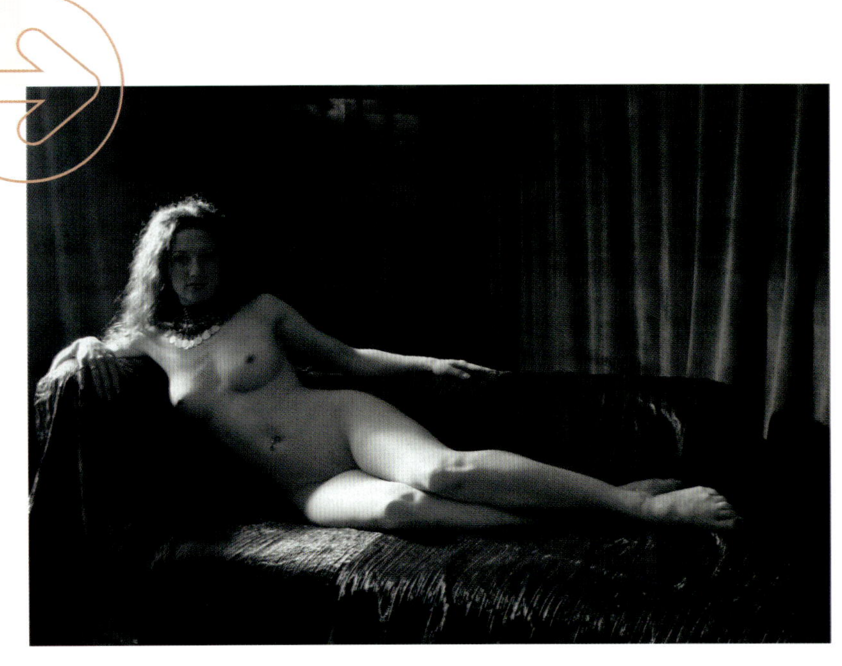

ADDING GRAIN

Graininess adds a nostalgic, romantic feel to images of the nude, suggestive perhaps of an early photograph or an etching. Elements has a *Grain* filter (*Filter* > *Texture* > *Grain*), but I find it less appealing than the judicious use of *Filter* > *Noise* > *Add Noise*.

This section explores the use of layers and filters as tools for creatively manipulating images. The techniques examined include muting colors, adding grain to images, and turning the model to stone.

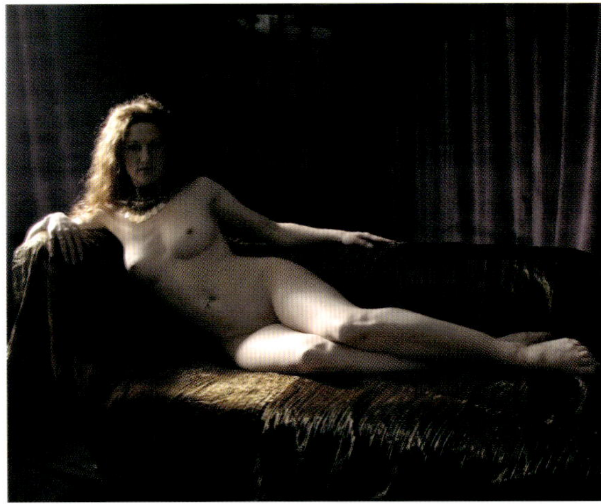

1 After checking the levels, begin by converting the image to b/w, by using *Layer* > *New Adjustment Layer* > *Gradient Map*. Then flatten the image and check the levels again. You may need to alter the levels slightly after applying the *Gradient Map*. In this example, I've raised the midtones.

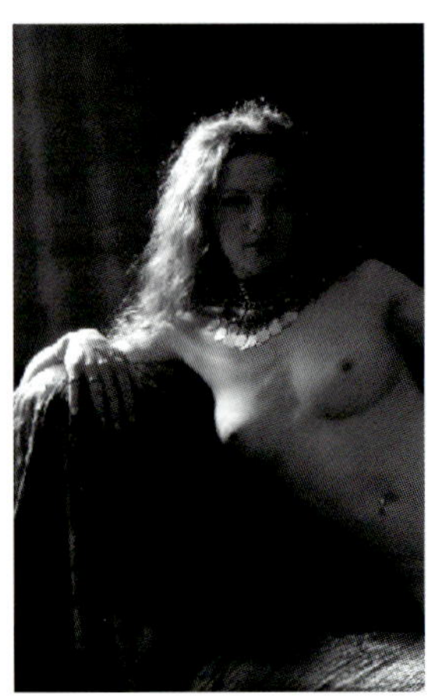

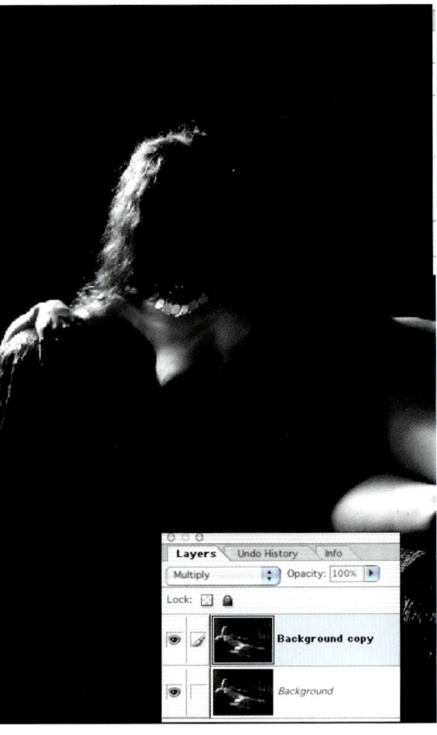

2 Duplicate the background layer and set the blend on the new top layer to *Multiply*. The result may be very dark in the dark areas, but notice that the highlights won't change much—that's how *Multiply* works in practice.

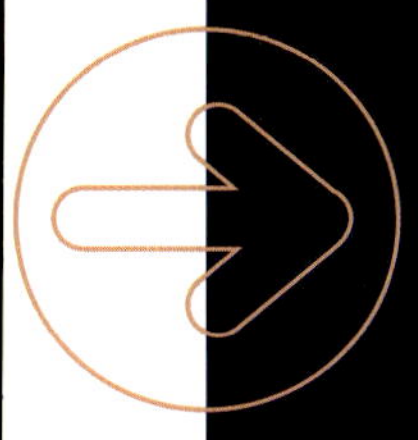

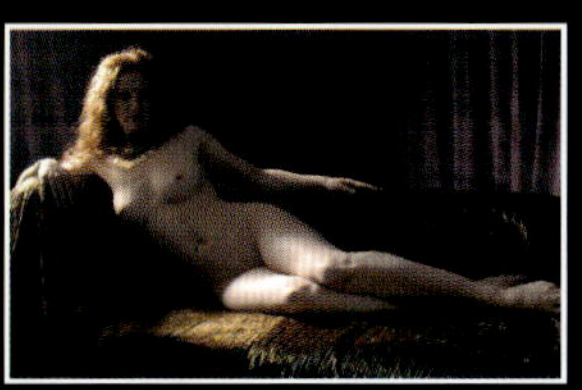

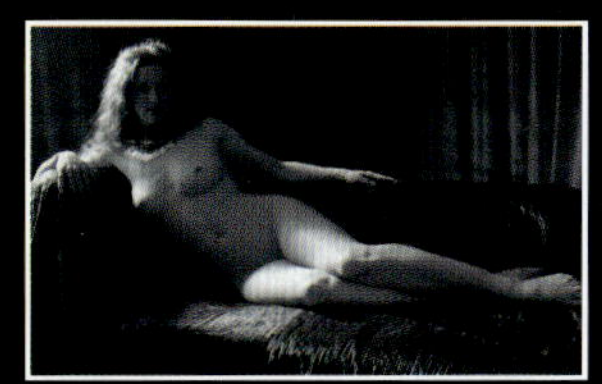

Image-editing programs such as Adobe Photoshop Elements are ideal for creating special effects such as adding color to selected areas of a black-and-white image.

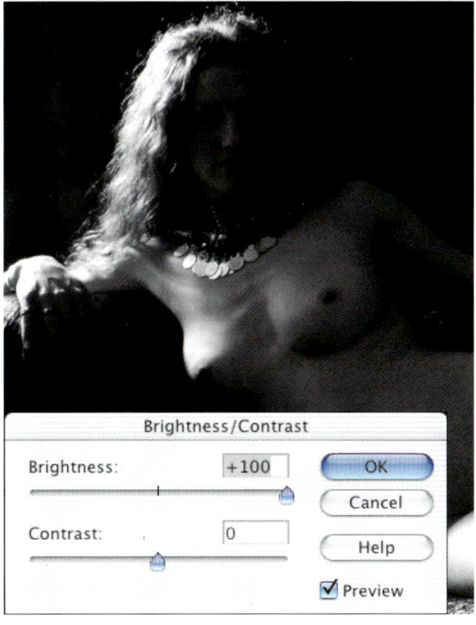

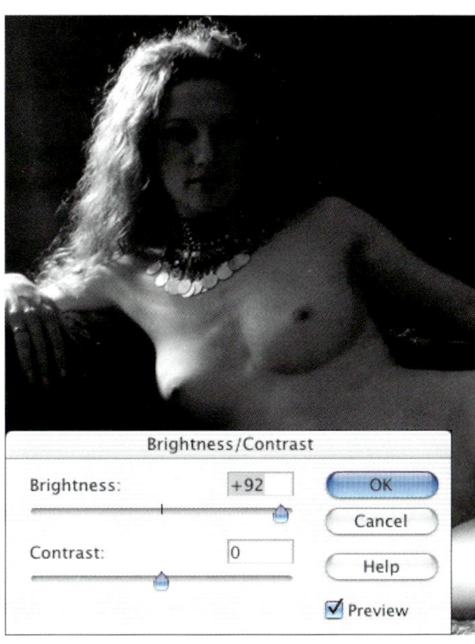

3 Now select the bottom layer and go to *Enhance > Adjust Brightness /Contrast > Brightness/Contrast*. Raise the brightness substantially. Because you're using the *Multiply* blend, the highlights won't burn out. Your aim is to make the picture look pretty much as it did before you added the second layer. In this case, I've brightened the bottom layer by 100%, then gone back and brightened it again, this time by 92%. I can check, by toggling the bottom layer off and on, that my two-layer version of the image looks just like the original.

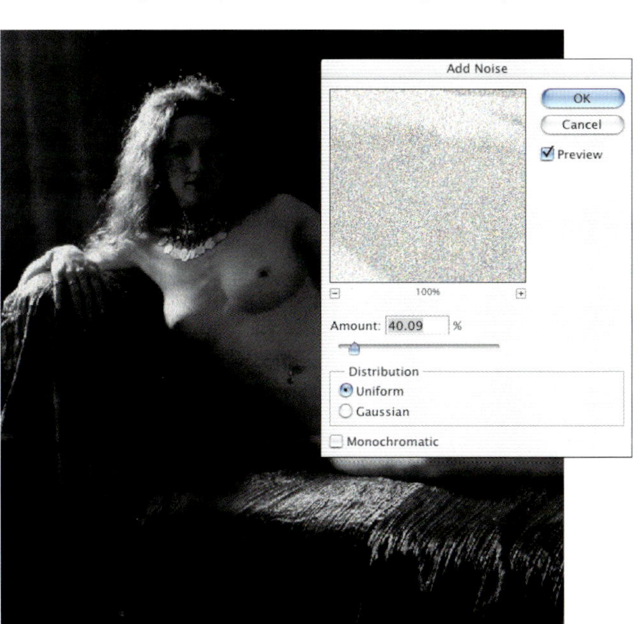

4 Still with the bottom layer selected, go to *Filter > Noise > Add Noise* and try out noise values between 20 and 45%. Use *Uniform Distribution*, and don't check *Monochrome*, which seems to make the noise more clumpy. When you're satisfied, click *OK*. Go to *Enhance > Adjust Color > Remove Color* to make the noise black-and-white.

FACT FILE

Adding noise

Adding noise directly to an image means that you'll get noise equally across the whole tonal range. This weakens the rich, dark tones of the original, as shown in the top example image here. In the bottom image, noise has been added to one layer using *Multiply* and appears only in the midtones and highlights.

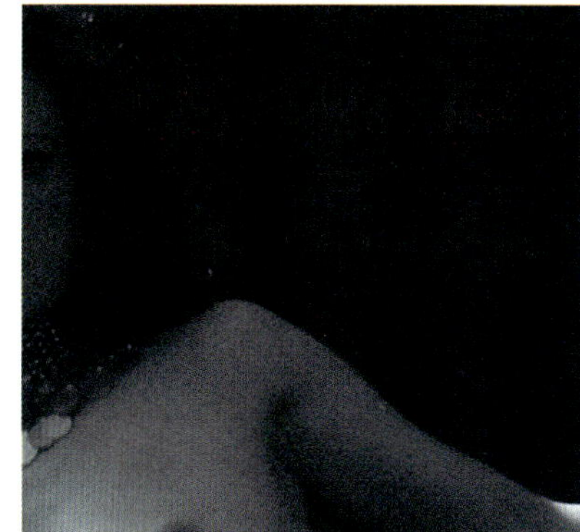

Bad noise

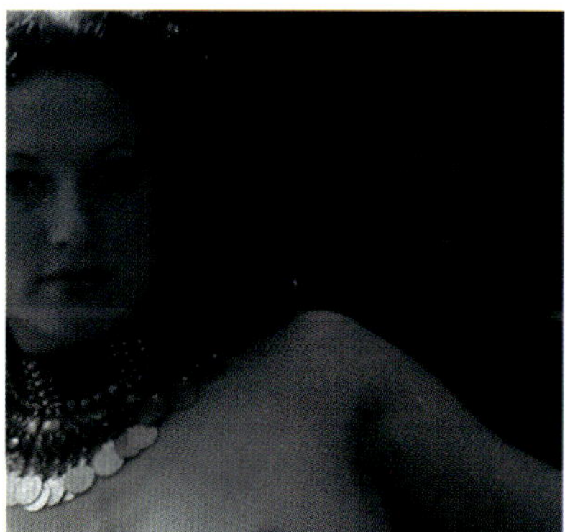

Good noise

PARTIAL COLOR

Layers and blend modes let you create images that are part monochrome, part color. This image was a happy accident, underexposed because a flash head failed to fire. The effect depends on the oversaturated skin tones.

1. First, duplicate the layer.

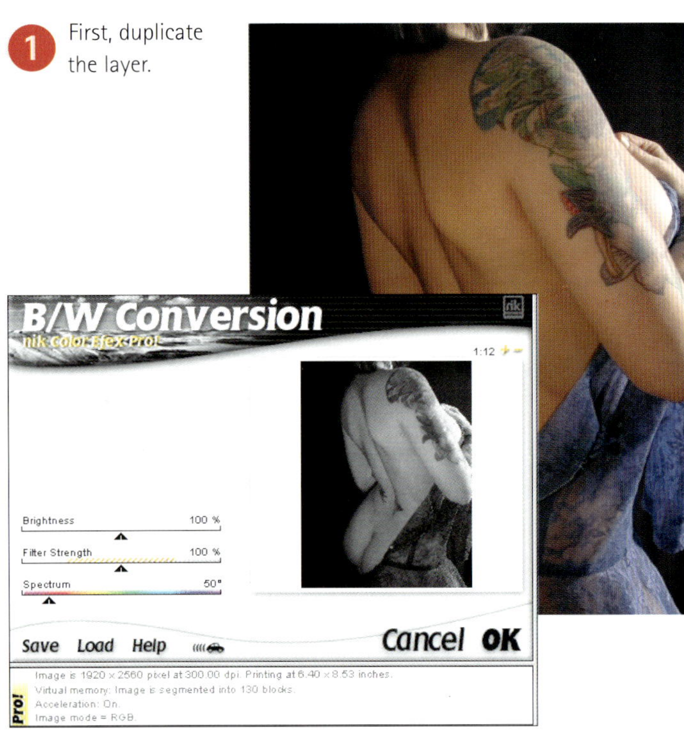

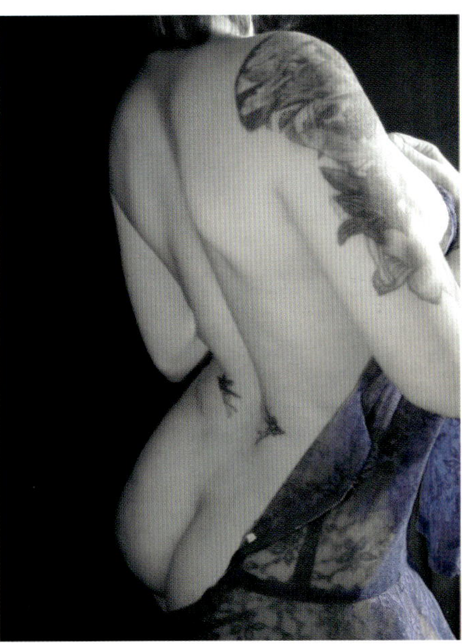

2. Make the bottom layer monochrome. I used Nikon Color Efex's *B/W Conversion* filter, with *Filter Strength* at 100% and *Spectrum* at 50°.

3. Set the blend for the top layer to *Lighten*. The rich blue colors of the layer below will show through, but leave the skin tones monochrome.

MUTED COLORS

Each blend mode has a distinct impact on different levels of brightness. *Screen* mode makes all colors lighter apart from pure black, but it has a greater effect on light colors than dark. You can see this effect at work in the image to the right.

You can achieve almost the same effect, but keep a little more saturation in the gloves, by using, on the top layer, *Layer* > *New Adjustment Layer* > *Gradient Map* and applying the *Black-to-White* gradient. Then set the blend mode of the adjustment layer to *Screen*.

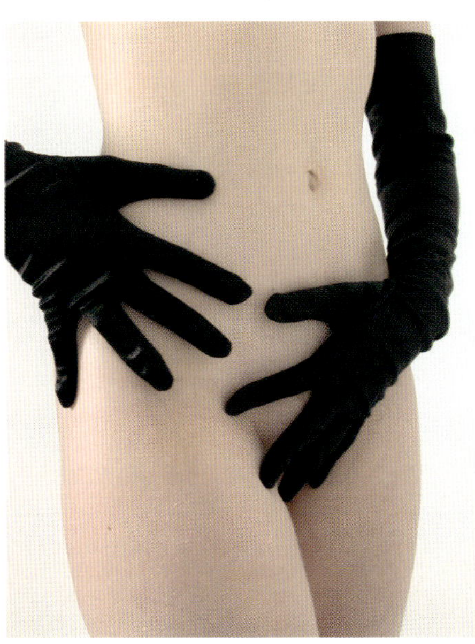

I wanted to make this image look less "natural," with a heightened contrast between the black gloves and the model's skin tones.

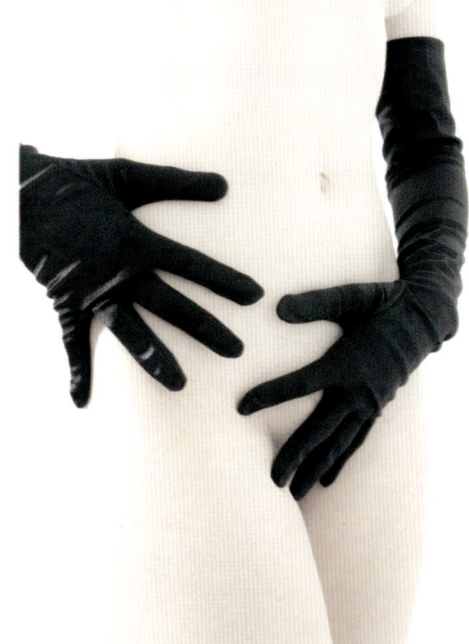

I created a duplicate layer and set the blend mode to screen. In this example it works well in producing the muted skin tones I wanted.

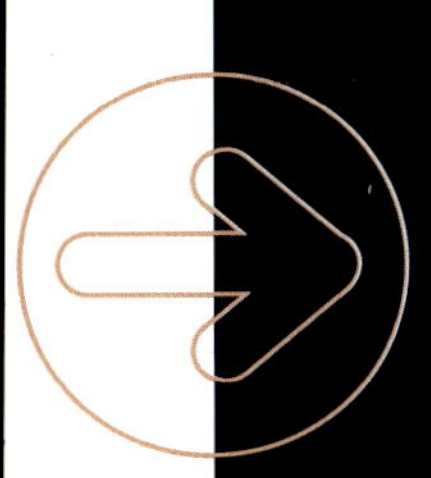

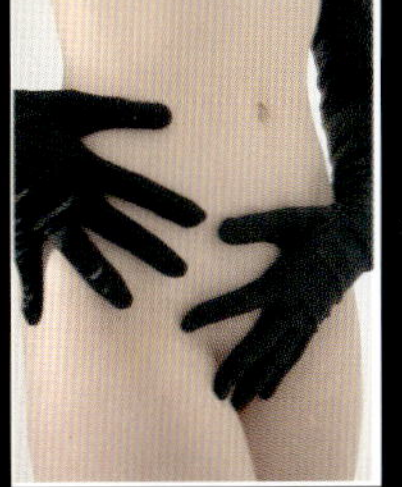

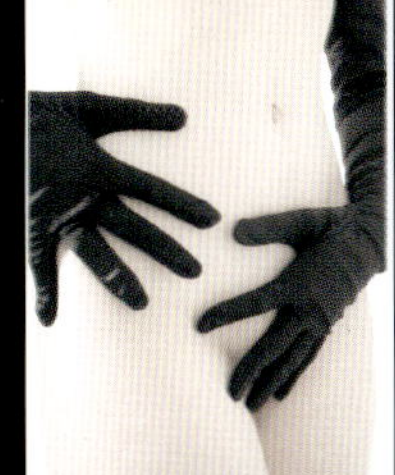

You can achieve almost any effect when you combine filters, selections, and layers together. The ability to transform your images in any way you please is the biggest single advantage of digital photography.

TIP

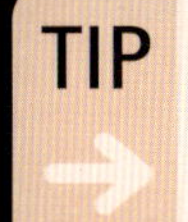

Look for different and original ways of combining black-and-white with color.

MIRROR PLAY

The internet is crammed with images of black-and-white models wearing bright red bikinis. The method of creating those pictures is the same as I'm going to demonstrate here, except that I've cheated, by picking a nice straight-edged shape to work with!

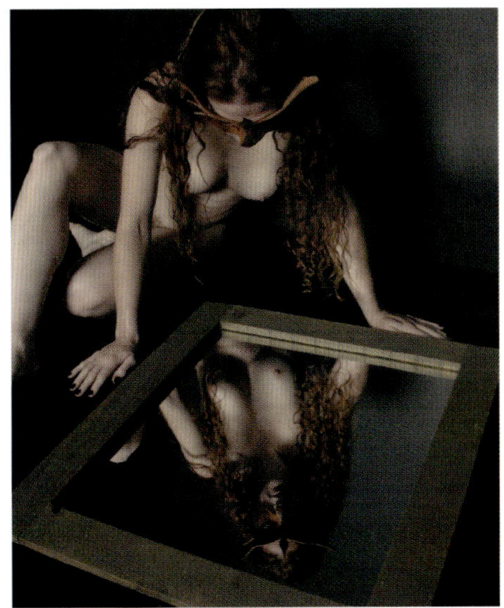

1. Before starting, use *Levels* to adjust the overall tone of the shot.

2. Using the *Polygonal Lasso* tool, make a selection of the mirror, including its frame.

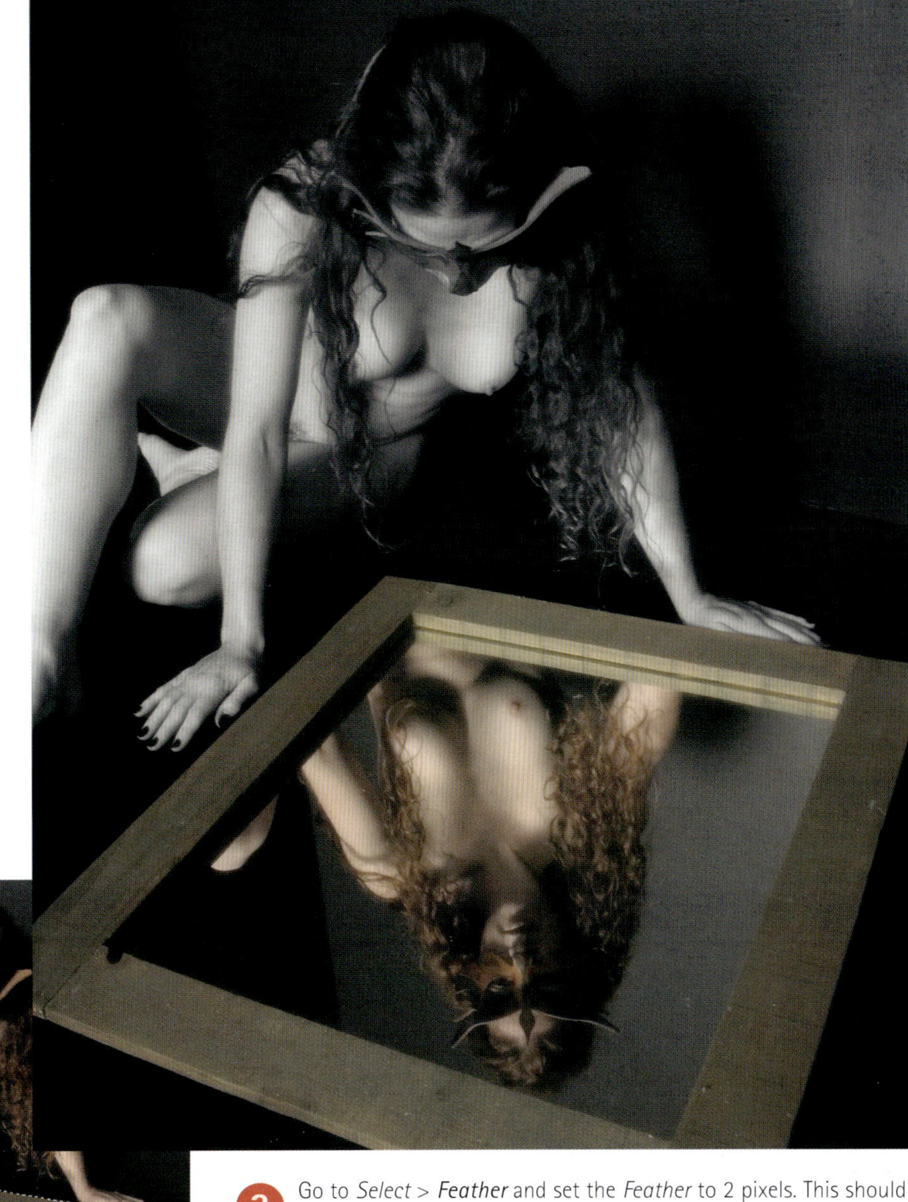

3. Go to *Select* > ***Feather*** and set the *Feather* to 2 pixels. This should be enough to give a smooth transition along the edge of the mask. Go to *Select* > ***Inverse*** and invert the selection. Go to *Select* > ***Save Selection*** and save the selection. Now go to *Layer* > *New Adjustment Layer* > ***Gradient Map*** and select the *Black-to-White* gradient. You see the gradient applied only to the model and her background, not to the reflection. Finally, to enhance the vividness of the reflection, apply Nik Color Efex's *Classical Blur* with a 35% setting to the selected area. A low-value *Gaussian Blur* (*Filter* > *Blur* > ***Gaussian Blur***) would also work well.

Creative manipulation

STONE PEOPLE

In this section we'll use the *Overlay* blend mode to create two very different images. Here, I wanted to combine the picture of the model's torso with a close-up of a fossil-filled chunk of Sicilian rock, to create a mysterious image in which the model seems to be sinking into, or emerging from, the rock.

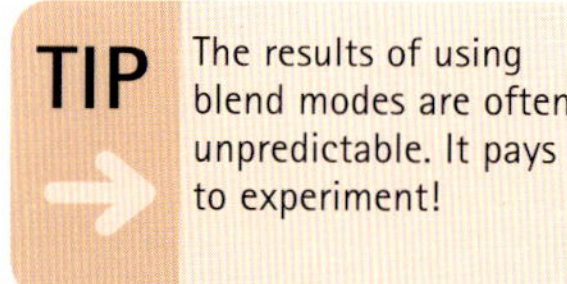

The results of using blend modes are often unpredictable. It pays to experiment!

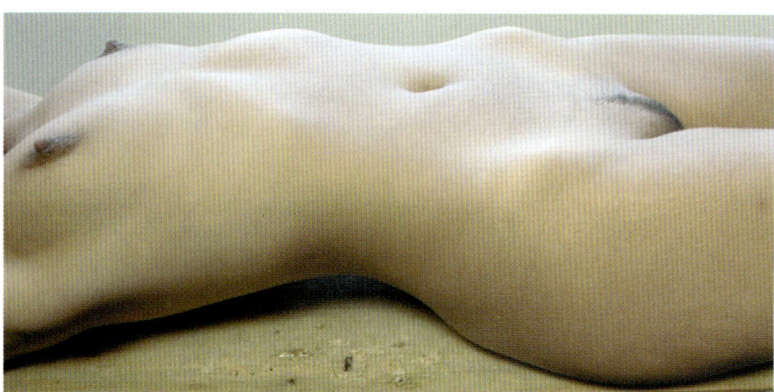

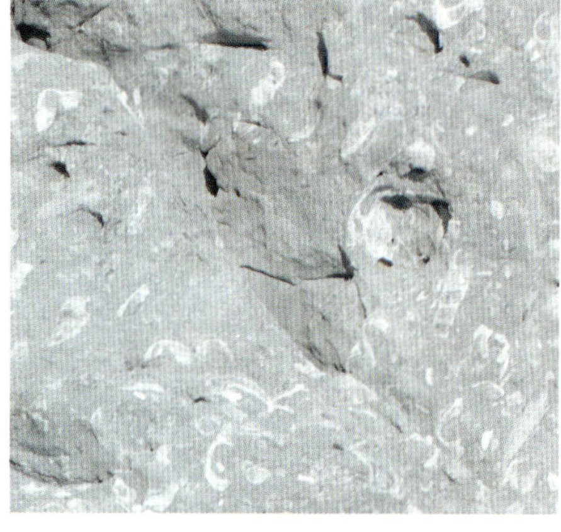

1 With both images open, click on the background layer of the stone picture in the *Layer* window, and drag the layer onto the picture of the model. It appears as a new layer. Then close the stone picture. I took these two pictures with different cameras, and the stone layer is smaller than the model. In this case, we can enlarge the stone layer without worrying about it losing sharpness.

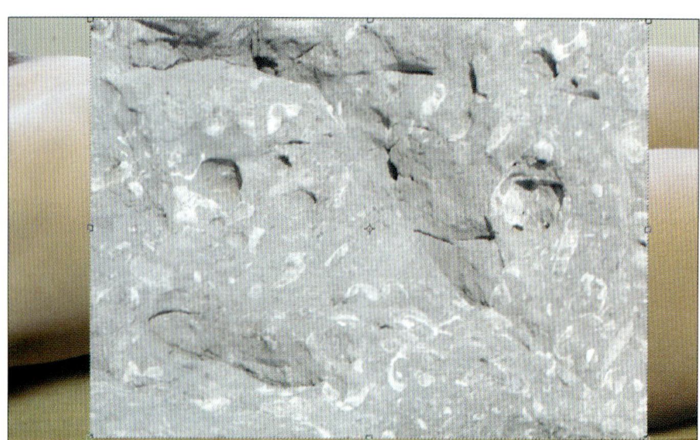

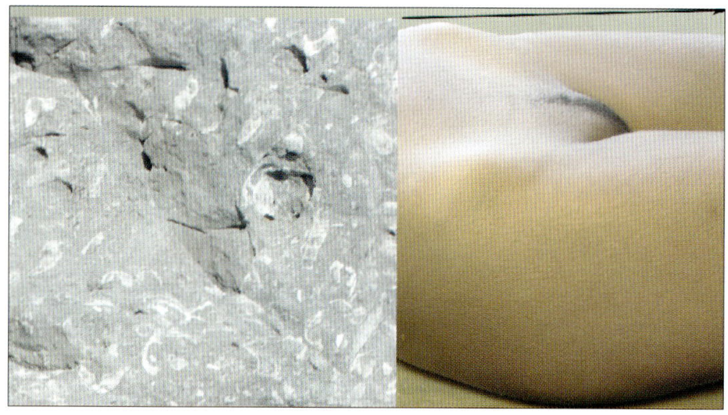

2 Using the *Move* tool, position the stone layer in one corner of the model layer. Make sure that the stone layer goes right into the corner—if it bleeds out beyond the edges of the model layer, that's fine. Now click in the corner of the stone layer that isn't touching the edges of the layer below, and drag it so that the stone layer extends right over the layer below.

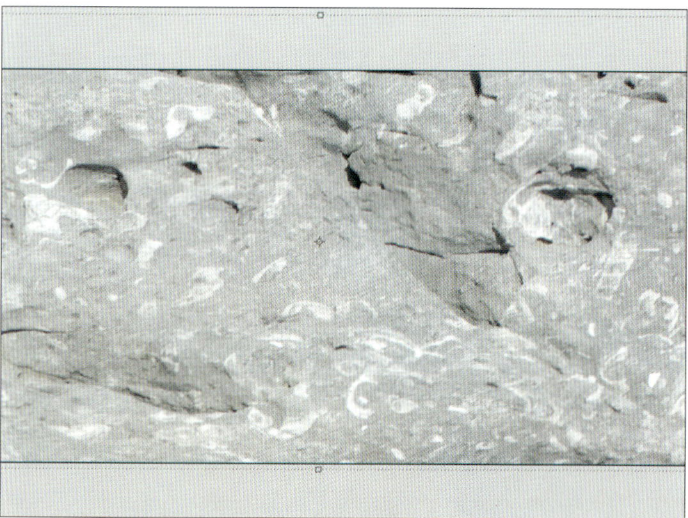

3 In this case, the aspect ratio of the picture is so different from that of the stone layer that you also need to drag the top edge of the stone layer straight up, so that it doesn't look too distorted.

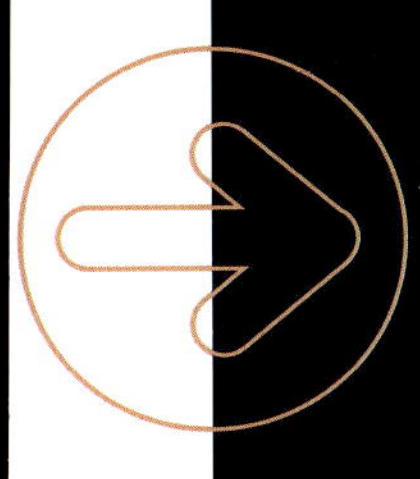

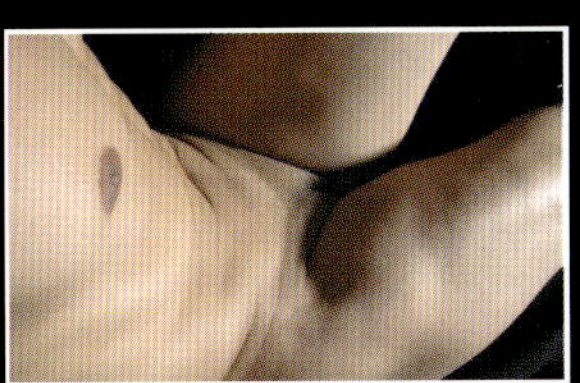

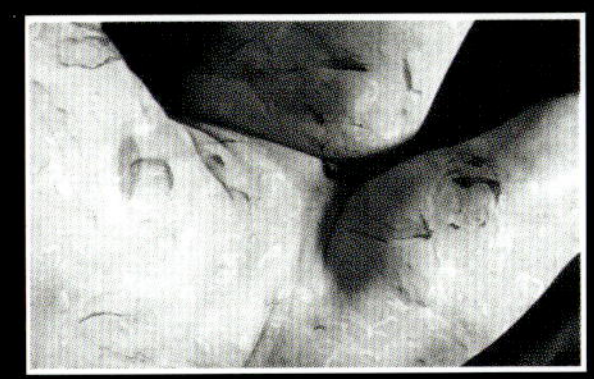

By compositing your nude photographs with other material, you can easily use layers and blend modes to create some stunning effects. For example, use a scanned background to give your subject's flesh a very different look.

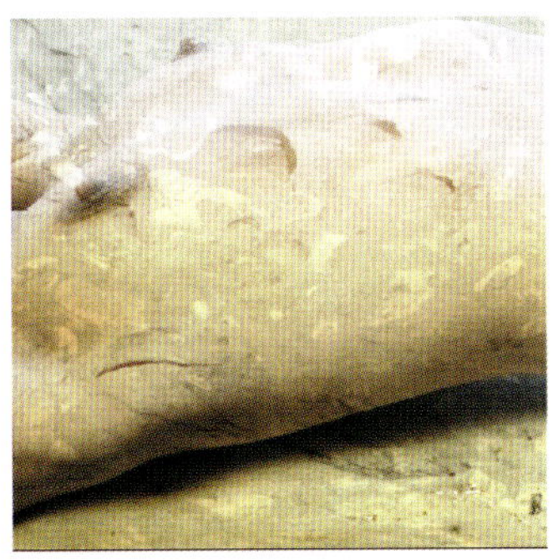

4 Set the blend mode for the top layer to *Overlay*. You will see the combined image.

5 You can still tinker with the stone layer, resizing it further, and/or rotating and repositioning it. To vary the overall color of the image, you can experiment with *Enhance > Adjust Color > Hue/Saturation* on the model layer. To produce a black-and-white image, apply *Layer > New Adjustment Layer > Gradient Map* using the *Black-to-White* gradient. The effect will be slightly different with either layer.

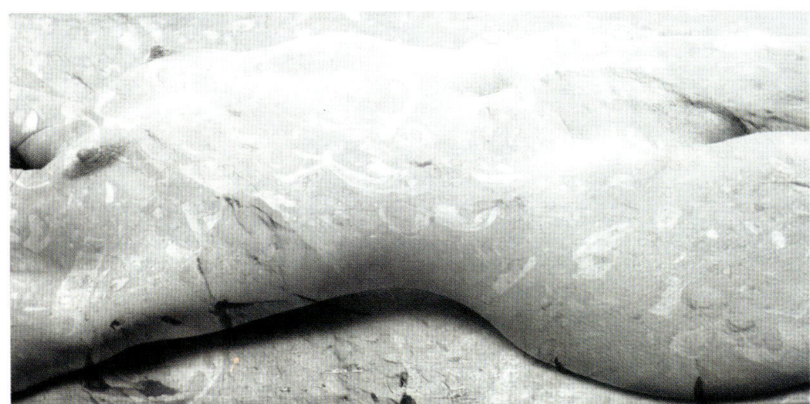

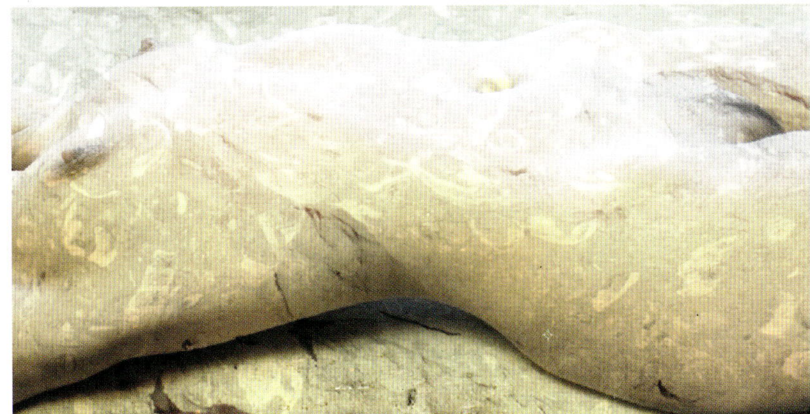

EXPERIMENTING WITH THE OVERLAY BLEND MODE

The same process produces different results when applied to a more dramatically lit image.

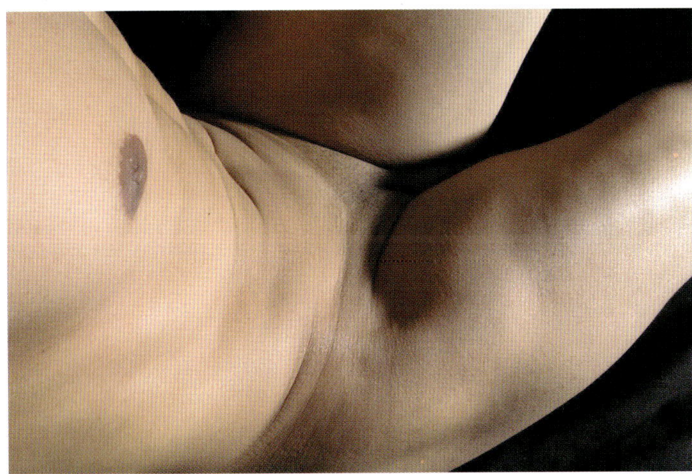

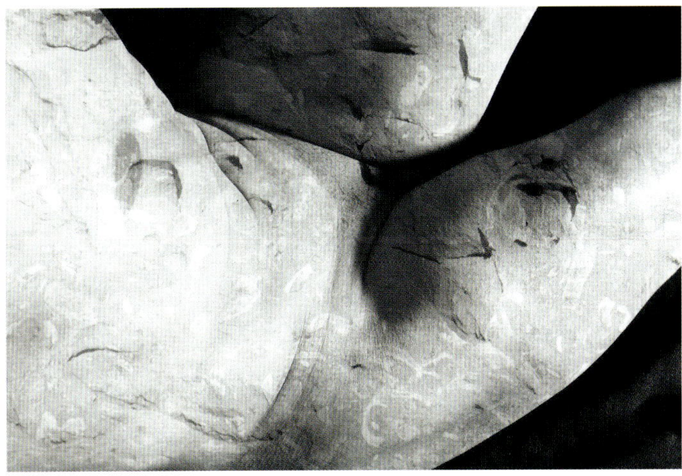

Montage

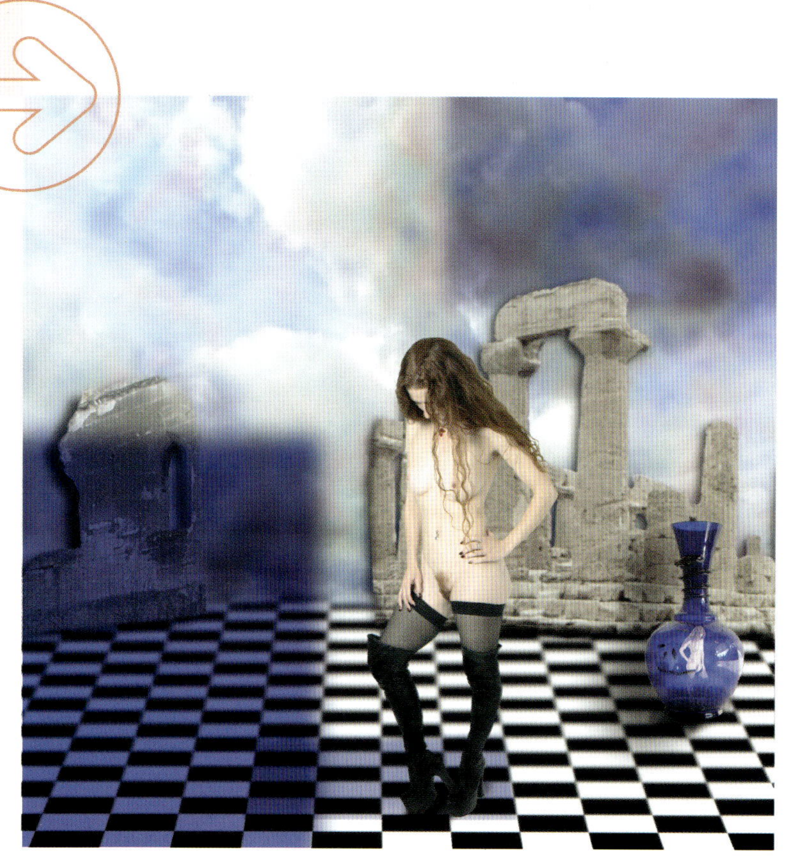

THE MONTAGE ELEMENTS

I wanted to create a dreamlike landscape in which the objects in the montage (illustrated individually below) were juxtaposed in a surreal, illogical fashion. The foreground checkerboard pattern was drawn in Elements, and the sky was a blend of real (photographed) clouds blended with Elements' digitally generated *Difference Clouds*.

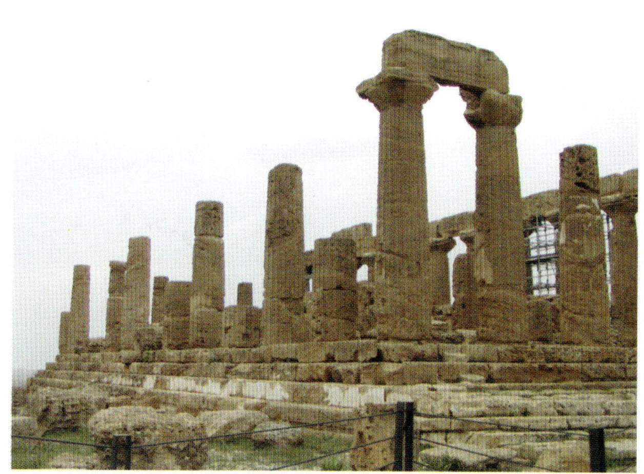

One of the buildings in the montage was a Greek temple from the Valley of the Temples near Agrigento, Sicily.

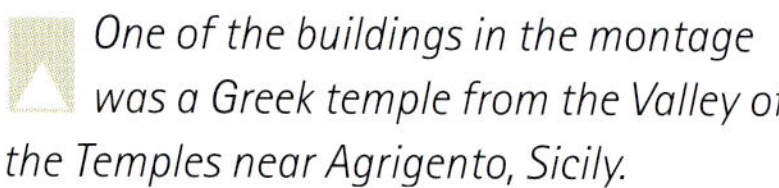

Montage refers to the combination of two or more separate pictures to form a new image. Programs like Elements, with their capacity to scale and blend layers together, make this easy to do. In this section I'm going to create a fantasy image that demonstrates these capabilities.

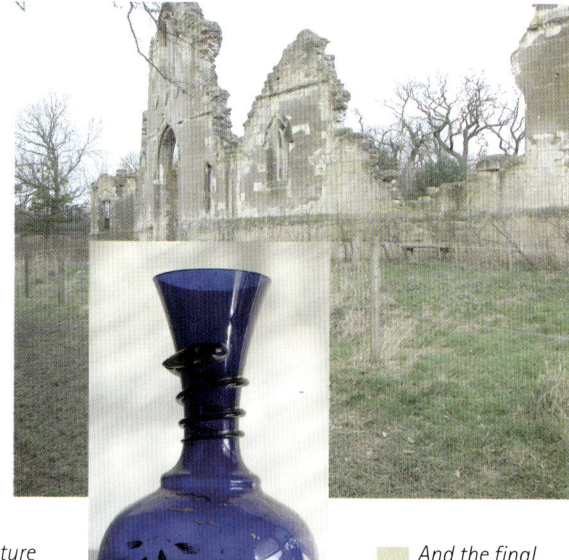

The serpent twined round the neck of this antique vase inspired me to call the image "The Serpent's Dream."

Another feature of the montage background was taken from an image of a fake medieval ruin near Cambridge.

And the final element was, of course, the nude model.

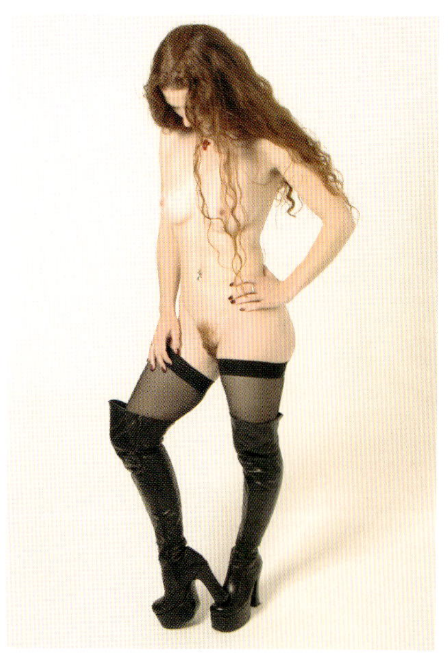

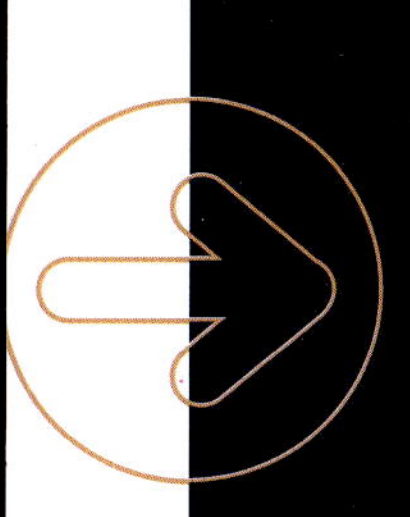
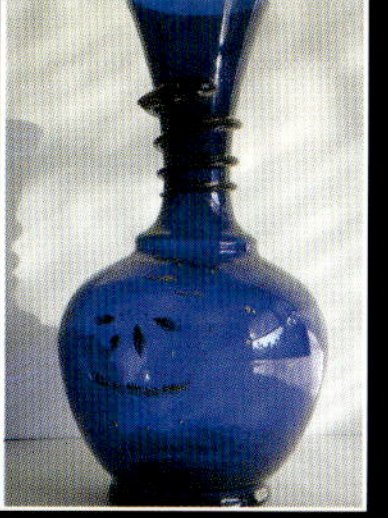
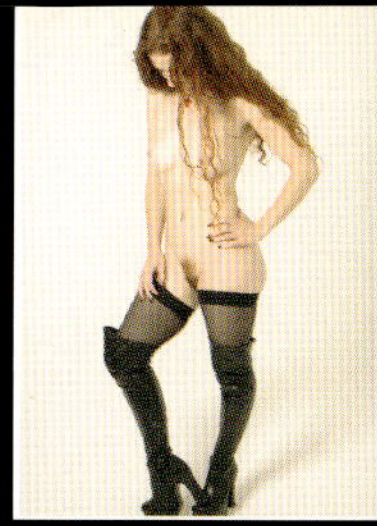

Using Photoshop Elements, it is very easy to create fantasy images made up from parts of several different photographs. The *Difference Clouds* filter and the *Perspective* tool are particularly useful in this genre.

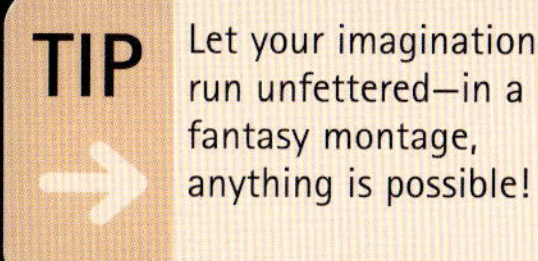

Let your imagination run unfettered—in a fantasy montage, anything is possible!

THE TILED FLOOR

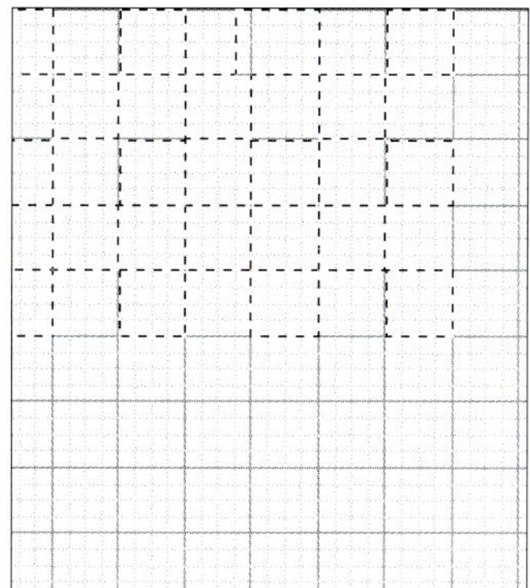

1 Create a new file of around 10 x 10 inches with a white background. Go to *Photoshop Elements* > *Preferences* > *Grid* and set the grid to ½ inch, and under *View* check *Grid* and *Snap to Grid*. With the *Marquee* tool set to *Add to Selection*, select every other square for a section of the grid.

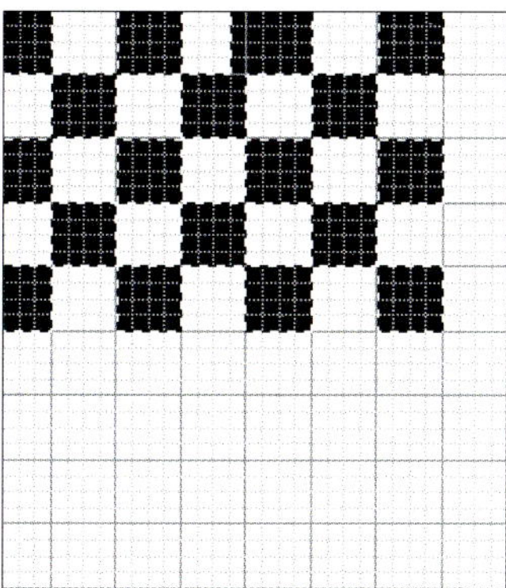

2 With the foreground color set to black, use the *Bucket* tool to fill the selected squares.

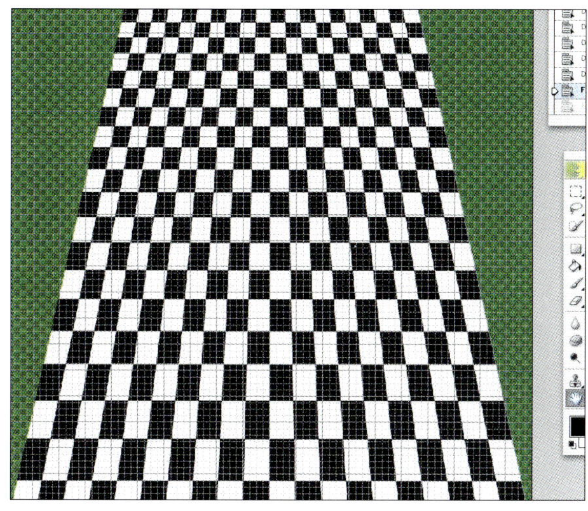

3 Select the *Move* tool and, while holding down <*Alt*>, click and drag in one of the black squares to copy all the black squares into an adjacent section of your image. To continue the pattern correctly, you may have to overlap the new section over the original by one row or column. Do this until the checkerboard pattern fills the canvas. In the *Layers* window, double-click on the *Background* layer and turn it into an ordinary layer. Go to *Image* > *Transform* > *Perspective*, and drag in the handles in either of the upper corners of the canvas to create a sense of perspective in the checkerboard.

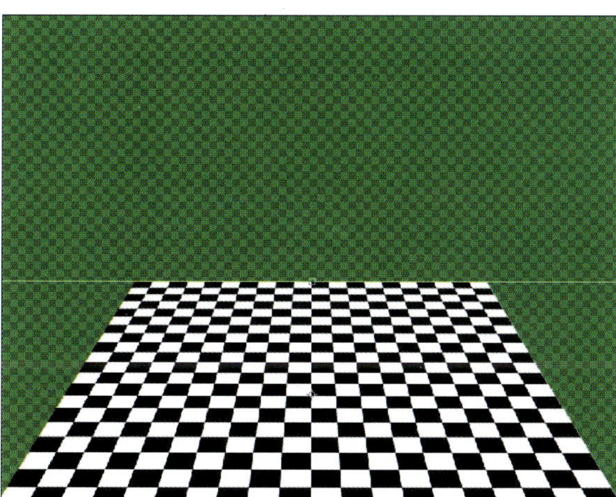

4 Uncheck *View* > *Grid*. Go to *Image* > *Transform* > *Distort*, then click in the top center handle and drag it straight down, so that the checkerboard looks like a tiled floor.

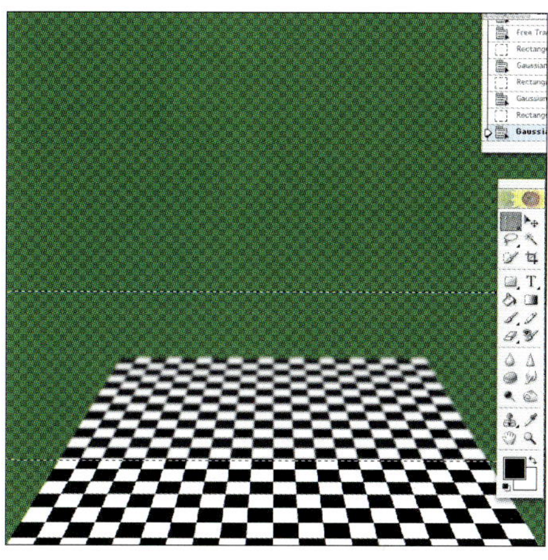

5 To complete the feeling of depth, follow the steps set out on pages 96–97 to create "graded" depth-of-field in the tiled floor, working from the "back" of the floor about halfway to the "front."

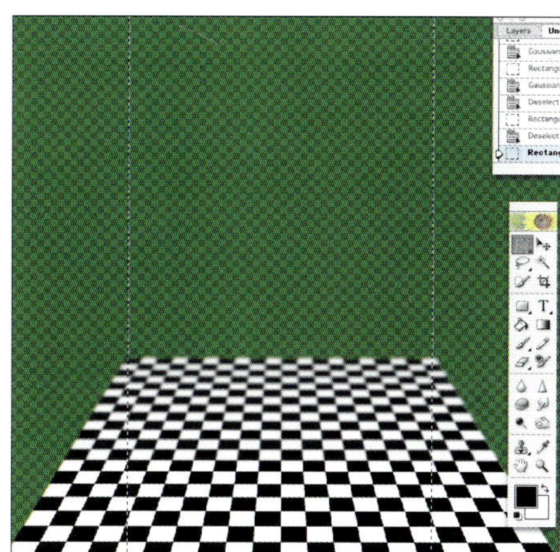

6 Finally, crop the image so that the tiled floor fills the foreground, without any space on either side.

Montage

THE CLOUDY SKY

You could create a cloudscape by using *Filter* > *Render* > ***Clouds*** and *Filter* > *Render* > ***Difference Clouds***, but using real clouds produces a more distinctive result.

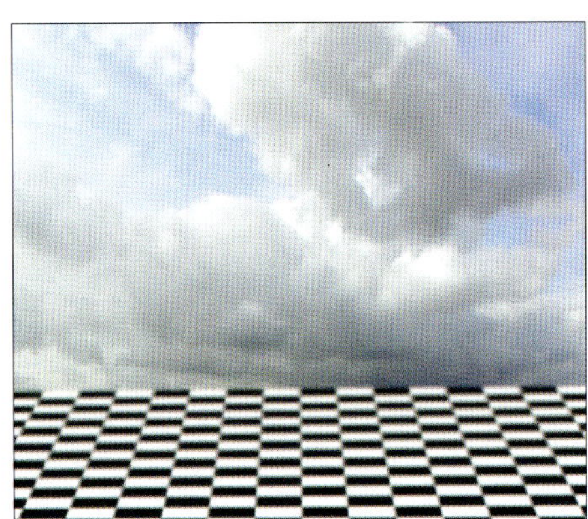

1 Copy your photographed clouds into the upper part of the image, by dragging their layer from the original photograph into the montage. They should appear in a new layer. Position them so that they just overlap the tiled floor. If they're too small and you need to increase the size of this layer, that's fine: any slight pixellation will be masked by blending the layer with digitally generated clouds in the next few steps.

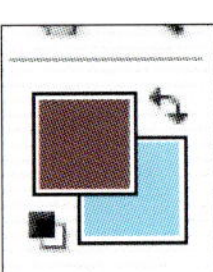

2 I set my foreground color to a deep red brown, and my background color to a rich sky blue.

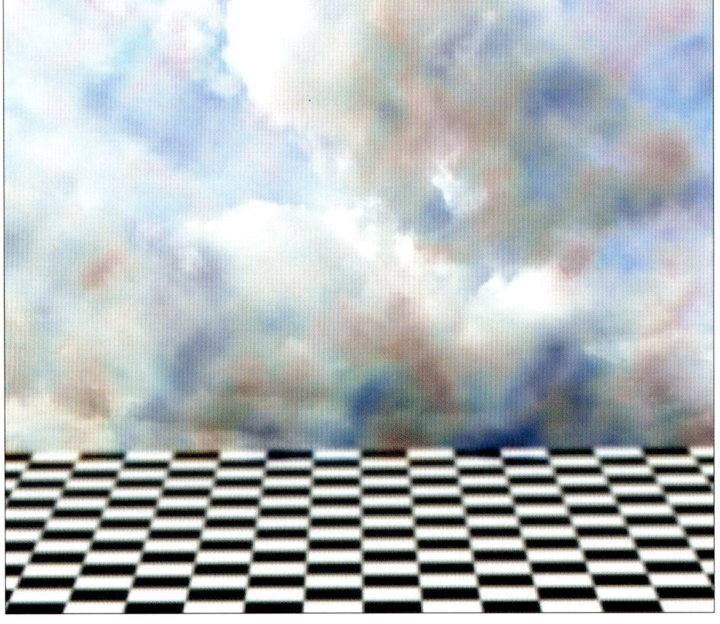

3 Create a new layer above the layer containing the photographed clouds and set its blend mode to *Soft Light*. In this new layer, use the *Marquee* tool to select the area above the clouds you created in Step 1. Go to *Filter* > *Render* > ***Clouds*** to fill this layer with digital cloud. Go to *Filter* > *Render* > ***Difference Clouds*** to create a dramatic cloudscape. You may want to try these two steps a couple of times, experimenting with changing the colors. When you're satisfied with the result, and keeping the layer of digital cloud still active, go to *More* > ***Merge Down*** in the *Layers* window to combine both cloud layers. If necessary, use a low setting of *Gaussian Blur* on the cloud layer to enhance the illusion of depth-of-field. With the *Eraser* tool set to a low *Opacity*, soften the edge of the cloud layer where it meets the tiled floor.

ADDING FOREGROUND OBJECTS

For each of the remaining objects, you need to follow these steps. Note that the first three steps are carried out on copies of the original files containing the objects, before you add the objects to the montage.

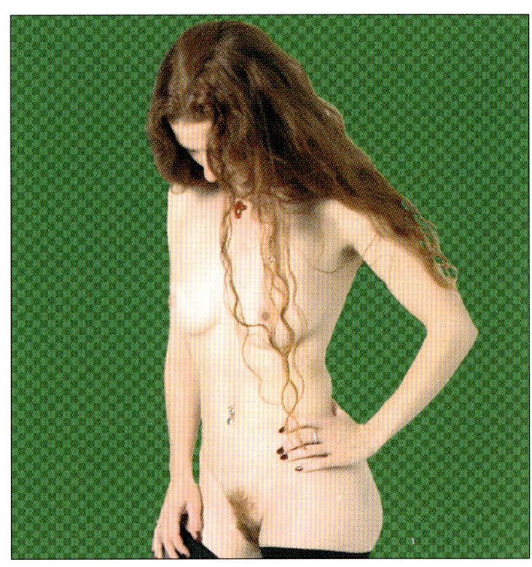

1 Make a copy of the original file containing the object. In this new file, double-click on the background layer in the *Layers* window and convert it into a normal layer. Select the object carefully and clear everything else from the layer so that the object is left surrounded by transparency. It may be easier to select the background than the object itself. Don't feather any of the edges as you make the selection. If you have selected the background, remove it by going to *Edit* > ***Clear***. If you have selected the object, go to *Select* > ***Inverse***, then *Edit* > ***Clear***. Copy each object by dragging its layer from the copy file into the montage. It's essential that each object has its own layer! Every time you add another layer, the overall look of the composition changes, so you may need to readjust earlier layers by repeating some or all of the next steps. Using the *Move* tool, <shift + drag> in the handle in one corner of the layer to scale it to the size you require. Use *Image* > *Transform* > ***Perspective*** and *Image* > *Transform* > ***Distort*** to make the layer fit into the overall design. Adjust the color of the layer as necessary.

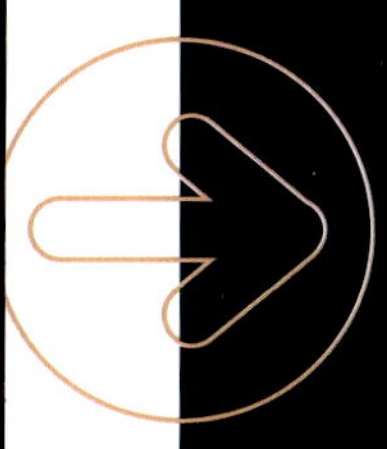

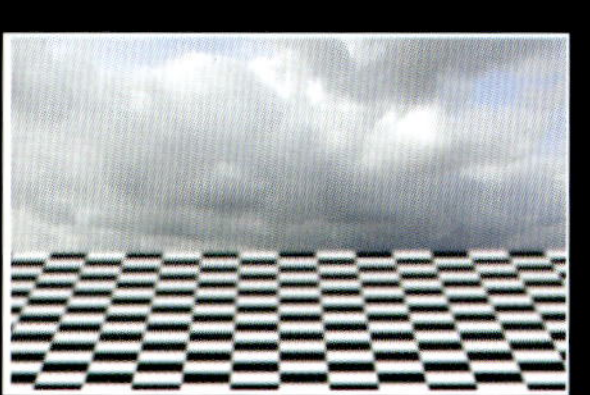

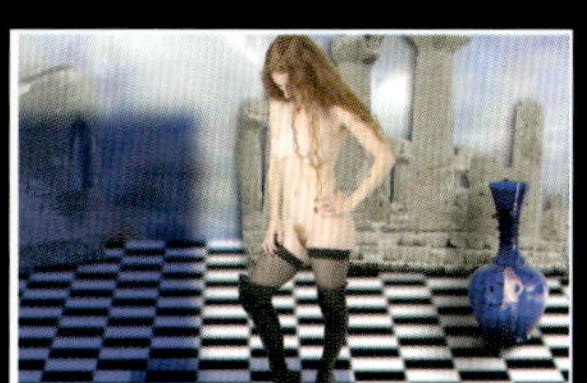

The various techniques demonstrated here lend themselves to almost any type of image. Try to resist the temptation to place too many elements in an image. Sometimes a more subtle approach is more effective.

PUTTING THE MODEL IN THE BOTTLE

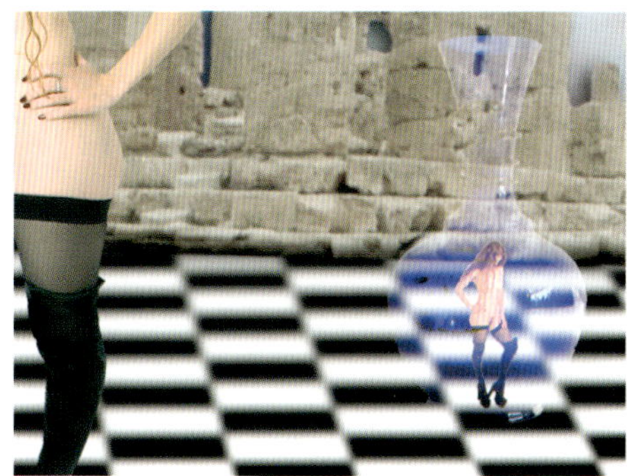

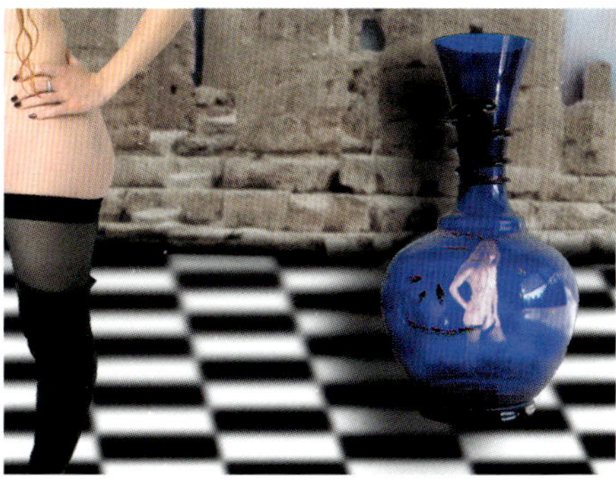

1 Carefully position and scale the bottle, making sure it's on a layer by itself. Set the blend mode of this layer to *Screen*. The results won't look right at this stage, but you need to be able to see through the bottle in order to carry out the next step. Carefully position and scale the image of the model that you want to appear inside the bottle. This layer should be immediately below the bottle layer. You see the model inside the bottle, but the background still looks wrong. In this example I've also used *Image > Rotate > Flip Layer Horizontal* to flip the model.

2 Create a new empty layer, underneath the layer containing the model in the bottle. In the *Layers* window, make the bottle layer active, and command-click on it. The bottle is selected. Make the empty layer you created earlier active, and go to *Edit > Fill*. For *Contents*, use *Black*. An area of black is created behind the bottle. Sightly reduce the *Opacity* of the layer, so that the tiled floor is just visible through the bottle.

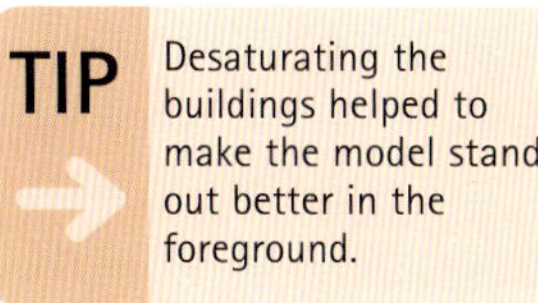

TIP Desaturating the buildings helped to make the model stand out better in the foreground.

3 Use *Enhance > Adjust Color > **Hue/Saturation*** to desaturate the skin tones of the model, in order to enhance the illusion of seeing her through the blue glass. As you build up your layers, you may notice places where the object wasn't perfectly selected. Use the *Eraser* tool, set to 100% *Opacity* and a small soft brush size, to tidy up any rough edges. In this example I found that the internal edges (around windows, etc on the buildings) needed particular attention.

SHADOWS UNDER OBJECTS

At this stage your objects may all look as if they're floating just above the tiled floor. You need to add shadows to bring them down to earth.

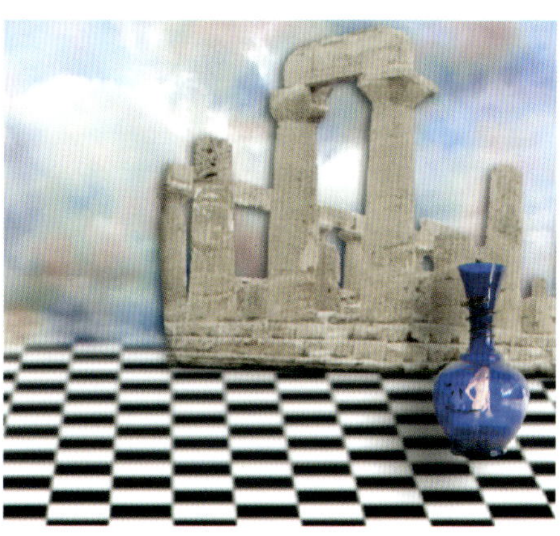

1 Create an empty layer below each object's layer. Using a small soft brush with about 50% *Opacity*, paint in a black shadow under each object, with every shadow on a separate layer.

FINALLY...

I found that the strangeness of the montage was enhanced by adding a series of soft-edged transparent colored shapes.

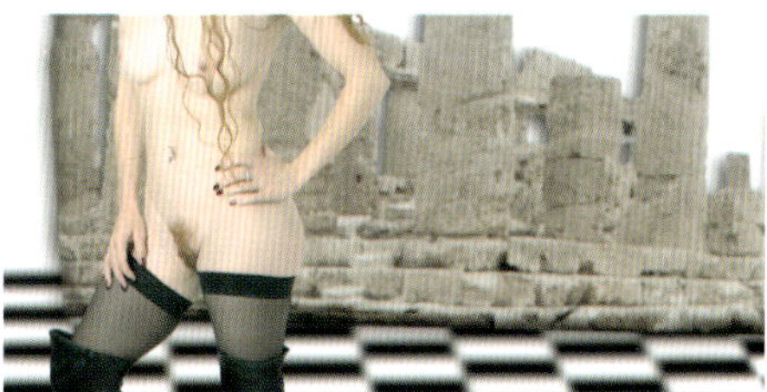

1 Create each shape on a separate layer. Use the *Marquee* tool with a 30-pixel *Feather* to draw the shape. Set the foreground color to a suitable color. Use *Edit > Fill > **Use Contents: Foreground Color*** to fill each shape. Adjust the opacity of each shape. Experiment with *Image > Transform > **Perspective*** and/or *Image > Transform > **Distort*** to alter the spatial relationship between each shape and the rest of the montage.

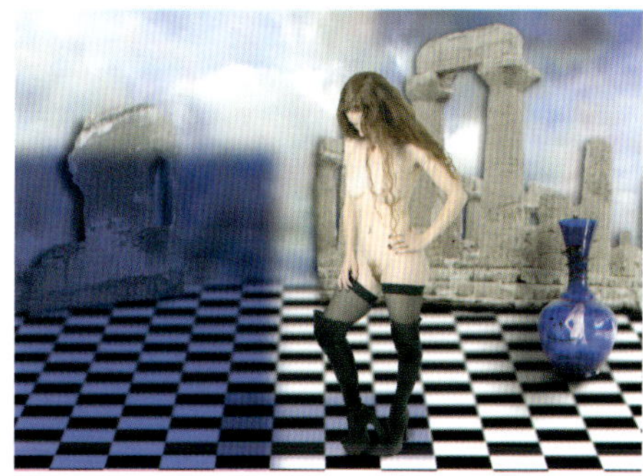

2 The final version of "The Serpent's Dream." You can go on tweaking and refining an image like this for ever, so always save a copy of it with all layers separate, before you flatten it..

Collage

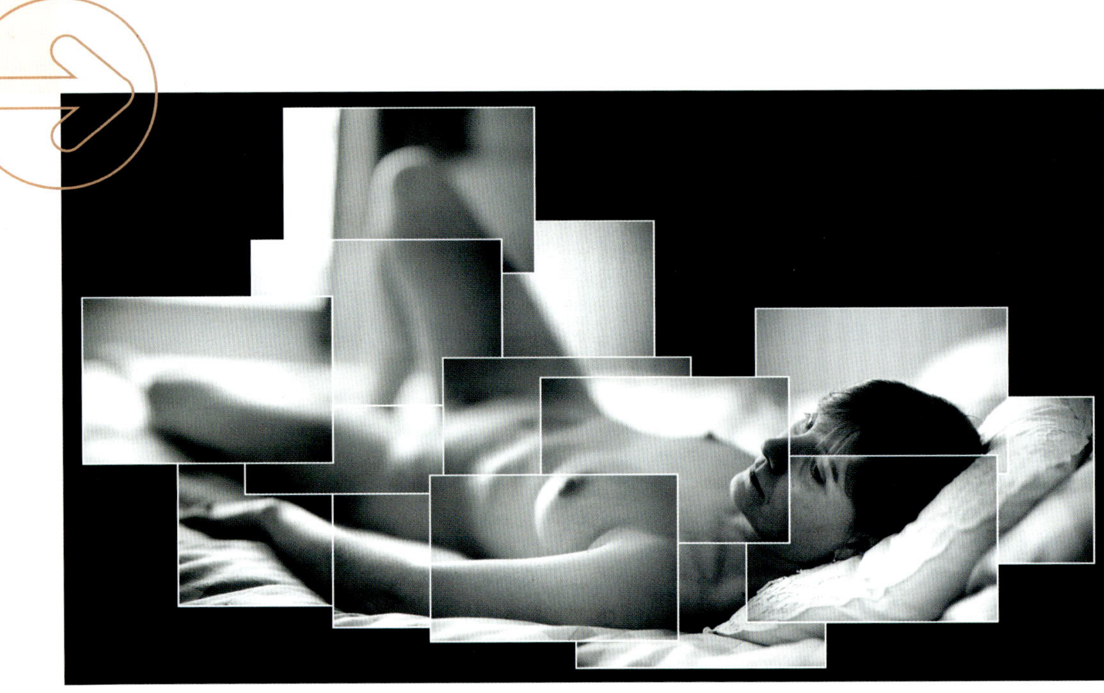

The collage image in its final form. Note how it follows the shape of the model.

Some of the separate images from which the collage is constructed.

Collages are made up of several separate photographs fitted together. Here we follow this process through, from shooting the photographs to preparing them for the collage and assembling the complete image. This example, created by Bruce Robertson, was shot on film and constructed from scanned negatives, but the process is just the same for wholly digital images.

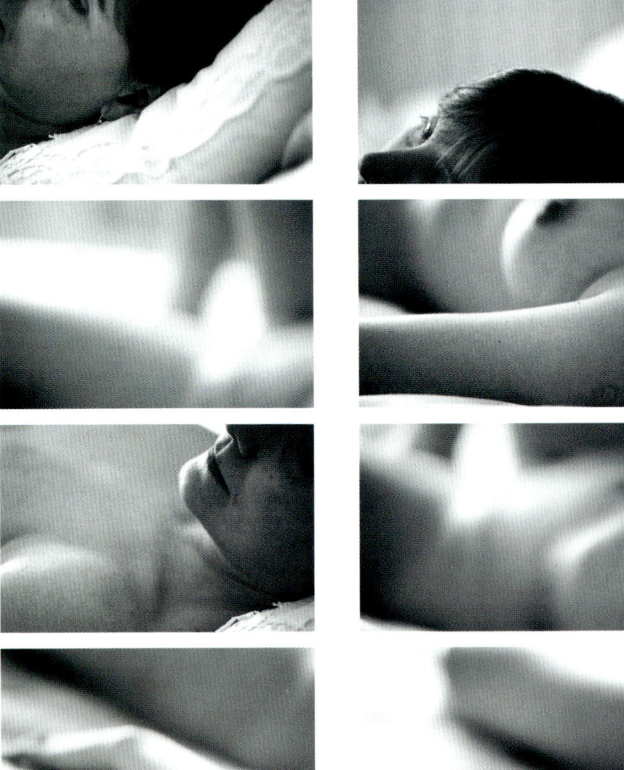

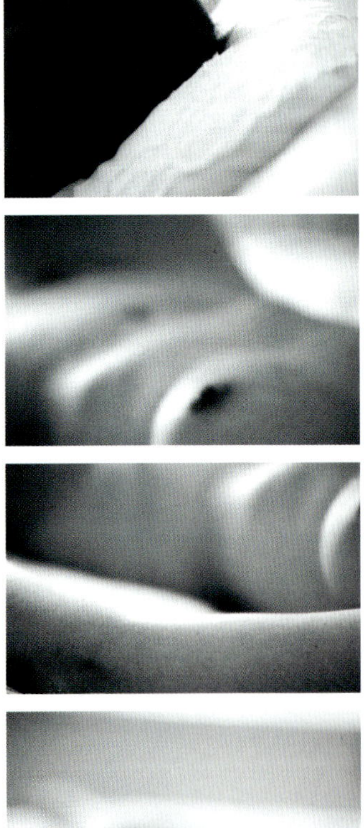

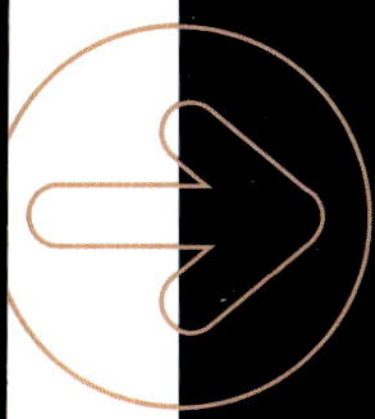

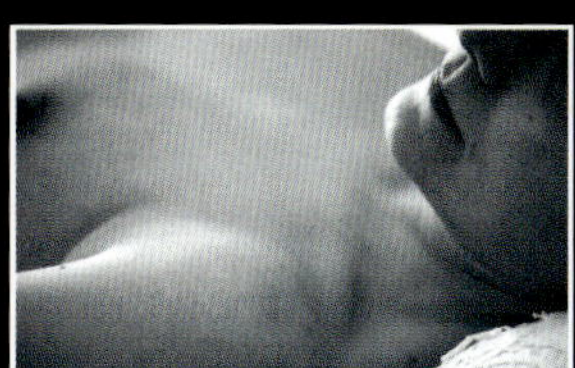

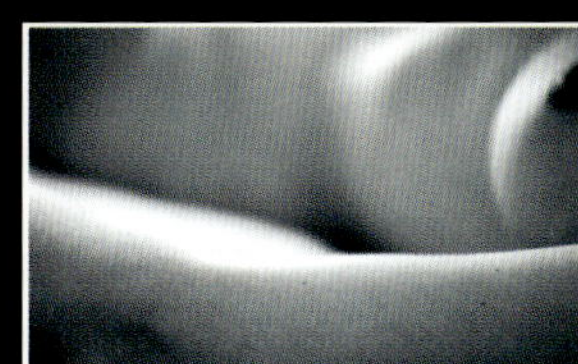

This collage effect, constructed from several different images, is easy to create with a working knowledge of layers. The result is more subtle than an overt montage, and still eyecatching.

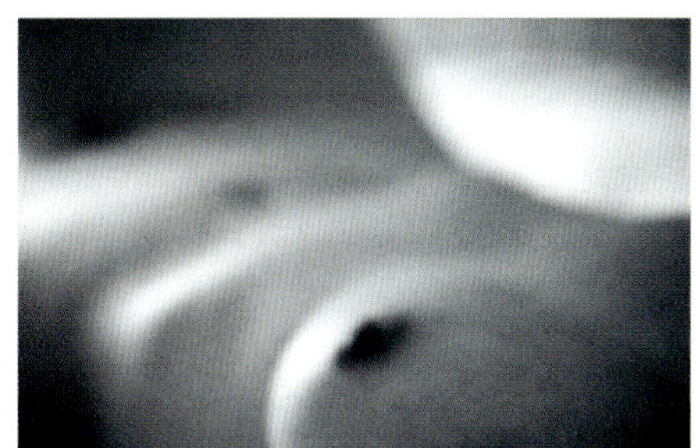

1 Review your pictures, and estimate the dimensions of the composite image, in tiles. In this example, the final image is six tiles wide by five tiles high. Decide roughly how large you want the final image to be (including any border), and create a new Elements file, with a black background, of that size (we'll call this the final file). In this example, the print size of the finished image is about 12½ x 7¼ inches. It's safer to make the image slightly larger than you finally want it: you can always scale it down later. As always, duplicate the files of all the separate photographs for safety. Scale each photograph to its "tile" size. In this example, the final image is six tiles across, but you need to allow for overlap, so make each tile about one quarter of the final size.

2 If you want the image to be black-and-white, convert the tiles to black-and-white and then go to *Image* > *Mode* > *Grayscale* to make them grayscale files (about one-third the size of an RGB file). Smaller file sizes will use up less RAM on your computer as you build up the collage. In this example, each tile has been given a white border. For each tile, double-click on the background layer in the *Layers* window to convert the layer into an ordinary layer. Then go to *Edit* > *Stroke*. In this example, 12 pixels worked well.

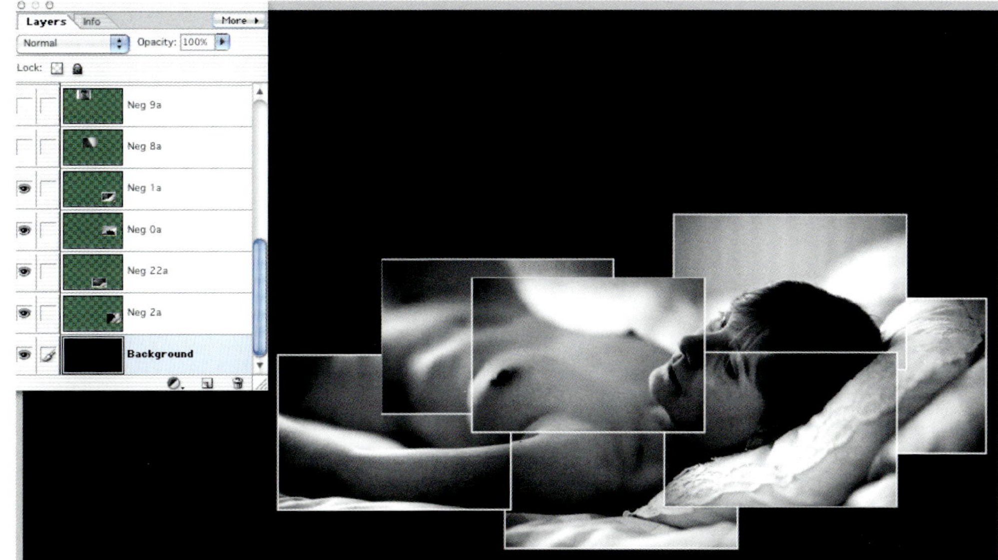

3 Now you are ready to assemble the collage. Tile by tile, click in the layer in the *Layers* window, and drag the tile into the final file. Check that Elements is placing each tile on a separate layer. Now position the tiles. Vary the amount of overlap to avoid creating too much regularity. Also vary the way the tiles overlap (that is, don't make a regular pattern like the tiles on a roof). Do this by dragging layers up and down in the *Layers* window. To help you concentrate on one section of the collage, it's often helpful to switch the other tiles off.

FACT FILE

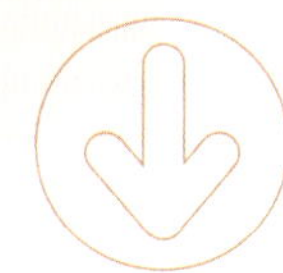

Photography for collage

To ensure good results for collage images:

▶ Set your camera to manual focus mode.

▶ Use a tripod, and don't reposition it or alter its height between shots.

▶ Frame the area you want to have in focus. When you've set the zoom and focus for that area, don't change them as you shoot the sequence.

▶ As you pan and tilt the camera to create the separate "tiles," follow the model's shape, but without forming a regular pattern.

▶ Some of the separate tiles will be hard to recognize as parts of the body. Work methodically to make it easier to identify each tile.

▶ The separate shots need to overlap, so you will probably shoot more tiles than you need.

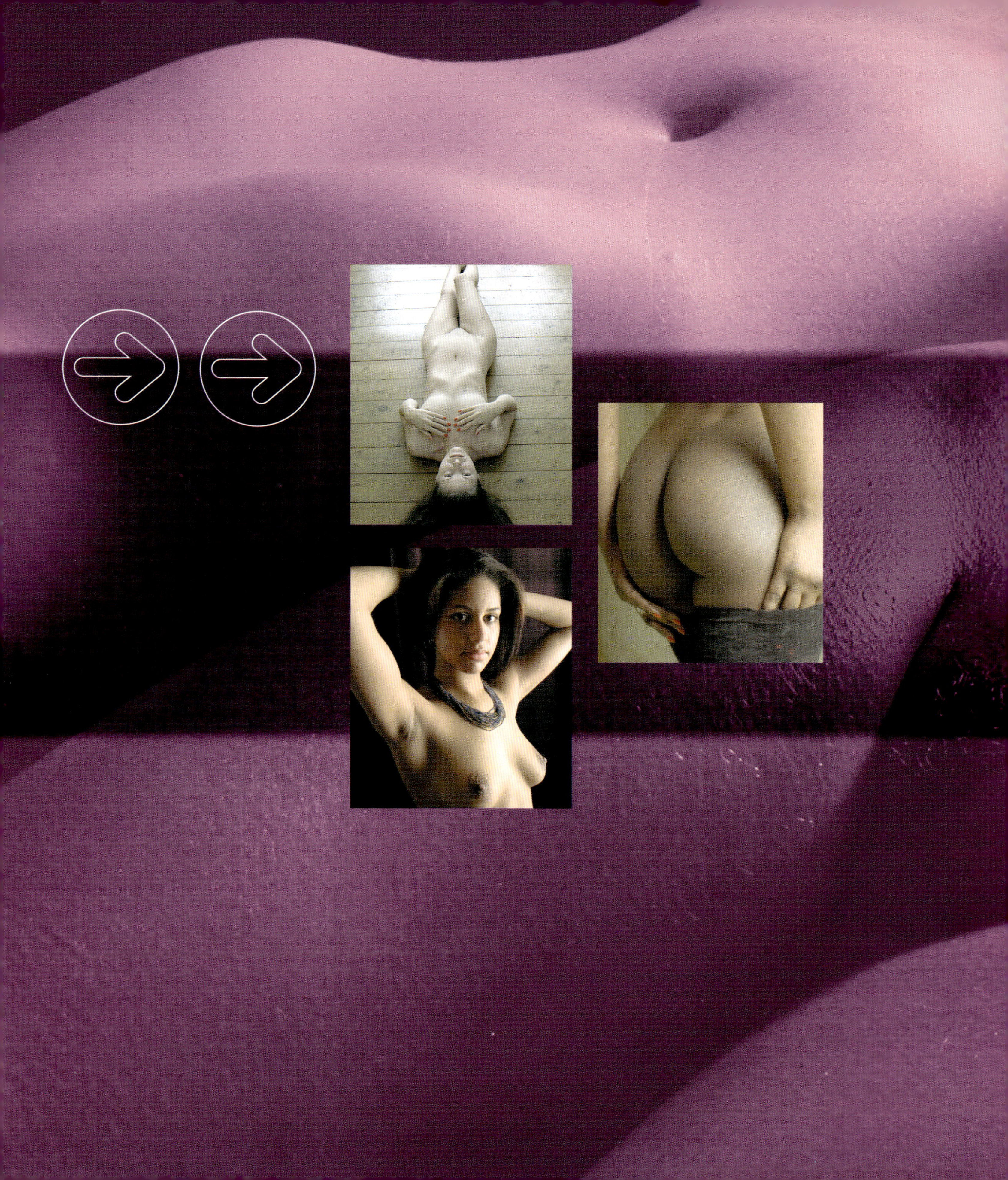

4 Showing and sharing

There's not much point spending time creating images if no-one else gets to see them! In this chapter we look at ways of putting your work on the web, from photography-oriented user-groups through to setting up your own website. We also look at assembling sequences of images into slideshows to distribute on CD-ROM. In a more traditional vein, we look into the use of inkjet printers to make high-quality prints, and explore different ways to frame and show them.

Getting the best from your printer

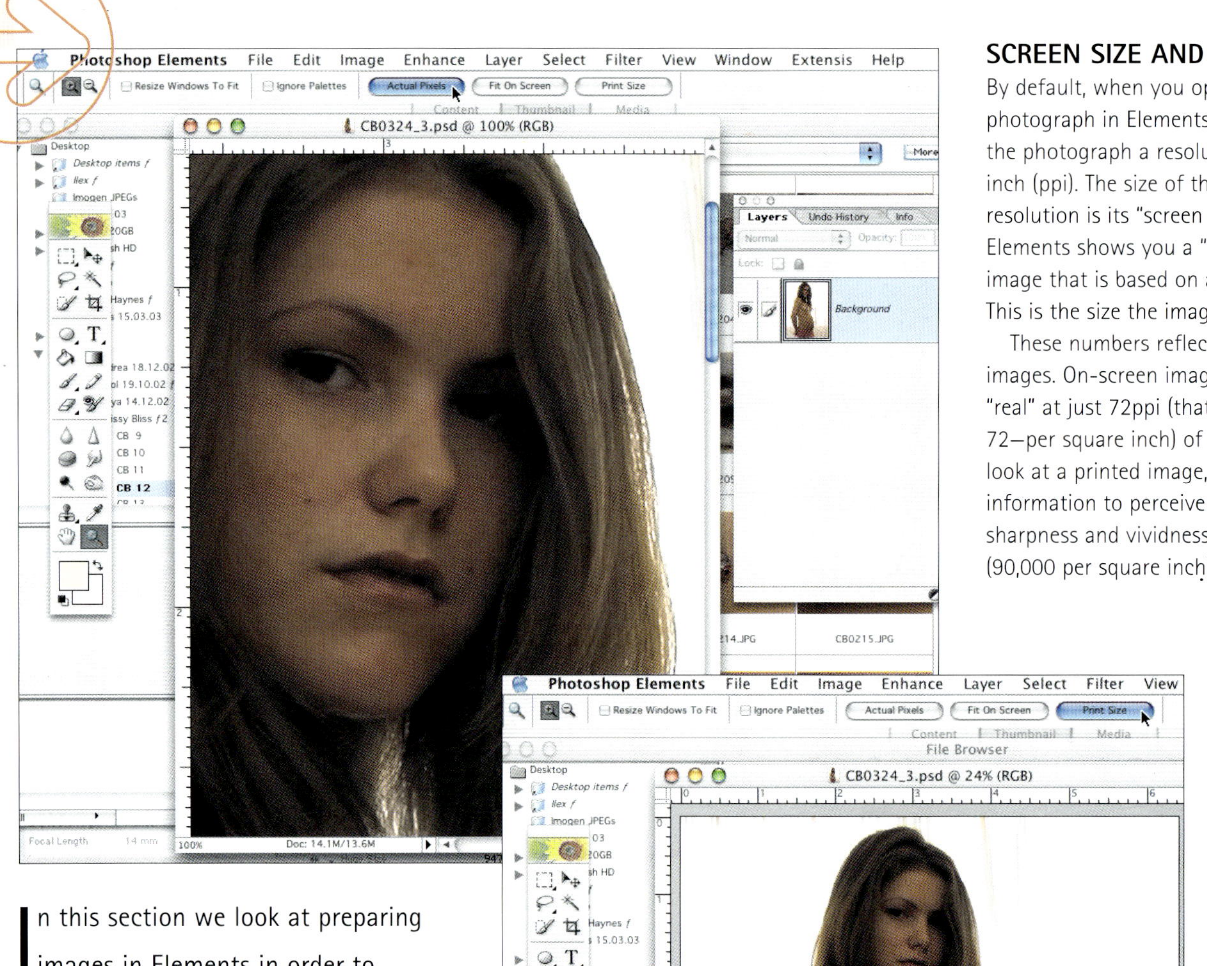

You can see the difference between screen and print sizes by selecting the Zoom *tool, then clicking on the* Actual Pixels *and* Print Size *buttons.*

SCREEN SIZE AND PRINT SIZE

By default, when you open a digital photograph in Elements, the program assigns the photograph a resolution of 72 pixels per inch (ppi). The size of the image at this resolution is its "screen size." At the same time, Elements shows you a "document size" for the image that is based on a resolution of 300ppi. This is the size the image will be when printed.

These numbers reflect the way we perceive images. On-screen images look sharp and "real" at just 72ppi (that is, 5184 pixels—72 x 72—per square inch) of the display. When we look at a printed image, we need more information to perceive the same level of sharpness and vividness—about 300ppi (90,000 per square inch) for an inkjet printer.

In this section we look at preparing images in Elements in order to achieve good, reliable output from your printer, and examine the difference between screen and printer resolution. This chapter deals only with preparing pictures to print on domestic inkjet printers. It's also possible to have photographic prints made from your images. If you do this, the photo-processing house you go to will tell you how they require your files to be formatted and presented.

CREATING BORDERS

Before you deal with the process of printing itself, consider whether you want the image to have a border. This will partly depend on how the image is to be framed or presented (which is covered on pages 132–133). If you would like to get away from the straight edges that the camera imposes on your image, there are a number of options for creating borders. There are commercial products like Extensis Photoframe *(www.extensis.com/photoframe/)*, which offer the digital photographer thousands of different patterns for frames and borders. Alternatively, you can draw your own. In this example, I chose to add an irregular edge by hand to my pictures.

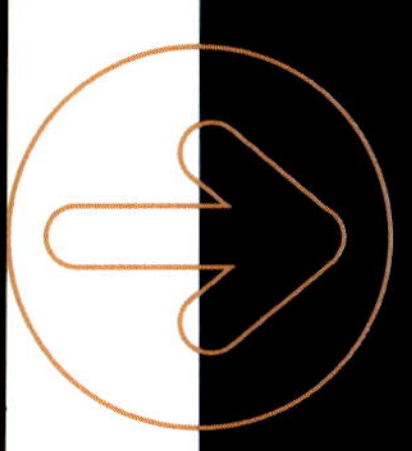

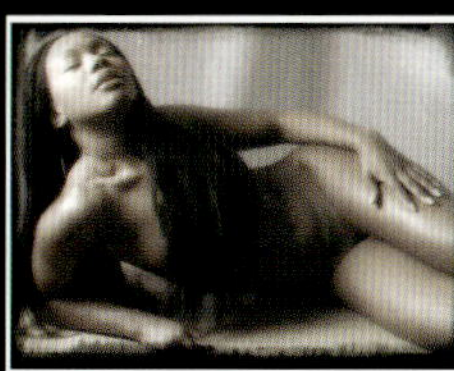

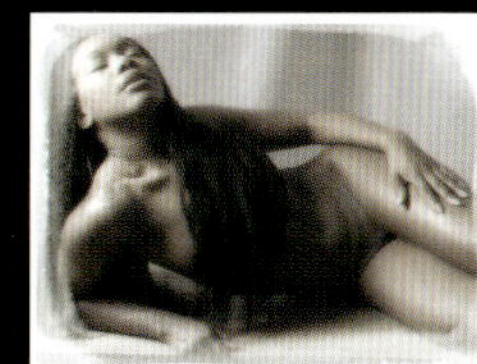

Before you attempt to print out an image, it is advisable to have an understanding of the relationship between image resolution and output size. What looks good on screen may often appear pixellated when output to a printer.

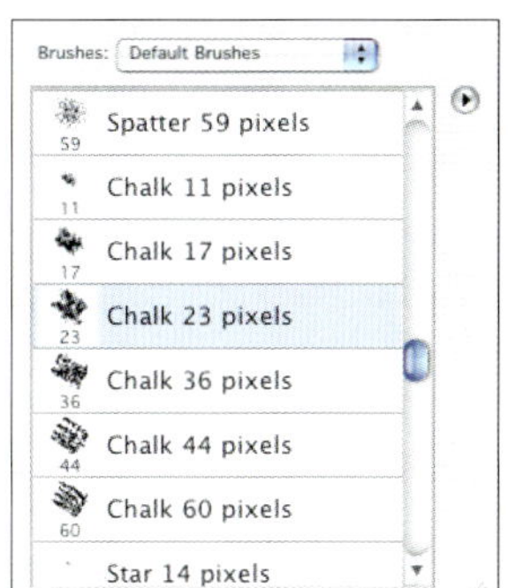

1 Add a new layer to the image for which you want to create a border. Go to *Image* > *Resize* > *Canvas Size*. Check the *Relative* box and increase the size of the canvas by adding 50 pixels to the width and height. This gives you some extra space to create the border in, without cropping the image too much. Select a rough brush, and choose white as the foreground color.

Adobe Photoshop Elements

The new canvas size is smaller than the current canvas size; some clipping will occur.

Cancel | Proceed

2 Make sure you have selected the top layer, and paint (not too precisely) round the edge of the image. Use the *Eraser* tool to correct any slips. Once you have created the border you want, go to *Image* > *Resize* > *Canvas Size* once more. This time, type in -50 pixels into the height and width boxes. When you see the warning message saying that you are about to clip the canvas, click on *Proceed*.

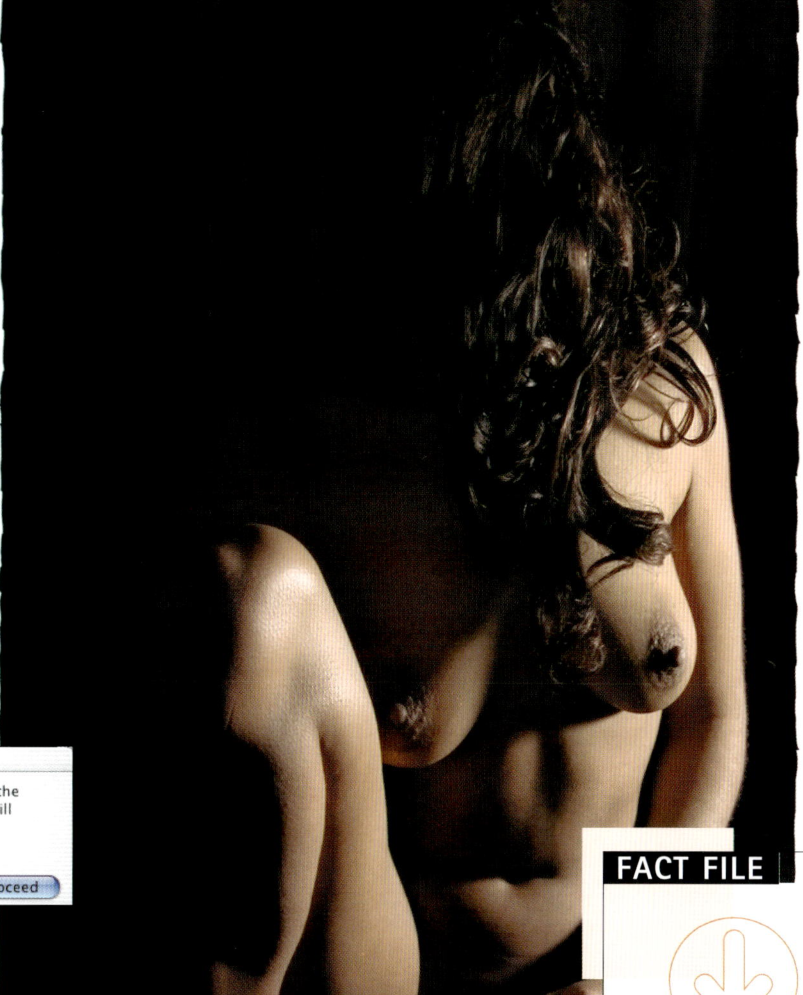

A homemade wiggly edge. Experiment with different brushes in Elements to decide which you prefer.

FACT FILE

Increasing the size of the printed image

You can use *Image* > *Resize* > *Image Size* to make your picture bigger. Beyond a certain point, however (about 120% of the original size), the image becomes noticeably pixellated. This is less of an issue when you are printing the whole of the image than it is when you have cropped the image severely and want to print a small area to the same size you print uncropped images.

Getting the best from your printer

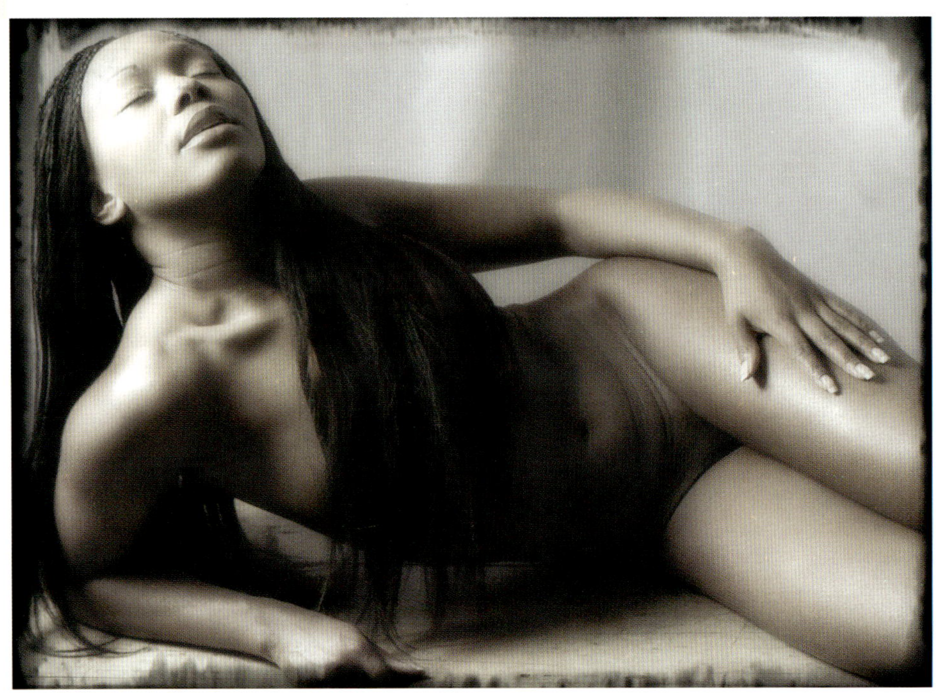

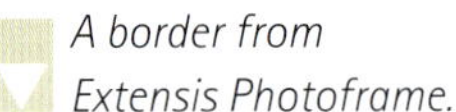

▲ *The same border in white and black.*

▼ *A border from Extensis Photoframe.*

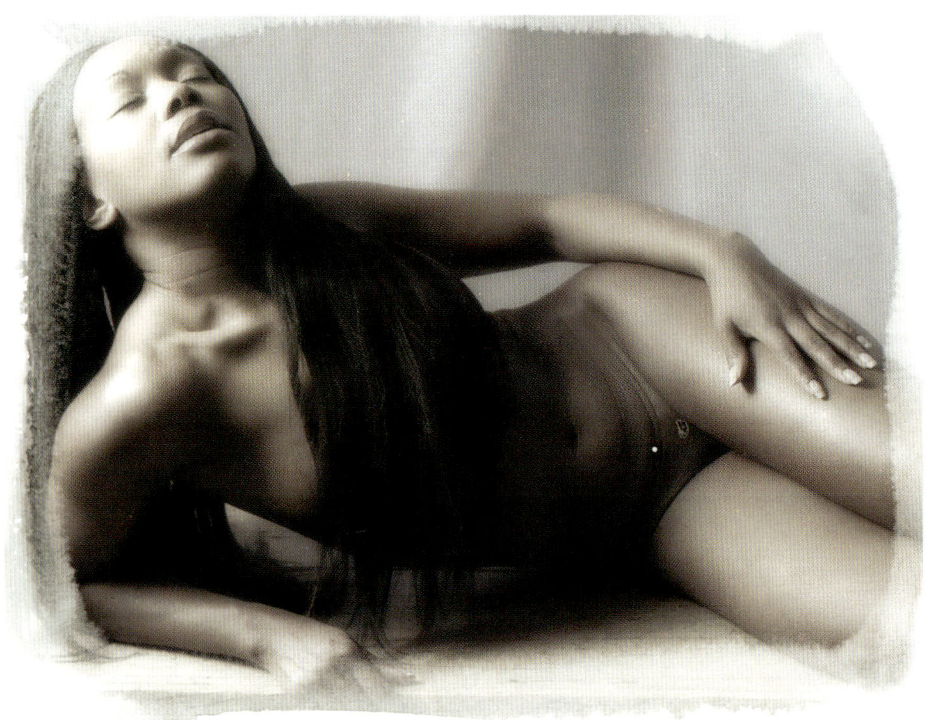

PAPER AND INK

Papers for printing photographs on inkjet printers are available in a wide range of qualities, weights, and finishes. Not all have equal durability, so you may want to check with the manufacturer about the archival properties of their papers (and inks). However, this is much less of an issue now than when inkjet printers first came onto the market.

You won't go wrong by sticking to the printer manufacturer's own paper and inks, but it's also worth trying out materials from other manufacturers. Traditional photographic paper-makers like Kodak and Ilford now also produce good inkjet papers.

PRINTING BLACK-AND-WHITE

The received wisdom is that printing black-and-white images with just the black ink in a color printer doesn't produce sufficiently dense blacks. On the other hand, printing black using all the inks may produce a color cast. I have found that one technique works better with some prints, and the other method with other prints. If you can dedicate one printer just to doing black-and-white, there are a number of ink systems available that in effect replace the color inks with black inks to provide richer blacks and better durability. See www.piezography.com and www.lyson.com.

PRESERVING YOUR PRINTS

Check the drying time for the paper you are using, and let the print dry for that length of time, lying it flat in a stable atmosphere. The drying time may vary from a few minutes to 24 hours. After that, prints should be stored out of the light, in boxes or wallets that shield them from atmospheric pollutants.

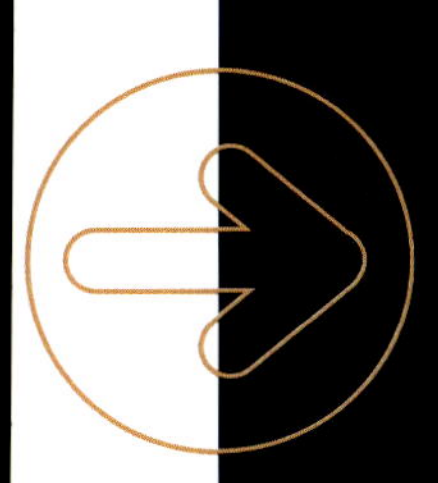

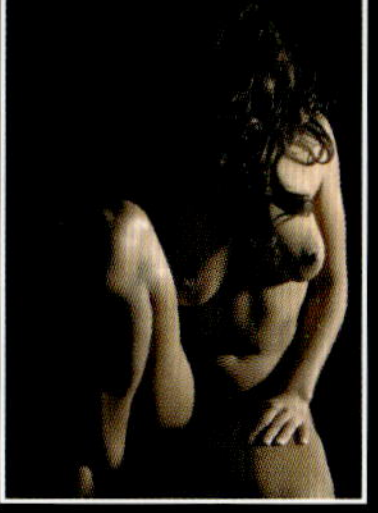

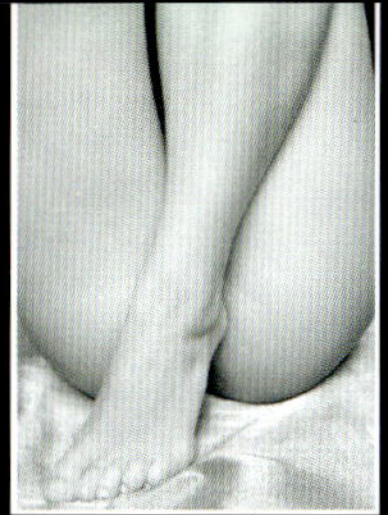

Effective color management is a key part of getting the best results from your printer. Different printers have different color management profiles, so make sure you set up your printer options correctly.

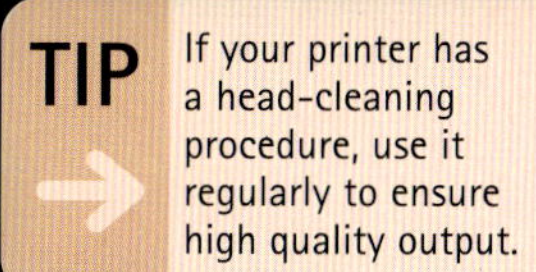

SETTING UP THE PRINTER

Let's look at the setup for a typical printer. This is an Epson Colour Stylus 880, but the interface and options for more modern printers and printers from other manufacturers will lead you through similar steps.

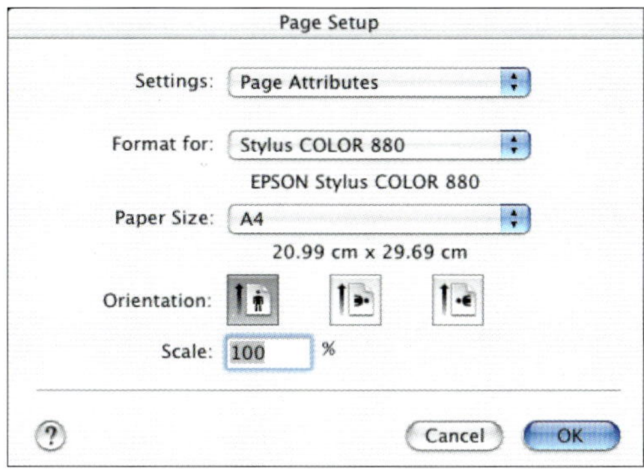

1 Go to *File* > *Page Setup* and check that the correct printer and paper size are selected.

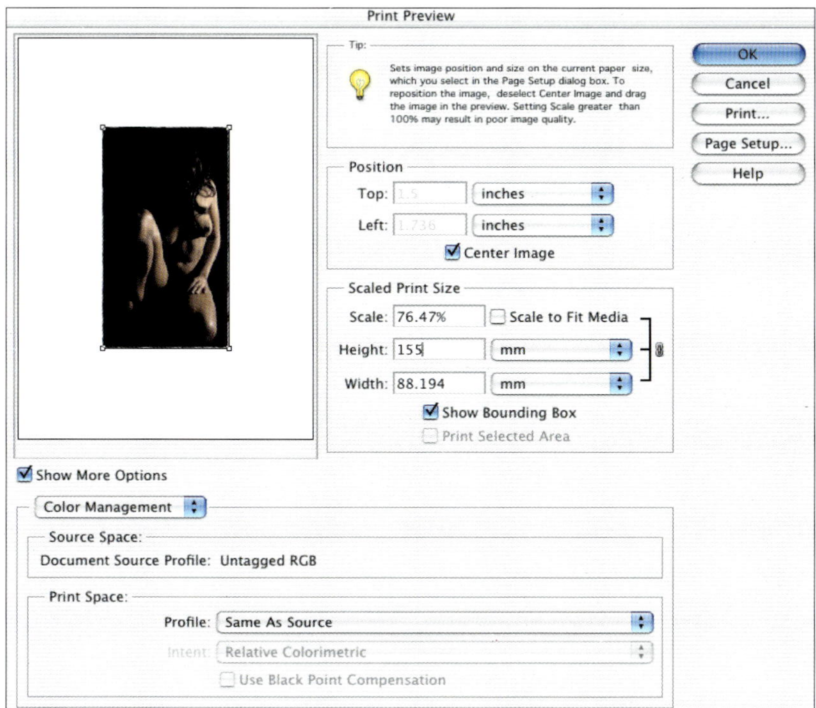

2 Go to *File* > *Print Preview* and set up the image size you want. You have the opportunity here to scale the image up beyond 100%. Using the printer's own software to scale images up produces better results than increasing the image size in Elements. Either way, you will find that there are limits to how far you can increase the size of an image above 100% before pixellation and other artifacts start to appear. Still in the same window, go into *Color Management* and set the print space to *Same As Source*. If you don't want the picture printed in the center of the sheet, use the *Position* options to locate it where you want it.

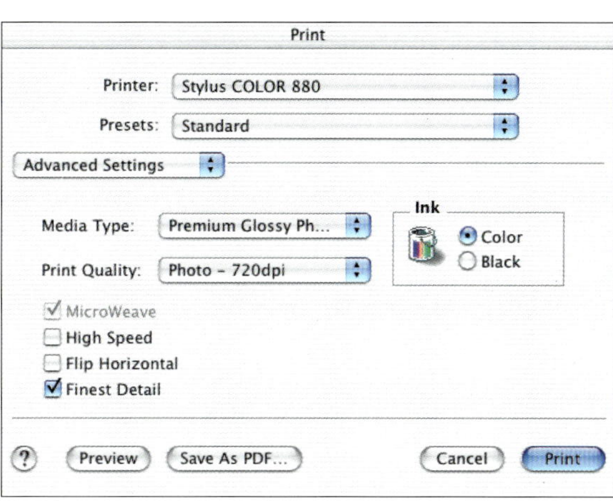

3 When you're finished with the *Print Preview* options, click on *Print*. The most important submenu is *Advanced Settings*. Here you choose the *Media Type* and the *Print Quality*. In this case I'm printing at 720dpi and I've also unchecked *High Speed* and checked *Finest Detail*. In theory, the more dpi you print with, the sharper and truer in color your pictures should be. However, after experimenting with different settings, I've concluded that there's virtually no visible difference on my printer between images printed at 1440dpi and at 720dpi with the *Finest Detail* option checked. The lower resolution prints faster, and uses less ink. In fact, if you print at 1440dpi and your image has areas of intensely saturated colors, you may notice a metallic sheen (called "bronzing") on the surface of the paper. This is caused by the printer laying more ink on the surface of the paper than it can fully absorb. Switching to 720dpi may cure this. When you're satisfied that you've configured the print job correctly, click *Print*.

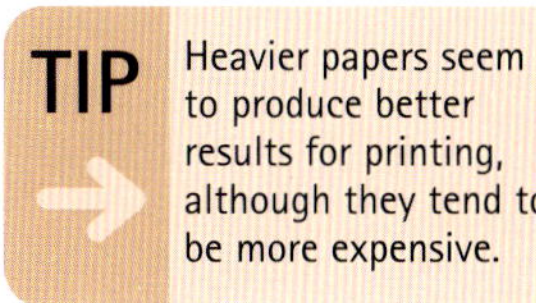

Presenting prints

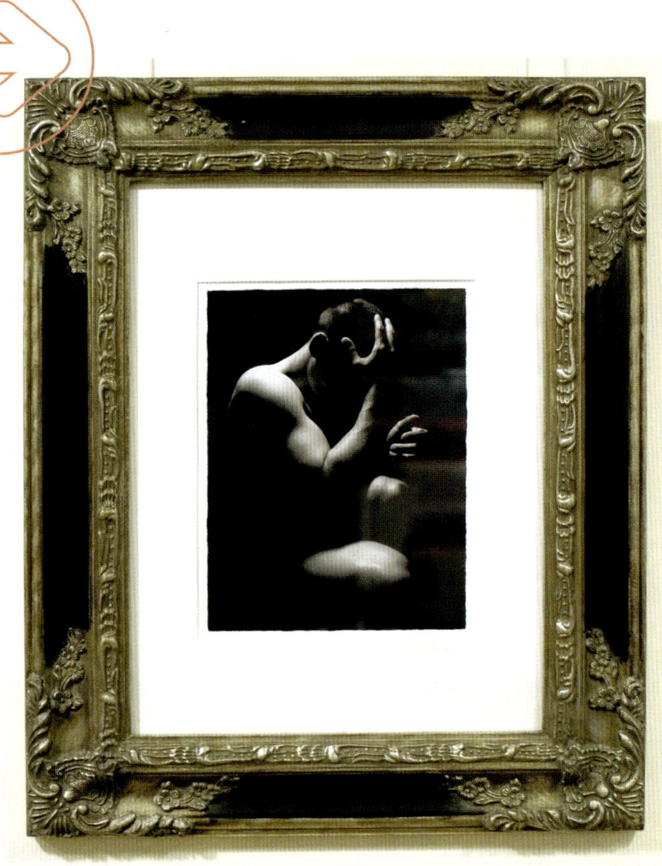

Rules are made to be broken! You wouldn't expect these ornate frames to work with black-and-white photography, but in fact they look wonderful.

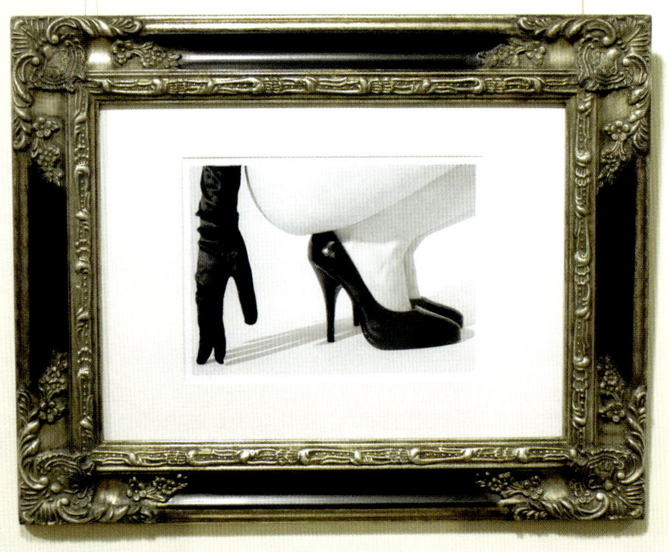

In this section we consider some options for framing prints, considering frame and image sizes, white space, and different borders. We also look at possible locations for exhibiting your work.

WHITE SPACE

It's important to consider how much white space you want around an image. This depends on the style of the frame, and on where you intend to exhibit your work. Some people exhibit their work without any white space, using a very simple frame and bringing the frame right up against the image. This can look spectacular when the pictures are shown, spaced well apart, in a large gallery.

I tend to print images with a lot of white space around them. Typically, the image itself ends up no larger than about 5½ x 4¼ inches, centered on a 10 x 8-inch sheet. The wide border makes it easier to see each image distinctly, without being distracted by its surroundings. This is helpful when I put work up in my home "gallery" as the pictures are close together. I also avoid straight edges.

FRAMING PRINTS

The simplest (and infinitely cheapest) option is to buy clip frames and frame your work yourself. Clip frames can work well esthetically. In effect, a clip frame doesn't have a frame; it's a very simple and modern-looking design, and it doesn't distract from the image. Clip frames also make it easy to swap images around.

Another option is to use ready-made frames with mounts. Most picture-framing shops sell precut mounts, but it's not expensive to have mounts cut to match more closely the size of your pictures .

Overall, I think simple frames work best. But, at the other extreme, large, flamboyant frames can work surprisingly well, particularly with monochrome images.

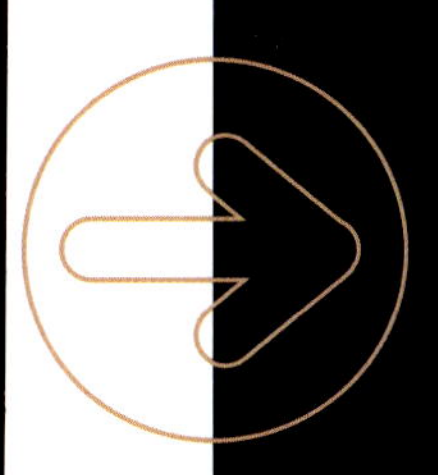

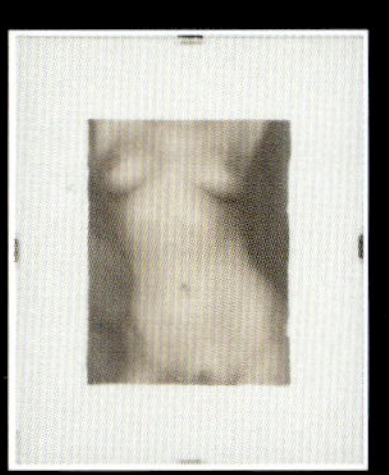

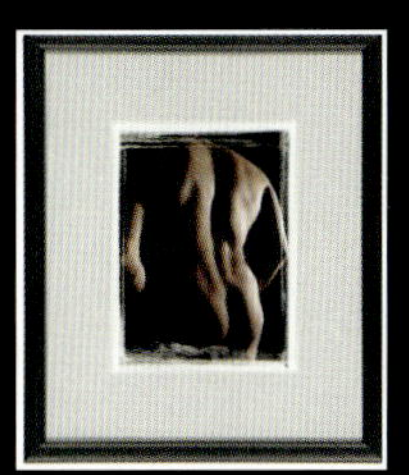

A picture frame can make or break an image, but selecting an appropriate frame is often a matter of personal taste. When framing a picture, do not overlook the importance of white space.

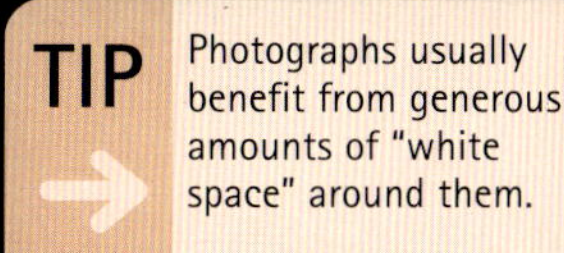

TIP

Photographs usually benefit from generous amounts of "white space" around them.

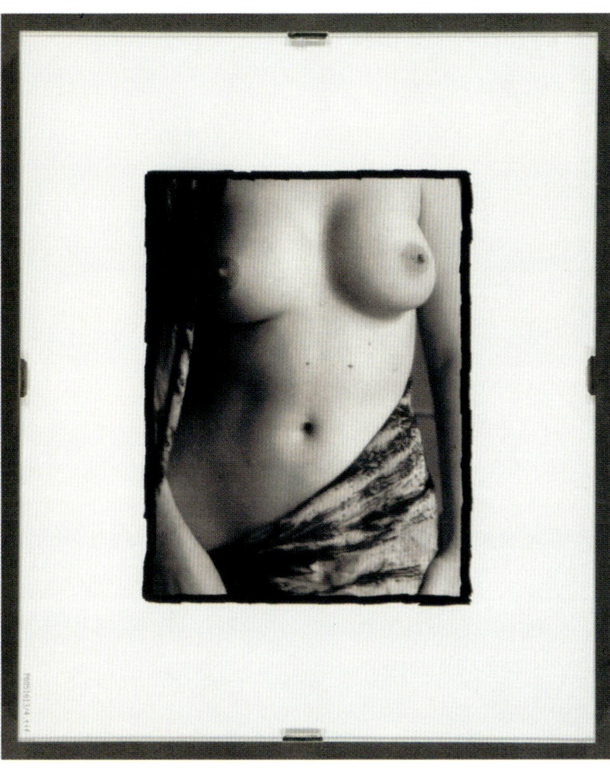

Three different methods of making borders for prints and framing them. The mount for the wooden frame was cut precisely to size for the print.

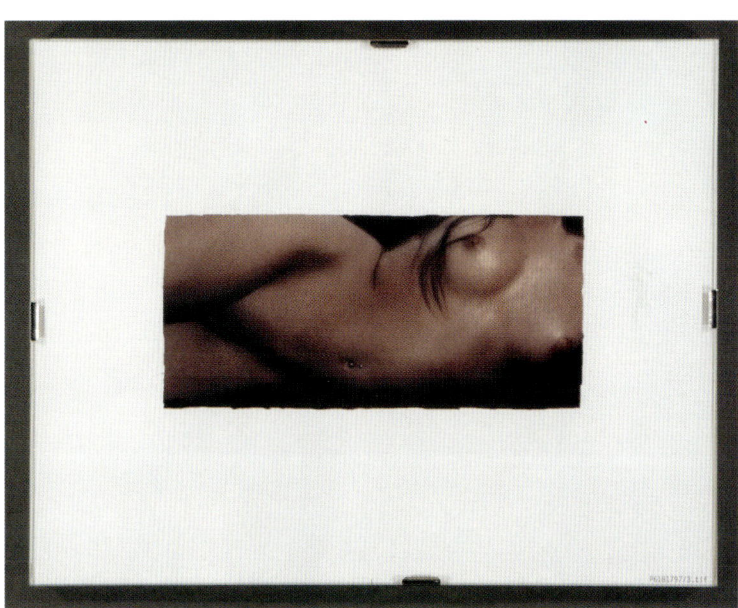

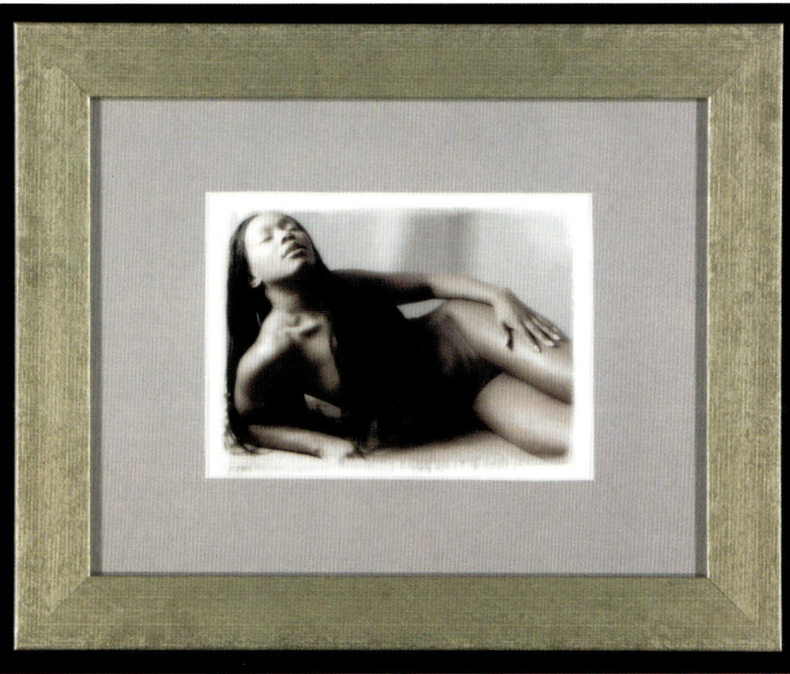

FACT FILE

Exhibiting work

Photographs need to be seen. At home you can make a "gallery" from quite a small area of wall. One benefit from having your pictures on display where you see them frequently is that it improves your critical sense about your own work. Other places to display your work could be your local photography club, local galleries, or picture-framers. Coffee bars often put on exhibitions of local artists' work and are also worth approaching with a carefully selected portfolio of your best images.

E-mail and CD-ROM

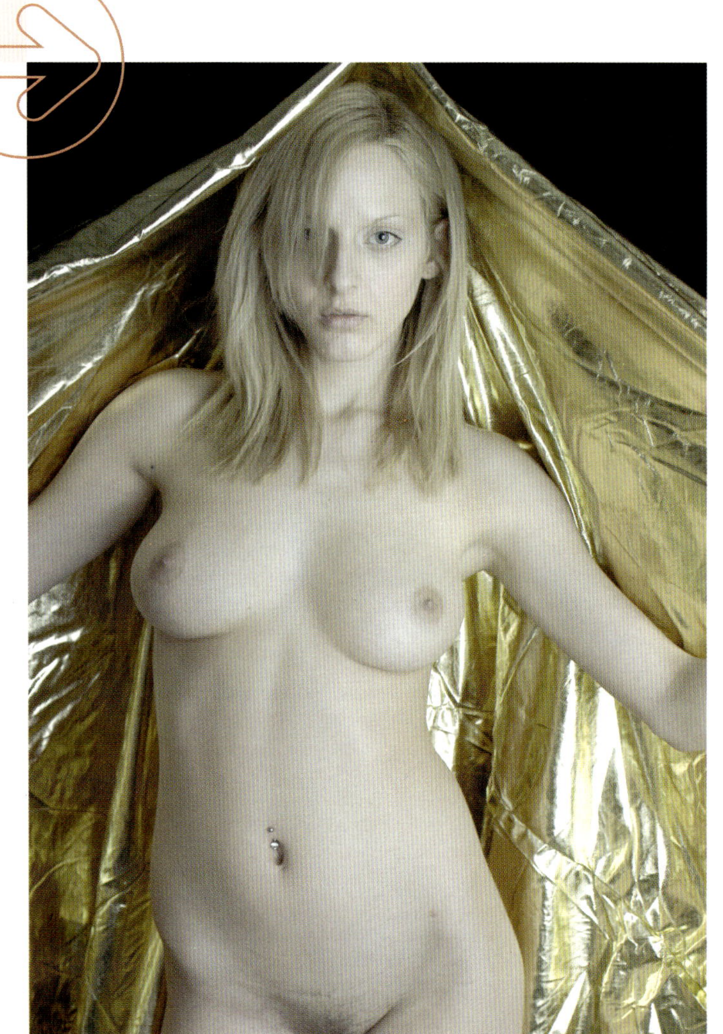

I f you want to share your pictures with friends, Elements offers an easy way of preparing images to send by e-mail. It also has a straightforward procedure for creating slideshows that you can burn onto a CD.

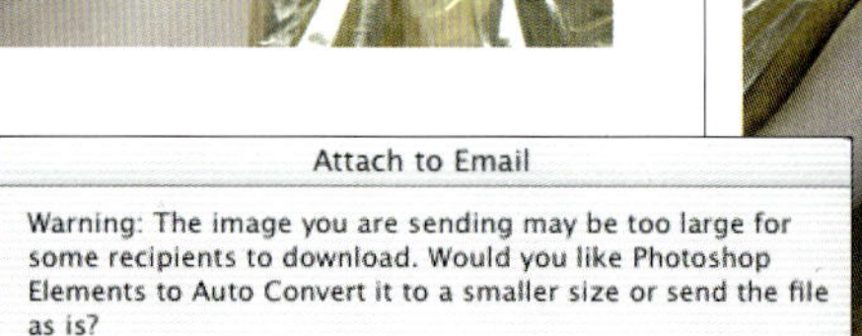

1 Open the picture you want to send, then edit it as necessary and save it. Now go to *File > Attach to E-mail*. If your image is bigger than 1200 pixels in either dimension, isn't a JPEG, or has properties that aren't supported by the JPEG format (for example, if it's a .psd file), the *Attach to Email* dialog box appears.

PREPARING PICTURES TO EMAIL

I'll use Elements to produce a good-quality smaller version of this 6-megapixel image, to e-mail to a friend.

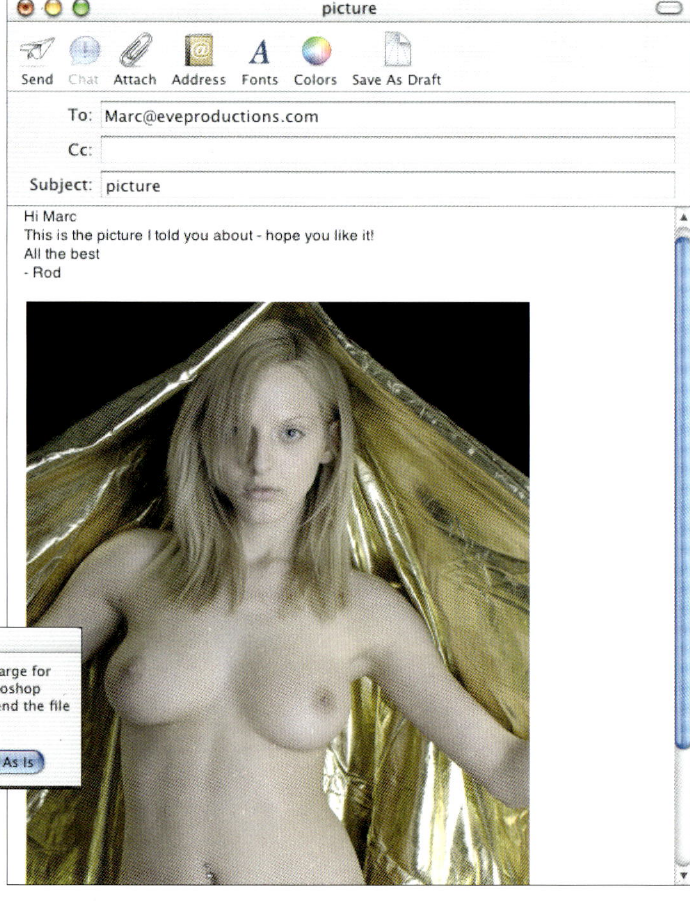

2 Assuming that you want to send the file in a form which will be easy for the recipient to download, click *Auto Convert*. Elements makes a smaller JPEG version of the file and loads it into your email browser. You then just need to add the recipient's address, a subject for the e-mail, and any text you want in the body of the message, and your e-mail is ready to send.

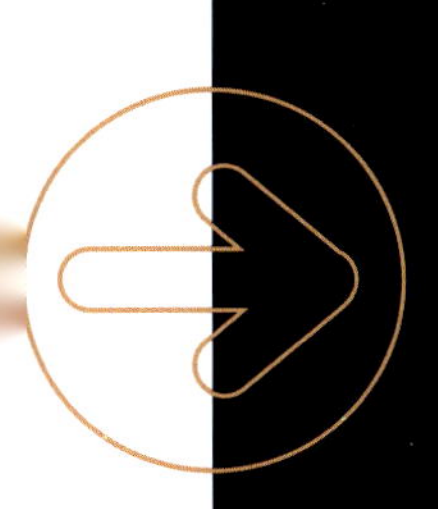

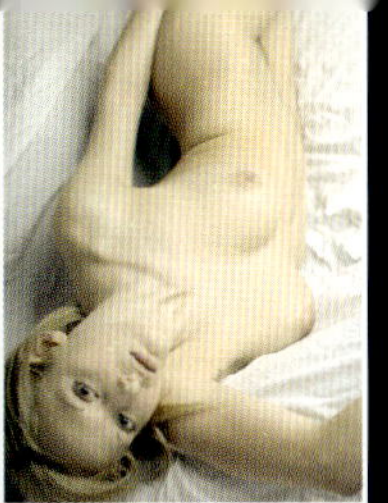

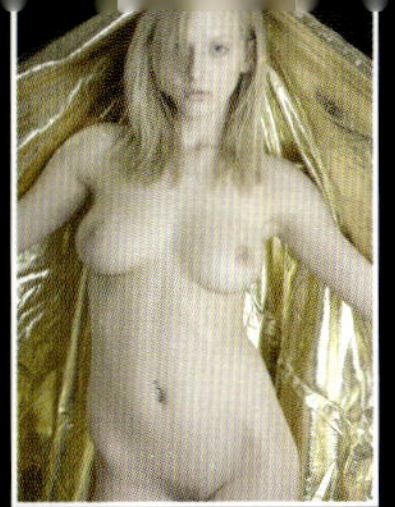

As well as printing out your pictures on paper, digital photography offers other methods of sharing your images. You can e-mail individual shots to a friend or create your own slideshows with custom soundtracks.

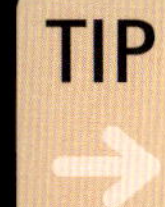

TIP Try to create a theme or sequence for your slideshow, rather than assembling images at random.

CREATING A SLIDESHOW

A slideshow is a sequence of images that plays automatically. Once you have made a slideshow, you can run it on your own computer or burn it onto a CD to send to friends. Elements assembles your JPEG images into a Portable Document Format (.pdf) file. Almost all computers have an application that reads .pdf files (usually Adobe Acrobat Reader) installed, but if not Acrobat Reader can be downloaded from www.adobe.com/products/acrobat/readstep2.html.

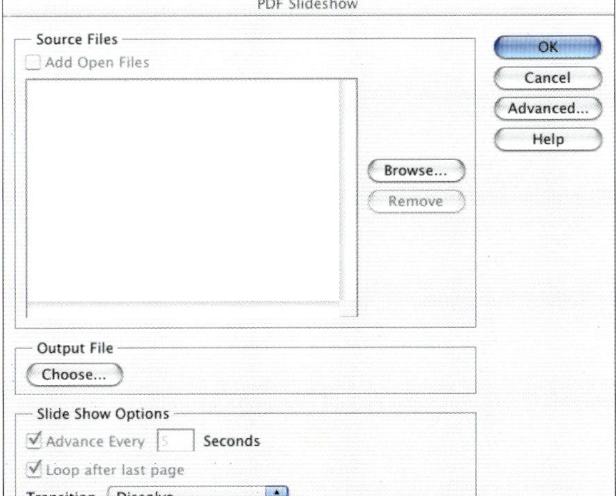

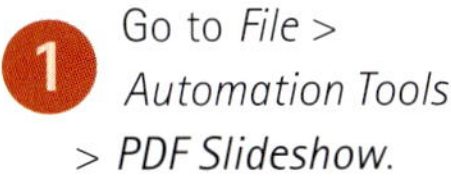

1 Go to *File > Automation Tools > PDF Slideshow*.

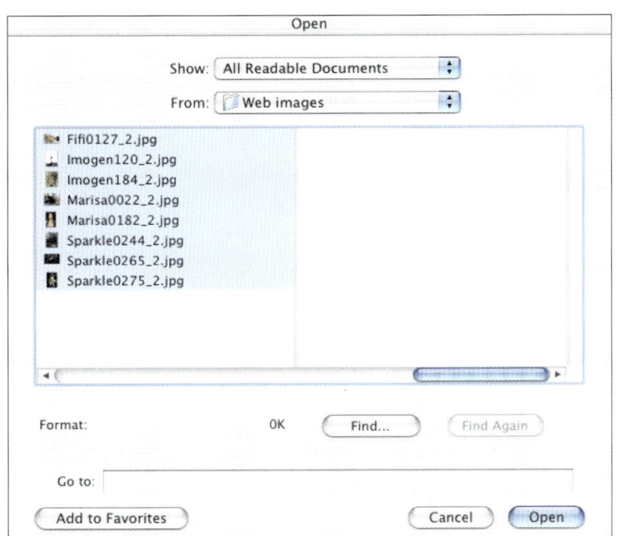

2 Use the *Browse* button to navigate to the JPEG files you want to include in the slideshow. Select the files (Apple-click to select more than one file at a time) and then click *Open*.

PDF Options
Encoding
ZIP
JPEG
Quality: 8 High
small file large file
OK
Cancel
Save Transparency
Image Interpolation

3 The file names will appear in the *PDF Slideshow* dialog box. To remove a file from the list, select the file-name and then click the *Remove* button. To rearrange the sequence of the files, click on a file name and drag it to a new position. In the *PDF Slideshow* dialog box, click *Choose* to set the name and location of the slideshow file, and then click the *Save* button. To compress your final PDF file, click the *Advanced* button to specify the quality you want for your JPEGs. (ZIP compression, which is also available, works best for images that contain large areas of a single color, so is unlikely to be appropriate for photographs.) *Save Transparency* doesn't apply here, but if you've included any low-resolution images and the recipients of your slideshow might want to print them, check *Image Interpolation* to anti-alias the images so that they print better.

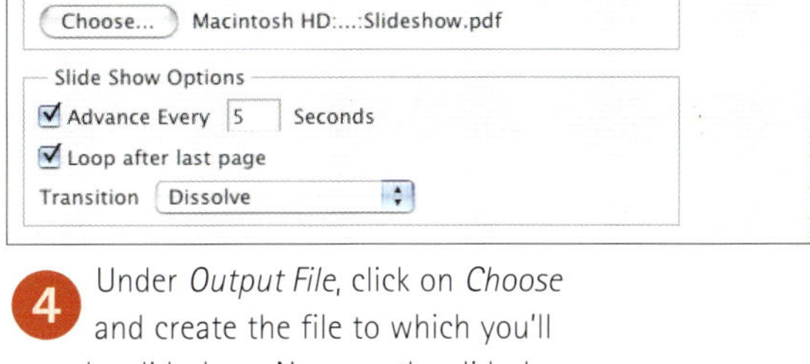

4 Under *Output File*, click on *Choose* and create the file to which you'll save the slideshow. Now set the slideshow options. In the *Advance Every* box, enter the number of seconds you want each slide to be on screen. To make the slideshow loop continuously, select *Loop After Last Page*. Use *Transition* to choose how a new slide replaces the one before it. Click *OK* to generate the slideshow. When the .pdf file has been made, you can burn it onto a CD.

Putting pictures on the web

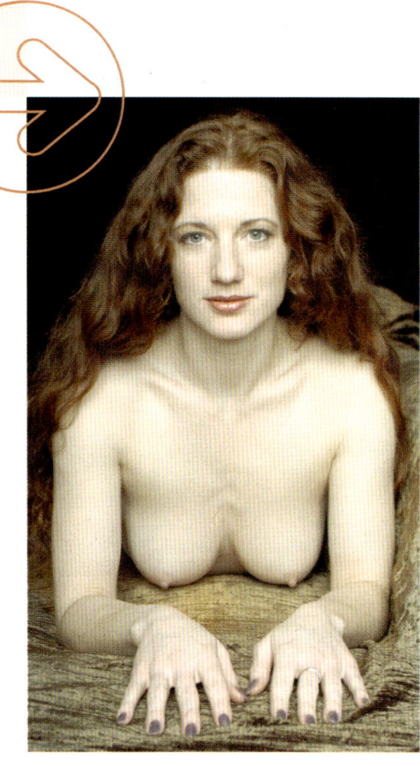

One of the best ways to bring your work to a wider audience is to put it on the internet. Elements provides tools to help you prepare images for the Web. We also look at how you can find places on the web to display your images.

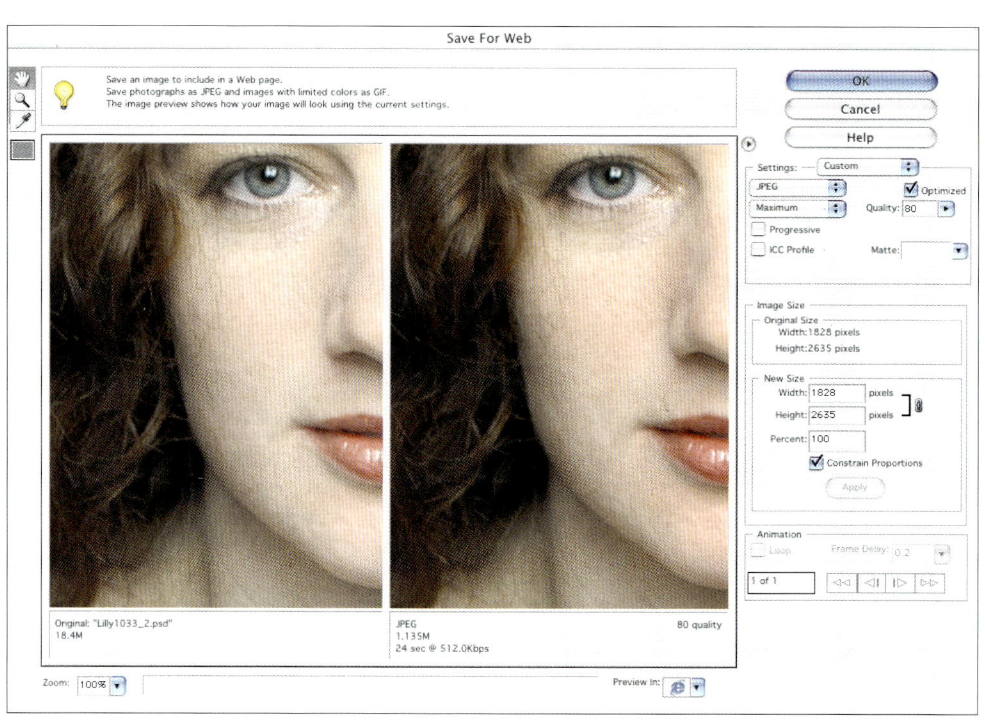

1 You have to start with a Photoshop (.psd) or .tif version (not a JPEG) of the image you want to make as a web-suitable version. Go to *File > Save for Web*. A new window opens, with your original image in the left-hand pane and the Web-optimized image (using the current settings) in the right-hand pane.

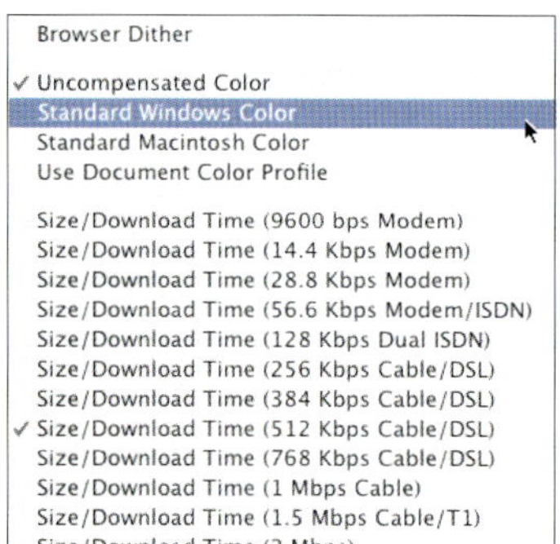

2 The screens of PCs and Macintosh computers have different brightness levels. Use the drop-down window to check that your image looks okay on both.

3 This is a question of "splitting the difference" so that the image is acceptable on both (but not perfect on either). If necessary, click the *Cancel* button to take you back to the main picture window, adjust the brightness of the image, save it, and then return to *File > Save for Web*. Now use *New Size* to set the size you want the image to be on the web. Assume that the viewer's screen is set to 1024 x 768 pixels, and that their browser window fills their screen. The biggest image that will fit on the screen at once, without them having to scroll the window, is about 600 pixels high. If your free service imposes maximum dimensions, use those, or at least don't exceed them. When you have decided on the image size, click *Apply*. Next you need to decide what quality you need. To see clearly the effect of changing the picture settings, use the *Zoom* control in the bottom right-hand corner of the window to zoom in to 200%.

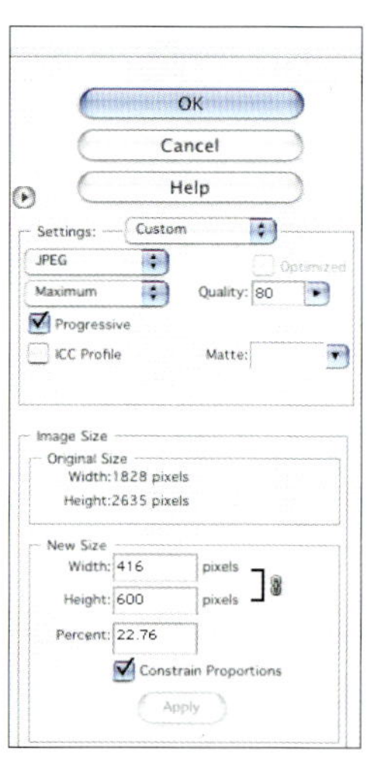

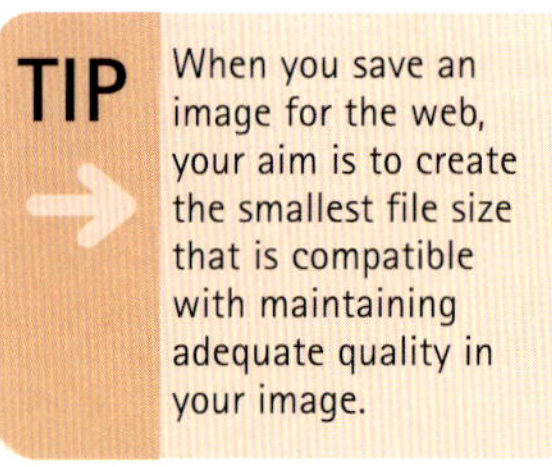

TIP When you save an image for the web, your aim is to create the smallest file size that is compatible with maintaining adequate quality in your image.

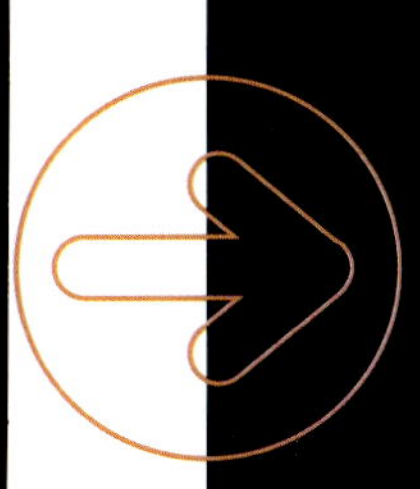

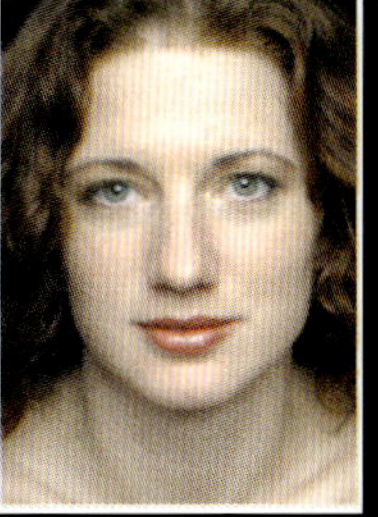

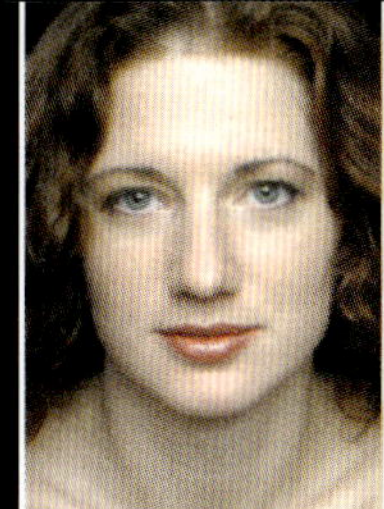

Save For Web is a feature that simplifies the process of preparing an image for placement on a webpage. To reduce the size of your photographs, image size and resolution are both adjusted during this procedure.

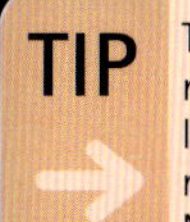

TIP To look right, images need to be made lighter on PC monitors than on Mac monitors.

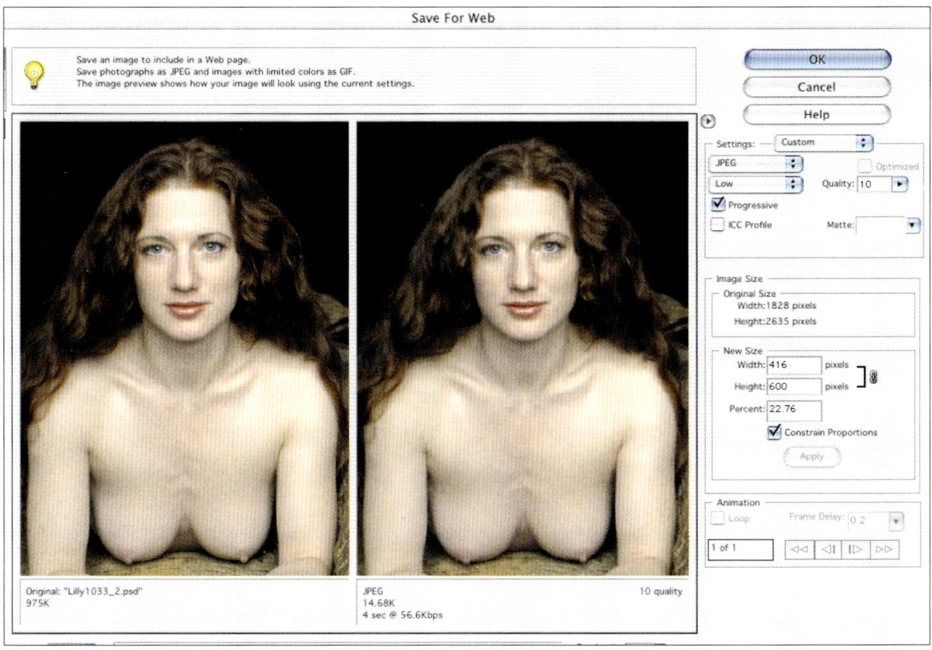

4 Now specify the settings for your image for the web. You can use the *Custom* settings option if you want, but the presets that are available should work for most images. The file format should be JPEG. Of the other options available, GIF is intended only for images with 256 colors or fewer, so is unsuitable for photographs. The same applies to PNG (pronounced "ping"). PNG24 produces high-quality images, but PNG24 files are larger than JPEG files and not all browsers can handle them, so JPEG is a better choice. Experiment with the quality settings. You should aim to use the lowest setting at which your image still looks good (that is, the colors aren't changed, edges are clear, and there's no pixellation).

5 Keep an eye on the download times, shown below the right-hand pane. You can use the drop-down window shown above to see how long it takes to download your image using different internet connections. You may want to check the *Progressive* box; this makes the image download in a series of passes so that it builds up gradually. This way the viewer sees a partial version of the image immediately, rather than having to wait for the whole image to download before anything appears on-screen. If you don't want this, then check the *Optimized* box to get a better quality/size ratio in the image. You can also use the *Preview* to see what your image looks like in a range of browsers (this will depend on which browsers you have installed on your computer). Have a final close look in the right-hand pane to check that you are happy with the quality of the image, and click *OK*. Finally, go to *File > File Info* and add a title (plus any other information you want) for the image.

File Info
Section: General
Title: Marisa
Author:
Caption:
Copyright Status: Unmarked
Copyright Notice:
Owner URL:
OK
Cancel

FACT FILE

Displaying photos on the internet

▶ Use a free Web service (e.g. Yahoo's www.photos.yahoo.com or MSN's www.photos.msn.co.uk). Some camera manufacturers also offer this service. The main drawback is that you have little control over how your images are presented. They may be shown next to adverts, or part-covered by pop-ups.

▶ Sign up to a photographic website such as www.onemodelplace.com or www.modelexpose.com. These are sites mostly aimed at showcasing models, but many photographers are also members. These sites aren't free: levels and categories of membership vary. You just upload your images into your own album within the site.

▶ Build your own website. You can use the free space offered by some Internet Service Providers (ISPs), or you can buy space from an ISP. Having acquired some space, you can build a site just using Elements' *Create Web Photo Gallery* command (*see page 138*), then upload it to your ISP.

▶ If you get serious about the internet, there's a wealth of software to help you create a more sophisticated site and take the pain out of programing. Packages like Macromedia Dreamweaver (http://www.macromedia.com/software/dreamweaver/) and Adobe GoLive (http://www.adobe.com/products/golive/main.html) let you create your site visually with little or no programing knowledge required.

Putting pictures on the web

MAKING A WEB PHOTO GALLERY

Elements provides a tool for you to prepare pictures for your own website. For further details, consult Elements *Help*, which is excellent on this topic.

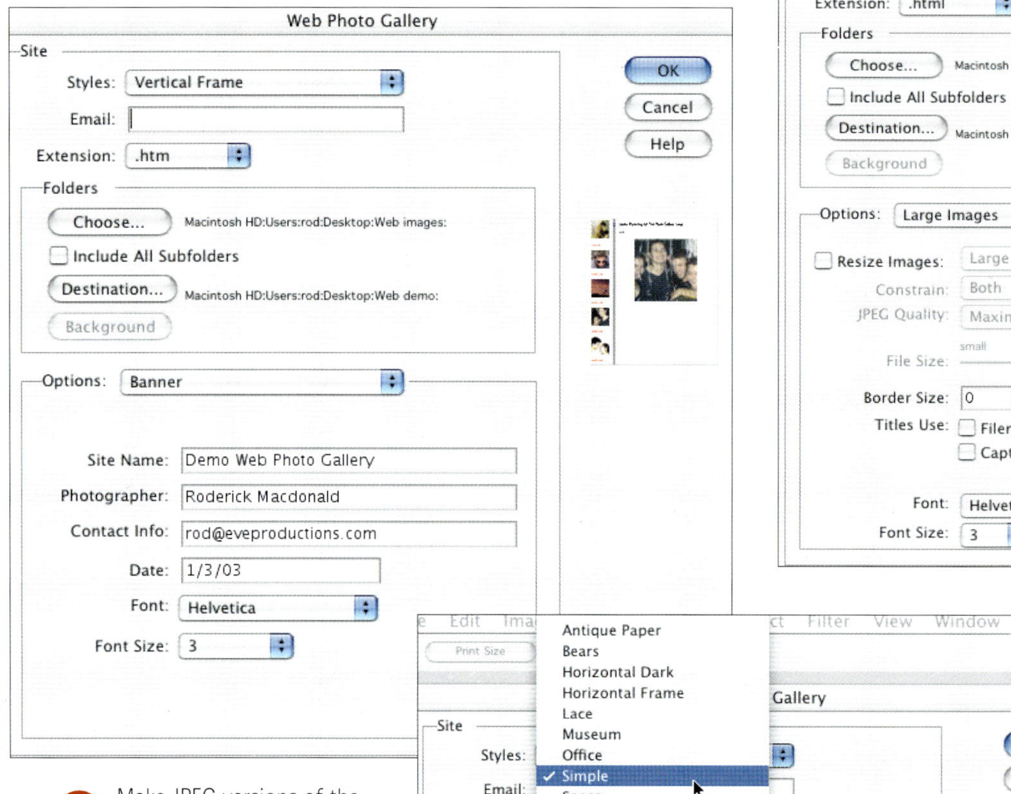

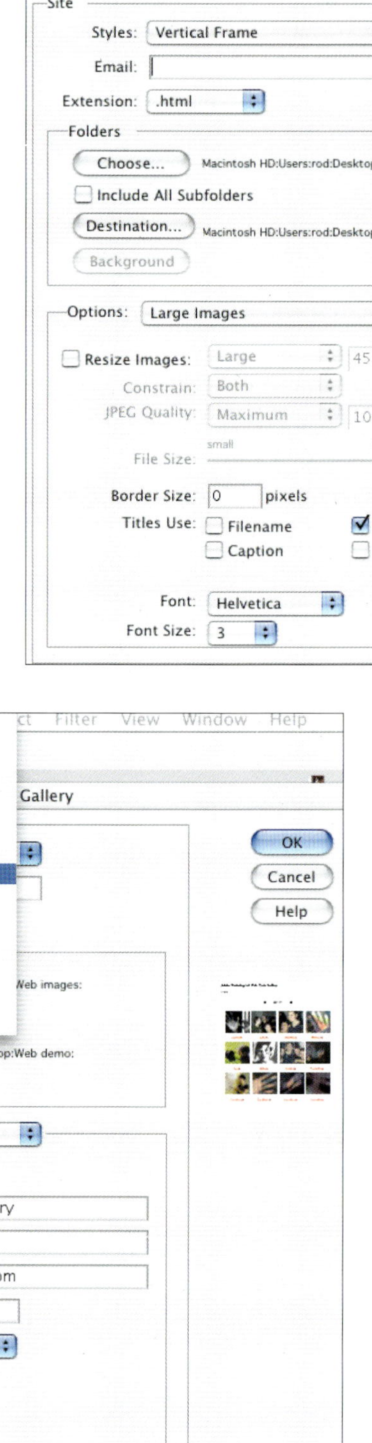

1 Make JPEG versions of the images you want in your gallery, as described on page 136. Gather these JPEGs into one folder. Go to *File > Create Web Photo Gallery*.

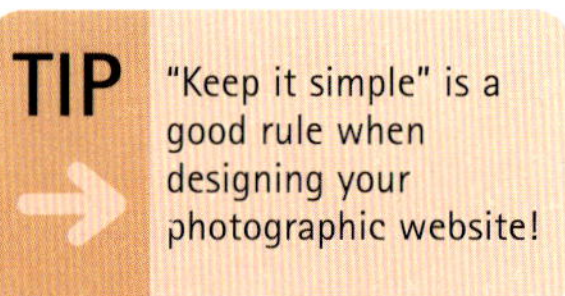

TIP "Keep it simple" is a good rule when designing your photographic website!

2 Choose a gallery style from the *Styles* pop-up. You see a preview of the home page for the chosen style on the right-hand side of the dialog box.

Web Photo Gallery
Site
Styles: Vertical Frame
Email:
Extension: .html
Folders
Choose... Macintosh HD:Users:rod:Desktop:Web images:
Include All Subfolders
Destination... Macintosh HD:Users:rod:Desktop:Web demo:
Background
Options: Large Images
Resize Images: Large 450 pixels
Constrain: Both
JPEG Quality: Maximum 10
small large
File Size:
Border Size: 0 pixels
Titles Use: Filename Title Caption Copyright Notice
Font: Helvetica
Font Size: 3
OK
Cancel
Help

3 In the *Folders* section, click on *Choose* and navigate to the folder that contains the pictures you want on your site. Select *Include All Subfolders*, if you need to include images in folders within this folder. Next, click on *Destination* and navigate to or create a folder to hold the files for the website. Some styles have additional options: consult Elements' *Help* for advice on these. To set options for the text banner that appears on each page in the gallery, choose *Banner* from the *Options* pop-up menu and fill as many of the boxes as you wish. Select *Large Images* from the *Options* drop-down. Because you have already optimized the JPEGs for this site, you don't need to change the size for *Large Images*. To label gallery pages, check the *Title* option.

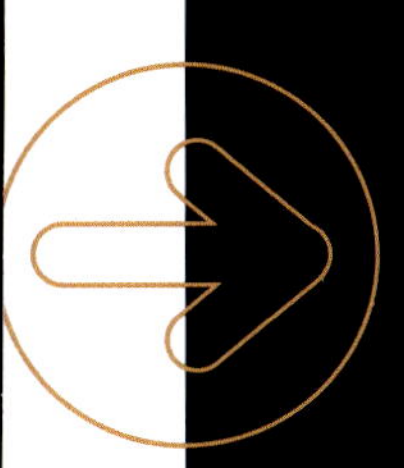

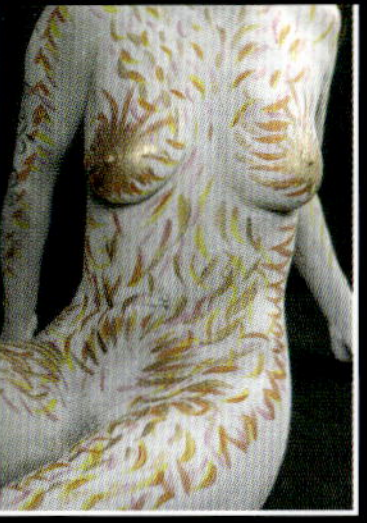

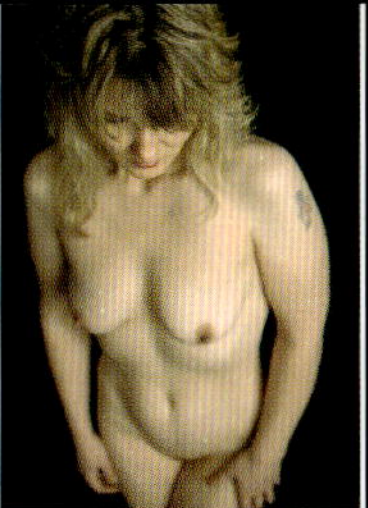

Adobe Photoshop Elements offers automatic web gallery creation. This is a method of presenting your work on the Internet to a worldwide audience. To do this you need to have an account with an Internet Service Provider.

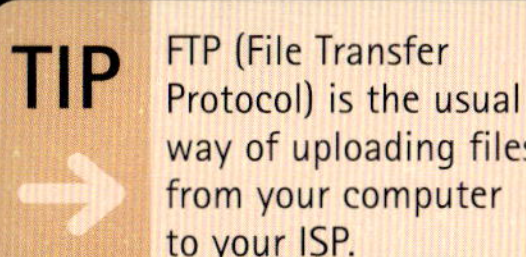

4 Now choose *Thumbnails* from the *Options* drop-down. You can stick with the default settings or follow the directions in the *Help* to alter them. Again, check the *Title* option.

5 Click *OK* to create the gallery. Elements creates all the necessary files and folders inside the destination folder you chose. The folder is ready for you to FTP to your ISP.

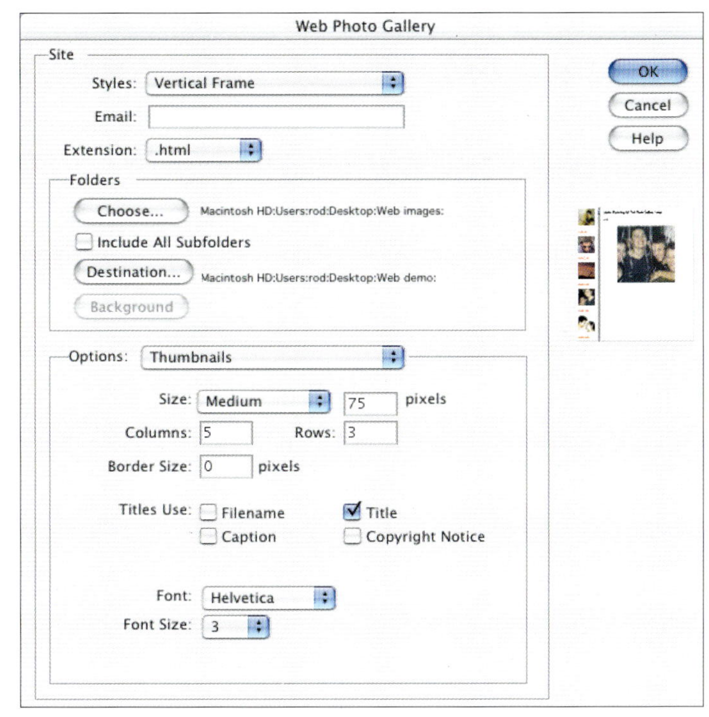

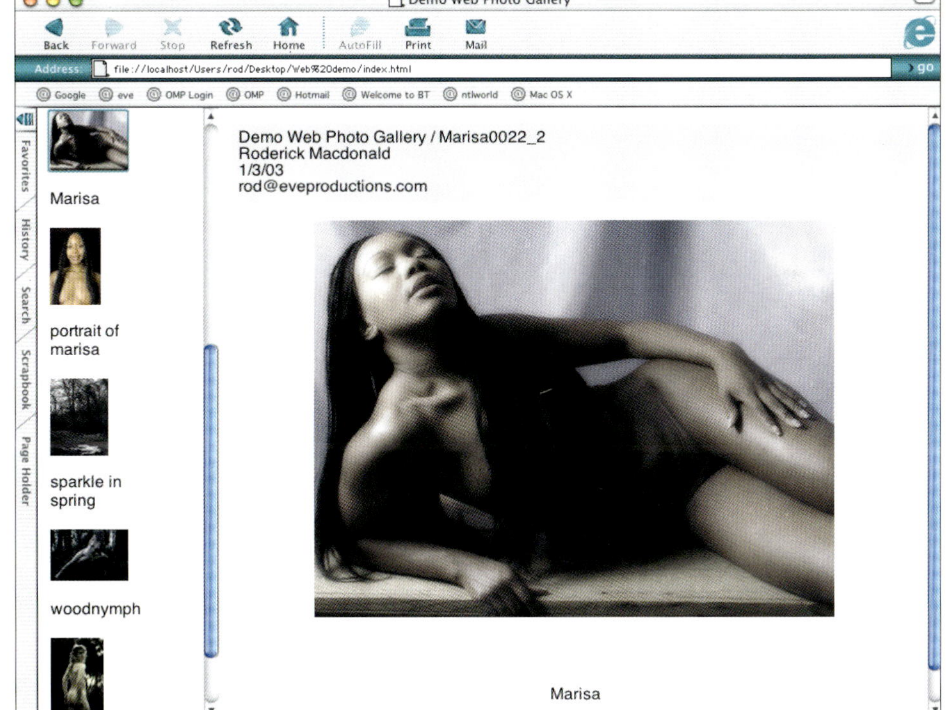

FACT FILE

A note on copyright

Essentially, unless you've previously assigned it in writing to someone else, you own the copyright in all the images that you have created yourself. So anyone who downloads a copy of one of your images and publishes it, on another website or elsewhere, without your permission, is infringing your copyright. There is very little you can do to prevent this happening—part of the nature of the internet is that it makes sharing content very easy. If copyright infringement is of concern to you, there are options within Elements' *Create Web Photo Gallery* menu that let you put a copyright statement right across the image. This should deter anyone from stealing the image, but could also spoil it! Alternatively, you could investigate digital watermarking, a process that invisibly marks your images and thus makes it easy to prove that you own the copyright on them. One company that produces software for this purpose is Digimarc (*www.digimarc.com*).

Glossary

aperture The opening behind the camera lens through which light passes on its way to the CCD.

application Software designed to make the computer perform a specific task. An image-editing program is an application, as is a word processor.

artifact A flaw created by processing that spoils a digital image.

aspect ratio The ratio of the height to the width of an image, whether on-screen or in print.

autofocus A system used in traditional and digital cameras to ensure that the subject of a photo will be in focus at the moment the exposure is taken. Several different models are used, varying in sophistication and application.

bit (binary digit) The smallest data unit of binary computing, being a single 1 or 0. Eight bits make up one byte. See also Byte.

bit depth The number of bits of color data for each pixel in a digital image. A photo-quality image needs eight bits for each of the red, green, and blue channels, making for a bit depth of 24.

bitmap An image composed of a grid of pixels, each with their own color and brightness values. When viewed at actual pixel size or less, the image resembles a continuous-tone shot, like a photograph.

blend mode Setting in the Photoshop Elements Layers palette, which controls how the pixels in one layer affect those in the layers below.

brightness The level of light intensity. One of the three dimensions of color. See also Hue and Saturation

byte Eight bits—the basic data unit of desktop computing. See also Bit

calibration The process of adjusting a device, such as a monitor, so that it works consistently with others, such as scanners and printers.

CCD (Charge-Coupled Device) A tiny photocell used to convert light to an electronic signal. Used in densely packed arrays, CCDs are the recording medium in some scanners and most digital cameras.

CD (Compact Disc) Optical storage medium developed by Philips. As well as the read-only CD-ROM format there are two recordable formats. A CD-R (Compact Disc-Recordable) can only be written to once, although it's possible to keep adding data in different "sessions." On a CD-RW (Compact Disc-Rewritable) the data can be overwritten many times.

cloning In an image-editing program, the process of duplicating pixels from one part of an image to another.

CMOS (Complementary Metal-Oxide Semiconductor) An alternative sensor technology to the CCD, CMOS chips are used in high-resolution cameras from Canon and Kodak.

CMYK (Cyan, Magenta, Yellow, Key) The four process colors used for printing, including black (key).

compression Technique for reducing the amount of space that a file occupies, by removing or squashing redundant data. Compression is either lossy (some data is lost altogether) or lossless (no data is permanently lost).

contrast The range of tones across an image, from the bright highlights to dark shadows.

cropping The process of removing contiguous parts of an image, leaving behind only the most significant portion.

depth of field The distance in front of and behind the point of focus in a photograph, in which the scene remains in acceptable sharp focus.

dialog An on-screen window in an application, used to enter or adjust settings or complete a procedure.

dpi (dots per inch) A measure of resolution in printing. See also PPI.

drag To move an icon or a selected image across the screen, normally by moving the mouse while keeping its button pressed.

feathering The fading of the edge of a digital image or selection.

file format A method of storing information (such as an image) in digital form. Common formats include TIFF, BMP and JPEG.

fill-in flash A technique that uses the on-camera flash or an external flash in combination with natural or ambient light to reveal detail in the scene and reduce shadows.

filter (1) A thin sheet of transparent material placed over a camera lens to modify the quality or color of light before it reaches the film or sensor. **(2)** A feature in an image-editing application that alters selected pixels for visual effect.

focal length The distance between the optical center of a lens and its point of focus when the lens is focused on infinity.

fringe An unwanted border effect around a selection, where pixels inside the selection jar with those in the background.

f-stop A measure of the aperture size of a photographic lens.

GB (gigabyte) Approximately one thousand megabytes or one billion bytes (actually 1,073,741,824).

gradation The smooth blending of one tone or color into another, or from transparent to colored in a tint. A graduated lens filter, for instance, might be dark on one side, fading to clear on the other.

grayscale An image made up of a sequential series of 256 gray tones, covering the entire gamut between black and white.

handle A small box-like icon used in imaging applications to manipulate picture elements.

histogram A map of the distribution of tones in an image, arranged as a graph with the horizontal axis running from the darkest tones at the left to the lightest tones at the right. The vertical axis shows the number of pixels in that range.

hot-shoe An accessory fitting found on most digital and film SLR cameras and some high-end compact models, normally used to control an external flash unit.

HSB (Hue, Saturation, and Brightness) The three dimensions of color, and the standard color model used to adjust color in many image-editing applications.

hue The pure color defined by position on the color spectrum; what is generally meant by 'color' in lay terms. See also Brightness and Saturation.

interpolation A procedure used when resizing a bitmap image to maintain resolution, creating new pixels by comparing the values of adjacent pixels.

ISO An international standard rating for film speed. The higher the film speed, the less light and the lower the shutter speed needed to get a correct exposure, but the more grain in the image. The same principle applies with digital equivalents and noise.

JPEG (Joint Photographic Experts Group) A lossy compression format for compressed image files. Higher levels of JPEG compression involve a significant loss of data, and therefore a lower-quality image.

KB (kilobyte) Approximately one thousand bytes (actually 1,024).

lasso A selection tool used to draw an outline around an area of an image for the purposes of selection.

layer A level of an image file used to hold discrete elements of an image, allowing them to be edited without affecting the whole.

luminosity The brightness of a color, independent of hue or saturation.

macro A mode offered by some lenses and cameras that enables them to focus in extreme close-up.

mask A grayscale template that hides part of an image, limiting changes to a particular area or protecting parts from alteration.

MB (megabyte) Approximately one thousand kilobytes or one million bytes (actually 1,048,576).

megapixel A rating of resolution for a digital camera, directly related to the number of pixels output by the CMOS or CCD sensor. The higher the megapixel rating, the higher the resolution of images created by the camera.

midtone The parts of an image that are approximately average in tone, falling midway between the highlights and shadows.

noise Random pattern of small spots on a digital image. Generally unwanted and caused by non image-forming electrical signals.

pixel (PICture ELement) The smallest unit of a digitized image—the square dots that make up a bitmap. Each pixel carries specific tone and color values.

plug-in Software produced by a third party and intended to supplement a program's features.

ppi (pixels per inch) A measure of resolution for a bitmapped image. See also DPI.

RAW A file format created by some high-end digital cameras, containing all the pixel information with no compression. Usually requires proprietary software supplied with the camera to view, adjust, and convert the files.

resampling Changing the resolution of an image either by removing pixels (lowering resolution) or adding them by interpolation (increasing resolution).

resolution The level of detail in an image, measured in pixels per inch for a digital image, or dots per inch for a printed one.

RGB (Red, Green, Blue) The primary colors of the additive model, used in monitors, digital cameras, and image-editing programs.

saturation The purity of a color, going from the lightest tint to the deepest, most saturated tone. See also Brightness and Hue.

selection A part of the on-screen image that is chosen and defined by a border, in preparation for manipulation or movement.

shutter The mechanical device inside a camera that controls the length of time during which the film is exposed to light. Many digital cameras don't have a shutter as such, but the term is still used to describe the electronic mechanism that controls the length of exposure for the CCD.

shutter speed The time the shutter (or electronic switch) leaves the CCD or film open to light during an exposure.

SLR (Single Lens Reflex) A camera that transmits the same image via a mirror to the film or CCD and the viewfinder, ensuring that you get exactly what you see in terms of focus and composition.

spot meter A specialized light meter, or function of the camera light meter, that takes an exposure reading for a precise area of a scene.

telephoto A photographic lens with a long focal length that enables distant objects to be enlarged. The drawbacks include a limited depth of field and angle of view.

thumbnail Miniature on-screen representation of an image file.

TIFF (Tagged Image File Format) A file format for bitmapped images, which can use lossless LZW compression. The most widely used standard for high-resolution digital photographic images once they have been edited.

white balance A digital camera control used to balance exposure and color settings for artificial lighting types with a different color temperature than daylight.

zoom A camera lens with an adjustable focal length, giving, in effect, a range of lenses in one. Drawbacks include a smaller maximum aperture and increased distortion over a prime lens (one with a fixed focal length).

Index

Acknowledgments

Thanks first of all to all the models: Andrea, Aylith, Bart, Becky, Carol, Catya, Chrissy, Christopher, Clare, DonnaMarie, Eulalia, Fifi, Ilonka, Imogen, Ja, Jackie, Jo, Liz, Maria, Marisa, Mel, Mercedes, Naomi, Red, RedLilly, Roxana, Solariss, and Zoë.

Next, to the colleagues at APU in Cambridge who generously tolerated my distracted state of mind while I was working on the book; in particular to the wonderful team in Media Production, whose advice and trenchant views helped me separate the wheat from the chaff.

Among the many friends who provided support, advice, and practical help I must thank in particular Susan Meredith and David Glover. Janet Croft helped me keep it together. Mike Nott's observations, during our rambles through the wintry Cambridgeshire landscape, had a decisive impact on the selection of certain images. Liz Girvan gave me the benefit of her detailed knowledge of the world of models and photographers, and Peter Chapman brought his finely developed esthetic sensibility to bear on many of the issues surrounding photography of the nude.

Ronan and Kieran Macdonald provided invaluable moral support. Don and Jessica Bailey gave tough but fair criticism.

Three Cambridge stores deserve a mention: Ark let me use their delightful attic for a location shoot. Dixie's secondhand clothes stall was a source of garments, great conversations, and inspiration. And Phil from Nomads was extraordinarily generous with his superb hoard of ethnic jewelry.

Rolo at Ilex came up with every piece of equipment I asked for. I'm very grateful, too, to the other artists whose work appears in the book. Mike and Sally, bodypainters extraordinary, provided the living art for the chapter on the painted body (pp 64-65) and Doreen Alvarez, Lindsay Martin, and Bruce Robertson contributed photography on pages 11, 61, and 124-5 respectively.